[0]

[2] Inv R

... at with a runcible spoon; And hand in hand, on the edge of the sand, They danced by the light of the moon, The

[3] Inv R.

[4] Inv R.

moon, the moon, they danced by the light of the moon.

Oct 17/66

To the those sweet melodies to you, dear Bob (Robert Craft) as a souvenir of our thirty years old friendship

Yours affectionately

Igor Stravinsky
Los Angeles
March 31, 1968

STRAVINSKY

Discoveries and Memories

ROBERT CRAFT

NAXOS

BOOKS

I am wondering how these incredible patterns of form and tone appear to any soul, how can the wonder and beauty of what you say come to us like that... All the miracles of the ancient barbaric, passionate world are there, and all the human heart is there.

Stark Young to Stravinsky
at the 1948 premiere of the 1947 version of the
Symphonies of Wind Instruments

To my son, Robert Alexander Craft,
and to my sister, Phyllis Craft Crawford

Published by Naxos Books, an imprint of Naxos Rights US Inc.

© Robert Craft 2013

www.naxosbooks.com

Printed and bound in the UK by Biddles, part of the MPG Printgroup, Bodmin and King's Lynn.

Design and layout: Hannah Whale, Fruition - Creative Concepts

All photographs of Stravinsky are the property of the author.

Front cover: Igor Stravinsky and Robert Craft at Paestum, Italy, October 1959. Both are looking down to avoid the many lizards on the path. Photograph by Robert Emmet Bright.

Frontispiece: Manuscript of the ending of *The Owl and the Pussy-Cat*, part of Stravinsky's gifting of the complete manuscript to Robert Craft.

Inside front cover flap: The author in the tenth-century Byzantine church of La Cattolica at Stilo, Calabria, 14 October 1995.

ISBN: 978-1-84379-753-1

Contents

AUTHOR'S PREFACE
'And looking back to whence I came'

I know it now, I knew it not,
But all too late I rew it,
I rew not that I knew it not,
But that I never knew it.

The Phoenix Nest, 1593

Recently the Friends of Historic Kingston, New York, invited me as a native son to speak in the city's National Historical Landmark, the Old Dutch Church (1659), which is surrounded by the tombstones of George Clinton (vice-president to Thomas Jefferson) and to Revolutionary and Civil War veterans, three or four of them my ancestors. I accepted, but with apprehension: would the pews be absolutely empty or, if not, very sparsely occupied by a few coevals, perhaps some music students and a sprinkling of Woodstock artists? Would anyone there remember me? I had left Kingston for boarding school at the age of twelve and only rarely returned. My other connections to the city were the graves of my family in Wiltwyck Cemetery, among them Charles Lang Freer, the founder of the Freer Gallery in Washington, D.C. But I am also linked to an antique shofar lodged at Kingston's Temple Emanuel.

After a concert tour in Israel in 1962, President Ben-Zvi had presented this precious relic to Igor Stravinsky. When the composer moved from his spacious California home to a small hotel suite in New York in 1969, he was obliged to divest himself of many of his most treasured possessions. Having heard me speak with veneration of Rabbi Herbert Bloom of Temple Emanuel, Stravinsky asked me to give the shofar in his name to this congregation. It still remains there. I had met Rabbi Bloom at age twelve with my friend and fellow-menace to neighbourhood peace, Robert Gross, who took me with him to Shabbat services. Here the rabbinical scholar opened my mind to the world of philosophy, particularly Spinoza's.

You must wonder how an inexperienced small-town student came to be associated with Igor Stravinsky? My musical life began at home, where my parents and sisters played the piano – my mother had been accepted at the New England Conservatory in Boston. Our parents took us to the Metropolitan Opera, New York, to see Balanchine's production of *Tannhäuser* and to hear New York Philharmonic concerts conducted by John Barbirolli. At age six, I became a soprano in the choir of St John's Episcopal Church whose choir director, an organist steeped in Bach, convinced my parents that I had musical talent that should be trained. So my next few summers, until 1937, were spent at a music school near Woodstock, where I audited classes by Percy Grainger and took piano lessons from Cassius Gould, who I now realise was a paedophile.

At Christmas 1937, during a school furlough, I heard the Rochester Symphony play the *Firebird* Suite conducted by José Iturbi. Enthralled, I made my way backstage to ask him about Stravinsky. Iturbi had played the premiere of the composer's Five Easy Pieces for piano four hands with him in Lausanne (8 November 1919), as well as the world premiere of the Piano-Rag-Music. Startled that a fourteen-year-old schoolboy knew about these remote concerts, Iturbi shared his fascinating recollections of the composer with me. On 7 April 1940 I heard a live broadcast of Stravinsky conducting *The Rite of Spring* with the New York Philharmonic in Carnegie Hall and resolved to dedicate my life to music, particularly his.

In 1941 I was awarded a scholarship to the Juilliard School. It proved disappointing. Only Igor Buketoff on the faculty was in the least interested in contemporary music and sympathetic to me. Stravinsky was ignored as well as deplored as an iconoclast, which redoubled my passion for his music. I organised student ensembles to perform the Octet, *L'Histoire du Soldat* and the *Dumbarton Oaks* concerto and presented them in programmes filled out with 'Brandenburg' concertos and Mozart serenades. The audiences at the Brooklyn Museum, Hunter College and the 92nd Street 'Y' were most enthusiastic.

I wanted to add Stravinsky's *Symphonies of Wind Instruments* to our repertoire and, finding that the music was unavailable, I wrote to the composer and asked for help in procuring the score. It seems that on the day my letter arrived, he had begun to prepare a revision of this work. A superstitious person, he regarded this coincidence as significant, and replied that he would like to conduct the premiere in one of my New York concerts. I was elated but answered that we could not pay his fee. He wrote again, offering to waive it, to everyone's amazement. The concert actually took place in Town Hall on 11 April 1948. Stravinsky conducted his revised *Symphonies* and *Danses concertantes*, and on the second half of the programme, I somehow navigated my way through his Symphony in C and Capriccio. The unlikelihood of this still makes it unreal: a twenty-three-year-old rustic with a nervous-wreck temperament and no experience as a conductor, save a single appearance with the Juilliard Symphony, sharing the podium with the world's most eminent composer-conductor! How could this have happened?

During Stravinsky's sojourn in New York for the premiere of his new ballet, *Orpheus*, I was with him every day. Stravinsky called me 'Bob' and I addressed him as 'Mr Stravinsky', and I never to the end of his life addressed him otherwise. Only his wife was allowed to call him 'Igor'. When Auden used 'Igor', Stravinsky glanced at him with a baleful eye. Russian friends, including new acquaintances, were encouraged to call Stravinsky by his first name with the patronymic 'Igor Fyodorovich'. His orchestra players addressed him as 'Maestro'; but this seemed banal, since every ordinary musician in the European music world was a 'maestro'. Stravinsky himself was very strict and formal in matters of nomenclature. The elder Sitwell brother was 'Sir Osbert', and such titles as Princess, Marchioness, Duke or Count were always observed. In Germany he was especially careful in distinguishing degrees of nobility; Count Salm was 'Urlaut Salm'. People of the highest intellectual and artistic stature addressed him and he them by last names only. Eliot and Stravinsky talked and wrote to each other using surnames alone. Vera did not follow any of these strictures, though in her old age most people called her 'Madame'. She called her husband 'Eager'. Only once, in his 27 May 1919 thank-you note to Schoenberg, did Stravinsky ever address another musician as 'Honoured Meister'. Stravinsky was very particular in his ordinary correspondence to address friends as 'Dear' and especially close friends as 'My dear', having learned that a British court case had convicted a gentleman on a charge of sodomy on the basis of the use of 'My'.

Stravinsky quickly realised that I knew and loved all of his music. After his return to Hollywood, we corresponded. At first I was a kind of factotum for some of his musical business in New York. His letters became increasingly personal, as well as candid about the musical scene. He invited me to attend his forthcoming concerts in Denver and then to visit him in his California home, which I did in July 1948. Before departing for the West Coast, he entrusted me with the task of inventorying the surviving materials, scores and orchestra parts of his music at the Boosey & Hawkes warehouse in Lynbrook, Long Island, which had been devastated by a fire. I next saw him in New York in February 1949, when he asked me to accompany him on a Boston Symphony concert tour (Cambridge, Boston, Carnegie Hall, Brooklyn and Newark). I also conducted a second concert with him in Town Hall, after which he encouraged me to spend the following summer with him and his wife, cataloguing his music manuscripts and archives only recently received from Paris. Eventually I became his co-concert and rehearsal conductor for more than two decades.

I have thought, but never before attempted to say, that Stravinsky must have seen resemblances of himself in me, traits and idiosyncrasies of character and personality. His most striking features are the abruptness of his movements, his nervous tension and power of concentration. These qualities, of course, were not a part of my makeup. So what could we have had in common? My love of learning, and my preoccupation with the musical classics and avant-garde music. Our only common characteristics were that we were both omnivorous readers and that we had a similar sense of humour, particularly of the sarcastic kind.[1]

The six weeks with him in New York following our 1948 concert was the greatest learning experience of my life. I had entered into a cultural world at its highest peak of which I knew nothing. Stravinsky spent hours with me in the Metropolitan and the Frick museums. He taught me how to look at pictures and sculptures, and instilled his own preferences in me. He introduced me to writers whose talk about poetry, from the classics to Eliot, was thrilling and left me appalled at my own pedestrian prose and inept attempts at writing poetry. I felt as if all my years of formal education were not worth an hour of this man's company, since everything he said was filtered through one of the most acute sensibilities of the century. Perhaps Stravinsky was simply rehearsing his English with me, because I did not understand any other of his five languages. He also, kindly, made me aware of the crudity of my manners, which perhaps did help to improve them. Although he did not refer directly to my deficiencies, I was a good observer, and particularly when we were in company with his friends I did learn much from his impeccable behaviour.

---

1   Dr Max Reinkel, a biochemist at MIT, was the first to note in 1949 the personal and medical similarities between us. Successive doctors agreed with him.

Acknowledgements

I wish to thank the English poet and master of maieutics, Craig Raine, for inspiring this book during four four-hour transatlantic telephone interviews; he is in no way responsible for its content. I must also express appreciation for the help and information I have received from Dr Ulrich Mosch of Basel, dean of Stravinsky scholars. The American writers Allen Shawn and Mark DeVoto were supportive and made valuable and important suggestions. I also thank Carol Archer, for her patience and tireless typing and devotion throughout the evolution of this book; Lise Steinhauer, for helping to bring it to its final form; my sister Phyllis Crawford and her daughter Kristin for their helpful input; and our editor-in-chief at Naxos, Genevieve Helsby. Above all, I thank my beloved wife, Alva, for numerous suggestions and improvements.

PART ONE
The Music

2

CHAPTER 1

A Collocation:
Stravinsky and Schoenberg

When the two deities of twentieth-century music met in Berlin in December 1912, the world was not yet aware that they had just revolutionised music history. Both had almost simultaneously composed what were destined to become their signature masterpieces. *The Rite of Spring* was begun in the summer of 1911 and finished in sketch score on 4 November 1912. *Pierrot Lunaire* dates from the spring and summer of 1912. After the first flight of *The Firebird* (1910) the younger composer was the more widely known, but Schoenberg, concert-touring as a conductor, was nearing the peak of his public career, which came three months later in Vienna with Franz Schreker's triumphant performance of *Gurrelieder*.

Diaghilev was in the audience when Schoenberg conducted the premiere of *Pierrot* in Berlin (after forty rehearsals) on 16 October, and determined that Stravinsky hear this astoundingly original creation. The impresario invited Schoenberg to attend the Ballets Russes' forthcoming German premiere of *Petrushka* on 4 December. Meanwhile, Schoenberg repeated *Pierrot* in Hamburg on 19 October, in Dresden on the 24th, Breslau on the 31st and Vienna on 2 November. He then returned to his home in Zehlendorf (Berlin) to prepare for orchestral concerts in Amsterdam on 28 and 30 November. Anton Webern joined him in Berlin for a few days.

At Diaghilev's insistence, Stravinsky arrived at the Adlon Hotel in Berlin on 20 November, primarily to rehearse the *corps de ballet* in Part One of the *Rite* but also to attend the Berlin premiere of *The Firebird* on the 21st; it was a stunning success, after which he was warmly congratulated by Richard Strauss. Probably Schoenberg and Webern, who was staying with him, were in the audience, but no evidence has surfaced confirming this. On 23 November, Schoenberg must have departed for Amsterdam to begin rehearsing *Pelleas und Melisande*. Returning to Berlin on 1 December, he heard *Pierrot* the same day under Hermann Scherchen, who had been touring with it in Stuttgart, Mannheim, Frankfurt and, finally, Munich, where Klee, Klimt and Schiele were in the audience. On 4 December Stravinsky, Diaghilev and Schoenberg attended a performance of *Petrushka* together. Stravinsky recalled that Schoenberg was 'very friendly and warm to me and seemed to be interested in my music'. Schoenberg wrote later, 'I really liked *Petrushka*, parts of it very much indeed.' Stravinsky heard Schoenberg conduct *Pierrot* at the Choralion-Saal on Sunday noon, 8 December. Stravinsky, in row 5, seat 5, was overwhelmed, writing to Russian colleagues about a 'new musical summit'. Schoenberg invited Stravinsky to dinner at his home following this concert. He vividly recalled the evening for the rest of his life and remembered meeting Webern there with the pianist Eduard Steuermann, who has left a memoir of the event. At a press conference in London a month later Stravinsky extolled Schoenberg as 'one of the greatest creative spirits of the age'.

After World War I Arnold Schoenberg founded The New Vienna Society for Private Musical Performances (*i.e.*, no critics) and wrote to Stravinsky on 24 April 1919, inviting him to send chamber music pieces, which he did. The new organisation gave the world premieres of the full instrumental versions of *Berceuses du chat* and *Pribaoutki* at one of these concerts. On 27 May 1919, Stravinsky's note to Schoenberg – 'Honored Master' – thanks him for presenting the Russian song cycles at the Society and includes a copy of his Three Pieces for String Quartet. On 8 June Anton Webern wrote to Alban Berg:

There was no more room in the hall. The concert was completely sold out. Stravinsky was wonderful. These songs are marvellous. This music is very close to me. I love it quite especially. There is something unmentionably moving in these cradle songs. How the three clarinets sound, and *Pribaoutki*. Ah, my friend, something quite marvellous. This realism leads us to the metaphysical.

The same programme included Berg's Piano Sonata, Op. 1 and an arrangement for four pianos of his orchestral piece *Reigen* in which Rudolf Serkin was one of the pianists.

In New York in December 1924, Leopold Stokowski conducted Schoenberg's *Herzgewächse* and Stravinsky's *Renard* on the same programme. Both pieces had to be repeated. The following month Stravinsky, now in New York himself, told a reporter for a Berlin periodical that whereas other composers wrote music for the future, he composed strictly for the present. Having suffered violent abuse from the European press, Schoenberg misinterpreted the remark as an attack on him and overreacted by composing Three Satires, which ridiculed Stravinsky quite personally. *Vielseitigkeit*,[1] the second Satire, refers to 'the *kleine Modernsky*'. The music is a four-part *a cappella* chorus that reads the same way both forwards and backwards, a musical somersault and a feat of contrapuntal art, praised as such by Stravinsky. Schoenberg's otherwise loyal disciple, the philosopher Theodor Adorno, criticised the Satires, writing to his composition teacher Alban Berg:

I am disappointed by the Satires. Would the preface not truly have sufficed? Does all this have to be chewed over compositionally... and must art be made out of art? And what sort of humour is this, who laughs about this, for whom has all this been written anyway? If Schoenberg (rightly) recognises

---

1   On New Year's Eve 1925 Schoenberg claimed that *Vielseitigkeit* was not intended to be performed: 'The title "Manysidedness" means that it can be read only by turning the paper around and reading it from end to beginning. The same music (if you call it music) would come out. This piece is merely *Papier Musik*.'

that today's objectivism is worthless and reactionary, then he should make better music than the other, and restrict his polemic to the literary kind, if at all, but not confuse achievement with opinion and achieve a puerile aberration! If he is doing it out of resentment – well then, he should find another way to deal with it. What seems tragic to me is that Schoenberg's last works have all been absolutely right in their conception – though neither has he overcome the listener. If nothing were to remain but this music we would have to despair... I can no longer ignore the realisation that, for Schoenberg, the twelve-tone technique did become a recipe after all, and functions mechanically, above all in the rhythm, which grows monotonous.

Werner Reinhart, the Swiss art dealer, had written to Stravinsky advising him that Schoenberg[2] would be conducting his new Serenade in the forthcoming Venice Biennale, thereby implying that Stravinsky might not wish to appear in the small, commingling city[3] at the same time, even though he had not yet been invited. Reinhart was evidently aware of Schoenberg's growing hostility to Stravinsky. Stravinsky wrote to the director of the Biennale, Alfredo Casella, asking him to find a place for a new Sonata in one of the programmes. Complying, Casella appealed to Reinhart to pay Stravinsky the same high fee he had guaranteed to Schoenberg, though Stravinsky would have to play his ten-minute Sonata in the smaller Teatro Malibran[4] on a mixed programme that included pieces by Carl Ruggles and Louis Gruenberg. Schoenberg was in the audience for Stravinsky's performance on the 8th; after the concert Stravinsky and Vera dined with Reinhart and his protégée, the Australian violinist Alma

---

2   Stravinsky was unaware that Reinhart had an equally close relationship with Schoenberg and had sponsored a performance of *Pierrot Lunaire* conducted by the composer in the Reinhart Winterthur mansion. Reinhart, who was also Stravinsky's concert manager in Switzerland, had commissioned *Histoire du Soldat* for 15,000 Swiss francs on 27 June 1918, and had sponsored a performance of *Renard* in the same Winterthur home three years before its authorised public premiere in Paris in 1922. In 1951 Reinhart planned to join the composer in Milan and travel with him to Venice for the premiere of *The Rake's Progress*, but this good friend died on the day of the composer's arrival in Milan.

3   Schoenberg lodged in a hotel on the Lido and arrived in the city for rehearsals more than ten days before Stravinsky.

4   Not in the Teatro alla Fenice, as mistakenly stated in all biographies.

Moodie with whom Stravinsky would soon give the premiere of his arrangement for violin and piano of excerpts from *Pulcinella*.[5] Schoenberg wrote to Webern later that evening, denigrating the Sonata and the musical direction it indicated but also describing the audience noise and antagonism that insulted the Serenade. As late as 7 January 1932, Schoenberg was still writing to Webern about the scurrilous reception of the masterpiece in Venice: 'My very dear fellow... I cannot forget the treatment [I received] at the Venice Music Festival; I do not want to forget it.'[6] In the hindsight of 2013, the Serenade opens a genuinely new path and is immeasurably more interesting than the music of the Sonata.

A festival of Schoenberg's music in Paris in December 1927 drew accolades from everywhere and greatly increased the composer's international stature. The Five Pieces for Orchestra were well received by a large audience, as was the Septet-Suite conducted by the composer. Working on *Oedipus Rex* in Nice, Stravinsky was fully informed of this success by his musical assistant, Arthur Lourié, whose letters do not conceal his own favourable impression of Schoenberg.

On 8 January 1928 Stravinsky heard his Octet on a programme with Schoenberg's Chamber Symphony, both conducted by Ernest Ansermet. Stravinsky's silence about this juxtaposition may be an indication of the depth of the split between the composers. When he attended the premiere of Schoenberg's *Accompaniment to a Cinematographic Scene* on 6 November 1930, conducted by their mutual friend Otto Klemperer, Schoenberg was absent, perhaps not entirely for the published reason (influenza), but because he had learned from Klemperer that Stravinsky would be in the audience. Stravinsky also heard Schoenberg's orchestrations of two Bach chorale preludes in Klemperer's Berlin premiere and again later in Paris at the Salle Gaveau, conducted by Igor Markevitch. Stravinsky

---

5   Stravinsky had promised the premiere to the violinist Paul Kochanski but Reinhart offered more money for a prior performance with Moodie. In compensation Stravinsky also accompanied Kochanski in his first performance of the piece.

6   Folklore claims that when Schoenberg conducted *Pierrot Lunaire* in Venice in the 1920s, after a passage in which the piccolo plays shrill, whistle-like high notes, someone shouted in imitation of a train guard, 'Signori in carrozza!' ('All aboard!'), provoking much laughter.

admired but said nothing about the music at the time. In 1960 when I opened some of Stravinsky's South American concerts with these transcriptions, he was dazzled by them.

After Schoenberg departed for America in the autumn of 1933, little was known in Europe of his continuing struggles. Stravinsky was in Los Angeles with Samuel Dushkin in 1935 and 1937, and during the second visit Klemperer managed to induce Schoenberg to attend a concert of the Los Angeles Philharmonic guest-conducted by Stravinsky. All that is known about this event comes from Klemperer, who testified that Schoenberg remarked, 'I could never bow like that', after seeing Stravinsky's Russian manner of bending from the waist following the *Firebird Suite*. But Schoenberg declined Klemperer's invitation to go backstage with him and greet his colleague.

Six years later Stravinsky himself became a refugee resident of Hollywood, living only a few miles from the Schoenberg home in Brentwood (West Los Angeles). Although the two men had several friends in common – Oscar Levant, Otto Klemperer, Ingolf Dahl, Peter Yates, Alma Mahler – they glimpsed each other on only a few occasions. The closest they came to meeting was in San Francisco in the last week of 1943.[7] On 26 December Schoenberg conducted the Ballet Theater premiere of his *Pillar of Fire* (*Verklärte Nacht*) choreographed and danced by Anthony Tudor, with Stravinsky in the audience. The Stravinskys were so enthralled that Vera titled her first California painting *Verklärte Nacht*. Stravinsky conducted the same company in a performance of *Petrushka* the following night, but by this time Schoenberg had returned to Los Angeles. During their three days in San Francisco the composers and their spouses dined separately with Pierre Monteux and Darius Milhaud, either of whom could have, should have, invited both parties but did not or perhaps dared not.

Stravinsky and Schoenberg were both contributing composers to Nathaniel Shilkret's *Genesis Suite* commissioned on 30 September

---

7   Sol Hurok had visited both composers in Los Angeles on the same day to obtain their signatures on their San Francisco contracts but did not mention to either of them that the other would also be performing.

1945. Stravinsky had already finished his piece, the cantata *Babel*, in April 1944. Schoenberg's contribution, the Prelude, was completed only a few weeks before the scheduled premiere on 21 October, but the date had to be postponed to 18 November for the reason that the difficult Prelude required more rehearsal time. Leonard Stein[8] reported that at a rehearsal, or perhaps recording session, the composers sat on opposite sides of the hall, and that after *Babel*, Schoenberg remarked, 'It lacks an ending; it simply stops.'

The next mention of the two men in the same place at the same time comes from the *Los Angeles Times* of 7 July 1948: 'The Stravinskys, the Schoenbergs, and the Thomas Manns attended the same dinner party in honor of Alma Mahler-Werfel at the Beverly Hills Hotel.' Since Stravinsky never mentioned this to me, I can only assume that either the newspaper was mistaken or that Stravinsky and Schoenberg were seated at different tables or on the same side of a long table. Bruno Walter, Eugene Ormandy, Erich Korngold, George Antheil, Italo Montemezzi and Ernst Toch also attended the party, which was held in the hotel's Crystal Room with its many tables. Ormandy conducted Mahler's Eighth Symphony in the Hollywood Bowl later in the month, a performance the Stravinskys bravely attended, as almost certainly did the Schoenbergs.

I was not yet living with the Stravinskys in January 1949 when I read the exchange of letters published in *The Saturday Review* (Letters to the Editor) concerning the *Dr Faustus* dispute between Schoenberg and Thomas Mann:

> The supposition of one reviewer that [Mann] obtained information about [my] technique from Bruno Walter and Stravinsky is probably wrong because Walter does not know anything about twelve-tone composition and Stravinsky does

---

8 Leonard Stein, Schoenberg's assistant, had known Stravinsky since 1942 when he asked Leonard's French-born wife, Marie, to translate the *Poétique musicale* into English, but she was involved on another project. Stein was the pianist in all my Schoenberg and Webern recordings in Los Angeles; he participated in some sixty rehearsals and recording sessions with Stravinsky present, also recording Schoenberg's Piano Pieces, Opp. 33a and 33b, and the Three Songs, Op. 48. Stein provided Schoenberg's copies of Webern's music for Stravinsky's use during these recordings.

not take any interest in it. The informer was Mr. Wiesengrund-Adorno, a former pupil of my late friend Alban Berg. Mr. Adorno is very well acquainted with all the extrinsic details of this technique and thus was capable of giving Mr. Mann quite an accurate account of what a layman - the author - needs to tell another layman - the reader - to make him believe that he understands what it is about. But still this was my property and nobody else's.

When Mrs. Mahler-Werfel discovered this misuse of my property, she told Mann that this was my theory, whereupon he said: 'Oh, does one notice that? Then perhaps Mr. Schoenberg will be angry!' This proves that he was conscious of his guilt and knew it was a violation of an author's right... It must have been very difficult for Mrs. Mahler-Werfel to convince Mann that he must do something to correct this wrong. Finally I sent him a letter and showed him the possible consequences of ascribing my creation to another person, which in spite of being fictitious, is represented like a living man, whose biography is told by his friend Serenus Zeitblom. Much pressure by Mrs. Mahler-Werfel had still to be exerted to make Mann promise that every copy of *Dr. Faustus* will carry a note giving me credit as the inventor of twelve-notes composition. I was satisfied by this promise because I wanted to be noble to a man who had been awarded the Nobel Prize. But Mr. Mann was not as generous as I, who had given him a good chance to free himself from the ugly aspect of a pirate. He gave as an explanation a few lines which he hid at the end of the book on a page where no one would ever see it. Besides, he added a new crime to his first in the attempt to belittle me: he calls me 'a (a!) contemporary composer and theoretician'. Of course, in two or three decades, one will know which of the two was the other's contemporary.

Arnold Schoenberg

Arriving at the Stravinsky home at the beginning of June 1949, I noticed that he had underscored the reference to himself in his copy of the magazine. I was upset by this, interpreting the statement as revealing Schoenberg's regret, not his anger, at Stravinsky's lack of interest. I now realised that I was coming to California with a mission. The pain of Schoenberg's paranoia is manifest in this blunt but dignified testament of the pureness of his pride, while Mann's righteous and flippant response sullies his reputation.

Mann himself confesses to his debt to Schoenberg in his notebook for *Dr Faustus*:

> We had Schoenberg to our house one evening. He told me about the new trio he had just completed, and about the experiences he had secretly woven into the composition – experiences of which the work was a kind of fruit. He had, he said, represented his illness and medical treatment in the music, including even the male nurses and all the other oddities of American hospitals. The work was extremely difficult to play he said, in fact almost impossible, or at best only for three players of virtuoso rank; but, on the other hand, the music was very rewarding because of its extraordinary tonal effects. I worked the association of 'impossible but rewarding' into the chapter on Leverkühn's chamber music.

On 23 October 1949 Stravinsky heard Schoenberg deliver an address at the Wilshire Ebell Theater thanking the Austrian Consul-General for the recently conferred Freedom of the City of Vienna Award. Stravinsky walked onstage afterwards with the intention of greeting Schoenberg but the honoree was swiftly whisked off by an Austrian official. Since I was in New York that day,[9] the Stravinskys attended the event alone, and I could not help to effect a meeting. On my return Stravinsky told me that Schoenberg had read aloud from a bundle of papers in his own large handwriting.

It has been asserted that in December 1949 I 'went to a Schoenberg matinée[10] in the Los Angeles County Museum, but Stravinsky stayed

---

9   On 21 October 1950 I conducted the Septet-Suite and *Pierrot Lunaire* in a Town Hall concert. Ross Russell, the proprietor of Dial Records, was in the audience and wrote to Schoenberg about the programme, saying, 'It was probably the first all-Schoenberg concert in America.'
10 The date of the Los Angeles concert was 22 January 1950.

at home', the implication being that he did not wish to go, though in truth he had been looking forward to the event. (His plans were interrupted by a surprise visit from his friend Baron Fred Osten-Sacken, who had just flown in from Mexico.) I heard the String Trio for the first time on that programme and was electrified by its opening measures, as I still am. Schoenberg was not present, but a broadcast of a recorded interview with him by the Bartók biographer Halsey Stevens was aired for the first time. The elderly composer's voice was fragile but Old-World aristocratic, and the German accent scarcely noticeable. He spoke with great dignity and humility, reflexively questioning almost every one of his own statements. The dialogue began with Stevens's remark about Schoenberg being a painter – which Schoenberg abruptly converted to the past tense, 'was' – as well as a composer. On hearing the interview I so wanted the experience of seeing and conversing with this great man that I resolved to meet him. This finally took place in his home on 6 July 1950, as described in my *Stravinsky: Chronicle of a Friendship*.[11]

Three months earlier, in April 1950, Stravinsky had heard *A Survivor from Warsaw* conducted by Dimitri Mitropoulos in Carnegie Hall. I went to the first performance and found myself sitting with Sam Dushkin and his accompanist Erich Itor Kahn, a Schoenberg pupil. Always wary of offending Stravinsky, Dushkin made me promise not to mention that I had seen him at the concert, but I was determined that Stravinsky should hear the repeat performance the next day. In 1950 Schoenberg was still a delicate subject; to broach that request would have been a bold step for me. Yet Stravinsky was with me at the second performance, and was as moved by the music as I had been, from the twelve-tone bugle reveilles at the beginning to the reduction of the orchestra to percussion alone – a stunningly robotic effect – to introduce the German sergeant's commands, and on to the unison male Jewish chorus hobbling most unmilitarily to the end. Afterwards I felt that this concert was a revelation in Stravinsky's discovery of Schoenberg.

---

11   New York: Alfred Knopf, 1972; reprint, Nashville: Vanderbilt University Press, 1994.

Meeting Schoenberg, I attempted to convey my own thoughts about the presentation of the *Survivor*, but he cut me short by criticising Mitropoulos for having instructed the Princeton male chorus to remove its robes, exposing white shirts at the beginning of the *Sh'ma Yisrael*. Though this had not especially upset me, I agreed with the composer that such showmanship was a distraction that blemished the dramatic climax. Moreover, since the choral ending lasts less than a minute in a work only slightly longer than six minutes, this robe-shedding puzzled the audience, having led it to expect a more extended piece. Stravinsky agreed with Adorno's publicised objection to the *Survivor*:

> The piece was intended for concert halls and therefore falls into the category of entertainment. To some degree it gives musical pleasure. Replacing suffering with aesthetic affirmation makes the unthinkable Holocaust to have some meaning. In the culture industry of the 1960s even genocide becomes cultural property.

Glenn Watkins's sensational *The Gesualdo Hex*[12] includes a discussion of the Schoenberg–Leibowitz correspondence 1945–50. The letters answer questions about Schoenberg's last-period compositions that have troubled every student of contemporary music. On 12 September 1945 René Leibowitz wrote and confronted the master on two issues: the return to octaves in the Piano Concerto and the abandonment of the twelve-tone system in *Kol Nidre* and the *Ode to Napoleon*, following that supreme creation, the Violin Concerto. Watkins rightly maintains that the transition from modal to tonal music and from tonal to atonal is a natural evolution, adding that traces of the older systems sometimes reappear in the newer ones, the modal in the tonal and the tonal in the atonal, which is Schoenberg's own explanation and the justification for the return to tonality in *Kol Nidre*. Watkins speculates that 'a group of performers,

---

12 New York: W.W. Norton, 2010.

both instrumental and vocal, would eventually begin to propose a historic kinship between a developing chromaticism in the Late Renaissance (with Gesualdo's music in particular) and the total chromatic explorations of the Schoenberg school'.

Watkins discreetly avoids the question of Leibowitz's copying the score of *A Survivor from Warsaw* and his *Partisan Review* polemics attacking Stravinsky on Schoenberg's behalf, which Schoenberg had not wanted; indeed, he criticised Leibowitz in print for his 'treatment of Stravinsky', who was displeased with the superficial arguments in an unsolicited rejoinder by Nicolas Nabokov. Neither does Watkins mention Leibowitz's duplicitous visit to Stravinsky during the November 1947 pilgrimage to Schoenberg nor, of course, Leibowitz's much later trips from Florence to Venice to see Stravinsky after the *Canticum Sacrum* and *Threni*. Moreover, no notice is taken of Leibowitz's own late recording of *The Rite of Spring* or of Schoenberg's anger on hearing Leibowitz's Paris recording of *Ode to Napoleon* with a female speaker (the manuscript specifies a baritone).

On 1 November 1950 I sent a copy to Schoenberg of his canon for the fortieth anniversary of the Concertgebouw, March 1928, thinking that he might not have it. He responded with the following note:

> November 4, 1950
>
> Dear Mr. Craft,
>
> I possess one copy of this canon. I want you to check whether the bass voice fits also to four parts. I cannot remember whether I planned it so. It seems to me that it should only be added when all the [other] three sing.
>
> With cordial greetings.
>
> Yours,
>
> Arnold Schoenberg[13]

I was deeply flattered by this question as to whether four voices, each in a different clef, would work harmonically by adding a bass

---

13   See the following page.

part (a cello with the C string tuned down to A). Stravinsky took the letter from my hands and wrote the canon in full score showing that the four voices (in Arnold, E[Schoenberg],[14] Concert, Gebouw) are harmonically viable. This was recorded with the Monday Evening Concert singers, and with Emmet Sergeant playing the cello part.

In a letter of 2 January 1951, to Fritz Stiedry, Schoenberg remarks, 'My young friend, Mr Craft... is slowly working himself into my music by performing my music a lot. And finally he will succeed.'

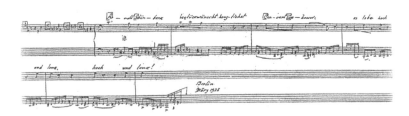

Schoenberg

Stravinsky's Resolution

News of Schoenberg's death in the last hour of 13 July 1951 was received in the Stravinsky home on the morning of 14 July. I answered the call and told Mrs Stravinsky, who waited to inform her husband until he was in his studio. Afterward she told me that he had suffered an attack of nerves and even real tears. About an hour later he emerged with a telegram to 'Mrs. Schoenberg', which the widow would tell Stravinsky was the first message of condolence that

---

14 *i.e.*, E flat

she received: 'Deeply shocked by saddening news of terrible blow inflicted to all musical world by loss of Arnold Schoenberg. Please accept my heartfelt sympathy. Igor Stravinsky.'

In the afternoon Schoenberg's relative and musical assistant, my friend Richard Hoffmann, who was born in Vienna and was a refugee to California via New Zealand, called me from the Schoenberg home with information about the funeral arrangements. Stravinsky prepared to attend but ultimately decided not to, fearing that his presence would be misconstrued. For forty years the composers' names had been automatically coupled yet they knew practically nothing about each other. On 19 July we were invited to dinner by Alma Mahler, whose home in the heart of Beverly Hills became the setting for a momentous event. After the meal her daughter, the sculptress Anna Mahler, joined us, gently cradling a box containing Schoenberg's death mask which she had made on the 14th, and offered to show it to Stravinsky. When she placed it on the cleared dining table, Stravinsky stood immobile as she carefully removed the protective wrappings. She then retreated, telling Stravinsky he would be the first to see the mask. He was mesmerised, gazing in silence for several minutes, then stepped back, took his coat, averted his eye, and indicated that he wanted me to drive him home. The silence continued throughout the next day and he never mentioned the experience. A religious and superstitious man, he may have felt that this transcendent life-death *coincidentia oppositorum* was brought about by an occult power. Somehow it had been destined that the two composers' creative powers must develop separately, and that Stravinsky, of all people, after a lifetime apart from his now deceased creative brother, should be the first to bow before his image.

Suddenly, on Schoenberg's death, the world was alive with him. Hermann Scherchen conducted the 'Golden Calf' music from *Moses und Aron* in the Teatro alla Fenice only weeks after the premiere there of *The Rake's Progress*. In the European cities that Stravinsky visited on his concert tour after his *Rake* performance, Schoenberg was being played with new interest. Stravinsky heard a tape of the Scherchen 'Golden Calf' in Cologne at the beginning of October.

In a letter of 13 April 1953 to her husband, then in Caracas, Vera Stravinsky described a breakthrough with Gertrud Schoenberg:

> On Sunday there was a concert by the New Music Quartet: Schoenberg, Webern and Berg. Bob asked Mrs Schoenberg if she would like to come to my house and go to the concert together. She accepted and arrived with her beautiful daughter. I gave them some Scotch. The first thing [Mrs Schoenberg] said was: 'This should have happened twenty years ago. It was not Schoenberg's or Stravinsky's fault, but people in between.' She is very nice, very direct, but very nervous. She talks a great deal and drinks copiously. She gives the impression of someone who has been hurt all her life.

What most intrigued the widow was a tour of Stravinsky's studio. She inspected this crammed but impeccably organised room with the greatest interest, comparing it to her late husband's and finding similarities. A high point was her discovery in the adjoining bathroom that Stravinsky and Schoenberg used the same Knize toilet water.

On Stravinsky's return to California in 1952 after two months in Europe[15] and several weeks in New York, we were invited to a dinner in the Schoenberg home. Stravinsky was fascinated by Schoenberg's serial sketchbooks and library which, to Stravinsky's delight, contained the three-volume German edition of *Siddhartha Gautama Buddha*, as well as orchestral scores of Verdi's *Falstaff* and *Otello*, collections of Romantic German poetry[16] and an unopened copy of Mann's *Dr Faustus*.

The first of California's memorial tributes was a series of four 'Evenings on the Roof' concerts of Schoenberg's music in the autumn, organised by Peter Yates. Since I conducted most of the music,

---

15 At this time Stravinsky had known *Erwartung* only from Mitropoulos' recording, hearing a live performance for the first time in Nicolas Nabokov's Paris festival in 1952. Stravinsky said nothing about it, but on his return to Hollywood told the *Los Angeles Times* that it was one of the great experiences of his European trip.

16 Schoenberg had a family connection to Heinrich Heine through the poet's great-grandmother Sara Lea Pressburg. See Carl Djerassi's *Four Jews on Parnassus*, New York: Columbia University Press, 2008.

Stravinsky came with me to all of the rehearsals and concerts. These four events filled the hall, and the performances of some of the pieces were American premieres. Stravinsky mentioned the strong tonal elements of the piece 'Eine blasse Wäscherin' and the flute solo, as well as the repetition of the same verse form in all twenty-one pieces. His only comment on *Pierrot Lunaire* was that he still did not like the *Sprechstimme* but lauded the composer for having transposed sentimentality into high art.

On 29 July 1953 George Balanchine came to seek Frau Schoenberg's permission to present a Schoenberg ballet. Since she knew nothing about ballet and thought that I could be helpful in discussing the matter, she invited me to a dinner barbecued on her lawn by the great choreographer – a master chef. He was embarrassed to be there in my company, fearing that Stravinsky, in the hospital recovering from a prostatectomy, would find out about the project. At table I convinced Mrs Schoenberg that the *Accompaniment to a Cinematographic Scene* could make an ideal ballet, whether abstract or in the style of such silent films as *The Cabinet of Dr. Caligari* – what Stravinsky and other Russians called the 'German Green Horrors'.[17] Mrs Schoenberg wanted *Verklärte Nacht* but Balanchine insisted that he needed a 'twelve-tone' work. I interposed that there were no other possibilities. Richard Hoffmann then mentioned that a ballet orchestra would not be able to play this difficult piece satisfactorily. Insulted by this speculation, Balanchine commented that the New York Philharmonic probably could not play it, but the New York City Ballet orchestra regularly performed more difficult new music. Soon afterwards he departed, accompanied by his wife, Tanaquil LeClerq.

The next event was the arrival of Willy Strecker, Stravinsky's long-time friend and the director of B. Schott's Söhne, Mainz (one of the music publishers of Beethoven and Wagner). Strecker had come with the goal of purchasing and publishing *Moses und Aron* for an immediate performance, and of undertaking a future *Gesamtausgabe*. The publisher spent most of his time with the Stravinskys and in fact

---

17   This is exactly what Balanchine did in his ballet *Opus 34*, presenting the short piece twice, each with a totally different interpretation.

was lunching with them on his way to the airport with the original manuscript of the opera in a briefcase when a telephone call from Frau Schoenberg summoned him from the table. He returned to tell us that she had persuaded him to hold the *Moses* manuscript on his lap throughout the flight back to Germany. He had tried in vain to convince her that it would be wiser to send the manuscript, insuring it to the limit, and seemed amused at her lack of concern about what would happen if the plane were to crash with him on board.

For me the great event came on 11 October 1953. After conducting Schoenberg's Wind Quintet in the Los Angeles County Museum that afternoon, I attended a dinner party at Mrs Schoenberg's which began with her presentation to me of one of my most treasured possessions, a paper on which, shortly before his death, Schoenberg had written: 'Encourage Craft. He will break the Schoenberg Clique.'

In 1954 the British critic Hans Keller submitted a review of Stravinsky's *In Memoriam: Dylan Thomas* to Boosey & Hawkes for its house magazine, *Tempo*. Ernst Roth, the editor, sent the proofs to Stravinsky and appealed to him to reject the title of the article, 'Schoenberg's Stravinsky'. Stravinsky answered, 'No, I am very proud of the title.' Roth, a Schoenberg nemesis, had been responsible for Universal Edition's decision to stop publishing Webern. As a dedicatee of one of Richard Strauss's *Four Last Songs*, Roth is now an immortal name in the U.K. for helping to convince the elderly Strauss to appear in London after World War II. Otherwise Roth spent his time secretly urging Stravinsky to oppose my malevolent influence. Erwin Stein,[18] the chief musical editor at Boosey & Hawkes, Schoenberg's pupil and, with Webern, a founding member of the 'clique', was now the principal editor of Stravinsky's music. Stein sought my influence in convincing Stravinsky to remove the boxed tone-rows in his soon-to-be published Septet score. At an earlier date (1947) Stein, always very friendly to me, had asked for my help in trying to restrain Stravinsky

---

18 This keen and insightful man died suddenly in 1958. In 1949 George Lascelles, the seventh Earl of Harewood (first cousin of Queen Elizabeth II) married Stein's daughter Marion, a concert pianist whose full name was Maria Donata Nanetta Paulina Gustava Erwina Wilhelmine Stein. When Schoenberg heard the news he exclaimed: 'That should make me the *Erlkönig*.'

from rewriting the *Symphonies of Wind Instruments* until he had seen all three versions of the proofs of the 1920 printing.

After the exultant *Moses und Aron* premiere (Hamburg, 12 March 1954), and hoping to arouse interest in California for all of her late husband's creations, Mrs Schoenberg organised an exhibition of his paintings at UCLA, which the Stravinskys attended. She and I had become friends in the early 1950s when I visited her regularly to talk about her husband. She was lonely and tended to imbibe liberal amounts of Scotch. During one of our teatime libations I heard her say that in old age, Schoenberg had admitted an aversion to the *Sprechstimme* in *Pierrot Lunaire*: 'If only the voice would keep quiet so that I can hear the music.' Stravinsky felt the same way, which is what he had meant by his reservations about the 'aesthetics' of the opus in his 1935 autobiography. Before my first recording of Schoenberg's Serenade, his widow invited me to rehearse the piece in the Schoenberg home, which I did for a small invited audience that included my Cal-Tech professor friend, Paco Lagerstrom.

On 12 September 1954, Stravinsky answered an invitation from Mrs Schoenberg to attend a broadcast of the Hamburg *Moses und Aron* tape on her lawn. He did not go, but not for the given reason of a conflict with the first rehearsal of his *In Memoriam: Dylan Thomas*:

> Dear Mrs. Schönberg, this day of September thirteenth [Schoenberg's birthday] must be kept high in every musician's mind and I am deeply regretful not to be able to attend your noble musical gathering to commemorate the great Arnold Schönberg. Most sincerely, Igor Stravinsky.[19]

The *Dylan Thomas* piece is a landmark on the Stravinsky–Schoenberg path. For Stravinsky as for Alban Berg, the principal cog in the twelve-tone method was the abolition of major-minor modes, but in the *Memoriam* piece Stravinsky found an alternative way, introducing the

---

19 The truth is that Mrs Schoenberg had deliberately not invited me, and Stravinsky would not attend without me. I had been having a romance with her daughter Nuria Schoenberg since 1951 but this came to an end in the summer of 1954.

modes into serialism by melodic and harmonic means. Erwin Stein wrote to Stravinsky on 3 November 1954:

> I saw the beginning of your *Canticum Sacrum* and am enormously impressed... One recognizes your mind and hand in every bar. I am fascinated by your contrapuntal style. Your twelve-tone rows will cause an upheaval in the music world and will keep the analysts busy. I do not know whether you should help them by the arrows you have indicated in the score... Is it necessary that the listener knows the rows or is it sufficient that he feels the unity of form which the rows provide?

Stravinsky returned the letter, writing in the margin, 'As always, I forgot to delete the arrows.'

Stravinsky heard *Die glückliche Hand* for the first time when I conducted it in a concert shared with him on 5 June 1961, at Royce Hall, UCLA. He conducted Symphony of Psalms and his Violin Concerto (with Eudice Shapiro) on the same programme but the novelty of the evening was the Schoenberg West Coast premiere. The widow remained in attendance throughout and at the end was very complimentary to me. Meanwhile, Stravinsky was greeted backstage by a contingent of Soviet composers sent to obtain his commitment to celebrate his eightieth birthday in Moscow, managing to delay a confrontation by inviting the Russians to his home the next afternoon and obtaining a postponement of the trip to September 1962.

Stravinsky's supreme show of respect to Schoenberg was in his refusal in London in 1964 to re-record *The Rake's Progress* unless Columbia Records consented to underwrite my five sessions for *Von Heute auf Morgen*.[20] This insistence, making possible the commercial recording of the Schoenberg opera, was Stravinsky's most magnanimous gift to his peer. It has been said that my 1964 'recording of Schoenberg's opera was made as usual in time left over from [Stravinsky's recording of] *The Rake*'. But since Schoenberg's

---

20 Columbia's producer of this record, John McClure, deserves much of the credit for realising the project and for his talents in following me through this difficult work.

orchestra was twice as large as Stravinsky's and required many different instruments (saxophones, piano, mandolin, harp, multiple percussion), this would have been impossible. On two or three occasions in the early Hollywood years Stravinsky had required only about half of his fixed three-hour sessions and given the remaining time to me to record short pieces employing the same ensembles.[21] In June 1957 during his seventy-fifth-birthday recording of *Agon*, Stravinsky rewarded me for preparing the premiere and subsequent recording by giving me a quarter-hour from the second of his *Agon* recording sessions to complete a passage from Schoenberg's Variations, Op. 31, making it possible for me to release this first commercial disc of the piece.

Instead of requesting scores directly from the publisher, Stravinsky tended to hide his acquisitions of Schoenberg's music. David Adams of Boosey & Hawkes was asked to procure the orchestral and piano scores of the Piano Concerto. A note of 9 May 1962 from John Roberts in Toronto informs Stravinsky that Schoenberg's *Prelude to Genesis* (in which score Stravinsky had a special interest) was photographed per his request before it was returned to the publisher. Stravinsky's letters asking his London publishers to obtain tapes of Schoenberg works from German radio stations also survive. Regarding the printing of *Abraham and Isaac*, Stravinsky wrote to Roth on 23 September 1963, instructing him to send the vocal score to Israel, adding that the Hebrew letters and spelling of the English phonetics should conform to State rules or university usage: 'This, incidentally, is how Schoenberg's *De Profundis* was first published: Hebrew on top, Latin underneath, English in the flyleaf.'

After the premiere of Stravinsky's *Abraham and Isaac* in Israel (1964), the *Paris Express* published an interview with him by Nicole Hirsch, which reveals that Stravinsky had refused the commission for

---

21 An instance of using leftover Stravinsky recording time surfaced in a 2011 note from Mark DeVoto: 'I had a talk with Bethany Beardslee last summer at the Bard College Festival, and she told me how she and Bob and The Columbia Symphony made the first-ever recording of Berg's *Altenberg Lieder* in a half-hour left over from the session that recorded Stravinsky's *Threni* in 1959. The record was a life-changing experience for me.'

the work and donated it to the fund for the restoration of Masada.[22]
He is quoted in the article:

> My baritone has a double role, that of a narrator who tells
> the story, and that of a singer who comments... The language
> inspired me to employ appoggiaturas, as in Arab chant... As for
> the serialism, it is perfectly natural; it is the *other way* that is
> exhausted. I cannot do otherwise... Schoenberg understood this.

In October 1964 the London *Observer* invited Stravinsky to
review *Arnold Schoenberg's Letters* (edited by Erwin Stein), recently
published by Faber. Stravinsky wrote a review, but the arts editor,
Terence Kilmartin, rejected it as too brief. When the paper's music
critic was sent to persuade me to write a replacement, I agreed only
on the condition that my independent comments would be published
as such. The reader can scarcely imagine my anger the next day on
finding Stravinsky's name attached to my review, accompanied by an
envelope containing the *Observer*'s cheque made out to him.

Gertrud Schoenberg dined at the Stravinskys' on 4 November 1965,
and on this occasion gave a facsimile of *Jakobsleiter* to Stravinsky.
She died on 18 February 1967, while the Stravinskys were in Seattle.

After a concert in Los Angeles by the touring Pittsburgh Symphony
in May 1966, I invited Elden Gatwood, the orchestra's first oboist (and
my friend from Juilliard), to lunch at 1218 North Wetherly Drive. He
had met the composer on other occasions, most recently in Warsaw
the year before; he was now sitting at the composer's right, and some
music talk began. A propos of nothing, Stravinsky asked Mr Gatwood
if he knew the Schoenberg Violin Concerto. The answer was that he
had heard it several times on records but did not know it. Stravinsky

---

22   Years later the mayor of Jerusalem, Teddy Kollek, asked Stravinsky to give his manuscript
of the work to the University of Jerusalem, which he did most graciously. Kollek gifted to
me a Hittite chariot ornament that he had excavated during his youth in Iran, understanding
that the entire project could not have taken place without my help.
   After Stravinsky's first concert tour to Israel, President Ben-Zvi gifted an ancient shofar
to him, which he placed on his mantelpiece in Hollywood. In September 1969 when the
Stravinskys moved from their large California home to their small New York apartment,
Stravinsky asked me to give the shofar to a synagogue in Kingston, New York, where I had
been a follower of lectures by the Rabbi Herbert Bloom.

then startled his guest by announcing, 'It is the greatest concerto ever written.' When I checked this anecdote with Mr Gatwood on 30 November 2010, he added that he had followed every step in Stravinsky's composing path in the twelve-tone Schoenberg direction without finding any Schoenberg sound in it at all. 'Stravinsky's serial music sounds like Stravinsky all the way.'

CHAPTER 2
Stravinsky and Webern

In March 1959, after nine hours of empty ocean en route from Honolulu to Tokyo, the Stravinskys and I landed on Wake Island, our first fuelling stop in that pre-jet era. We scuffed through pink coral dust to an air-conditioned canteen where we were startled by the roar of a landing eastbound Swissair flight. The atoll was so narrow that the two airplanes that were parked side by side filled the tarmac. As the arriving passengers disembarked from a mobile stairway, we were climbing back onto our Pan Am aircraft when a young man shouted at me from the parallel gangway: 'Aren't you Robert Craft?' – apparently he had recognised Stravinsky next to me – 'I want to thank you for your Webern records.' I was dumbfounded. This was the coincidence of a lifetime: Wake Island, that speck in the ocean; a virtually unknown composer; and the one-in-a-billion likelihood of encountering anyone acquainted with my recordings of his music.[1]

My 1957 Webern album had transfixed Stravinsky, and the discovery of the Viennese composer became the main musical event in the Russian composer's post-*Rake's Progress* life. Stravinsky first heard Webern's orchestral Variations in October 1951 in Baden-Baden,

---

[1] Imagine two strangers, seated together on a flight from Perth to Addis Ababa and finding that they were both reading the same novel by Eça de Queiróz.

listening to a tape recording of it again and again.[2] Ten days later, in Munich, Karl Amadeus Hartmann, the organiser of a Stravinsky concert there and the last musician to have known Webern intimately, talked at length to Stravinsky about him, describing him as a botanist and temperamentally a recluse. The composer of the *Rite* was pleased to learn that, like himself, Webern was small, fanatically fastidious and dedicated to exactitudes. (Karl Amadeus added that Frau Webern was 'shrewish' and a 'compulsive housekeeper' who intimidated her husband, obliging him and their guests to remove their shoes before entering their home.) Also like Stravinsky, Webern was capable of angry outbursts on hearing worthless music, as when he and Hartmann attended a concert together at the Vienna State Opera. According to Hartmann, other musicians ostracised Webern and went out of their way to avoid him. As for his intellectual preoccupations, he was especially fond of Hölderlin's cosmology and of Heraclitus ('Oneness diversified within itself'), which the composer wrote down in Greek letters.

Stravinsky was fascinated by Hartmann's imitations of Webern's deft hand movements as he unwrapped and rolled out his scroll-like manuscripts; but what most captivated the Russian composer was Webern's always edifying analyses of music, which began with a dissection of the first measure of Schoenberg's *Erwartung* and concluded with Webern's own piano Variations, which Hartmann called a 'miracle of sound supremely constructed'. Bemoaning his inability to follow the technique of these 'serial interweavings', Hartmann nevertheless thought they 'contain the divine afflatus'. The reader should try to picture the gentle, heavy-set Hartmann speaking

---

2   Although Stravinsky never heard a coherent performance of the score, it would remain his favourite Webern opus. The work requires only two metronomic tempi, a fast (160 for the beat) and a slow (112 for the beat), but with 120 changes of metre in only 180 bars it is admittedly difficult to commute between these speeds, and made more so by the many silent downbeats and 'off-the-beat' rhythmic constructions. Other obstacles are that neither of the two tempi continues for more than a few bars, and almost all are moderated by *ritardandi* and *accelerandi*. In addition, fermatas are frequent, and breaks occur between the six variations as well as in a silent bar. Recordings seldom observe Webern's dynamic and other markings, and performances of the Variations, Op. 30 seem to swerve through the six and a half minutes in what often sounds like a single wobbly speed. Also, the F sharp trumpet note in bar 166, instead of the F natural blare, is a painful mistake in most recordings.

quietly but passionately to the thin, diminutive, wide-eyed Stravinsky. Later, in 1956, during Stravinsky's six weeks in Munich's Red Cross Hospital, Hartmann was a daily visitor.

Paul Collaer, the Flemish music director of Belgian Radio and a pioneer Stravinsky biographer, was our host during his concert tour in Belgium in 1952. As Webern's first champion in post-war Western Europe, Collaer greatly stimulated Stravinsky's interest in and knowledge of the Austrian composer by connecting him to the polyphonic masters of the Flemish Renaissance. Collaer played tapes of Webern's cantatas while telling us that the first of them, *Das Augenlicht*, refers to the sparkle in the eyes of his daughter Amalie Waller, to whom the piece is dedicated.[3] This personal touch appealed to Stravinsky who, having just heard a performance in Paris of the hothouse *Erwartung*, was already veering towards Webern's crystalline, linear style. Observing this, I felt that if Stravinsky had not already accepted a dinner invitation from his friend Queen Elisabeth he would have returned directly to California to complete his 'Lyke-Wake' Cantata. The next stage in his Webern orientation would take place in New York in the winter of 1952–3 at the New York apartment of Arthur Berger, where the New Music String Quartet played Webern pieces for his great new admirer.

As for late-period Webern, few listeners have heard it as yet, in the sense that coherent performances were unknown before the present decade and the Naxos releases. Further progress requires a variorum edition. For only one example, the printed score of the first song of Opus 18 differs from the manuscript in eight places and the metronomic indications vary in different printings, as do dynamics and phrasings everywhere.

Stravinsky was especially intrigued by stories of Webern's manner of conducting and his fights for more rehearsal time. We heard descriptions from Stravinsky's Hollywood physician, Dr Max Edel, who as a young man had attended Webern's Workers' Symphony Concerts. Marcel Dick, violist of the Kolisch Quartet, tells the story

---

3   In an afternoon with her at the Sacher Hotel in Vienna in October 1956, I found her charming, though she annoyed me by ridiculing all of her father's music as a hoax.

of Webern rehearsing Mahler's Ninth Symphony and Schoenberg's orchestrations of Bach. Webern was allotted only two rehearsals but by the end of the first was

> still tinkering with the third measure of one of the Bach Preludes, fussing about it, tickling out this sound and that. When Webern conducted a performance, there was nothing like it by anyone, but Schoenberg calculated that to rehearse Mahler's Ninth enough to have satisfied the conductor would have taken seven and a half years. The next morning at the second and last rehearsal Webern was, of course, unable to continue, and his place was taken by Erwin Stein.

Stravinsky was amazed by Webern's letter to Hermann Scherchen on his forthcoming BBC performance of the composer's instrumentation of the Bach *Ricercar*. The conductor had written to the composer asking exactly what he meant by the word *rubato* in the fugue subject that begins the piece. Webern replied in part:

> The subject should be played with movement every time, even with all the later additional counterpoints, *accel.*, *rit.*, and so forth, finally merging into the *poco allargando* of the last notes of the subject. For myself, I feel this part of the subject, this chromatic progression, to be essentially different from the first five notes, which I think of as being very steady, almost stiff (*i.e.*, in strict tempo; for the tempo is set by this phrase), and which, in my view, finds an equivalent in character in the last five notes. More precisely, I intend the *rubato* like this: faster G via F sharp to F, then holding back a little on the E flat (accent provided by the harp), and again *rubato* on the trombone progression where the instrument has a crotchet rest in bar 6. By the way, G to E flat is also five notes, and if you count the E flat as a link twice; to the inner ear this crotchet in bar 5, the tied E flat on the horn plus the crotchet rest of the trombone, is heavily stressed, a dividing point from the beginning and from the end. I have orchestrated it as such. Well now, if you count

the E flat twice you again have five notes. The construction
therefore appears to me as follows: Five notes, then 4 + 1 and 1
+ four, which is twice five, and at the end another 5 notes! And
these central twice-5 notes, the actual centre of the structure,
I feel to be quite different in character from the beginning and
from the end. The latter leads back with the *poco allargando* to
the stiffness of the opening – not appearing in the answer. In
dynamics this means that you must make a strong difference
between the *pp* of the first 5 notes and the *p* of the central
notes! And in the last five notes return *molto diminuendo* to *pp*.

I hope I have made myself understood. I must add that of
course the subject must not appear too disintegrated by all
this. My orchestration is intended (and I speak of the whole
work) to reveal the motivic coherence. This was not always easy.
Beyond that, of course, it is supposed to set the character of the
piece as I feel it. What music it is! At last to make available, by
trying through my orchestra to express my view of it, was the
ultimate object of this bold undertaking. Is it not worthwhile to
awaken this music from the seclusion of Bach's own abstract
presentation, and make this unknown, or unapproachable,
music available to everyone? ... One more important point for
the performance of my arrangement: nothing must be allowed
to take second place. Even the softest notes of the muted
trumpet must not be lost.

On returning to California, wanting to fix the analysis in his memory,
Stravinsky made a calligraphic copy of Webern's entire orchestral
score of the *Ricercata*.

One of the most absorbing of all Webern's revelations of his
thought processes occurs in a letter to a friend asking him to try to
obtain a commission for the Variations, Op. 30 from Paul Sacher:

> I settled on a form that amounts to a kind of overture based
> on variations – the orchestra is small: flute, oboe, clarinet,
> bass clarinet, horn, trumpet, trombone, tuba, celesta, harp,
> timpani, strings – and there is a synthesis in formal respects,

'horizontal' and 'vertical'. Basically my overture is an adagio form, but the recapitulation of the principal subject is in the form of a development, so this element is also present. Beethoven's *Prometheus* and Brahms's *Tragic*, for example, are overtures in adagio form, not in sonata form! But with me all of this evolves from the basis of a theme and a certain number of variations [six]. The theme is periodically structured from material elements. Repetition in a new form.

Webern had composed a tone row but a day later changed its second half, turning the last six notes into the retrograde of the first six. The intervallic patterns thus divided restructure the series into three groups of four notes, each one both harmonic and motivic; *i.e.*, vertical as well as horizontal. The composer noted the four new forms in a different colour pencil – black, red, blue and green.[4] He also used the green pencil to identify a new beginning on page five of the draft and to change the tempo marking from 'very animated' to 'lively', eventually the definitive tempo of the piece. Webern added:

On first looking at this score the reaction will probably be, 'Why, there really is nothing in it.' But because the person concerned[5] will miss the many, many notes he is used to seeing in R. Strauss... it would be vital to say that here in my score a difficult style is present... [I]t does not look like a score from the pre-Wagner period either – Beethoven, for instance – nor does it look like Bach. Is one to go back still further? Yes, but then orchestral scores did not yet exist! ... An orchestrated Josquin, perhaps?

Webern became the focus of European musical regard in the late 1940s with America joining in a little later (about 1952),[6] thanks in

---

4   I used Webern's score of Schoenberg's cinematic accompaniment music, Op. 34 when conducting it in Lausanne in 1956 and was pleased to see some of his corrections in coloured pencil. For example, Webern had rewritten Schoenberg's four quarter-notes (crotchets) in a bar of three as four dotted eighth-notes (quavers), which is more exact.

5   Paul Sacher, director of the Basel Chamber Orchestra.

6   See Glenn Watkins in the chapter 'A Collocation: Stravinsky and Schoenberg'.

the largest measure to the efforts of René Leibowitz, whose early influence was acknowledged even by Elliott Carter. By the mid-1950s a Webern 'movement' seemed to dominate the music world, albeit based on a misunderstanding concerning the traditional-classicist origins of this *avant-la-lettre* modernist. My own early Webern records increased interest in the composer, notably Marni Nixon's and Leonard Stein's performances of the songs with piano in which the accuracy of intonation was worthy of the composer, though Toni Arnold's 2011 recording of the same music supersedes this.

———

Anton von Webern was born in Vienna on 3 December 1883, to a family ennobled in 1731 by the Habsburg Emperor. Although the child's home environment was not musical, he was given piano lessons from the age of five. His parents did not oppose his choice of career but they considered their son's pieces 'too nervous' and 'all over before they start'. Like his contemporary Stravinsky, Webern married his first cousin and fathered four children, the first of whom arrived six weeks after the wedding. The new grandparents were so shocked by this peremptory appearance that they did not invite the young family to visit at Christmas, though financial support continued.

Webern seems to have been the first major twentieth-century composer deeply versed in Renaissance polyphonic music. He received a doctorate from the University of Vienna in recognition of his transcriptions of the second book of Heinrich Isaac's *Choralis Constantinus* and Johannes Brassart's *Sacris solemnis*, learning mensural notation and the construction of the isorhythmic motet from the latter. Webern's essay on the Isaac transcription proclaims the Netherlandish style of the sacred works of Josquin, Pierre de la Rue and Isaac as the apogee of musical art, further contending that 'in comparison with Ockeghem and Obrecht, there prevails in Isaac's work a much greater liveliness and independence of the individual parts'. Webern must have been stunned by *Pierrot Lunaire*, the polyphonic masterwork of the twentieth century, but why did he not confide this to his diary or a sketchbook?

The axial event in Webern's life, his decision in the autumn of 1904 to study with Schoenberg, is also, and inexplicably, not mentioned in the diary. Apart from their hyper-intensive creative personalities, the affinity that developed between teacher and pupil can be attributed in some measure to their provincial backgrounds, materially straitened circumstances and, perhaps, small physical statures. When Schoenberg's wife eloped with the young painter Richard Gerstl in 1908, it was Webern who convinced her to return and persuaded Schoenberg to receive, if not to forgive, her. If Webern had not been one of Schoenberg's closest intimates, this would have been an inconceivable intrusion.

The most shattering experience of Webern's own life heretofore was the sudden premature death of his mother in 1906. This is generally accepted as the underlying cause of his later 'nervous breakdown', but the hostile public reaction to his Five Pieces for String Quartet and Six Pieces for Orchestra, both written in her memory, undoubtedly contributed. A year after the premiere of *Pierrot*, when Webern began to show signs of emotional instability, Schoenberg advised him to consult a psychoanalyst, and for three months in the autumn of 1913 Webern was a patient of Freud's former associate Alfred Adler, whose reputation had been established by his success in the treatment of the inferiority complex. The only communications concerning Webern's progress are said to be in his still unpublished letters to Schoenberg, whose new works had evidently inspired him but also destroyed his self-confidence.

Webern could be described as a nature mystic or, in his own words, a 'metaphysical theosophist'. Though a Catholic, he believed that Beethoven's birthday should be celebrated on a par with Christmas. Reserved and introspective, he was also an autochthonous Austrian nationalist warped by an 'unshakable faith in the German spirit which indeed has created, almost exclusively, the culture of mankind'. A rustic, his early music employs cowbells, guitar and mandolin; his preferred avocations were mountaineering and the study of alpine plants and flowers. He spoke a Tyrolean dialect but, except for Church Latin, Italian musical terminology and the etymology of philosophical words in Classical Greek, knew no foreign tongue.

Webern's mystic-botanical inclinations help to explain his close friendship beginning in 1926 with the like-minded poet and painter Hildegard Jone, a married neighbour in nearby Mödling who wrote the verses for all of his future vocal works. She was apparently too 'spiritual' and 'pure' to have been his paramour, but the qualitative decline from Webern's previous selections of poetry by Goethe, Rilke, Trakl, Stefan George and Avenarius (Richard Wagner's nephew) to Jone's naïve pantheistic texts is puzzling. For Webern, another attraction would have been her descent from Beethoven's friend, the Countess Deym.

Webern's career as composer is chiefly remarkable for postponements of premieres, the ridicule of audiences, and the vilification of critics biased in principle against his Schoenbergian music. As a conductor Webern vacillated in his choices of employment and abruptly resigned from most of the jobs he accepted. By the age of forty, nevertheless, he had become an esteemed conductor, highly regarded both for his fiendish exactitude and musical depth.

As a young man Webern held posts as *répétiteur* and assistant conductor at the Vienna Opera and at opera houses in Danzig, Prague and Stettin but, because he baulked at having to prepare music he found contemptible, none of these appointments lasted very long. Beginning in the early 1920s after Schoenberg's Vienna Society for Private Performances had disbanded, Webern persisted for longer periods in respected conducting positions in Vienna. He directed the Singverein and the Workers' Symphony Concerts from 1922 to 1933, as well as the RAVAG (Austrian Radio) until his dismissal in 1934 after presenting a programme of the *verboten* Mendelssohn. His repertoire ranged from Bach to Glazunov but he focused on Beethoven and Mahler, presenting more of the latter's music than any other conductor at a time when it was rarely played. The attraction of opposites here is ironic since Mahler's pieces include some of the longest ever written, while Webern's are notoriously the shortest. 'If a programme is too long,' Schoenberg quipped, 'add a piece by Webern.' And whereas a Mahler symphony may seem like an *omnium gatherum*, every Webern opus is exclusive unto itself, never digressing from its own confined character and inner logic. The shock of Webern's music – and it is still there – is in its intensity of concentration. Next to Schoenberg, Mahler was the most important influence in the life of the young composer. He learned the art of conducting exclusively by observing Mahler.

In 1932 Webern conducted the first concert of American music, Ives included, in Vienna, though it was not advertised as such. He also led a male chorus in Mödling but resigned when it refused to accept a Jewish vocal soloist. After this he wrote to Schoenberg in Boston of 'feeling the most vehement aversion against my own race because of the anti-Semitism of so many of its members'. Even at today's distance, Webern's blindness to the impending catastrophe of the National Socialist Party seems incomprehensible. It had quickly condemned his music as 'degenerate', banned its publication and performance, and later forbidden him, as a disciple of Schoenberg, to conduct and teach, thereby depriving him of his only sources of income. Yet he seems not to have contemplated emigration, no doubt realising that with his large three-generation family, lack of money or prospects of support elsewhere, a move would have been impossible. Contrast his situation in 1933 with Schoenberg's, a world-renowned composer with a contract to teach in Boston, only two dependents and many American friends, all factors facilitating his move to the United States. Webern's vain belief in the supremacy of German culture was ultimately responsible for his violent, premature death.

An adamantine streak in Webern's personality emerges during the many crises in his career. The temporary break with his idol Schoenberg and the move away from him in Mödling soon after moving there only to be near him exposes this obduracy, as does Webern's abandonment of the directorship of the Workers' Concerts after years of successful and enthusiastically received performances, simply because a trombone player criticised his rehearsal procedures. His instant but permanent departure, with a refusal even to listen to the entreaties of the other players, seems irrational. Before the *Anschluss* (1938) he had been dismissed from a teaching position at the Vienna Israelite Institution for the Blind. After it, he became increasingly reclusive, his livelihood dependent on private teaching, sporadic conducting engagements in London (the BBC), Zurich, Barcelona, Winterthur and Vienna, and on such journeyman's jobs as arranging, proofreading and evaluating (*i.e.*, rejecting) new music submitted for publication:

> [X's] *Four Songs* are entirely amateurish, miserable, cheap! Indescribable. [Y's] *Albumblätter* is impossible! [Z's] Violin Concerto: I cannot recommend it. Inventions clearly based on Grieg... How poor it all is. Constant irrelevant modulations... Since we are being driven about all the time there is no idea of form.

On 7 June 1944, as the Russian Army advanced westward, two of Webern's daughters and their children fled to the town of Mittersill in the Pinzgau Mountains where one of their families owned a house. On 24 July Webern and his wife joined them there, but on their return to Vienna on 18 August he found an order to report for 'labour allocation'. Conscripted into service as an air-raid warden, Webern was uniformed and assigned to living quarters. He wrote to Frau Jone: 'I am not allowed to live at home any more, snatched utterly from my work. My duties are roughly those of a mason, carrying sand and hods and so on. Endless grind from 6 a.m.'

On 14 February 1945 Webern's son Peter, an army recruit, was killed in the bombing of a train in Yugoslavia. On 31 March, a few days before the Russian occupation of Vienna, the destitute, starving sixty-one-year-old composer and his wife set out on foot for Mittersill, trams no longer being available to civilians or not running at all. Mercifully, on reaching the rail terminal at Neulengbach they were able to purchase tickets for the remainder of the journey. Their daughter Amalie met them and brought them to her home where Webern, suffering from dysentery and malnutrition, shared a small house with sixteen other people.

The local choirmaster Cesar Bresgen, who had met Webern before, left a recollection of him at this time as 'repeatedly busy at a shabby little table with a pencil and compass occupied with geometrical figures or lines and signs'. Bresgen describes seeing him on a mountain path and hearing him talk about 'flowers, fungi, ferns, mosses, lichens'. Webern wrote in a letter to Berg:

> It is not the beautiful flowers in the usual Romantic sense that move me. My object is the deep, bottomless, inexhaustible meaning in all. I got to know a tiny plant, a little like a lily of the valley, homely, humble, hardly noticeable, but for me it contains all tenderness, emotion, depth, purity... I want to progress in the purely physical knowledge of all these phenomena. That is why I always carry my botany lexicon with me.

During the summer of 1945 the U.S. Army dispatched soldiers to Mittersill to curtail black-market activities and illegal currency exchanges between the residents and its own personnel. A curfew and blackout had been imposed on the neighbourhood where Webern's Mattel son-in-law, a suspect in this trafficking, resided. On 15 September Webern shared a meal at the Mattel home. Afterwards he stepped outside to smoke a cigar, American contraband undoubtedly provided by his son-in-law. Not understanding a 'hands-up' order by an American soldier posted outside the building, Webern struck a match and was shot three times in the chest and abdomen. (Contradictory versions of this unwitnessed savagery have appeared, but the three bullet holes were visible on a wall of the house for many years.) The American marksman, alleging that he had been assaulted with an iron bar - though Webern would have been too weak to lift, let alone wield one - was acquitted. A Gregorian Requiem Mass was held in Mittersill's small Baroque church. Five people followed the coffin to the cemetery.

The biography of Webern's creative mind is more difficult to comprehend than that of the man, simply another artist brutally treated at the hands of life. But the analyses of the music are often of little help to the listener. One of the most important discoveries in Webern's sketchbooks is that this supposedly abstract composer was actually responding to his natural world impressionistically - or expressionistically - and more subtly than the 'Ultima Thule' from the world of Strauss's *Alpine Symphony*. In fact, Webern had outlined an extra-musical programme for the Quartet, Op. 22 before composing a note:

> 1st movement: Quiet (Annabichl, mountains), perhaps Variations
>
> 2nd movement: Slow; Introduction to 3. (Schwabegg)
>
> (Soloists only)
>
> 3rd movement: Rondo (Dachstein, snow and ice, crystal clear
>
> air, cosy, warm, sphere of the high pastures) – coolness of
>
> the first spring (Anninger, first flora, primroses, anemones
>
> [hepataica, pulsatilla])
>
> IInd secondary theme (Soldanella, flowers of the highest region)
>
> Theme (IIIrd time) The children on ice and snow
>
> Repetition of 1st secondary theme. (Sphere of the alpine roses)
>
> IInd secondary theme, light, sky. IV.
>
> Coda: outlook into the highest region.

Ernst Krenek, who grew up in the same landscape as Webern and knew him well, defended him against accusations of 'cold cerebralism and of reducing music to meaningless calculations', memorably remarking that 'his music evokes the image of the tense stillness of the highest mountain peaks'.

In conversation with Stravinsky, Krenek extended the topographical image, associating the extremely wide intervals characteristic of Webern's Opus 22 Quartet with the jagged contours of the Styrian Koralpe which had been visible to Webern from his family home; his father was buried at Annabichl, his mother at Schwabegg. The Quartet's second movement is obviously a game, and the suggestion that it might be a game of 'children on ice and snow' is intriguing, though the specification actually refers to a third movement that was not included in the piece.

In comparison, most of Schoenberg's music is overtly programmatic, but of course not in conventional ways. Webern's exploration of the twelve-tone system is manifoldly different from that of its progenitor, as Schoenberg himself quickly understood. Curiously, Krenek was surprised that the twelve-tone technique of Webern's Trio attaches complete forms of the series end to end, but since it was his first entirely twelve-tone work, this seems only natural. (The recording of this work by the top-class Emerson Quartet destroys the second movement by crashing through full-stop red lights and ignoring road signs indicating changes of speed.)

Webern's next composition, the *Symphonie*, uses more than one series simultaneously and aims in a completely new aesthetic direction: the compounding of a Beethoven sonata form with the polyphonic purity of the sixteenth-century Netherlanders. Hereafter Webern pursued a course of simplification (call it reductionism), the Concerto, Op. 24 becoming virtually diagrammatic. Schoenberg contemporaneously explored ever-greater involutions, during which his aesthetic sometimes seemed to revert to Brahms, never more so than in the 1936 Violin Concerto dedicated to 'Anton von Webern'.

Most performances of Webern's music follow only minimally the composer's directions *vis-à-vis* tempi, dynamics, phrasing, articulation and expressive character. Of these elements, tempo is the most important, yet only one recording of the *Symphonie* (Naxos) presents the music near the speeds of Webern's metronomic indications, with the result that the masterpiece described by Virgil Thomson as 'spun steel' often sounds as limp as a melting Dalí watch looks.

The first movement of the *Symphonie* is distinguished by its spaciousness, sense of continuity, regularity of metre and pulsation, and ethereal sounds. From the start the listener is aware of underlying structures – horizontal and vertical symmetries, mirrors, palindromes and, more specifically, the Venn diagram for four terms – but musical pleasure is only subliminally related to such formal concepts. The second movement, in contrast, consists of eight discrete variations and a coda, all clearly distinguished by changes of instrumentation and tempo. Halfway through are two curious, interlude-like bars, strikingly reminiscent of Debussy. Both melodically and harmonically the music here (repeated minor thirds) is manifestly tonal. Webern had conducted a piece by Debussy on 17 April 1928, only shortly before composing this part of the *Symphonie*. What *can* be conjectured is Webern's realisation that the return to triadic harmony in Schoenberg's 'Eine blasse Wäscherin' legitimised his brief flirtation with tonality.

A study of Webern's songs with instruments ought properly to begin with the Latin canons for Maundy Thursday and Good Friday, if only because of their brevity and accessibility, simple linearity and limitation to either one or two instruments. His next song cycle, *Three Traditional Rhymes*, is immeasurably more difficult to absorb because of the great increase in rhythmic complexity and the density of the three-part instrumental accompaniment. *Rhymes* contradicts the assertion that Webern's vocal music is 'absolute', as opposed to 'programmatic'. In fact, the songs 'express' the emotions and reflect the meanings of the texts through extensions of traditional formulae as well as through new ones. In the opening lyric, pulsation, metre and tempo are regular throughout in correspondence with the simplicity of the verse, even though the triplet rhythm (violin/clarinet) is new. In the second song the *forte* dynamics, the grumbling rhythmic patterns in the viola, vividly evoke the scourging and crown of thorns in the text. The third song, the death agony on the cross, is also expressionistic. The singer's unaccompanied shriek on C sharp *in alt* on the word 'Rette' at the apex of the piece is dramatic realism. The rhythmically vaporous instrumental ending is one of the most subtle Webern ever wrote.

The next and last of the instrumental song cycles, like the first of the *Rhymes*, begins with a pastoral love lyric. The exuberant mood of the second song is suggested by the strumming guitar at the beginning, and the continuing sequence of joyous high and low vocal leaps are literally breathtaking for the singer. The language in dialogue form suggests a parallel to Lower Austrian roadside shrine carvings with painted iconic images. The third song, a Latin hymn, begins softly with a duet for the accompanying instruments intoning single melodic lines, but the music that follows is a song of religious exaltation.

The Trio marks Webern's biggest single step towards the perfect fusion of his materials. If the songs with instruments are static and can be compared to intricately carved jewels, each expressing an emotion inspired by a poem or prayer, the Trio, in contrast, contains scudding movement, development and variation. Webern wrote to Schoenberg that the tempo and dynamic markings in the Trio had cost him a great effort, and that he needed 'time to understand what I have written'. It is a revealing remark: the calculations in the composing process ultimately depend on the indefinable 'force that through the green fuse drives the flower', as the poet wrote. Webern's diary tells us that the Vienna premiere 'went very well, even if only a few listeners understood something of it'. A Berlin performance prompted a congratulatory letter from Schoenberg, but in Stettin the opus was boisterously rejected and, at an International Society for Contemporary Music concert in Count Chigi-Saracini's palace in Siena, provoked audience ructions. Someone shouted an appeal to Mussolini to close down the festival. Webern, who was not present, described the fracas – as told to him by Berg – in a letter to Schoenberg: 'During the first bars of the second movement the restlessness became so great that Kolisch [the violinist] decided to call a halt.'

As with the Trio and the *Symphonie*, the Quartet for tenor saxophone, violin, clarinet and piano raised the question of whether to give the piece a third movement, two-movement pieces being a cornerstone of Webern's aesthetic practice at the time. On 9 September 1930, he wrote to Berg, who did not answer the questions but responded: 'This Quartet is a miracle... [T]here is nothing in the entire world of music production that attains even approximately such a degree of originality' (19 August 1932). Webern revealed what few would have suspected: that the Scherzo third movement in Beethoven's G major Piano Sonata, Op. 14 No. 2 was a model for the second, *giocoso* movement, which includes insider jokes such as the re-use of the metronomic unit of the slow movement for the fast one and a final Presto for only one note.

The String Quartet, Op. 28 is arguably the most economical, concise and perfectly structured of all of Webern's late music. He tells us that the piece is thematic, and the theme is BACH, and every aspect of its construction interrelates. The series is limited to only three intervals: a minor second, a minor third and a major third. Webern seems intent on reducing the possibilities and imposing ever larger limitations on himself, even though already many years before he had composed the shortest and most extreme opus in modern music in his idea-packed Bagatelles.

No wonder Stravinsky was mesmerised by Webern, whose influence is most obvious in *A Sermon, A Narrative, and A Prayer*. On the tenth anniversary of Webern's death, Universal Edition urged Stravinsky to write a blurb for the review *Die Reihe*. Stravinsky complied because the publisher had been sending manuscript facsimiles of Webern's music to him, along with a photocopy of Webern's transcription of part of Heinrich Isaac's *Choralis Constantinus* and a facsimile of the orchestra score of Berg's *Lulu* used in the 1937 Zurich premiere – which Stravinsky gave to me and I, in turn, presented to George Perle, the late, highly esteemed Berg scholar and composer. Stravinsky's declaration is the only published tribute of the sort that he ever paid to a contemporary composer:

> The 15th of September 1945, the day of Anton Webern's death,[7] should be a day of mourning for any receptive musician. We must hail not only this great composer but also a real hero. Doomed to a total failure in a deaf world of ignorance and indifference he inexorably kept on cutting out his diamonds, his dazzling diamonds, the mines of which he had such perfect knowledge.

---

7   Stravinsky-Webern history must be corrected before a mistaken assumption becomes myth. When I visited Webern's grave at Mittersill in 1955, Stravinsky was not with me but in Lugano, where I rejoined him in time for his concert with the Swiss-Italian Radio Orchestra.

CHAPTER 3
Stravinsky and Balanchine

Since the time of Tchaikovsky, the relation of ballet
and music has changed. Before that master's time, the
composer was commissioned to write a series of numbers
to fit in with the dancing. Now the ballet composer writes
a composition to which the dancers must apply their art.
It is their work to fit in their dances.

Igor Stravinsky

I first met George Balanchine on 5 April 1948 in Stravinsky's suite in the Ambassador Hotel on Park Avenue. When I entered the room the two men were locked in discussion about their forthcoming production of *Orpheus*. My intrusion surprised Mr B. but not Stravinsky, with whom I had an appointment. He introduced me in English, then explained my presence in Russian. A few moments later, the prima ballerina Maria Tallchief came to fetch her husband for a rehearsal. Speaking English only, she reminded him of the time, but the two men continued their conversation for another half-hour, now in English. I understood that Stravinsky's macaronic American speech was more coherent than Balanchine's, which tended to omit verbs and abandon sentences midstream.

My perspectives on Balanchine differ from other people's because I was never in his presence *without* Stravinsky. Robert Gottlieb's book describes him as 'always calm, always courteous, and without the slightest touch of intimacy even in close contact'. This is mainly true, but I observed other sides of Mr B. as well. Alone with Stravinsky (and me), the great choreographer was often outspokenly critical of Lincoln Kirstein, who had brought Balanchine to the United States, co-founded the New York City Ballet with him, and remained his lifelong sponsor. Balanchine complained to Stravinsky about their double-billing and their promotion as equal partners: 'What does he *do*?' This comment may upset balletomanes, though some Balanchine associates were aware of his true sentiments. I doubt that he was completely candid about this even with Suzanne Farrell (a Kirstein groupie). Gottlieb is also mistaken about the choreographer's perpetual calmness. He could be explosive, vindictive and surprisingly jealous. Spotting Serge Lifar talking to Vera Stravinsky backstage in the State Theater at the end of the 1972 Stravinsky Festival, Balanchine abruptly retreated in another direction.[1] In Saratoga that same summer, he publicly avoided his protégée and intimate associate Karen von Aroldingen when he saw her strolling with me. Further, he could be demeaning about older women, even such long-time friends as Mme Lucia Davidova. But these are peccadilloes in the larger history. The man created a new kind of beauty as great as that of any artist of his time.

In New York I dined regularly with the Stravinskys and Balanchine in the Russian Tea Room, at Mme Davidova's and at Balanchine's apartment where, most memorably after midnight Russian Easter services, he prepared the paschal delicacies himself but tasted none of them. After Stravinsky's death I still saw Mr B. frequently, since he asked me to suggest outlines for programmes in the Stravinsky Festival planned for June 1972. The project was a consuming passion for him. The final decisions were his, of course, and he ignored my advice not to play the early Symphony in E flat, as well as my pleas to present *Petrushka* and *Les Noces*. I knew that he would refuse the

---

1   In 1928 Balanchine's *Apollo* choreography was scarcely noticed in the press, whereas Serge Lifar's glamorous dancing of the title role made him world famous.

former because it belonged to the world of Nijinsky and Fokine, the latter because it had been the domain of Bronislava Nijinska and Jerome Robbins.

One unforgettable experience with Balanchine was the 1965 filming in Hamburg of the 'Terpsichore' Variation in *Apollo*. ('Terpsichore, combining in herself both the rhythm of poetry and the eloquence, reveals dancing to the world, and thus among the Muses takes the place of honour...') Rolf Liebermann, the then director of the Hamburg Opera which in 1962 had invited the New York City Ballet to the German city for the celebration of the composer's eightieth birthday, now wanted to teach the ballet to a new generation of dancers. Liebermann's aim was to reveal a model of the prima ballerina's performance and provide a lesson for the opera orchestra of the authentic stylistic character of the piece. The two creators of the 1928 work now disagreed about tempi, the choreographer arguing for the much slower original, Stravinsky insisting that 'this is 1965 and I am taking the 1965 tempo'. Stravinsky as a conductor was often cantankerous and indeed was so when rehearsing the *Apollo* violin cadenza: he conducted every note, further humiliating the player by asking for agogic changes on most of them. Long inured to the composer's spiteful side, Mr B. simply asked Suzanne to dance 'Terpsichore' at both tempi, first snapping his fingers at the 1928 metronome speed in order to demonstrate that the piece could achieve its elegant seductiveness only at this more leisurely pace. Stravinsky eventually compromised, but neither Balanchine nor his muse was satisfied with the result.

Balanchine's primary aim in Hamburg was to obtain a recording of Stravinsky's new five-minute Variations, which the choreographer envisaged as a solo for Suzanne to dance three times, each with different choreography. The day after the recording session of the Variations we flew to London, where we listened repeatedly to the edited tape in Stravinsky's Savoy Hotel room, despite the intrusion of a BBC film crew. The snag this time was that the two Russians, speaking English together for the film, were scarcely able to understand each other, particularly regarding the pulsation in the three twelve-part variations. Balanchine's hand movements while chanting a slow 'cha,

cha, cha' puzzled Stravinsky, who would otherwise have explained that pulsation was not an obstacle since one instrument in each of the groups of twelve plays a steady tactus. As the BBC team was leaving, one of the workers asked: 'Mr Stravinsky, is it more difficult to compose in old age?' A broad smile unfolded as a prelude to the rapier response: 'Oh, for you I am old, but not for me.'

In Hollywood the two artists were together almost daily. At home Mr B. addressed Stravinsky with synaloepha as 'Igorfyodorovitch', somehow compressing the given name and the patronymic into a single syllable. Unknown aspects of the choreographer's personality emerged in his intimate conversations with the composer while they spent hours together listening to a wide range of music. In one of these sessions they heard an assortment of tapes by Yannis Xenakis,[2] from the Golden Age of cacophony, along with the Jack-the-Ripper scene in *Lulu*, which Mr B. wanted to choreograph for Suzanne, changing the scenario to display the charms of Ishtar, the Babylonian–Assyrian goddess who rescues Tammuz from the underworld by shedding another layer of her clothing at each of seven gates.

In Los Angeles in the 1950s, the Stravinskys and Balanchine were together almost every day during summers with the City Ballet at the Greek Theater in Griffith Park. It was here that Stravinsky urged Balanchine to revive *The Nutcracker* and to create *A Midsummer Night's Dream*, both of which were initiated in rehearsals as early as 1953. I remember a Sunday afternoon lawn party given for the ballet company at the Stravinsky home, when he slipped away to his studio to write down a musical idea. That evening he confided to me that on entering the room he quickly retreated after glimpsing Mr B. tenderly engaged with a young ballerina on the floor beneath the piano. Mr B. often visited the composer in his last years in Hollywood, always trying to lift his spirits and encouraging him to compose even

---

2   Mario Bois's book, *Près de Strawinsky*, reveals that Xenakis was published by Boosey & Hawkes through the influence of Stravinsky. Souvtchinsky gave several scores to Stravinsky, who pronounced them 'remarquable'. The music was at an opposite aesthetic from the older man's recent works, and Stravinsky was fully aware that the editor E. Roth would reject them. When Stravinsky relayed this response to Bois, the composer's answer was: 'What do you want? He loves *Der Rosenkavalier*.' Nevertheless, Xenakis received a contract for the publication of his complete works.

a few bars for a very short ballet which he predicted would be 'like an atomic pill'.

After the Stravinskys moved to New York in September 1969, Mr B.'s visits to the composer in the Essex House became less frequent, as he could not bear to see his dear friend so ill. At the private service held on the evening of the composer's death, Balanchine was drawn and pallid, but his nervous blinking had stopped, and he maintained his inimitably dignified composure. Following the ritual, he bowed to Mrs Stravinsky, kissing her three times through her veil in the Russian tradition. Taking my hand, he quietly thanked me 'for all you did for him', then walked to the flower-laden bier and knelt there praying until he was alone in the room.

A decade after Stravinsky's death I was especially close to Balanchine during his experiments with cuts in the first part of *Apollo*. He treated me with great kindness and sought my opinion, as if I had authority over Stravinsky's wishes in the matter. In truth, I did not care for the excisions in this crystalline masterpiece and said so, but Balanchine soon made up his mind to restore the original.

The real genius of Balanchine was discovered posthumously by Alastair Macauley, who described the connection between Stravinsky's music and the choreography:

> *Movements* seems to begin symmetrically... with a corps of six women (corresponding to the orchestra) arranged to the right and left, until we notice that the lead male–female couple (the piano) is off-center... All kinds of spatial tensions are going on here: a delicate one occurs when the two halves of the corps move not symmetrically but as two parallel units. Watching, we feel this as mystery, and the actual steps of the choreography making us feel that the mystery arises out of the music – keep asking new questions, taking bold steps to conclusions unforeseen... The ballet becomes most startling when we feel, in its later stages, how far from any step-for-note it proceeds. Balanchine, plucking out unheard rhythms, seems to connect Stravinsky to the music of the spheres.[3]

---

3   *The New York Times*, 28 January 2009.

CHAPTER 4

Stravinsky on Composing and Conducting

On Composing

Stravinsky's own commentaries on composing are more revealing than any other writing about him and his work. They are not extensive, though others remain to be discovered, translated and gathered into a volume worthy to rest on a shelf not very far below Mozart's letters. When Stravinsky began to give concerts in 1923, interviewers in comparatively remote cities seemed able to extricate more personal material from him than those in the musical capitals of the world, where he was better known but also more cautious. Music critics in Copenhagen, Warsaw and the American Mid-West in 1925 managed to gather more material than those in London, Paris and Berlin; for only one example, the story of Debussy's gift of his walking cane to him is revealed in a Danish newspaper interview of 1924.

Stravinsky preferred speaking to writing, which he thought too time-consuming. His *Conversations* books began as talk, then deteriorated into my writing, which he liberally remoulded, cut and corrected. It has been said that I sometimes put words in his mouth; this is true only because I was keenly aware that I could not substitute for the originality of his images, the precision and concision of his language. I understood that he would write about himself only in collaboration. The 'as-told-to' books previously published under his name, *An Autobiography* and *The Poetics of Music*, were ghostwritten respectively by Walter Nouvel and Roland-Manuel.

My advantage over these precursors was that I could provide direct quotations from Stravinsky, though that still raises questions of distinguishing authorship. More than half a century later, readers are becoming able to distinguish between our voices. My rebuttal, in any case, is that an alloyed Stravinsky would be preferable to no Stravinsky. Philip Glass, questioned in *Time* magazine as to the greatest composer of the twentieth century, replied, 'Stravinsky', and mentioned parenthetically, 'with the help of his mentor, Robert Craft'. Without Plato we would have had little of Socrates; without Plutarch, little Lycurgus; without Pensacola's James Macpherson, no Ossian (that favourite book of Napoleon, Goethe, Brahms – in his Opus 17 – and Schoenberg, who composed music for Goethe's Ossianic poem *Darthulas Grabgesang*); and without Gertrude Stein, no *Autobiography of Alice B. Toklas*. A. E. Housman's *Classical Papers* contends that much classical literature is similarly corrupted. In the dialogues with Maecenas, it seems that Horace wrote most of the answers to his own questions.

Apparently Stravinsky attached little importance to what he said to journalists, considering their writings largely impertinent as well as impermanent. Since he did not bother to collect his published interviews, almost all of those found in his archives were sent to him by admirers. A new generation of scholars would be wise to ransack the newspaper files of every city in which Stravinsky appeared as conductor, pianist, or duo-soloist with his son Soulima or the violinist Samuel Dushkin. New Russian critics have begun to mine the early Stravinsky years in the publications of his native land, but the results of this research have not yet been published in the United States.[1]

---

1   Among the interviews that merit publication are the programme notes for the 1933 Stravinsky-Dushkin English tour, which included Manchester, Liverpool, Cambridge, Oxford and London. Some of them are signed 'I.S.' and some 'Edwin Evans' (the father of Lady Natasha Spender, widow of Sir Stephen).

The following excerpt from the 1929 Budapest magazine *Magyarsag* provides a convenient introduction to Stravinsky's philosophy of composing:

> Creativity can endure if it is necessary and natural... Whatever I do, I find natural, and I always know what I must do. This is the essence of creation: to select the material and then purify it. Usually one problem occupies my mind and I build my work around it. Often I start with technical problems, together with spiritual and philosophical ones which reinforce or develop one another. Frequently a certain grouping of instruments attracts me, and I imagine that I will try to create something with a defined instrumental combination. But I am never in a hurry. I have time, my thoughts are maturing in me, and only when I feel the time is right do I start to work. This logic restrains me from working until the technical solution and the creative idea are in one hundred percent correlation. When I start to work, I am not certain what I am going to do, but I know exactly what I want to do. The creative process is very complex. One must limit the portals of what is called inspiration, which is popularly thought to be an onset of emotion that sets the creative imagination in motion. I disagree with this conception. Composition begins with an appetite or taste for discovery, and the emotion is borne after the discovery, following rather than preceding the creative process.

In April 1931 Stravinsky was in Trieste for a concert with the local orchestra under the direction of Rhené-Baton, the second conductor of *The Rite of Spring*, in London in July 1913, after Diaghilev had dismissed Monteux for refusing to make cuts in the ballet. In the 1931 visit, Stravinsky spent much of his time between rehearsals with his aptly named friend, though we do not learn from their talk whether R.-B. followed Diaghilev's dictates about the cuts. Their conversations would have been enlightening about the *Rite* and much more.[2] But *Il Piccolo di Trieste* did publish an important interview:

> The principal element and determining factor in the composer's work is hearing. If my ear is not pleased, my creative instinct does not respond. The ear has its own appetite, and it assembles, assimilates, orders and elaborates the construction... but I use the word 'appetite' in the spiritual sense, as St Augustine uses it in describing the appetite of the soul, which both exalts and sublimates itself as it gains more appetite for Light and for God. Both the imaginative faculty and our musical ear are sterile without light, grace and guidance from above. (23 April 1931)

In the right-wing French review *Gringoire* on 27 October 1937, Stravinsky addresses the subject of composition:

> Style is not a framework into which the work is inserted, but the work itself. Form is not a means to an end, but creation itself. Human work is conceivable only in form. The Russian word *stroi*, loosely translated as agreement [expresses what I mean]: we need a working agreement between ourselves and the surrounding chaos. When I compose, a great number of musical combinations occur to me. I have to choose and to select. But what standards should I use? Simply that only one form pleases me and the others do not. The result resembles a predetermined physical or chemical experiment. All that we are able to do is to surrender ourselves to the course of the experiment that is being conducted in and by us.

In Munich following a recital with Dushkin on 2 February 1933, an interviewer elicited other beliefs on the subject:

---

2   Stravinsky did mention that Rhené-Baton agreed with the composer's opinion that the cause of the scandal at the *Sacre* premiere was provoked by the dancing - pigeon-toed, stomping, jumping - and not by the music. Stravinsky framed a review of the second performance of *Sacre* that proclaims: 'Les spectateurs de la première représentation conserveront longtemps le souvenir du joli chahut provoqué dans la salle par les danses si particulières de M. Nijinsky.'

In art, emotion is understood. The issue is something else
that the Greeks called *poiesis*, 'to know how to do'. Music is a
matter of technique, culture and knowledge. It is a finality, as
significant as philosophy or mathematics. Emotion is for the
audience. Rhythm, to my understanding, becomes music itself.
Thus the works of Bach, whom I consider the imperishable
model for us all, consist only of rhythm and architecture.
Rhythm is integral and dominant, but the Romantics made an
ornament of it, a flourish.

In March 1933 the composer told the critic János Fáthy for the
publication *Pesti Hírlap* in Budapest:

If you perceive in me a proponent of a new classicism, then you
misunderstand. My art is aiming in a canonical direction. For
me, all great and pure art must be *ecclesiastical* in spirit, the
spirit built on the concept of recognition through knowledge.
I want the audience not just to hear the music but also to
recognise and to hear it. To hear and to comprehend are not
the same. On the basis of familiarity and habit it is easy to hear
and at the same time recognise the works of the old masters.
Today's music must be listened to in such a way that passive
hearing extends to active recognition and knowledge. In other
words, the hearing must be free of all that is familiar, habitual,
inherited.

One of the most engaging of Stravinsky's remarks on the creative
process came years later from an interview in New York on 25
February 1945, published in the paper *Pour la Victoire*:

I have no *manière* in composition, and I do not try to obey any
preconceived system. My aesthetic resembles that of certain
Latin authors, and of Pascal. I have a general idea before I
compose, but ideas come to me only while I am composing,
following each other, each one the logical consequence of its
predecessor – though more than ideas, obviously, are needed
to compose music.

While in Brussels for the first performance of Symphony of Psalms, 13 December 1930, Stravinsky made an important admission to an interviewer intent on drawing parallels between himself and Le Corbusier: 'For me constructive form is predominant and in all of my music, even in the early years. It seems to me that the tendency of all art today is constructivism.' Finally, another personal declaration exposes another perspective:

> It is harder to be a composer than anything else in the world today, first because the many noises that one must hear and guard against – the streets, neighbours, the radios – even when the radio is turned off, the vibrations that I know are going on waiting to be released in malevolent sounds from that little box – have the power to disturb. A doctor confirmed for me that inside one's ears are the instruments for balancing the whole body. One tiny muscle is drawn tightly all the time with the effort to receive and transmit the sensations made by the music I am hearing in my mind, together with the impressions or interruptions of the outside, and this affects the whole nervous system.

Turning from the philosophy of composing to the act itself, I had many opportunities to observe and sometimes even assist Stravinsky during the last two decades of his life. I was inexplicably and uniquely privileged to witness the creative struggles that took place in his Hollywood studio. In the analyses of completed and published compositions, I quote from Joseph Straus of Princeton, whose survey on Stravinsky's path of discovery in his sketchbooks following the *Rake* is admirably clear as well as eloquent:

> Stravinsky's late works differ from his earlier ones in striking and profound ways. During the final two decades of his life, every major work was almost shockingly new, right down to its original, and ever-changing, principles of structural formation. The works in this period describe a succession of compositional firsts, including his first works to use a series (Cantata, 1952,

Septet, 1953, *Three Songs from William Shakespeare*, 1954);
his first fully serial work (*In Memoriam: Dylan Thomas*, 1954);
his first work to use a twelve-tone series (*Agon*, 1954–7); his
first work to include a complete twelve-tone composition
(*Threni*, 1958); his first work to make use of twelve-tone arrays
based on hexachordal rotation (*Movements*, 1959); his first
work to use the verticals of his rotational arrays (*A Sermon,
A Narrative, and A Prayer*, 1961[3]); his first work to rotate the
series as a whole (Variations, 1965); his first work to rotate the
tetrachords of the series (*Introitus*, 1965); and his first work
to use two different series in conjunction (Requiem Canticles,
1966, his last major creation).

The pattern of innovation is remarkable, persistent, and
unprecedented. I can think of no other major composer, at
a comparably advanced age and pinnacle of recognition and
success, who so thoroughly altered his compositional approach,
or whose late works differ so greatly from his earlier ones. While
there is some truth in the cliché that Stravinsky always sounds
like Stravinsky, nonetheless the late works differ radically
from the earlier ones at every level, from their deep modes of
musical formation to the rhythmic and intervallic details of the
musical surface. Furthermore, Stravinsky's late works are not
only radically different from the earlier ones, but are highly
individuated from each other as well. There is no major work
in this period in which Stravinsky did not try something new.[4]

---

3   The latter part of this masterpiece, from the stoning of St Stephen, contains the most
    dramatic music in all of Stravinsky's late works. He wrote this, inspired by Dante: 'Him I
    saw bowed to the earth by death / which weighed upon him now, but of his eyes, he made
    ever gates to heaven.'
4   Matthew Arnold's deploration that 'old age is incapable of emotion' is belied by such
    masterpieces as Richard Strauss's *Four Last Songs*, Schütz's Christmas Oratorio and Act
    Three of *Parsifal*. Kenneth Clark's features of an old-age style are: 'A sense of isolation,
    loneliness, the snuffing out of the lyric faculty, and the choice of tragic themes.' Clark
    thought that the old-age style began with Donatello's St Anthony high reliefs in Padua. The
    writer also maintained that 'the act of creation became a torture... Michelangelo grumbled
    about every job he undertook.' Also Monet created his own marvellous late manner out of
    infinite pain. Clark archly stated that 'All old people are bored and irritated by the company
    of their fellow bipeds.'

The music of Stravinsky's first American years dismayed many of his loyalists, particularly the lighthearted American-style pieces: the *Circus Polka*, the *Norwegian Moods* and *Scherzo à la Russe*. The opus that antedated these, *Danses concertantes*, began well but ended poorly. The score had a great rhythmic vivacity and a new twist in its melodies in which many mistakenly detected a debt to Copland. The orchestration was a marvel and many listeners gave it an A-minus. Surprisingly, all of these five productions, extending to the Sonata for Two Pianos, were jolly in mood with no suggestion of the horrors that had closed down Europe. But these early pieces are amazingly varied and fresh, and they all give promise of new dimensions to be explored.

Stravinsky's participation in the bellicose mood that came with Pearl Harbor began in the Symphony in Three Movements on 6 February 1942, soon after the completion of the *Danses concertantes* and before he conducted its premiere. Stravinsky announced that the symphony had been conceived as a piano concerto – even though the instrument is not employed at all in the sketches – until he had already written a considerable part of the opus. But the chronology of the work is bewildering, even though not starting at the beginning is characteristic of the composer, who famously said: 'You have to know what you are introducing before you can introduce it.'

The first music is the passage now at bars 71–80. The next section, bars 59–70, was followed by a draft of the third movement through the canon for bassoons, bars 146–9. Next came sections in the first movement, bars 34–56 and bars 81–93. The first four bars of the symphony are repeated (in a different key) at bars 105–7, though in the second part of the closing melody the notes are twice as long. On 15 June 1942 he completed a draft of the first movement that is still without indications for piano. Can we imagine the piece at all without the rippling piano triplets that introduce the second section, formed of the sparkling tritone-related ninth-chord that was, as revealed by Mark DeVoto's landmark essay *Boris's Bells, by Way of Schubert and Others*, employed in bar 15 of *The Firebird*? The piano finally appears at bars 143–172, noted in the manuscript as 'New with piano'. It should now be said that the sections from bars 71–80 and 59–70 were separated out of the manuscript as if complete in themselves.

The most remarkable digression in the composition is that Stravinsky rewrote the third movement after a two-year hiatus. The second movement occupied him for a month from 15 February 1943, and the third movement from 7 August to 14 October 1945. The interruption was devoted to the creation of the *Ode* and the new version of the 'Danse sacrale'. In December 1943 he composed the Kyrie and the Gloria of the Mass. On 12 April 1944 he completed *Babel* for the *Genesis Suite*, which would not be performed until November 1945.

But the major work of 1944 was *Scènes de Ballet*, in which Stravinsky's full innovative powers spring to life. Somehow the prospects of this alien opus rejuvenated him. It was written under a deadline but he could not be rushed. He began at the very end of the piece, then turned to the beginning and produced music as brash and as new in harmony, sonority and, especially, rhythm as anything he had done in thirty years. The Introduction is exuberant and newly suspenseful. The irregular lengths of the opening chords – four beats, five beats, one beat – actually replace the concept of metre. This feeling continues for several bars until a 5/8 metre appears, though this is not immediately perceived since the music begins on the second beat after a silent first beat. A debonair main theme is then introduced in the violas in 5/8 metre with a solitary timpani note at the heretofore silent beginning of the bar. This rhythmic playfulness continues until the ballerina's classical ballet number, which would have puzzled any audience, except that there was no audience at the premiere since the opening music had to be cut because the musicians were so bewildered by the rhythms that they could not play it. The ending of the ballet, the apotheosis, is no less astonishingly new. The pulsation of the entire movement is in offbeats and totally devoid of any feeling of metre. The succession of *fortissimo* chord shifts – two beats, 4, 2, 2, 4, 4, 2, 6, 4, 2, 2, 9, 6, 9 – is thrilling and hardly less suspenseful than places in *The Rite of Spring*. The concluding, much-too-long chord is a lapse that can only be attributed to Stravinsky's high spirits since he wrote after it, '18th August, Paris is no longer German.' The Stalingrad victory had elated him, and the turn in the war during the composition of the piece must be understood as expressions of his ebullience. Stravinsky had captured the American spirit of wartime Broadway and not just in those Benny Goodman riffs. I was there, and writing this I am feeling an intense nostalgia for the Billy Rose Theater on Sixth Avenue in 1944.

I have here detailed in chronological sequence Stravinsky's phenomenal ability to compartmentalise his mind and juggle music of incredible diversity of style and content.

On Conducting

Stravinsky endorsed Schoenberg's first statement about his principles for his new Society for Private Musical Performances in Vienna: use less well-known players 'so as to avoid irrelevant virtuosity and individuality'. Stravinsky called them 'grandstanding distractions'. Excerpts from reviews reveal more of his musical philosophy:

> I demand that conductors of my music respect my intentions strictly, and inject their own aesthetic as little as possible.
> (10 January 1924, Antwerp)

> Tempo is the basic problem of conducting[5]... A creative aspect exists in the treatment of tempo... [A] change of pulse-rate cannot be imposed upon a human being without endangering him. Similarly the tempo in music must be regarded with utmost care... The proof of this is found in the tempo of a march, which varies from nation to nation. These variations are not deliberate or calculated but natural, corresponding to the physical properties of that people, their walking stride.
> (8 December 1930, Mannheim)

---

5   On 19 September 2012 the New York Philharmonic opened its season with a performance of *The Rite of Spring*. The reviews of this event unanimously mention the extremely slow tempo of the final dance ('Danse sacrale'). The score offers no option concerning the pace of the piece, the metronomic marking indicating 126 to the beat. A too-slow-tempo destroys the music. In the same week, the Manhattan School of Music student ensemble a few blocks north on this same street gave a commendable performance of the piece conducted by George Manahan.

One of Stravinsky's observations is of primary importance: 'Often the tempo is not too slow or too fast, but the performance makes it feel this way.'

Astoundingly, a Stravinsky scholar has identified Beecham, Koussevitzky and Ziloti as the 'three conductors to whom Stravinsky perhaps owed [the] most'. Is there no debt to Pierre Monteux for teaching us to conduct the changing metres in *Petrushka* and the *Rite*? The composer himself must have learned this from Monteux. In fact, the critic's chosen three are among those to whom Stravinsky was the least indebted. Beecham conducted only two or three Stravinsky pieces, Ziloti only the very earliest, and Koussevitzky only the first Russian and a few later performances of *The Rite of Spring* (God knows how). He also led the premieres of the Piano Concerto, the *Ode*, the U.S. premiere of the Symphony of Psalms, and – disastrously – the world premiere of the *Symphonies of Wind Instruments*. Koussevitzky commissioned Nicolas Slonimsky to re-bar some of the *Rite*, but this version has apparently never been played. In truth, Ansermet and Stokowski performed more of Stravinsky's music than any others of their time, though in 1925 Stravinsky himself declared Chicago's Frederick Stock 'the best conductor of my music; in some cases he does it better than I do'.

Though Stravinsky praised his friend Otto Klemperer's performances of *Oedipus Rex* and the Piano Concerto after criticising the conductor's opening tempo ('it should sound like Savonarola'), Klemperer was not temperamentally suited to Stravinsky's music and played little of it. He never attempted the *Rite*. Nevertheless, Stravinsky concurred with Schoenberg's judgement that 'Klemperer does know and understand Beethoven to a really quite exceptional degree and has the ability to feel his heroic quality, having fire and spirit enough himself not to fail in the task. He is tyrannical but this quality would be to the advantage of the undertaking as a whole.'

Stravinsky insisted that I accompany him to every Klemperer performance in my Los Angeles years, especially of the 'Brandenburg' concertos, a revelation for me.

Stravinsky's autobiography commends Fritz Reiner, who substituted for Stokowski in the 1925 Philadelphia performance of the Piano Concerto, but Reiner did not conduct Stravinsky's music with any frequency after that and, like Klemperer, never attempted the *Rite*. Stravinsky chose Reiner to conduct the 1953 American premiere of the *Rake* at the Metropolitan Opera but his tempi were sluggish. After an *Esquire* interview in which the composer cited this, the offended 'Amico Fritz' wrote a rebuttal and thereafter kept his distance. The good relationship was re-established with Reiner's telegram to Stravinsky on his seventy-fifth birthday: 'Laudate eum in cymbalis bene sonantibus Laudate eum in cymbalis jubilationibus Alleluia cliens devotissimus fidelis. Fredericus Reiner.' (The conductor had been performing the Symphony of Psalms.) In the summer of 1968 the two musicians found themselves on the same steamship from New York to Genoa, and Reiner sent a bottle of champagne to Stravinsky's table every evening.

In America in the 1950s the composer admired William Steinberg's recording of *The Rite of Spring* as the only one that attained the metronomic tempo of the 'Glorification of the Chosen One'; on meeting him in the Hollywood home of composer Eric Zeisl, Stravinsky complimented the conductor. At this period Stravinsky greatly admired Antal Doráti, giving him hours of instruction about conducting *Petrushka* and the *Rite*. Stravinsky also appreciated Bernardino Molinari and Sir Georg Solti, who studied *Oedipus* with the composer before performing the work in Los Angeles. After Sir Georg conducted the Paris premiere of *Moses und Aron*, the present writer was introduced to him by Rolf Liebermann, the then director of the Paris Opéra, at a party at Fouquet's. Until Sir Georg's death in 1997, he always honoured me when preparing Stravinsky pieces by telephoning to ask how certain passages should be done. When he asked me if the concert-ending for *Petrushka*, which he was doing in Vienna, was authentic, I replied in the affirmative but added that the ballet ending is the greatest moment in the piece and said, 'Forgive me, Maestro, but *Petrushka* isn't *Petrushka* without the original ending.' He agreed but answered that the Viennese trumpeters could not play it, and mentioned that he found himself in the same position as Stravinsky in Vienna in 1913.

One of the European conductors who most interested Stravinsky was Hermann Scherchen, whose performance of the *Soldat* in Weimar in 1923 satisfied all of the composer's requirements. In gratitude, he granted Scherchen's request to perform the first part of the *Rite* as a separate work. Relations between Stravinsky and the conductor cooled when the composer discovered that Scherchen's dedication to Schoenberg was deeper. Stravinsky nevertheless continued to respect Scherchen and treasured his late-in-life recordings of Bach. In Berlin in 1956 the two men spent late-evening hours together after Scherchen's performance of Henze's *König Hirsch.* In London two months hence, the conductor came to my rehearsals of the *Canticum Sacrum* and invited me to join his summer studio at Gravesano.

Stravinsky was harshly critical of symphony orchestra conductors for their ignorance of the colossal organ repertory of Bach, and especially of the three-part counterpoint in the manual parts of the Six Sonatas (no pedal) written for the composer's eldest son, Wilhelm Friedemann, to help establish him as an organist in Dresden. Here Stravinsky was influenced by Nadia Boulanger, who had not only performed numerous Bach cantatas for him but also taught Bach's organ music to him.

Following a press conference in Tokyo in April 1959, the *Asahi Evening News* quoted Stravinsky's own assessment of the three best conductors of his music as 'Pierre Monteux, Fritz Reiner and Robert Craft, who is a very good and active conductor of my works – the old ones, the new ones, and even those not yet written'. In fact, David Atherton[6] and I are the only conductors to have performed Stravinsky's complete works. Most others play only the popular Diaghilev-period pieces, though the Psalms and the two symphonies have become repertory staples. Oliver Knussen, one of the exceptions, regularly allows his audiences to hear late Stravinsky pieces along with *Le Baiser de la fée.*

---

6   The British musical establishment presented a retrospective of Stravinsky's published works under Atherton's direction, and Vera Stravinsky was favoured with a visit by ex-Prime Minister Edward Heath, who flew to New York to receive her blessings.

Stravinsky as a conductor could be ruthless. At the beginning of a Hollywood recording session of the *Fée* in the late 1960s he shouted at the horn player, James Decker, one of the greatest masters of the instrument and a good friend, because of two burbles in the difficult horn 'Valse' in the First Tableau. Standing next to Stravinsky on the podium, I gently reminded him that the orchestra had not had time to warm up. A few minutes later a young clarinettist missed a note in the notoriously awkward fingering in the fourth-scene cadenza and the composer spoke harshly to him. The player, who worshipped Stravinsky, broke down in tears, whereupon I came to the young musician's defence. Stravinsky considered this an affront and, turning to me, said, 'Tu est très impertinent.' He spoke to me in French so that the orchestra – who were shocked by the confrontation – would not understand. I flinched and withdrew to the back of the hall,[7] embarrassed and humbled. By dinner time he had sent a deeply felt note of apology to me. This was the only occasion when Stravinsky ever spoke to me in this way. But recording sessions are always a strain because of the time limits, the repetitions and the accidental interruptions from page-turns, chair squeaks, nasal purgations, incompletely muffled coughs and outside traffic noises.

I also came to the aid of the late Charles Rosen in his recording session of *Movements* with Stravinsky. The famous pianist could not follow Stravinsky's beat in one place, and the composer instructed Ingolf Dahl, who was playing the celesta part, to take over the passage on the piano while I played the celesta in Dahl's place. But here it must be said that *Movements* was very new and Stravinsky did not yet know how to conduct it.

I dreaded Stravinsky's confrontations with other conductors. After my performance of *Threni* in Town Hall, New York, in 1959, Leopold Stokowski came to a small reception where Stravinsky took me to him saying, 'This is Stokowski, if you want to meet him.' I was deeply

---

7   This was in the American Legion Hall, Los Angeles, where Jerry Lewis, recipient of the 2009 Lifetime Oscar Award, attended many Stravinsky recording sessions incognito and took numerous photographs of him. We learned this only after dining in Mr Lewis's restaurant at the juncture of Holloway Drive and Sunset Boulevard. On a second visit to the restaurant, the actor displayed his imaginatively arranged Stravinsky photo album for us.

ashamed at hearing these words. After all, Stokowski was the most understanding of *The Rite of Spring* of anyone who ever meddled with this great work, realising that only one dancer is required in the ballet, the victim in the final 'Danse sacrale', which explains his reason for staging it with Martha Graham alone. But Stravinsky was never very kind to Stokowski, who lived less than a mile away in the Hollywood Hills during his movie-making period (*One Hundred Men and A Girl*). The statement seems cruel to the man who supported Stravinsky's music in the 1920s with large amounts of money and performed more of his early music than anyone in America for many years. The present writer attended Stokowski concerts in New York in the early 1940s and thought some of them, including his rendering of Schoenberg's *Pelleas und Melisande* in the 56th Street Mosque, qualified him as one of the all-time great conductors. I still possess a valuable miniature score of *L'Après-midi d'un faune* dated 'Février 1926' and containing the previous owner's notation that Stokowski's metronome speed (the score does not have any) in a performance of 25 May 1939 was 104 to the quaver. The score belonged to a pupil of Nadia Boulanger and is inscribed: 'À ma chère petite bien-aimée comme Prélude à l'avant-midi d'un amour'.

Posters of Stravinsky were all over New York when the Stravinskys attended Leonard Bernstein's performance of *The Rite of Spring* in June 1966. At the end, when he gestured to Stravinsky in his loge, the explosion of applause compelled the composer to stand and acknowledge the cheering, screaming audience. To escape a barrage of flash bulbs, he left the hall on his wife's arm and walked backstage to the conductor's green room where glasses of Scotch were proffered. When Lenny finally completed his dozen or so returns to the podium and sought respite himself, Stravinsky asked to see the score, turned to a page near the end of the 'Danse sacrale', pointed to the high horn theme in crotchets, and remarked wryly, 'There is no *allargando* here.' Lenny had nearly doubled the length of each beat, saying that he passionately loved these measures and was simply following Stokowski in the over-emphasis. This, of course, increased the pent-up aggravation beneath the composer's complaint – but by this time the whisky had taken effect and Stravinsky's innate graciousness returned. The evening ended in several of those inevitable, affectionate Bernstein hugs.

The kinesthetic correspondences between a composer conducting his own music and the gestures of the music itself have never been more apparent than in the 1965 BBC film of Stravinsky in close-up, directing the last ten minutes of *The Firebird* in the Royal Festival Hall. The responses to his small, sharp, sudden beat, free of descriptive and rhetorical flourishes, produce precise, accentuated attacks with the utmost rhythmic clarity. The absence of preparatory upbeats is notable, as is the 'grabbing' of a chord instead of 'cueing' its component players, which most conductors do with outstretched arms. The viewer also observes that Stravinsky's stance on the podium is forward-tilting, with the weight of his body on the toes in accordance with the strong upbeat and dance-like emphasis of his music.

Stravinsky has been caricatured holding a metronome in his right hand as he conducts, an apt depiction since strict – as opposed to *rubato* – tempo was his principal concern. For him, dynamics, articulation and phrasing were less important than the establishment and maintenance of a *tempo giusto*. Not that he was indifferent to the innumerable nuances and shadings between *piano* and *forte*, but he believed that these variations were circumstantial, dependent on acoustics and on physiological as well as psychological factors affecting the conductor. He maintained that degrees of volume have to be adjusted anew with every orchestra and hall. Above all, Stravinsky was a stickler for balance.

A BBC film confirms that eye contact was essential to Stravinsky's communication with his players. A glance in the direction of an oboist conveys meanings, musician to musician, that cannot be verbalised or indicated by flailing arms. He condemned all pretences of facial expression – ecstasy, agony, heroics – as one might anticipate in a composer who likened his ideal conductor to a bell-ringer in a church,[8]

---

8   In June 1914 Stravinsky notated the bells of St Paul's in London, and when he lived in Venice he worked out diagrams of the second bell catching up and overtaking the first, the third overtaking the second, and so on.

pulling the rope to set the clangings in motion at the proper speed and nothing else.

Most surprising in the film is the commanding power of Stravinsky's tiniest signals. Some of this was due to his status as the music's absolute authority but still, at eighty-three years of age, his hand and upper-body movements reveal an astonishing vitality. Among such colleagues as Toscanini, Klemperer, Stokowski and Monteux, Stravinsky was only a time-to-time maestro, not a continually practising one. But by 1926 he had memorised *The Firebird*, *Petrushka* and most of *The Rite of Spring*, including the final pages in which eye contact is not possible because the players do not have time to look up to the conductor and back to their parts. He could give flawless performances of these first three ballets but was less reliable with later works and quite unable to conduct those of his final period.

Stravinsky's conducting style changed over the years. I do not know exactly when he dispensed with batons, though he continued to use them in orchestra pits when conducting stage works. Only a very few musicians remain to testify to a change in his technique in the period immediately before I knew him. My source was the late Roger Voisin, the trumpet player of the Boston Symphony (as well as chamber ensemble groups formed within in performances of the Octet and *L'Histoire du Soldat*). At Boston University in 1997, Voisin told me that Stravinsky had conducted 3/8 and 3/16 bars in his fast-tempo music by rapidly outlining small triangles with his finger[9] instead of, as in later years, conducting the threes with a single scoop. Voisin amusingly demonstrated how the composer would beat a fast 2/4 passage with the right hand moving between waist and shoulder, then reduce the area for the intralaminar three-beat a few inches in front of his solar plexus. In bars of fives and sevens, Stravinsky would combine these patterns, which meant that 2+3 or

---

9   The Canadian documentary *Stravinsky at Eighty* includes almost a half-hour of footage showing him rehearsing the *Ragtime* and the Royal March in *Soldat* and beating all of the fast three-, five- and seven-metre bars in the way that Voisin described, but Stravinsky was frequently late with the following downbeats.

3+2, 2+2+3 or 3+2+2 had to be firmly established in rehearsal. In the rhythmically most complex music with constantly changing metres, this could cause confusion if Stravinsky happened to forget whether he had decided that a two should precede a three or vice versa, and outlined the sequence the wrong way around.

Whereas conductors generally try to act out how their audiences should feel about what they hear, Stravinsky was content to let the music speak for itself to the extent, in the ostinato in the Fourth Tableau of *Petrushka*, of folding his arms and leaving the beat to the bass drum. In *Agon* he did not conduct the castanet dance, but obliged the orchestra to follow this instrument's ostinato rhythm. In fast-tempo music such as Kastchei's Dance in *The Firebird*, he decreased the size of his beat, and in the 5/8 section of the overlapping syncopated canon near the end of *Petrushka* he did not conduct at all but left the players to 'do their own thing'.

In December 1928 Stravinsky told James Joyce's friend Eugene Jolas:

> A month ago, I came to Paris to record *Firebird*. This was my second recording experience; *Petrushka* in London was my first. Nothing could be more strenuous. Striving for the best possible performances, one must repeat the piece endlessly; one's weariness accumulates, and when nerves are about to snap, the violinists' arms to succumb, and the mind to go blank with the monotony of the task, that is the moment when one must be perfect for the 'take' that is still to be recorded. Never have I experienced such exertion. The idea of being my own critic, listening coldly to myself in front of an apparatus without taking part in the orchestral action, powerless to correct any weakness, any mechanical defect, makes even the most cruel of criticisms pale by comparison. Imagine, moreover, that after one satisfactory trial performance, the piece is repeated three more times and the final recording will be chosen from one of these.

At rehearsals and recording sessions, Stravinsky often wore two pairs of glasses, one on his forehead[10] (which was sufficiently recessive to hold them in place) to look at the orchestra, the other to read the score. Since he could not whistle, he would ask me to do it for him, correcting notes or a figure for a player. If he was nearby, Stravinsky would sing what he wanted, albeit lower than the actual pitch. His speaking voice equalled Sarastro's in its sepulchral range but was soft in its sonority and sharp in enunciation. Changes of temper were sudden, and the tempo of his speech could accelerate with changes of mood. His most curious method of demonstrating the quality of certain string sounds was to raise his head and stretch and tauten his neck to create a sound box in his throat against which he would flick his middle finger. The desired sonority was that of a hollow or string-bass harmonic. Like Wagner, he preferred wooden to metal flutes. When playing the Two-Piano Concerto, Stravinsky dabbed glue on his fingertips which, on drying, increased the percussive edge of the sound.

Stravinsky was extremely sensitive with percussion instruments and knew more about how to play them than any other composer I have known. To understand exactly how these instruments should sound was vital to him. He would demonstrate to timpanists and bass-drum players how close to the rim of the instrument it should be struck and with which mallet, stick or felt. (Two kinds of drumsticks required in the original *Soldat* score are now extinct.) The sizes of drums were critical to him, and he was obsessive about the accuracy of timpani intonation. He seemed to know more about the harp than most of its players and once remarked that 'harpists spend ninety percent of their lives tuning their harps and ten percent playing out of tune.' Walking to the battery sections of orchestras, he would demonstrate how to play a tambourine, a triangle, a bell, a tam-tam,

---

10 One of the most striking features of Stravinsky's anatomy was the small size of his head. Two busts by Marino Marini are often criticised for inaccuracy in this regard, but I was present in 1950 when these sculptures were made and photographed next to the living head and can testify that the measurements are exact. Phrenology, the nineteenth-century notion that the weight of the brain is a gauge of cognitive power, has been disproven. I still possess a leather box containing Stravinsky's full-dress collars, which extend only halfway around my normal-sized neck.

drawing from this last a tornado-like glissando by rubbing the circle of the rim. Small wonder that he delighted in the bouncing quality of cimbalom notes, an instrument he mastered soon after his discovery of it in a Geneva café in 1915 (and after having it restrung in a logical, not in an alternating left–right, fashion). During the Swiss years he tried to employ his teacher Aladár Rácz on a permanent basis as a cimbalomist-secretary. In 1946 I observed Stravinsky playing the instrument at a rehearsal of the Ballet Society's revival of *Renard* and remember him beaming with pleasure throughout. The rarity of the instrument was a great disappointment to him. When I conducted the unfinished 1919 version of *Les Noces* in Berlin in 1969, the two cimbalomists had to be flown in from London.

Towards the end of his life, Stravinsky preferred the greater orchestral clarity of his 1943 revision of the 'Danse sacrale'. One of his last performances of *The Rite of Spring*, in Stockholm in 1961, preserves a rendition of this unknown ending, but he did not know the score well enough, not having seen it in eighteen years. Nevertheless, and to my amazement, he began to make changes and corrections during the rehearsal which were apparently never incorporated in a later edition. David Schiff, one of our most intelligent critics of contemporary music, was the first to notice, as he wrote to me:

> At three after rehearsal [36] Stravinsky rescored the original five-note motive in the trumpets as a hocket between trumpets 3 and 4 and the trombones – a very subtle effect, I would think. On your recording, however, it sounds like the trumpets are playing as in the original version. For a composer the comparison of the two versions is endlessly fascinating because Stravinsky seems to have scrutinized every note and eliminated every trace of fat, but I want to make sure that the published score of the revision represents his final version – or were there final revisions of the revision?

The arrangement contains improvements such as the eight horns doubling the strings in the first chord, but the rewriting of the wind parts sacrifices the power and volume of the whole, and the tam-

tam part is missing. Stravinsky used the 1943 version of the *Rite* in Venice in 1958, which I had rehearsed for him with the Hamburg Philharmonic, but he did not use it in 1960 in Mexico.

Stravinsky's recorded legacy is a controversial subject. Most of the records he made after his 1956 thrombosis cannot be accepted as fully embodying his wishes. The chief obstacle is that I rehearsed the music for him, both to conserve his strength and to provide an opportunity for him to decide what he wished to do differently. On the whole he followed my examples. But so do early Stravinsky recordings raise questions concerning the authenticity of the performances. His own conductor's score of *The Rite of Spring* contains his calculations of timings made to determine where the record-side breaks should occur to fit his 1940 New York Philharmonic recording on 78-speed discs. The necessity of accommodating the limited time frames had a procrustean effect on his tempi, both fast and slow, though this 1940 performance is one of the fastest of the 200 or so now on the market.[11] A nagging question is that of which of the three very different speeds of the final section of the Symphony of Psalms in his three recorded performances – as well as in the unreleased fourth recording made in Hollywood in 1960 – is the most 'authentic'? Some musicians maintain that it would be the earliest because that is closest to the date of the composition. I demur for the reasons that the performers were insufficiently familiar with the music. And shouldn't second, third and fourth thoughts be respected as well? When the question was put to Stravinsky, he simply said that each tempo reflected his thoughts and physical and mental condition at the time the recording was made.

---

11 The 'Danse de la terre' in Stravinsky's 1960 Columbia *Rite* is considerably slower than the indicated crotchet = 160, but most performances are too slow because conductors foolishly try to attain the clear pitch of every semiquaver of the cellos in the whole-tone scales near the end.

CHAPTER 5
Stravinsky and Gesualdo

The poet and editor of the Oxford review *Areté*, Craig Raine, once asked me, 'Isn't the greatness of a composer rooted in his ability to see himself in the mirror of the past and to see new linguistic elements which he can use?' I answered in the affirmative but emphasised that this would apply only during a comparatively recent period. The music of the great polyphonic era – Josquin to the Medici Codex, and on to Monteverdi – was not available to Mozart and Beethoven. The Baroque composers knew little of the giants of the *trecento*, *quattrocento* and *cinquecento*. As for Stravinsky, his knowledge of pre-Bach composers was meagre until 1932 when Nadia Boulanger opened vast new territories, starting with Monteverdi. Very little, if any, of the music of his predecessors, extending as far back as Pérotin and Gregorian chant, has been transcribed.

Shortly after Stravinsky's move to the United States, the American scholar Helen Hewitt published a new edition of the first printed collection of polyphonic music, Petrucci's *Odhecaton* of 1501 (Cambridge, MA, 1942). Boulanger presented this seminal publication to Stravinsky that same year in Boston, where they often worked together at the Edward Forbes House, and later at the Arthur Sachs home in Mendocino. Mlle Boulanger assisted Stravinsky in several capacities, correcting the orchestral parts of the Symphony in C and proofreading the Two-Piano Sonata, the 1943 score of the 'Danse sacrale', and the Kyrie and Gloria of the Mass.

In Berkeley in the 1940s, the musicologist Manfred Bukofzer introduced Stravinsky to the music of Matheus of Perugia. From this *trecento* composer Stravinsky borrowed the concept of alternating instrumental and *a cappella* passages in the Agnus Dei of his Mass. Bukofzer continued to enlighten Stravinsky with the music of John Dunstable, which became the foundation of Stravinsky's passionate interest in and extensive collection of old English music, including madrigals, lute songs, the complete works of William Byrd and a rare edition of Thomas Tallis, the latter a gift from William Glock. In the 1950s and 1960s Ernst Krenek remapped Stravinsky's path of discovery to Ockeghem and early Flemish polyphony.

My contribution to Stravinsky's new passion began in 1952 when I brought to his attention the music of Don Carlo Gesualdo, the Prince of Venosa, with which Stravinsky soon became as enraptured as he was with the development of chromaticism in other sixteenth-century composers. This led to a correspondence with the musicologist Edward Lowinsky; Stravinsky then read Lowinsky's fascinating, if outdated, *Secret Chromatic Art in the Netherlands Motet* and wrote a preface to one of the musicologist's later books. Stravinsky began to experiment with the combining of serial techniques and the intricate techniques of the medieval and Renaissance composers and was soon followed by younger musicians. One of the latter, the American Charles Wuorinen, handsomely thanked Stravinsky by composing a beautiful Reliquary for him, interwoven with fragments of the great composer's unfinished last composition.

In Hollywood in 1950 I learned that the few Gesualdo madrigals available in modern notation were strewn with errors of transcription. Copies of the original part books, which were extremely rare at the time, were printed in Naples, Ferrara, Venice, Genoa and the village of Gesualdo, located about fifty mountainous miles from Naples. Books V and VI as well as the *Responsoria* for Holy Week were all published in part books by the Neapolitan printer Simone Carlino on the composer's own music-type printing press installed in his castle in Gesualdo. Molinaro's famous score edition in 1611 was not published until after Gesualdo's death; it enabled performers to see what others were singing and made the music available for the first time.[1]

The Library of Congress acquired a copy of this set, apparently in the early twentieth century, from which my friend and collaborator Lawrence Morton procured some sixty microfilms of madrigals of Books IV, V and VI. We immediately determined to transcribe them from the early seventeenth-century notation for eventual performances at our Los Angeles Monday Evening Concerts. Working in our respective homes, we spent many late nights in this pursuit, telephoning each other as dawn approached to play on the piano passages of music that from a harmonic point of view could be mistaken for creations from the period of *Parsifal.* The thought that we were hearing music that had probably not been performed for hundreds of years was thrilling. But the astonishing discovery that such marvels of voice-leading and harmonic progression could have occurred to a musician four centuries earlier was almost beyond belief. Of course I showed these treasures to Stravinsky, who was even more fascinated by them, and as impatient as we were to hear the music in its living vocal colours.

The work of transcribing lasted two years, as Morton and I were not educated in the notation of the period. The durations of the accidentals were a problem in the *Responsoria* where one had to learn by trial and error that, for example, a series of C sharps would have a sharp sign repeated for each and every C sharp, while a flat before a series of B's (or E's or A's) was understood to remain in effect for the following succession of the same pitch without a repetition of the accidental. That is to say, flats and sharps were treated differently. Our next step was to assemble a quintet of singers with pure tone qualities, perfect pitch, master musicianship, and a willingness to devote hours and drive long Los Angeles distances to Stravinsky's home where the rehearsals took place. The principal

---

1   In 1987 a facsimile edition of Molinaro's scores became generally accessible. The original 1611 books were available in the intervening centuries in the Biblioteca Nacional de España and published in Madrid during the period of the Spanish rule of the Parthenopean territories. Under Philip II, Gesualdo's father was elevated to the rank of Prince of Venosa and hence became the principal representative of the Habsburg crown in Basilicata.

aim of the present chapter is to reveal the extent of Stravinsky's participation.

At first the composer provided helpful suggestions at rehearsals but his involvement deepened as we became more engrossed. I watched him intently for the emotional effect, thinking that the haunting melancholy of the music was alien to his temperament, but he seemed not to be disturbed by the pathos. He made copies of several pieces and his manuscript ink score of *Io pur respiro* can be seen today in the Sacher Stiftung in Basel. Only when Stravinsky moved to the sacred music from the secular did he become personally involved, composing the missing vocal parts. In this he seemed deliberately to avoid what appeared to be the indicated, obvious harmonic solutions. When we finally heard his completions in *Illumina nos*, the singers, having anticipated academic resolutions, were perplexed and, I suspect, disappointed by its fusion with the sixteenth-century composer. Some of Stravinsky's rhythms surprised the singers – from bars 22 to 32 of *Assumpta est*, for example, and in the inverted part introduced at the beginning of *Illumina nos*. But his harmonic 2nds and 7ths are all within the possible range of the earlier composer, and dissonances of Stravinsky's kind, though not characteristic of Gesualdo, seemed more natural in the religious music than would have been the case in the malinconia of the madrigals.

Between 1957 and 1960 Stravinsky composed, or recomposed, four works by Gesualdo of which the most important – though best known as a ballet – is a translation from voices to instruments of three madrigals titled *Monumentum Pro Gesualdo di Venosa ad CD annum*. Although this ingenious instrumentation, unique in music history, has been misunderstood and maligned by oafish critics, Stravinsky's own account of his recomposing process is admirably lucid:

> I first thought of translating a group of Gesualdo madrigals for instruments in 1954, but concluded that it could not be done. Then in February 1960, I re-examined the last two books, and chose three examples that I could instrumentalise and hence clarify the contour of the music. My translations attempt to define and distinguish instrumental and vocal.

In the first of the three reworked pieces I compressed the music to phrases of three plus two, in the instances where Gesualdo has three plus three, but I did not tamper with the rhythmic structure of the second and third pieces. The relief elements in the second are provided by octave transpositions and the rotation of the instrumental combinations. The character of the music is further transformed by the timbre and articulation of the brass and double-reeds, so that the madrigal becomes an instrumental *canzona*. To impose a sense of movement on the saturating chromaticism of the final piece, I divided the orchestra into its sexes – strings, brasses, woodwinds, and horns (hermaphrodites, with or without mutes), hocketing them from group to group. The hocket is a rhythmic device, after all.

A crucial development in this brief chronicle of the Gesualdo adventure took place in Tokyo in the spring of 1959 when I received a letter from the musicologist Dr Glenn Watkins; he had heard my 1957 Columbia Records Gesualdo recordings, though my first recording was issued in 1954 by Sunset Records through the influence of the composer David Raksin and his girlfriend, the popular singer Peggy Lee. Watkins wrote to me in Tokyo of *Tristis est anima mea* and *Aestimatus sum.* This was the beginning of a long correspondence, from which I learned that we also shared a fascination with Japan[2] and that he spoke and wrote Japanese fluently, having served in the translation and interpretation section of General MacArthur's

---

2   Stravinsky's knowledge of Japanese art and theatre long predated ours, and with wonderful consequences, his *Three Japanese Lyrics* of 1912 being widely regarded as one of his finest chamber music creations. He told Hans Pringsheim of the *Asahi Shimbun,* 5 May 1959: 'I have long been fond of Japanese art and I used to own some prints by Hokusai and Hiroshige, and I have the feeling that some of the prints I used to own are included amongst the views of Mount Fuji by Hokusai and the fifty-three stages of the Tokaido by Hiroshige that I have seen here today. [Stravinsky is referring to an exhibition of Ukiyo-e masterpieces in Osaka.] Unfortunately, many of my most treasured possessions disappeared during the First World War. [The reference is to the looting of his home in Ustilug.] I became interested in Japanese wood block prints in 1912. What attracted me was that this was a two-dimensional art without any sense of solidity. I discovered this sense of the two-dimensional in some Russian translations of poetry and attempted to express this sense in my music.'

headquarters during the American Occupation. Dr Watkins was then teaching at the University of North Carolina at Chapel Hill but would soon join the musicology faculty at the University of Michigan, Ann Arbor, as chairman of the department. I knew from our correspondence that our musical interests were identical. Equally mesmerised by Gesualdo, we were also disciples of Schoenberg and Stravinsky. Glenn had just published the first modern edition of Gesualdo's *Responsoria* for Holy Week and was already transcribing and editing other volumes of his collected works to be published by the Hamburg firm, Ugrino Verlag, whose chief editor, Wilhelm Weismann (an intimate of Anton Webern), had recently come to my Hamburg Radio broadcast of Webern's orchestral Variations.

My first meeting with Glenn took place in December 1959 at a post-concert reception for Stravinsky in a Fifth Avenue penthouse. I had invited Glenn to this affair and I introduced him to the composer but that evening Gesualdo was only mentioned, not discussed. We fixed an appointment for a free day during the following week, which was difficult to arrange because Stravinsky had another Town Hall concert to conduct.

Glenn and I talked about Alban Berg and together attended a tape-editing session for my forthcoming recording of his Three Pieces for Orchestra. A slowly rising chromatic passage drew Watkins's comment: 'Ah! The drowning scene in *Wozzeck*.' When I responded with 'The origin of the passage for both surely comes from the conclusion of *Erwartung*, don't you think?' We knew at once that we had connected and knew it conclusively during my recording of Schoenberg's Violin Concerto in Toronto in June 1962 at the re-entry of the full orchestra after the third-movement cadenza. I rehearsed this passage a dozen times, not to improve the performance but for the beguiling sonority of the doubled upper-woodwind melody that had thrilled Glenn, Stravinsky and myself.

After the Stravinskys' return to California, copies of Gesualdo's music and that of his Neapolitan contemporaries arrived from Ann Arbor regularly. Stravinsky's attention was first drawn to three incomplete sacred motets, two of them for six voices and one for seven, but all three had missing parts. Glenn, meanwhile, had transcribed the incomplete six- and seven-voice motets and, on discovering the missing canon parts, sent the whole to Stravinsky at the Bauer in Venice, where he completed them in August 1959. I should have sent Morton's and my transcriptions of these pieces to Watkins first, who would have found important flaws, but I did not do so because this modest man would not have wished to add his name to manuscripts that had been partly rewritten by Stravinsky.

As a surprise for me, Stravinsky secretly orchestrated the three madrigals that he would publish under the title *Monumentum Pro Gesualdo*, inscribing the original manuscript to me in 1960: 'To Bob, who made me do it and I did it, Love Igor Stravinsky.' In July 1960 Glenn, who was ecstatic at the prospect of hearing the instrumentation, came to Hollywood for the recording of the work and Stravinsky presented him with an autograph copy of the manuscript prior to the recording session, which took place the next day.

Stravinsky conducted the first live performance of the *Monumentum* in Venice on 27 September 1960, in the Palazzo Ducale's Sala dello Scrutinio. Since this palazzo did not have elevators, Stravinsky had to be borne up the hundred stairs in a palanquin. The irony of the event was that Neapolitans and Venetians do not appreciate each other's musical cultures. Gesualdo himself, who had lived in the Doge's Palace briefly after his second marriage and heard much Venetian music, including the Gabrielis', cared for none of it.

In the spring of 1960 I brought the *Monumentum* score to New York, where, on 3 May, George Balanchine and I studied the manuscript in my room at the Gladstone Hotel. I urged him to choreograph it, after obtaining his promise not to reveal my role in this to Stravinsky until the ballet was ready to be performed. Mr B. immediately recognised that it would be the perfect companion piece for Stravinsky's *Movements* and, indeed, they have been danced in tandem ever since.

By this time another Gesualdo scholar, Professor Ruth Adams of UCLA, began to share her knowledge and enthusiasm with us. She had discovered a Gesualdo psalm in the lost manuscript of the beautiful *Salmi delle compiete* in the Naples library named for St Philip Neri. She came to rehearsals and, of course, to the recording sessions. Our vocal artists included the mezzo-soprano Marilyn Horne, one of the great voices of the twentieth century and the greatest modern-period *bel canto* Rossini singer.[3] She became a virtual member of the Stravinsky family (and, between times, my typist); I am proudly responsible for convincing her to learn the part of Marie in *Wozzeck*; when the soprano at Covent Garden was indisposed, Marilyn triumphantly replaced her. In 1968 Stravinsky dedicated his instrumentations of two Hugo Wolf songs to her. He also dedicated his Shakespeare Songs to our soprano Grace-Lynne Martin. Cora Lauridsen was our contralto and Charles Scharbach, a piano-tuner with the perfect ear necessary to provide the exact harmonic foundation pitches, our basso. Richard Robinson, our tenor, would become Stravinsky's ideal voice in all of his subsequent tenor music. Richard Levitt, the other tenor in a six-part madrigal, later achieved fame for his recordings of Landini and Monteverdi's Vespers.

For countless hours between 1953 and 1960, the Stravinsky home throbbed with Gesualdo. Aldous Huxley[4] attended many of the rehearsals, translating and correcting the texts for us as well as improving our Italian pronunciations. In 1956 and again in 1958 Stravinsky himself visited the feudal town of Gesualdo. The end date of our Gesualdo period – 1 March 1964 – was marked by a CBC broadcast from Toronto of the Holy Saturday Service of *Tenebrae*, which incorporates Gesualdo's settings of four *Responsoria* as well as his *Miserere* and *Benedictus*.

In May 1964 we spent a week with Glenn in Ann Arbor, where Stravinsky conducted *Perséphone* in the final concert of his Philadelphia Orchestra series and I conducted his Symphony in C and Schoenberg's Five Pieces. Afterwards we drove in two cars to Toronto, thereafter the centre of much of Stravinsky's recording activity and where, in 1967, he conducted in public for the last time. Glenn was present at many of our Toronto recording sessions,

---

3 Stravinsky also gave to her two photographs of Rossini, autographed by that composer.
4 Curiously, he did not approve of any of the madrigal texts, though Gesualdo set some of the thirty-one expressly written for him by his friend Torquato Tasso. Huxley also seems not to have known about Montaigne's visit to Tasso in his deranged old age. An engraving of him in this condition survives.

including my broadcast of Gesualdo's *Semana Santa* music with the Gregorian chant for the liturgy, and in Princeton in September 1966 for rehearsals and the premiere of the Requiem Canticles.

Glenn Watkins's *The Gesualdo Hex*[5] is the first factually reliable account of the composer's psychotic life. Born in Naples in 1566 (not 1560), he married his beautiful twenty-year-old cousin Maria d'Avalos,[6] whose notorious infidelities soon compelled Don Carlo to commit uxoricide in order to restore his honour. He planned to do this by informing his spouse that on an appointed date he would leave his Naples palace, San Severo, ostensibly to go on a hunting expedition, then returned to surprise his wife and her latest lover, the Duke of Andrea, *in flagrante delicto*. Adding insult to fatal injury, Gesualdo ordered one of his servants to help carry out the murder of the pair, after which the composer galloped to his heavily fortified seventh-century castle. As these were crimes of honour, the cuckold was not prosecuted. Seeking a liaison to one of the most musically progressive courts in all of Europe, he soon arranged to marry Leonora d'Este, the cousin of Alfonso II, Duke of Ferrara,[7] whose predecessor, Duke Alfonso I, had been the husband of Lucrezia Borgia, among others, and is assumed to be the murderer–narrator portrayed in Browning's *My Last Duchess*. Gesualdo's journey to Ferrara was clearly motivated more by the rich musical life in the city, home of the ur-chromaticist Nicola Vicentino and the esteemed madrigalist Luzzasco Luzzaschi, than by the marriage to Leonora. Before returning home to his castles in Venosa, Gesualdo and Taurasi, the bridegroom visited Venice for some weeks to observe the city's musical life, and eventually returned to Basilicata via Barletta aboard one of the Doge's private galleys.

For as long as Leonora could postpone the trip she did not join her husband. She finally journeyed overland by way of Florence to Gesualdo, where she discovered that his castle was also the residence of his favourite concubine, who seems to have been a witch. The elixir

---

5   New York: W. W. Norton, 2010.
6   Her portrait is in the same church in Naples in which Gesualdo is buried, facing the Palazzo San Severo.
7   After all, Orlando di Lasso, the 'first truly international composer', had come with his full choir on a pilgrimage to Loreto in the 1580s and stopped for four days at the court of Ferrara.

she prepared for the prince was a mix of her own menses and his semen (a less digestible cocktail, one supposes, than Donizetti's in *L'elisir d'amore*). Leonora also became aware that the genius composer she had married was an algolagniac and promptly informed her brother, now in Modena (after the death of the Este Duke, Ferrara was escheated to the Vatican), that she was returning to stay with him. The documentation of the Gesualdo story is voluminous but his historical notoriety is due less to his music[8] than to his villainy and to the renown of his uncle Carlo Borromeo, the principal intellectual force behind the Counter-Reformation.

In December 2011 *The New Yorker* published a review of *Hex* that revived and greatly expanded worldwide interest in Gesualdo's biography and music. Ironically the only music by him readily available to concert- and theatre-goers is the *Monumentum*, Stravinsky's orchestral transcription of madrigals presented regularly by the New York City Ballet. Almost all of Gesualdo's music is for vocal ensembles, only a very few of which are able to perform the music in tune. Stravinsky's instrumentation is therefore a rare treat; we should be grateful to Stravinsky–Balanchine, who received no recompense for opening a new world of chromatic-harmony polyphony.

The *New Yorker* review does not mention the most important study of the composer before *Hex*, Antonio Vaccaro's *Carlo Gesualdo, Principe di Venosa, L'uomo e I tempi*, Edizioni Osanna, Venosa, 1982 (second edition, 1989). The volume is illustrated by facsimiles of the frontispieces of most of the madrigal part-books published at Ferrara, Gesualdo, Naples and Genoa as well as an attractive portrait, replicated nowhere else, of the composer's second wife, Leonora d'Este. Many letters are reproduced, including some in Gesualdo's beautiful handwriting to the Duke d'Este and one from 'El Rey Filippo II' of Spain (dated 4 January 1594, Madrid). The book also displays the complete correspondence between Gesualdo and Torquato Tasso,

---

8   John Milton, who wrote five beautiful sonnets in the Italian language, was probably the first Englishman to have known Gesualdo's music. During the poet's visit to Italy in 1638-9 he became friends with Galileo and with the composer's librettist Torquato Tasso. Milton purchased several books of Gesualdo's music in Venice and sent them to London. Milton also read the Cosenza poet Serafina della Salandra's *Adamo Caduto* and borrowed substantially from it in *Paradise Lost*, in some cases with lines taken *totidem verbis*.

as well as the composer's letters to the Duke of Ferrara written from Florence in 1594, and to Cardinal Federico Borromeo immediately prior to his canonisation in 1612.

Gesualdo's last testament, compiled only five days before his death, reveals that he had suffered a life of inner torture for his crimes and fiendish behaviour. The document appeals to the 'Holy Father', asking for the forgiveness of his sins and pleading to 'take my soul up unto the place of salvation'. The 'most glorious Virgin Mary' and the 'glorious apostles S. Peter, S. Paul, S. Michele, S. Carlo, S. Maria Magdalene, S. Catherina of Siena and S. Francis' are beseeched to 'intercede for me in spite of my infinite wickedness, and sins committed against His divine precepts, that through His Grace my soul be gathered unto eternal life'. It seems that the murderer had a conscience and repented, if only at the last minute.

Vaccaro reveals that Gesualdo's principal heir was the as yet unborn child of his daughter-in-law Donna Polissena Fürstenburg; he gave 200,000 ducats to the mother and the same amount to his own niece Donna Isabella Gesualdo. Since the newborn proved to be a girl, a clause in the testament bestowed on her a dowry of 100,000 ducats. Through the Fürstenburg marriage European history changed and the Gesualdo power moved north under this new name. In 1957 Stravinsky became a friend of Prince Max Egon zu Fürstenburg and spent several days as a guest in his Donaueschingen palace. When the prince died two years later, Stravinsky composed an *Epitaphium* 'as a tombstone for him'.

Gesualdo was generous in his distributions to the family heirs, particularly his paternal uncle Cardinal Alfonso, Archbishop of Naples, thus enabling him to build the church of Sant'Andrea della Valle in Rome, which would become the setting for the first act of *Tosca*. Much of the will consists of sums of money to have Masses said in memory of the deceased – as many as 1,000 to San Marciano de Fuento – with alms to be distributed by the church officials. Five hundred Masses were to be celebrated at the altar of the Chapel of St Gregory in Rome. A special request of the testament directs that perpetual alms be given to the friars of the composer's own church of Santa Maria delle Grazie in Gesualdo in the form of bread, meat and wine. Also a church was to be erected in honour of his uncle San Carlo Borromeo and six Masses were to be celebrated daily in his name.

An interesting Gesualdo connection emerges from recent discoveries concerning links between John Shakespeare, father of William, and the Jesuits. In 1767 a copy of Carlo Borromeo's spiritual testament was discovered hidden in the roof of the Shakespeare house in Stratford. John Shakespeare, a recusant Catholic whose own spiritual testament was supposedly signed both by him and by Borromeo, may have been in Milan during the plague of 1578 when he would have met Cardinal Borromeo. The martyr Edmund Campion, a member of the clerical entourage that travelled from Rome to the Emerald Isles and the central figure in the Stratford Papal underground, was sequestered in Stratford in 1580 when John Shakespeare signed the 'Spiritual Testament of Catholic Faith' brought by the Jesuits directly from the Milan Counter-Revolution's ideologue, Borromeo.

That Prince Carlo of Venosa could have been in Milan at the same time is possible but it is only known for certain that he visited the city before his 1594 marriage to Leonora d'Este in Ferrara. In Milan he was fitted for a suit of armour to be worn in the jousting tournaments popular in Ferrara. This armour and that of the horse are on display in the Konopiště Castle south of Prague, a structure now better known as the residence of the Austrian Archduke Franz Ferdinand who spent the last years of his life there shooting animals, as if he sought single-handedly to exterminate the wildlife of Bohemia. He kept a register of 171,337 animals, all of them taxidermied before his assassination at Sarajevo, which led, in turn, to the deaths of millions in the Great War.

CHAPTER 6
Stravinsky in Canada and the U.K.

Stravinsky has been a venerated figure in Canada since his 1937 concerts in Toronto and Montreal. Arriving in Toronto on an overnight train from New York, he went directly from the Hotel Royal York to a rehearsal in Massey Hall, pausing briefly for an interview in the hotel lobby, in which he mentioned having just finished reading his first novel in English, *The Sun Also Rises*,[1] and indiscreetly referred to his most renowned patron, Benito Mussolini.

Toronto became the centre of Stravinsky's life as a conductor from 1962 to 1967 when he gave concerts there and recorded more than twenty of his works. The city's orchestras, choruses, directors, audiences and critics received him with more cordiality and intelligent appreciation than those in any other city this side of the Atlantic, with the possible exception of Boston during Koussevitzky's reign. Canadian Television filmed him extensively, most notably aboard the SS *Bremen* between New York and Germany, and in conversation with Nicolas Nabokov in the composer's Hamburg hotel room, footage that forms probably the most precious cinematic portrait ever made of a great composer.

---

1   Hemingway wrote to Stravinsky asking to meet him, no doubt because of the author's interest in Gustavo Durán, a pupil of Nadia Boulanger.

Stravinsky's Toronto connection in the 1960s can be attributed to Glenn Gould, who had recommended me to guest-conduct the CBC Symphony and in 1961 invited me there to record Schoenberg's Piano Concerto with him. We became fast friends, and he soon persuaded me to perform such unlikely pieces as Strauss's *Der Bürger als Edelmann*. I reported to Stravinsky on the high calibre of the CBC musicians, which led to a concert in Toronto honouring the composer's eightieth birthday. Gould's role is ironic in that he was an enemy of Stravinsky's music, and even turned down a request from CBS New York to record the Capriccio with its composer. Stravinsky never knew this but was fascinated by Gould both as musician and person.

When I first attended a Gould recital with Stravinsky (*intermezzi* by Brahms and Berg's Sonata) at the Wilshire Ebell Theatre in Los Angeles in the late 1950s, the composer expressed a desire to meet the pianist. This eventually came about through Leonard Bernstein in New York in January 1960 when all three participated in a programme that began with Bernstein conducting Gould in the Bach D minor Concerto and ended with Stravinsky and the *Firebird* Suite. An affinity between the composer and the pianist was immediately manifest, which still perplexes me, as does Stravinsky's remark, 'He is very handsome'[2] – a word I never heard the composer use in reference to any other male. Two years later, in January 1962, after our arrival from Los Angeles in a blizzard in the middle of the night, Stravinsky and Gould somehow managed to breakfast together in our Toronto hotel. During the following week Gould came to my rehearsals in Massey Hall, sitting with Stravinsky while I worked with the orchestra. The subjects of their conversations were remote from the new-music scene, the pianist soliciting the composer's opinions on such unlikely topics as the chamber music of Max Reger, heard in the St Petersburg of Stravinsky's youth.[3]

The CBC director of music, Geoffrey Waddington, delegated John Roberts,[4] the young president of the Canadian Music Centre, to

---

2   See Chapter 12: Amorous Augmentations.
3   In December 1907 Stravinsky attended a concert in St Petersburg in which Reger conducted his Serenade in G.
4   The go-between who had arranged the Gould breakfast.

shepherd the Stravinskys through our first and all future appearances in the city. Roberts kept a chronicle of Stravinsky that unavoidably includes my function:

> The electricity generated by Robert Craft seemed to keep Stravinsky's traveling household in running order... [T]he Stravinsky suite in the Park Plaza Hotel was full of flowers and light... There were perpetual long-distance calls to and from the U.S. and other countries and one felt that because Stravinsky was like the center of gravity in the music of our time, wherever he was the international world was also.

Among the nuggets preserved by Roberts during this first visit is Stravinsky's remark that he 'loved the piano music of Schumann', followed by the comment that while his own music is 'not dependent on interpretation, Schumann's is'. Stravinsky added that 'Moritz Rosenthal was the greatest interpreter of Schumann's piano music I have ever heard', and that 'hearing him play [it] was a very beautiful experience'. Roberts then asked Stravinsky about his own influence on contemporary music, to which he replied: 'I never thought about this; I live neither in the past nor in the future but in the present.' Two unrelated observations followed: 'Once I disliked Wagner for the right reasons. Today I like him – but also for the right reasons' and, 'I have just discovered Bruckner, a wonderful and moving composer with a very individual concept of space and time, but someone who would never be understood by the public.'

Sitting next to Stravinsky while I rehearsed *Zvezdoliki* (1911) in Massey Hall,[5] Roberts offers a picture of the composer in a unique situation:

---

5   On 4 April 1913 Stravinsky wrote to his Russian publisher Jurgenson asking for an update on the printing of the *Zvezdoliki* score and parts: 'In May, probably toward the end, a concert is planned for which I have been asked to give *Zvezdoliki*; thus I am turning to you with a request to hasten the printing and to do the parts. It can be checked in manuscript at your place and the rest we will do at rehearsals... This concert is very important. It will be dedicated to contemporary music, the newest trends of the various nationalities: from Germany Schoenberg, from France Debussy, from Hungary Bartók, from Russia – I.'

For Stravinsky the recording of *Zvezdoliki* was a great moment because it was the only one of his works he had never heard. Suddenly, Stravinsky tugged at one of the many pencils which he kept in his top breast pocket and in a deft manner began to revoice a bar here and a bar there over many pages. Stravinsky wanted to stop Bob so that he could talk to him about this. But the rehearsal was intense. Bob Craft was the protagonist and the clock was the antagonist. Soon it was the break and Bob, rubbing his head with a towel, rushed to Stravinsky and asked him to take over. When the rehearsal recommenced I expected Stravinsky to instruct the musicians about the revoicings he wanted. This did not happen. Afterward, when I asked him why, he replied: 'You have no idea what it is like to feel yourself young but to be imprisoned in an old man's body.'

He could not return to the spirit of 1911 to revise the music.[6] The reader can only try to imagine him hearing *Zvezdoliki*, composed a half-century earlier, for the first time and wishing to make changes in this harmonically, orchestrally and chorally most modern of all his works. The reason he had not yet heard it was that Debussy, to whom it is dedicated and who had played it four-hands with Stravinsky, considered it unperformable, suggesting that 'it might be done on Sirius or Aldebaran'. I was euphoric after the rehearsal, having been haunted by *Zvezdoliki* ever since conducting its American premiere in November 1949 in Carnegie Hall.

In late April 1962 we were back in Toronto to record *A Sermon, A Narrative, and A Prayer* and Schoenberg's Violin Concerto. This time Stravinsky was interviewed in French by Maryvonne Kendergi from the University of Montreal. She questioned him about his great enthusiasm for Schoenberg's Concerto played by Israel Baker in my half of one of Stravinsky's concerts. He came to all of our rehearsals for this powerful work, inviting Mme Kendergi to follow the score with him. She noted that

---

6   *Zvezdoliki* was presented in Boston by the BSO under Richard Burgin in 1962, the chorus using an English translation by Nicolas Slonimsky. In 1969 Michael Tilson Thomas repeated *Zvezdoliki* on one of his Spectrum concerts with the BSO.

he pointed his finger to every fault less than a second after Craft corrected it. When I asked what he thought of having the Concerto on the same programme as his own works he answered: 'But this great master is dead and you are going to hear a work of mine that I have just completed and composed in my own serial manner, *A Sermon, A Narrative, and A Prayer.*'

After the last rehearsal Stravinsky traced the contour of his hand with open fingers and autographed the palm as a gift to Kendergi.[7]

Their entire interview should be translated and published, even though one of Stravinsky's remarks seems to confute this: 'I find that French cannot be translated; it must stay in French so that the language becomes music. When I said this to Debussy, he professed to have the same rapport with words as I do: he always considered words as *matière musicale.*' The Kendergi exchanges also include a discussion of Symphony of Psalms, which Stravinsky referred to 'as a kind of Te Deum'. He added a dig against reviewers' classifications of himself: 'Stravinsky *manière*, Go to Hell; Stravinsky *Russe*, Go to Hell; Stravinsky *classique*, Go to Hell. More exactly, *Envoyons-le* to Hell, because that is where the Devil is found.'

In November 1962 we returned to Toronto to record the Symphony in C. I was there two days in advance to prepare the orchestra for Stravinsky. Reviewers have noted that his Toronto recording differs markedly from his 1952 version with the Cleveland Orchestra. This was inevitable since he had not had time to rehearse the piece at all

---

7   Stravinsky sometimes traced his hand in autograph albums. In one case he did so in the booklet of a female pianist in Warsaw. Sergei Prokofiev later was asked to inscribe his name next to Stravinsky's but the younger composer added a wisecrack about the older. The page, reproduced in a Paris newspaper on 20 December 1933, did not amuse Stravinsky. He complained to Prokofiev, who replied: 'It is time to forget that whole period when you spoke badly about my music.' But Stravinsky always spoke badly about Prokofiev's music, which the older composer thought had declined after his return to the Soviet Union. Though Diaghilev had a strongly independent mind in musical matters, one sometimes wonders if his opinions concerning Prokofiev were influenced by Stravinsky. In a letter of 8 March 1915, the impresario wrote to Stravinsky that 'Prokofiev brought a ballet to me, the subject is a St Petersburg confection... [A]s he puts it, "the score is just plain music devoid of any attempt at Russianness". And that is an apt description: it is plain music and quite awful so that everything will have to be done over again... I am counting on you. Prokofiev is talented but he yields to influences and is evidently more naïve than his former arrogance would indicate. I will bring the piece to you, for it needs a complete overhaul.'

in Toronto but merely followed my broadcast of it. This Toronto talk must include a note about Franz Kraemer, who produced Stravinsky's final concert, *Pulcinella* and *Oedipus Rex*, in the city in 1967 with Marilyn Horne singing Jocasta and Jean-Louis Barrault as Speaker. Kraemer became a good friend of the composer during the summer of 1963 in Santa Fe, sitting with him during the rehearsals for the U.S. premiere of *Lulu*. Since Kraemer had been a pupil of Alban Berg during its composition, we heard interesting anecdotes. We next saw Kraemer in London in 1965, when Stravinsky invited him to join us backstage in his Royal Festival Hall concert with the BBC Symphony Orchestra. A year later Franz gifted his correspondence from Berg to Stravinsky, who placed it with two of his treasured autographed photos of Berg.

The Rake's Progress should be respected as Stravinsky's monument to eighteenth-century English culture. Continental prejudice against the use of the language in music appears in an interview titled *Strawinsky ha detto*, published in dialogue form in the *Feuilles musicales* of Lausanne at the time of the opera's premiere. Italian musicologist Emilia Zanetti[8] had been hounding Stravinsky for the interview, which began in Milan a week before the Venetian premiere.

> Z: *For some years, Maestro, you have affirmed your wish to compose an opera in English. What are the reasons for your attraction to a reputedly anti-musical language?*[9]

> S: After having written music with Russian, French and Latin texts, the moment to take an interest in English prosody presented itself. And if one knows that language, it is easy

---

8   Zanetti had worked at UCLA with the musicologist Walter Rubsamen, who wrote the first account of the death of Schoenberg. One of her letters to Rubsamen had been sent by mistake in an envelope addressed to me while he received the letter intended for me.

9   In the present writer's opinion, Stravinsky's English songs are his greatest: the 1952 Cantata, the Shakespeare Songs (especially the one from *The Tempest*), the Dylan Thomas memorial, the 1961 Prayer, Eliot's *a cappella* chorus, and the farewell opus, *The Owl and the Pussy-Cat*.

to imagine the quantity of problems I had to resolve. Still, I do not see why English would be an anti-musical language. Things become what is demanded of them. Had I needed a full, sweet and sonorous language, I would naturally have turned to Italian. English has other musical resources. But to consider it anti-musical is to persist with a prejudice contradicted by two centuries of English vocal music – the sixteenth and seventeenth – and by an artist of the stature of Henry Purcell.[10]

Z: What was the nature of the 'provocation' that Hogarth's prints engendered in you? Was it of a visual or a dramatic order?

S: Above all, a theatrical order. What first struck me in Hogarth is the dramatic character of the art, evident in his method of narrating through a sequence of images about morality which readily translate to the stage. I wanted to respect his concept, keeping not only the original title, but also the best possible Italian translation: 'carriera' of a rake, rather than 'progresso', conveys the irony implicit in Hogarth's choice of the English word 'progress'. But something else in Hogarth attracted me as well. I recognised the quintessence of that particularly eighteenth-century English which I wanted to put to music. The colour and the society of London at that time had so many elements that lend themselves to musical interpretation. (Auden has understood this magnificently, making use of ancient English locutions, and I in turn have responded by employing equivalent musical mannerisms.)

Z: Are the modifications to the Hogarthian narration your work or that of your librettists? How did your collaboration with Auden develop?

---

10 A great admirer of Purcell, Stravinsky possessed and was familiar with the Englishman's complete works. He even wrote an instrumentation of the *Funeral Music for Queen Mary* (which I performed at the Monday Evening Concerts).

S: After having decided to take the subject of my opera from Hogarth's prints, I asked my dear friend Aldous Huxley to advise me as to which person would be most suitable to undertake the composition of the libretto. 'Auden,' Huxley replied, 'there is no one better than he.' I communicated this to my publisher in London, Ralph Hawkes, who was enthusiastic. The project started to become reality. Taking advantage of Auden's presence in New York, I invited him to join me in Hollywood. There, in one week, the plot of the work took shape through Auden's initiative, with all of the variables in accordance with Hogarth. It is also Auden who proposed Kallman's collaboration, the extent of which I was not initially aware.

I was already familiar with the poetry of Auden, whom I also admired for his collaborations in the domain of film.[11] That admiration only increased during our work together. He is a poet in the most authentic sense of the word, which is to say in the ancient Greek meaning. *Poiesis* (that is, 'to make' in English – the concrete 'to make' rather than the indeterminate 'to do') – that is to create with complete and absolute technical mastery of the material. The versification must fit exactly, as happens with a good fugue (*Z: With that, Stravinsky crossed and uncrossed his hands, showing the strength and flexibility of his grip*). One could never extol too highly the virtue of technique, nor insist too strongly on the intrinsic bond that art has with technique. To speak of inspiration, on the other hand, is suspect. One can cite many brilliant inspirations aborted by the absence or insufficiency of technique, never the contrary. Look at the painters. Monet, Manet, Cézanne, Picasso are great painters because they are great artisans. As for me, I begin with technique and finish with inspiration.

Z: Had you planned since the beginning to write a normal-length opera?

---

11 Stravinsky first became aware of Auden through the 1936 film *Night Mail*, which opens with the poet's reading of his poem of the same name about the royal Scotland-London mail train.

S: We would have to agree on the meaning of 'normal' because *La finta giardiniera* [Stravinsky found this Mozart opera boring] is also normal. Do you mean an opera that takes a whole evening? In that case I can assure you that that was my intention from the beginning. I wanted a 'full-length ship'.

Z: *Could you tell us, Maestro, whether a motif or a harmonic principle or even a musical idea was the point of departure in the creation of your opera, as, for example, the harmony of the 'Augures printaniers' was for the* Sacre?

S: For each case there is an appropriate solution. In that of the *Rake*, the framework and sonorous dimensions as originally conceived were the point of departure: a small orchestra, few characters, a limited chorus. In short, 'chamber music', as in *Così fan tutte*. That should make clear how and why I insisted that the world premiere take place in a setting such as the Fenice – rather than the Metropolitan Opera, which was the first to request the premiere of my opera – or the Scala. Of course the work would be free to make its own way later and be presented in larger venues. But the opera's baptism had to take place in the setting for which it was created.

The chronological order of the composition corresponded directly to the development of the opera. I began with the first measures of the opening – neither an overture nor an 'important' prelude, but simply with the equivalent of 'On va commencer'. The last measures I wrote are those that end the opera.

Z: What attracted you to the Italo-Mozartian model with its compartmentalised construction?

S: Although opera has always interested me, I have no taste for music drama and believe in it even less. Musorgsky, for example, is undeniably a great artist, but *Boris* does nothing for me.

Z: And the Debussy of Pelléas et Mélisande?

S: Even less. Music drama, which implies a total absence of form, is powerless to establish a tradition. But to me, art without a canon (*l'art acanonique*) is of no interest.

Z: Doesn't the cult of form risk thwarting an authentic expressive force?

S: But naturally. Except that expression cannot be isolated or separated from artistic substance; expression is a consequence and not an antecedent to art. To want it the other way, giving equal primacy to expression, is to confuse art – in good faith or bad – with improvisation. Likewise, and for most people, freedom is synonymous with ease.[12] The first condition of any true art is a healthy preparation and implementation. One must possess the object. The imprecise is suspect.

Z: Should the very clear position you have taken with The Rake's Progress *be interpreted as an act of faith in the future of opera, or only the work of a solitary and free artist celebrating the flower of a civilisation?*

S: I cherish true opera and repeat that I do not believe in music drama; I think therefore that one must take this into careful consideration and follow the path indicated by the music.[13]

---

12 '*The New York Times* has for far too many years been giving the title *Arts and Leisure* to its arts section. Art has nothing to do with leisure.' (Stravinsky)
13 On 5 December 1946 Stravinsky was en route to Montreal for concerts, which involved a change of trains in Chicago, during which he saw an exhibition of Turner, Hogarth and Constable at the Chicago Art Institute.

Among anglophone musicians, Sir William Walton, Sir Colin Davis, Sir Adrian Boult, Eugene Goossens, Reginald Stewart of the Baltimore Symphony Orchestra and Oliver Knussen also have places in Stravinsky history. In 1951 Walton was to have dined with the Stravinskys at his home in Ischia, which was near the house where Ibsen had written *Peer Gynt*. But this had to be cancelled because Stravinsky had incipient pneumonia. Stravinsky respected Walton's Shakespeare film scores and the Viola Concerto; in Hollywood, Aldous Huxley brought the Waltons to the Stravinsky home, where they spent a jolly afternoon together. As for Sir Colin, Stravinsky had consulted backstage with him after his performance of *Oedipus Rex*, reading through the score with him, readjusting tempi, and recommending changes in style and articulation. In Stravinsky's last years Sir Colin's recording of *Messiah* gave him great pleasure. I introduced Knussen to Stravinsky during a rehearsal for a concert in the Royal Festival Hall in 1965, and the composer was delighted by this fourteen-year-old's intelligence and vivacity. Lotte Klemperer also has memories to share of Stravinsky and her father in the Festival Hall, where he once conducted a late-evening Beethoven concert that was followed by a midnight *Oedipus Rex* led by its composer, with Cocteau narrating.

The brilliant and precocious Benjamin Britten's analysis in his diary entry for 12 February 1936 says the twenty-two-year-old composer had heard a performance of *Oedipus Rex* conducted by Ansermet at Queen's Hall that same evening. He recognised the piece as 'one of the peaks of Stravinsky's output; this work shows his wonderful sense of style and power of drawing inspiration from every age of music, and leaving the whole a perfect shape, satisfying every aesthetic demand'. Britten goes on to claim that 'the established idea of originality' dies a slow death – forgetting to say whether the originality of *Oedipus* or the lack of it makes it easy

> to see why the later works of Stravinsky are regarded with such disfavour. The combination of set, stylized sections in the music, the Latin words... give the impression of an impersonal comment on Sophocles rather than a re-enaction of the drama... One London gentleman expressed amusement at Jocasta's

> great and beautiful aria... But perhaps it is a compliment in
> itself to have stirred him to any emotion at all.

This keen criticism covers not only the saliencies of the masterpiece, but it also confirms the general unpopularity of Stravinsky in England at this time. A contributing factor mentioned in the same diary claims that:

> The enthusiasm of the conductor did not seem to have spread
> to the performers. The chorus sang with dull tone and not
> much vitality. The attitude of the orchestra seemed the same;
> while the soloists seemed quite at sea. Oedipus was entirely
> miscast... A bel canto voice was needed, not a Tristan.

It should also be said that Stravinsky rated Britten's all-around musical skills among the very highest, particularly as accompanist to Peter Pears and as conductor. It is not known that the older composer studied the younger's opera scores as lessons in English word-setting before creating the *Rake*. The animosity that arose in later years between them was ignited when Auden gossiped to Stravinsky that Britten had told him that he liked everything about the *Rake* except the music.

In 1991 I was asked to review *Notes in Advance*, the recently published memoirs by Sir William Glock, Stravinsky's BBC friend. This surprised me, since I did not know him well and knew nothing at all about British musical politics. Reading the book, I suspected that what was really wanted was a favourable blurb from Stravinsky. I soon realised that I could not provide anything except a few revisions included here only reluctantly, because Stravinsky long believed, rightly, that his music, after the triumphant early Diaghilev ballets, was less popular with London audiences than with those of the continental cities. Stravinsky pointed out that Edinburgh was the only important musical city in which he had never conducted; he had only visited the city once, for an imported German performance of *Wozzeck*. Here is Glock:

In 1957 the [Dartington] Summer School Department had been honoured by a fortnight's visit from Stravinsky. In December 1956 he had come over to London to hear the first performances there of his new *Canticum Sacrum* and of his arrangement of Bach's canonic variations on *Vom Himmel hoch...* given at St Martin-in-the-Fields with Robert Craft conducting. The performances went well, and Stravinsky seemed very content. He and Vera Stravinsky and Robert Craft were staying at the Savoy... and my wife and I were at that time in charge of the International Music Association in South Audley Street, which had an excellent restaurant where we dined together [after the concert]... [T]his visit in December 1956 left memories of a splendid concert, of conversations that blossomed to an accompaniment of Montrachet, Mission Haut-Brion, and Château Latour 1944, of warmth and kindliness, of the promise that the Stravinskys and Robert Craft would come the next year to the Dartington Summer School and of a first sketching out of the programmes.

This says nothing of the other guests at that post-concert banquet – Michael Tippett, Stephen Spender, Peter Heyworth, Edward Clark and his wife Elizabeth Lutyens. These last two, together with Edwin Evans and Lord Berners,[14] were among Stravinsky's long-time British musician friends. But Stravinsky did not 'come over to hear' his new pieces. He came to conduct them at St Martin-in-the-Fields but, on doctors' orders, was forbidden to fulfil the commitment. He was seated in the front row next to Ralph Vaughan Williams but did not recognise him, and no one thought to introduce the two elderly composers. No promise was made that night to visit Dartington the following year. This agreement was reached several days later between Glock and myself, and Stravinsky was not included in the original invitation.[15]

---

14 In a letter to Randolph Churchill of 26 September 1941, Evelyn Waugh informs his correspondent that 'Lord Berners has written the dullest book yet seen.'

15 The truth is that he and his wife wanted a vacation and decided at a late stage to come with me.

Glock's memoirs cite a letter from me shortly before our arrival at Dartington in August 1957 saying that the Stravinskys' 'requirements' were 'a car, a supply of excellent Bordeaux and freedom from star-gazers'. In acknowledgement, Glock described both the home in which we would be accommodated and our housekeeper, 'a young woman of infinite tact and charm and with a cordon-bleu training'. He fails to note that the Stravinskys arrived in Dartington via Plymouth, where their transatlantic liner transferred them to a tender that took them to the harbour. Instead, Glock's memoir complains that Stravinsky seemed to be 'bundled off a lot of the time by the other two to London for rehearsals under Robert Craft, to Tintagel, to Salisbury Cathedral, to Bath...' In actuality we left Dartington for London by train on the day after our arrival, not because the 'woman with infinite tact and charm' who brought the first breakfast to my room was as naked as anyone in Manet's *Lunch* – and though fully dressed when she brought Stravinsky's to him, he was still clad only in his underpants. The composer wanted to spend hours in the British Museum, the National Gallery, the Victoria and Albert and the Tate, where he was amazed by the predominance of gold paint on Turner's palette. Stravinsky also wanted to enjoy London's deluxe hotel services, and of course was not 'bundled' at all. (Vera would have preferred to stroll on the beautiful green manses that adjoined the Dartington house.)

The chauffeur-driven Rolls to Salisbury was sponsored and arranged by *Life* magazine to obtain Gjon Mili photographs of Stravinsky in the cathedral and at nearby Stonehenge. Our first excursion was to Exeter Cathedral, not Tintagel. We spent a day exploring Roman Bath with the great Greek scholar H. D. F. Kitto, a charming and erudite guide who claimed, not quite believably, never to have visited the Roman ruins there. He gave numerous reasons for his detestation of everything Roman, and said that his archaeologist son sailing from Corinth back to Italy became ill at the sight of Venetian decadence. We returned to Dartington by way of Glastonbury and medieval Totnes.

Glock's other misinformation includes the statement, 'In the evening the three of them often played multi-lingual Scrabble', a game none of us had ever heard of. On our return to Dartington after the London weekend we dined regularly at the home of Leonard and Dorothy Elmhirst, the American owners of the famous progressive Dartington School, which was rented by the music school in the summer.

Glock's résumé of Stravinsky's activities in Dartington is also skimpy. The book mentions the stage production of *L'Histoire du Soldat* but not the translator, not the director, not the actors, and not my attractive assistant, Judith Jackson. Nothing is said about the hours that Stravinsky spent listening to tapes by and with Schoenberg's pupil, the Spanish composer Roberto Gerhard, nor even our unidentified California neighbours, the Hollywood String Quartet, who gave a sturdy account of a late Beethoven masterpiece. The most consequential event of the Dartington experience was the seating next to Stravinsky of Arthur Waley, in that he inspired the composer to read his translation of *The Tale of Genji* by Lady Murasaki Shikibu. Two years later the composer made an excursion to the lady's beautiful home near Lake Biwa, where the book was written a thousand years ago.

———

After the negative reception of *Les Noces* in 1925, Diaghilev persuaded his friend H. G. Wells to write an open letter which was distributed to the audience of the following performances of the work:

> Writing as an old-fashioned popular writer, not at all of the high-brow set, I feel bound to bear my witness on the other side. I do not know of any other ballet so interesting, so amusing, so fresh or nearly so exciting as *Les Noces*. I want to see it again and again, and because I want to do so, I protest against this conspiracy of willful stupidity that may succeed in driving it out of the programme.
>
> One of our guardians of culture treats the amusing plainness of the backcloth with its single window to indicate one house and its two windows for the other, as imaginative poverty – even he could have thought of a stove and a table – and they

all cling to the suggestion that Stravinsky had tried to make marriage attractive and failed in the attempt. Of course they make jokes about mothers-in-law; that was unavoidable. It will be an extraordinary loss to the London public, if this deliberate dullness of its advisors robs it of *Les Noces.*

The ballet is a rendering in sound and vision of the peasant soul in its gravity, in its deliberate and simple-minded intricacy, in its subtly varied rhythms, in its deep undercurrents of excitement that will astonish and delight every intelligent man or woman who goes to see it. The silly pretty-pretty tradition of Watteau and Fragonard is flung aside. Instead of fancy-dress peasants we have peasants in plain black and white, and the smirking flirtatiousness of Daphnis and Chloé gives place to a richly humorous solemnity. It was an amazing experience to come out from this delightful display with the warp and woof of music and vision still running and interweaving in one's mind, and to find a little group of critics flushed with resentment and ransacking the stores of their minds for cheap, trite deprecations of the freshest and strongest thing that they had had a chance to praise for a long time.

H. G. Wells

PART TWO
The Man

PART TWO
The Man

CHAPTER 7

Roots and Religion

Dushkin to Stravinsky, ranting over a printing error:

Igorfyodorovitch, even God makes mistakes.

Stravinsky (shouting):

Especially God!

Igor Stravinsky's family tree reveals a primarily Slavic ethnicity with Lithuanian,[1] Polish, Ukrainian, Belorussian and German strains. A 1962 letter from Stasys Stantvaras of 404 'K' Street, Boston, convinced the composer that his Stravinsky side was Lithuanian:

> The root of your name, STRAV, is not Russian. Is it possible that your grandfather or great-grandfather came to Russia from Lithuania?[2] You see, dear maestro, *Stravinsky* is a very common word in Lithuania. Even the old Prussian language, which as you know is very close to Lithuanian, has the word

---

1 The opening melody of *The Rite of Spring* is the Lithuanian national anthem.
2 In the late 1960s Stravinsky received a letter from a Dr Grydzewski, editor of a Polish émigré weekly published in London, informing him that his great-grandfather Ignace Ignatievich Skorokhodov was mentioned by Niesiecki in 1778 as a Lithuanian Chamberlain, or 'Podkomorzy litewski'.

STROVO (flow). In Lithuania you will encounter such words as
STRAVA and STREVA (the name of a river), STRAVYS, STRÈVYS,
STRAVINSKAS and STRAVINKSKIS (a proper name) and other
similar words resulting from Polish influence on Lithuanian
names. Excuse me for troubling you with such questions, but
your reply would be of great interest. Your answer will not be
understood as any theft from Russian music.

Stantvaras then directs the composer to *The Encyclopedia Lituanica*,
published in Boston, in which a biographical entry about him was due
to appear: 'The twenty-sixth volume has just been issued, so I cannot
tell you whether my Stravinsky biography will appear in volume
twenty-seven or twenty-eight because the letter "S" in our language
contains an enormous amount of entries.'[3]

Stravinsky's religious background was Russian Orthodox and
Roman Catholic. His mother's family were wealthy landowners, her
maternal grandmother, Maria Romanovna Kholodovskaya, having
received a large inheritance from her step-grandfather, Fyodor
Ivanovich Engel, whose father and grandfather were rewarded with
titles of lesser nobility for their participation in the Russo–Turkish
wars. Maria's father, Roman Fyodorovich Furman, became Privy
Councillor to Tsar Nicholas I. The parents of Stravinsky's mother,
Anna Kirillovna Kholodovskaya,[4] apparently objected to their
daughter's marriage to Fyodor Ignatievich Stravinsky[5] because he was
an artist and therefore a social inferior, but also because his parents
were divorced, after which he was reared in a state lyceum. The
composer's father is nevertheless the primary figure in this family's
arboretum because of his exceptional musical talents, artistic gifts
and intellectual abilities.

Looking at the photographs of Stravinsky's ancestors, the reader
should be reminded that photography was then in its infancy. The
subject had to remain motionless for at least twenty minutes, trying
not to blink. Both sides of the Stravinsky family were frequently

---

3   The complete work comprises thirty-six volumes.
4   1854–1939.
5   1843 to 2 November 1902.

photographed throughout the later decades of the nineteenth century, though this medium was then a luxury. The composer kept a gallery of these images in a cupboard in his studio, only very rarely showing them to guests. A noteworthy photo taken in July 1895 at the Elizabeth Spa, Bad Homburg, shows the thirteen-year-old Igor standing in the centre at a distance from his parents with a large assembly of people behind them. This positioning, with Igor at the front and centre, would become the standard format in group photos throughout his life, partly because of his diminutive height, a matter of supreme sensitivity for him.

Igor's father was renowned for the beautiful and polished tone of his bass voice, his histrionic talents, his gifts as the designer of his own opera costumes,[6] his dapper clothes and his bibliophilia. His private library was among the largest in all Russia, and he was known for his friendships with writers and composers, notably Dostoevsky, Turgenev and Musorgsky, all of whom had slept in what later became Igor's bedroom. Igor's tenth-birthday gift from his father was a copy of Turgenev's *A Sportsman's Sketches*, which may have awakened the boy's appreciation of literature. Photographs of his father standing on one of his library's ladders convey his pride in the collection, but a fall from one of them in 1900 resulted in an injury, for which he was treated by Wilhelm Roentgen in Berlin. Whether this accident had a connection to the sarcoma from which he died is not known. Many of the book titles suggest that Fyodor Ignatievich was a liberal. Surprisingly in despotic Tsarist Russia, his shelves included three different Russian editions of *Das Kapital*. When the library was nationalised after the Revolution, Igor's mother was appointed curator, but the collection was ravaged following her emigration to France in the autumn of 1922.

The outer stage curtain of the Mariinsky Theatre is embroidered above the bottom fringe with gold-framed medallion textile portraits of Fyodor Ignatievich and a few other renowned Russian musicians. Further evidence of his artistic stature is his present tomb in St

---

6   After the New York City Ballet's Russian tour, George Balanchine gave a complete set of colour photographs of these to me.

Petersburg's cemetery of the Alexander Nevsky monastery, the Necropolis of the Great Masters, close to the graves of Tchaikovsky, Musorgsky and Rimsky-Korsakov in a section reserved for national heroes. Astonishingly, Fyodor Ignatievich's remains and those of his youngest son, Gury,[7] were exhumed during the Soviet era from humble graves in the Bolkov cemetery and reburied in the cemetery of the Novodevichy monastery. In 1936 they were again exhumed and interred together in the Alexander Nevsky cemetery, where an imposing life-size bronze monument was erected for them.

The complexities of Fyodor Ignatievich's personality may stem from his abandonment after his parents' divorce when he, the youngest of their three children, was enrolled in the Nezhin Lyceum. Fyodor's father, Ignace Ignatievich Stravinsky (1809-1893), was Roman Catholic, but Fyodor's mother, Alexandra Ivanovna Skorokhodova (1817-1898), was Russian Orthodox. Fyodor's parsimony and meticulous book-keeping, his intractable moods and objurgations appear to have been inherited by Igor. This least-favoured child's hypochondria, anality, short man's 'Napoleon complex' and indomitable ego would make him a perfect subject for a psychobiography. A study of the man by a professional analyst[8] would have to trace these neuroses back to the nursery and examine Igor's confession that he was estranged from his father ('At dinner he never spoke to me'). Igor was also alienated from his hyper-critical mother, a distinguished pianist with outstanding musical gifts who seems otherwise not to have been close to the third of her four sons. Unlike his brothers, Igor was not suckled by his mother[9] but by a wet nurse and subsequently by his German nanny, Bertha Essert.

In his late teens Igor had shown exceptional talent as a painter, most evident in his landscape[10] of the Lubomirski castle on the Bug

---

7   Gury Fyodorovich Stravinsky (1884-1917).
8   Late in life Stravinsky became interested in Freud, purchased the complete works in the Strachey translation and read several volumes, beginning with *Moses and Monotheism.*
9   In the next generation, Igor supervised the choice of a wet nurse for his own children. The composer's elder son reports: 'In Switzerland, my father went to an agency and was presented with several young bare-breasted women drawn up in a row. Each of these squirted some of her precious liquid into a cup, which was handed to my father for his appreciation.'
10 Now in the Fondation Igor Stravinsky, Geneva.

River,[11] but not yet as a composer. In 1901, hoping to prepare their son for a practical career, his parents enrolled him in the Faculty of Law at the University of St Petersburg where Tchaikovsky had been a student. Stravinsky earned a 'half-course diploma', with philosophy as his major interest. His letters provide the most revealing account of his early years. His first compositions brought him a measure of fame, and subjected him to journalistic intrusions for autobiographical information. Thus he wrote to G. N. Timofeyev on 10 March 1908:

> I began to study piano playing under A. P. Snetkova, the daughter of the violinist at the Mariinsky Theatre. At eleven I entered St Petersburg School 27, where I was a desultory student and behaved myself no better. At the end of the fifth grade I entered the Gurevich School, where I finished my intermediate education. I then enrolled in St Petersburg University, where I remained for eight semesters. My parents wanted me to become a pianist and gave me the opportunity to study with good teachers. For two years I took lessons with L. A. Kashperova, but was attracted to composing from the beginning.
>
> In my earliest childhood I could not write down my improvisations, which I ascribe to my lack of theoretical knowledge: I wrote them in ignorance... In my University years I came to know the family of N. A. Rimsky-Korsakov, which quickly accelerated my development. At this time I composed many comic songs on texts by Kuzma Prutkov.[12] In 1903-1904 I composed a large Sonata in F sharp minor, making use of numerous comments from N. A. Rimsky-Korsakov.

On 28 July 1908 Stravinsky wrote to Rimsky's widow saying he had completed a piece for orchestra 'in tribute to the great memory of our dear immortal Nikolai Andreyevich, my best piece to date'. Other letters detail Stravinsky's efforts to establish a performance of the work, but nothing survives of his reactions to his creation when it was

---

11 Near his wife Catherine's family home in Ustilug.
12 Stravinsky briefly returned to Kuzma Prutkov in July 1914, and though Alexander Benois convinced him of the inferiority of the texts, a sketch page for the music survives.

performed, and the score has disappeared. On 12 May 1909 he wrote to Rimsky's son-in-law, Maximilian Steinberg, about the commissions to orchestrate 'The Song of the Flea' for Chaliapin, and inquired about the rehearsals of the two Chopin pieces orchestrated for Diaghilev. Another letter complains of Cherepnin, who had promised to write from Paris 'about the way the Chopin pieces' instrumentation came out, but of course, I heard nothing'.

In spite of his late start as a composer, the speed and extent of Stravinsky's development from age twenty-seven to twenty-nine, from *The Firebird* to *Petrushka* to *The Rite of Spring*, are without precedent or succession in the history of music. The earlier commissioning of Stravinsky's orchestrations of Beethoven's and Musorgsky's settings of Goethe's 'The Song of the Flea' were initiated by the conductor Alexander Ziloti, but it was the famed bass Chaliapin, a friend of Igor's father, who finally chose the *parnishka* ('lad') over Glazunov and Rachmaninov to orchestrate the Musorgsky version[13]. Stravinsky's subsequent discovery that Rimsky-Korsakov had attempted to steer the prestigious commission to Glazunov is undoubtedly the origin of the younger composer's disaffection for his then recently deceased teacher. As late as 25 March 1924, Stravinsky told a critic in Madrid:

> Tchaikovsky's music is very easy, for which reason he has been considered vulgar. In reality he is the most Russian of Russian composers. I acknowledge the great merits of Musorgsky and Borodin, the only composers of 'The Five' who interest me, but I prefer Tchaikovsky. To make Russian music it is not necessary to wear an oriental kaftan. I am referring, above all, to Rimsky-Korsakov. I felt true admiration for him when he was my teacher, but now I perceive the artificiality of his Russianism and orientalism.

As for Stravinsky's ethnicity, evidence exists of German–Jewish blood on his mother's side through his great-grandfather Roman

---

13   See Arkady Klimovitsky's analysis (published in Russian and English) of a facsimile edition of Stravinsky's original manuscript of his orchestration of Musorgsky's 'Flea'.

Furman and Roman's mother, Yelizabeta Engel Furman. I am unaware whether records exist of compulsory conversions from Judaism to the Russian Orthodox Church in Catherine the Great's time – she herself had converted from Lutheranism to Russian Orthodoxy – but both of Igor's parents were born within the Pale of Settlement established by Catherine in 1792, his father in the territory of Minsk, his mother in Kiev. Peter the Great had hoped to establish a culture centre and home for outstanding artists in St Petersburg. Among these, more than a century later, was the basso Fyodor Stravinsky.

Igor did not spend his teenage summers with his parents in St Petersburg but in Ustilug, Volhynia, where he lived with the family of his first cousin and future wife, Catherine Nossenko,[14] whose father was the physician of the local stetel. The village was ninety percent Jewish, and many inhabitants of this community subsequently emigrated to Palestine. During his first concert tour in Israel in 1962 Stravinsky was warmly received by descendants of Ustilug émigrés, who proudly showed him a photograph album of his friends and admirers in the stetel.

It has been noted that the composer's Diaghilev-period friends, including the most intimate of them, Lev ('Lyovushka') Bakst,[15] the Ballets Russes's principal set and costume designer and the creator of several costumes for the original *Firebird*,[16] regarded Igor as Jewish. When Diaghilev failed to engage Bakst to execute the décors and costumes for Stravinsky's miniature opera *Mavra*, commissioning the inferior artist Léopold Survage instead, the offended Bakst wrote to Diaghilev, blaming the 'intervention of the Yankel[17] Shtravinsky'. In a June 1921 letter, following the rumpus over Koussevitzky's botched London premiere of the *Symphonies of Wind Instruments*, Diaghilev scolded Stravinsky for 'having too many Jewish friends'. Ironically,

---

14   Ekaterina Gavrilovna Nossenko (1881-1939).
15   Born Lev Samoilovich Rosenberg, he was one of the very few with whom the composer was on *tutoyer* terms. (Picasso was another.)
16   Most of the décor was by Alexander Golovine, but Diaghilev did not admire his work. Golovine's *Firebird* costumes can be seen for the first time in *The Salon Album of Vera Sudeikin Stravinsky*, edited and translated by John E. Bowlt, Princeton University Press, 1995.
17   This Yiddish diminutive for 'Jacob' was the name of Gogol's despised money-lender.

the sister of Yelizabeta Engel was Diaghilev's great-grandmother, hence Stravinsky and the impresario were cousins once removed.[18]

Stravinsky was inexplicably slow to realise that Hitler's Germany would immediately ban his music and his concert touring on his classification as a Jew. In 1936 Stravinsky and his son Soulima[19] performed the Two-Piano Concerto in Baden-Baden on condition that no Nazi musicians participate in their concert, which Stravinsky's German publisher, Willy Strecker, achieved after shrewd political manipulation. Father and son also performed the piece in Copenhagen later that year but travelled there by airplane, with only a fuelling stop in Hamburg. Ironically, the composer's first open conflict with Nazism occurred when the German edition of his autobiography deleted his anti-Wagnerian remarks. Yet Stravinsky spent nearly a week in Berlin in February 1938 recording *Jeu de cartes* for Telefunken with the Berlin Philharmonic, a secret visit because the publisher Schott wanted to promote the piece with a recording and not a public performance (Stravinsky had previously recorded his Violin Concerto with Dushkin in Germany).[20] In May 1938 the Düsseldorf exhibition *Entartete Kunst* ('Degenerate Art') had targeted Stravinsky as a Jew by featuring an enlarged photograph of Jacques-Émile Blanche's painting of him under the caption, 'Wer ist Jude?'[21] This was followed by months of futile official-level protests by the composer through the French ambassador André François Ponçet[22] (whose son would marry Marion Sachs, daughter of Stravinsky's close friend since 1924, Arthur Sachs).

I might add here that during my own last visit to the Soviet Union in 1981, the official Intourist guides, KGB types, pressed me for information about the composer's Jewishness, insisting that 'Stravinsky' is not a Russian name, but Polish–Jewish.

---

18   W. H. Auden's companion, Chester Kallman, also claimed descent from the Furman branch of Stravinsky's ancestry.
19   Sviatoslav-Soulima Igorievich Stravinsky (1910–1994).
20   I was able to purchase a copy in New York in 1941.
21   'Is he a Jew?' Oddly, this portrait is still referred to in biographies as a stereotypical description of Stravinsky: 'The nose, the lips, the ears... with a certain overdone elegance in his tailoring to hint at more remote, Eastern European, perhaps Jewish origins.' The same book also describes *me* with the adjectives 'edgy... complex, quick, almost Jewish'.
22   1887–1978.

Some scholars might argue that Stravinsky's Jewish identity is evident in his creations. Certainly he is the greatest modern-era composer inspired by Old Testament subjects: the Symphony of Psalms, *Abraham and Isaac*, the Lamentations of Jeremiah (*Threni*), *The Flood*, *Canticum Sacrum* (the *Canticum Cantoricum, Deuteronomy* and *Psalms*), *Babel* and *The Dove Descending* (the Pentecostal *Shavuot*). Even the offensive phrase in the 1952 Cantata is an adaptation of the Hebrew text from Deutero-Isaiah, made famous in Handel's *Messiah*: 'The people that walked in darkness have seen a great light.' Stravinsky's Christian music comprises a smaller category: Mass; Requiem Canticles; *A Sermon, A Narrative, and A Prayer*, the sacred *a cappella* choruses; and *Les Noces*, in which the actual marriage ceremony is sung without instrumental accompaniment, following the Russian Orthodox rule.

The only text I have read from Stravinsky's student law library is the volume on religious philosophy by Nesmielov, whose work the composer's wife Catherine also read and re-read. The style, at least in the translation by a Hungarian friend of the film director Tony Palmer, is thorny, but the book takes on greater significance in light of Stravinsky's own heritage. Nesmielov is concerned with what he calls

> Christian Jews, who never discussed their own religion... [but] adopted Christian dogma to the extent that it conformed with Jewish dogma, while in essence their beliefs remained unchanged... Christian Jews wished to recall the sad fate of the Jewish people and to discuss the prophecies from the point of view of their own first Scripture. But some Jews had come to believe in Christ because they doubted their own doctrines. Otherwise, no one would ever turn to any faith, since it is not possible to seek what one already possesses. Scepticism in itself is not necessarily indicative of disbelief.

Stravinsky wrote in the margin of this passage, 'Very good', 'Magnificent' and 'Man, for the sake of his interest in science, may choose to believe that there exists no God whatsoever.' While composing the pagan *Rite of Spring* he seems to have been an agnostic. The mockery of Christianity in *Renard* is blasphemous, and so is the parody of 'Ein' feste Burg' in *L'Histoire du Soldat*. In 1915 Stravinsky refused to compose the ballet *Liturgie* for Diaghilev on grounds that to present Russian Orthodox rituals on stage would be sacrilegious. Other marginalia in Nesmielov reveal that Stravinsky had been reading Kant, who presupposes that reality exists on two levels: the phenomenal, which can be known, and the noumenal (*Ding an sich*), which can only be postulated. The mystic Stravinsky naturally accepted the Kantian distinction.

Stravinsky's parents seem not to have professed any religion until the death in 1917 of the composer's younger brother Gury (from peritonitis at Iaşi, Romania), after which his mother became a member of the Russian Orthodox Church (*not* after the deaths of her oldest son Roman in 1897 or her husband in 1902). Stravinsky was baptised in the Nikolsky Sobor, a few blocks from his home and on the same side of the Kryukov Canal, but on our visit to this church with Soviet guides in 1962 he seemed to have no recollection of the interior of this most beautiful of the city's rococo buildings. Nor did he seem to remember the synagogue, the largest of the five in St Petersburg, which was clearly visible from the Stravinsky apartment on the transpontine side of the canal.

One would expect that the resurgence of the composer's wife's tuberculosis in 1914, followed by his affairs with Coco Chanel (1920-1) and thereafter with Vera de Bosset, would have consumed him with guilt, but he did not embrace the Russian Orthodox Church until 1925. He attributed this transformation to the 'miraculous' cure of an abscessed finger wrought by God, with whom he was on personal terms and who heard and responded to his prayers with a sign. He had prayed for the finger's cure in a church at Laghet, near Nice, before his departure for Venice on 7 September 1925. The orisons were made manifest in Venice the next day when he walked on stage to play his new Sonata and found that the stigma had disappeared. A few days after the Venice concert, the sign of 'God's personal intervention' came to Stravinsky in a vision in a church in Fiesole, but he never revealed the nature of the vision.

Matthew Arnold's *Culture and Anarchy* characterises the governing forces in man as 'Hebraism' and 'Hellenism'. The uppermost tenet of Hellenism is to see things as they really are, while that of Hebraism is good conduct and obedience. Arnold maintains that 'the essence of Hellenism is "spontaneity of consciousness", and that of Hebraism is "strictness of consciousness"', and that the complete person should embody both. No Stravinsky biography has examined his mature religious beliefs, a driving force in his life as a composer. He believed in 'intentionality', not Brentano's but the single kind set forth in St Anselm's argument that 'if God is thought about, He thereby exists in the understanding'.

Though Stravinsky and Jacques Maritain had been friends in France from 1925, their relationship grew closer at the University of Chicago during World War II. A letter from the philosopher, 23 July 1934, offers the only convincing explanation of Stravinsky's universally misunderstood pronouncement that 'music is powerless to express anything at all'. After praising the composer for his concept of 'the victorious power of the creative effort and the effacement of the individual by his achievements', Maritain adds:

> ...as philosophy – and Thomist philosophy – I agree with you on music and the expression of emotion. But I myself believe that there also exists something different, which I would describe as the creative emotion or creative intuition through which the artist unknowingly expresses himself in his works.

More mystically minded than ratiocinative, Stravinsky strongly disagreed with Maritain's Thomistic precepts. An interviewer in Barcelona, 25 March 1928, wrote:

> We talk about the intellectual and spiritual good which St Thomas Aquinas embodied. But now Stravinsky is deeply interested in the great mystics. We ask him about St John of the Cross, about St Theresa of the Perfect Jesus, and his eyes suddenly brighten with admiration... He comments on various saints – Jerome, for one – and religious philosophy –

Soloviev, among others – and we discuss Ramón Llull at length;
Stravinsky is deeply interested in this great mystic.

On 4 May 1932 Stravinsky drafted an agreement lending his
collection of 'religious objects belonging to me' to an Orthodox
Church. Most of these objects were acquired after 1925, when
Stravinsky embraced the faith and actually installed an altar in his
home in Nice complete with a live-in priest, Father Podosenov[23]. The
composer lists fifty-one items, among them

> a reproduction of the Holy Shroud of Turin; eight sections of
> iconostases; an image embroidered in silk of the decapitation
> of John the Baptist; four large wooden candlesticks; a bronze
> chandelier; priests' robes in white, yellow, and violet silk;
> lectern robes; altar coverlets in ten colours of silk and velvet;
> patens in silk with embroidered cherubs. These possessions
> were lent temporarily to the Ecumenical Parish of Nice as
> long as the Archpriest Nicolai Podosenov remained the Father
> Superior. Igor Stravinsky, Isère, 4 May 1932.

Stravinsky believed that his creative gifts were God-given.[24] He
prayed before an icon every morning before composing, and the
drawings of the Crucifixion attached to the flyleaf of the Symphony
of Psalms sketchbook, and of the Russian cross at the end of the
Polymnia Variation in *Apollo*, as well as the church calendar dates
found in other post-1925 music ('I. Stravinsky, after Friday Confession,
April 9, 1926' on the cover of the Serenade in A) testify to the fervour
of his faith.

Stravinsky sent donations for the Monastery of St John on Mount
Athos through his spiritual advisor there, Father Gerasim. An
especially impassioned letter from Stravinsky dated 12 July 1932

---

23 In 1928 George Balanchine described 'the stultifying religious atmosphere of the priest
    dining with the family as depressing and gloomy beyond imagination'. A parallel exists
    between Stravinsky's situation and that of the choreographer after the latter's wife, Tanaquil
    LeClerq, was stricken with polio in 1956, which helps to account for the choreographer's
    interpretation of *The Flood* as more Russian Orthodox than Old Testament.
24 'First ideas are very important. They come from God. And if after working and working and
    working, I return to these ideas, then I know they are good.' Letter to Dushkin, 1931.

survives along with the receipts that, characteristically, he preserved. His wife sent twenty-five francs for each prayer from Mount Athos. An icon of Father Gerasim graced the composer's night table and accompanied him on his travels during the last thirty years of his life. The Stravinsky I knew always wore religious medals, gold and silver crosses and amulets dangling on fine gold chains under his clothing.

Stravinsky devoted more composing time to 'Sektanskaya' (1919), his first religious, though heretical, opus, than to any of his secular creations of similar length. In addition to increasing his knowledge of Russian folk music and its texts, his July 1914 research in Kiev also influenced his philosophy. He returned to Switzerland with copies of Tereshchenko's[25] *Byt Russkago Naroda*, as well as Ivan Kireyevsky's song collections and his post-Hegelian writings about Khomyakov's 'integral reason philosophy', which includes pre-conceptual and non-cognitive elements.

At some point in 1914, Stravinsky became interested in the Khlisti, the controversial sect later led by Rasputin, who also preached a doctrine that abandoning oneself to sin is the truest humility. Since Stravinsky's Luciferian pride conflicted with his striving for Christian humility, he must have denounced the cult before the Holy Monk's disgrace and protracted assassination.[26]

———

On 18 June 1950 I witnessed Stravinsky's birthday confession, which began by lying spread-eagled and face down for a motionless hour on the floor of the Russian Orthodox Church on Micheltorena Street, Los Angeles. Suffocating from the incense, even denser than the smog through which we had come, I waited until the penitent arose and followed a priest behind a black screen, where another hour of confessing took place. When we finally returned to his car, the

---

25 Tereshchenko wrote to Alexander Blok in March 1913: 'There is something frightening about Diaghilev. He does not walk alone. Art, he says, is a stimulus to sensuality. There are two geniuses, Nijinsky and Stravinsky. Everything else about Diaghilev is terrible, including his active homosexuality.'

26 See the chapter 'Amorous Augmentations'.

composer swallowed most of a flask of Armagnac and then, since he had been fasting for twenty-four hours, consumed a four-course breakfast from a basket prepared by his cook, Yevgenia Petrovna. He did not speak and his mood was petulant. He revealed the cause to me only hours later: the Father Confessor had asked for an autograph. After this, Stravinsky discontinued his formal religious observances, with the exception of a midnight Russian Easter service in a church nearer his home in 1953. Thereafter, two of his children converted to the Roman Catholicism of their spouses, and perpetually proselytised their father to do the same.

I should avow my own guilt in Stravinsky's lapse in his Russian Orthodoxy. He understood that I considered myself a 'secular humanist', remote from metaphysical beliefs, at least at that time. In Santa Fe in the summer of 1950, he purchased a wood-panel Santo painted by a local Indian artist and a silver cross and gave them to me without a word, but the gesture was obviously intended to bring me 'back' to a church to which I had never belonged. At the same time he tried to discourage me from reading the 'anti-Christians' D. H. Lawrence and Aldous Huxley.[27]

In the autumn of 1944 the Stravinskys were staying in the Santa Barbara home of Arthur Sachs, along with another houseguest, the Abbé Elzéar Fortier from Montreal, who undoubtedly affected the composer's decision to write a Roman Catholic Mass. The Kyrie and Gloria were conceived and composed at this time, though the deepest roots of Stravinsky's Mass are still enigmatic. The ban on musical instruments in Orthodox services seems unlikely to have been the sole reason for the composer's setting of the Latin text, which was his own explanation, together with a wish to revive a traditional model (stylistically *quattrocento*) of a modern Mass. Remote as can be from his concert pieces of the period, the Mass – composed immediately after the Broadway musical *Scènes de Ballet* – was intended for liturgical use, and he was upset on hearing that Ernest Ansermet had

---

27 Auden vehemently argued that Huxley should be placed on the Vatican Index. Nicolas Nabokov and I often referred to the poet who attended early morning Mass daily as 'Bishop Auden'.

conducted the premiere on the opera stage at La Scala with female sopranos and altos, disregarding the manuscript's specification of an all-male choir. When the music was performed by the Roger Wagner Chorus on 8 December 1949, for the Holy Day of Obligation service in the Church of St Joseph, Los Angeles, the composer knelt throughout. He first conducted the work in a joint concert with me in New York in March 1949, and again in Palermo, Catania and Rome in November 1963. The last, in the Church of Santa Maria Sopra Minerva, was in observance of the funeral of President Kennedy in Washington.

The Mass was the first work that Stravinsky entrusted to me to rehearse for him. One evening in February 1949, I recruited Juilliard friends to play the double wind quintet while a Stravinsky friend managed to find an empty room in a recording studio in Rockefeller Center. On that occasion he heard the full instrumentation for the first time.[28] Perhaps because I had sung in a boys' choir, this Mass made an indelible impression on me. On a train to Boston the next day, Stravinsky revised the score, lengthening the choral responses in dialogue with the soprano and alto solo duo in the Gloria. During this trip I tried to convince him to remove the mutes from the solo trumpet part and from the brass in the choral responses. The muted tone quality seemed inappropriate; thus he rejected my suggestion on the surprising premise that volume was more important than sonority, but he relented when the full chorus was added.

In May 1955 Stravinsky accompanied his daughter Milene on a pilgrimage to the Portuguese Shrine of Fátima, the scene of the Virgin's appearance to a shepherd's three young children. The composer never mentioned this visit, except to remark that the cathedral esplanade is twice as large as St Peter's Square in Rome.[29] While the shrine's effect on him remains unknown, the architecture and pastel colours of Lisbon delighted him (as he wrote to me from there). Stravinsky, his daughter, and her husband flew back to New

---

28 The Kyrie and Gloria were performed at a concert at Harvard University before this date in an arrangement of the instrumental parts for two pianos by Claudio Spies.

29 At Easter 1954 Igor, Vera and Theodore Stravinsky heard Pope Pius XII deliver a sermon from the balcony of St Peter's. When the crowd below applauded, an annoyed Stravinsky resolved never again to attend such public exhibitions.

York and on to California virtually in silence. Despite the exhausting flights, on reaching home the next evening Stravinsky asked to hear music.[30]

---

30 I chose Bach's canonic variations on 'Vom Himmel hoch', which we played four-hands. Before the end of the year, Stravinsky began his orchestration of the work, inscribing it: 'Robert Craft gewidmet.'

CHAPTER 8
Diaghilev, *Liturgie*, Goncharova and *Les Noces*

In Florence in 1915 at the beginning of the Great War, Serge Diaghilev, isolated from Parisian friends and minions, allied himself with the Futuristi and summoned his fellow Russian-exile collaborators to join him in Florence. In a bravado declaration of patriotism, his closest female patron, Misia Sert[1], refused to leave the French capital, but Léonide Massine came promptly, as did Sergei Prokofiev. Fokine, in Biarritz, pledged his loyalty to the impresario but remained in France. Though horrified by the slaughter of the young male populations of Europe's most civilised nations, Diaghilev mentions the war only to assure the world that the Ballets Russes would go on unveiling the grandeur of Russia in Spain, Portugal, Monaco, Switzerland, the United States and Argentina.

---

1   This free-spirited Polish lady was described by Diaghilev as 'the only woman on earth whom I could possibly love'. She was bisexual and once shared a sleeping compartment on a train to Venice with the entirely lesbian American, Hoytie Wiborg. As Misia settled in for the night, Hoytie descended from the upper berth, pounced on her and, panting and heaving, declared her love. 'Oh, all right, if that's what you want,' Misia apparently said. A short time later, she added annihilatingly, 'Is that all you know how to do?' Readers of *Misia* by Gold and Fizdale still wonder about Misia's greater expectations. She became Diaghilev's spokesperson and exercised a powerful influence over him, being a trained musician, and, after her second marriage, a woman of considerable wealth who continually gave money to both Diaghilev and Stravinsky during World War I. When Diaghilev stopped paying Stravinsky for presenting his ballets, he turned to Misia for help.

Though more widely known as a *bon vivant* than a cross-bearer for suffering humanity, Diaghilev was suddenly impassioned by a vision of a ballet based on the unlikely subject (for him) of scenes from the life of Christ. The impresario exhibited clerical garments, silver icons and bejeweled iconostases, candelabra, gold crosses, and thuribles, all to be borrowed from Orthodox churches. This exhibition of the allure of ecclesiastical Russia was to be called *Liturgie*.

Diaghilev wrote to Stravinsky, immersed at the time in the composition of *Svadebka* (*Les Noces*) in the Alpine village of Château d'Oex, informing him of the idea of displaying the sacred ceremony as theatrical pageantry. The composer was shocked. Blasphemy aside, the insurmountable obstacle to this conception was that the music would have to be purely choral, instruments having been banned from Orthodox services since their Byzantine beginnings. Nevertheless, sketchbooks show that he did enter some notations for *Liturgie*. Diaghilev invited Stravinsky to Florence for discussions with the Yugoslavian sculptor Ivan Meštrović, with whom the impresario had begun to plan his new creation. Having explored the wonders of early Byzantium in Ravenna, Diaghilev and the sculptor were convinced that the time-frame should be the fifth century, thus limiting the visual aspect to low, rounded arches, domed pillars and mosaics.

The most qualified spokesman on the subject of Diaghilev's religion was his closest lifelong friend, Valechka Nouvel, who wrote to Stravinsky the day after Diaghilev's death in August 1929 declaring, 'His mysticism is of a pagan, not a Christian order. Instead of faith, he had superstition.' Another letter to the composer written on the same day and on the same subject came from his publisher friend Gabriel Paichadze: 'A large part of your life was connected with Diaghilev and his sudden death must have staggered you. You were the only person whom the deceased regarded in a different light than everyone else. In his own way he loved you, and in his own way he was jealous.' The last phrase here has never been understood by Diaghilev biographers.

Another obstacle for the composer was that in January 1914 his wife had suffered a virulent attack of tuberculosis and could not be left alone with their four young children. Diaghilev persisted, alternately pleading with and ordering the composer in telegrams, announcing train reservations and munificent hotel accommodations, as well as hinting at threats about future collaborations. These last intimations preyed on Stravinsky, who knew that only Diaghilev could produce *Les Noces*. The composer finally agreed to come to Italy for a single day in November, by which time Diaghilev had moved to the Hotel Continental in Rome. But Stravinsky continued to postpone his trip, and the Avezzano earthquake of 13 January 1915 provided a further excuse for delay; the tremors were felt as far away as Château d'Oex where, Stravinsky reported, his dresser 'hopped across the room' towards his bed. He eventually arrived in Rome on 8 February 1915, remaining there until the 15th. The extension of his visit can be attributed to stimulating meetings with Rodin and the Futuristi – Marinetti, Pratella, Boccioni, Cangiullo, Depero and Balla. In 1917 Diaghilev presented a Futuristic ballet with a 'cast' of coloured electric lights flashing on and off, singly and in combinations, in conjunction with the orchestral colours of Stravinsky's *Fireworks*.

On 15 June 1914 Stravinsky had heard a 'Grand Futurist Concert of Noises' in London, during which Marinetti expatiated on *The Art of Noises* and Luigi Russolo conducted his *Two Noise Spirals*. The instruments displayed in this concert included 'Buzzers, Whistlers, Rattlers, Exploders, Murmurers, Cracklers, Thunderers, Gurglers and Roarers': in short, an enlarged version of what Americans call a 'skiffle band'. Stravinsky was greatly impressed and went backstage to greet Marinetti. The composer's enthusiasm greatly encouraged Diaghilev.

A fascinating letter from Diaghilev, in Rome, to Stravinsky of 8 March 1915, reveals something of the evolution of *Liturgie* and of the impresario's proleptic powers:

> After thirty-two rehearsals for *Liturgie* we have concluded that absolute silence is death, and that there can be no absolute silence in any airspace. The action must have some accompaniment, not musical accompaniment but sounds. The source of the sounds must not be revealed, and the passage

from one to another must not be detectable to the ear. The sounds must flow into each other. No rhythm exists because the beginnings and ends of the sounds are imperceptible. The proposed instruments include bells (with tongues wrapped in felt), sirens, whirring tops, Aeolian harps, psalters, guzli and sistrums [Ethiopian rattles]. Please cable me whether you could come with us to Milan for a day. You will see a lot of new workshops. Please do this, as it is important for the future.

Diaghilev's prescient mind scoops Varèse, John Cage, Bang on a Can and the many percussion ensembles of the late twentieth century.

Stravinsky accepted Diaghilev's invitation, joining him in Milan in March 1915, and became acquainted with Pratella's arsenal of percussion instruments, the 'intonarumori'. Indeed, the Futuristi so interested Stravinsky that their influence in both *L'Histoire du Soldat* and *Les Noces* is a feature of these pieces. While Stravinsky was in Rome in February 1915, he played the first two tableaux of *Les Noces* for Diaghilev, who was so overcome by the music that his parting words were, 'Finish *Les Noces*. I am in love with it.' A letter from Stravinsky to Misia of 24 July 1916 refers to his playing of *Noces* for Diaghilev 'seven months ago in [her] apartment on the quai Voltaire'. *Liturgie* was postponed until after the completion of the first *Noces* sketch-score; thus *Noces* overtook *Liturgie*. Stravinsky also played portions of *Noces* for the impresario and Prokofiev in Milan's Hotel Continental as early as 14 April 1915.

Two years later Stravinsky gave the completed manuscript of the *Noces* sketch-score to Diaghilev in Les Diablerets, Switzerland, the bulk of it in July, and the remainder in October 1917, after which the two men departed together on the same train, Diaghilev returning to Italy and Stravinsky accompanying him as far as Aigle. The contract for *Noces* was signed during this trip, despite Stravinsky's failure to understand that the agreement would be nullified because the Russian Revolution had rendered him a 'stateless person' whose works were not protected by copyright.

After hearing *Noces*, Diaghilev nevertheless continued to toy with his original ideas for *Liturgie*. This is substantiated by documents in

Natalia Goncharova's[2] hand. Her reputation as a painter of Russian folk art (primitive imagery, costumes, ceremonies) and religious art (icons, vestments) made her the most qualified choice to design the sets and costumes for both *Liturgie* and *Noces*. After assigning her to work on *Noces*, Diaghilev revived her interest in his religious ballet, for which she had already completed numerous sketches, some of which were inscribed to Stravinsky in Morges in 1915. Partly because she continued to work on *Liturgie* until 1916, we learn more about Diaghilev's concepts from her letters than from any other source. The stage spectacle was to have consisted of eight danced episodes demarcated by purely musical interludes: The Annunciation, The Nativity, The Adoration of the Magi, The Sermon on the Mount, Palm Sunday, The Passion in the Garden of Olives, The Ways of the Cross and Golgotha. Goncharova also mentions that the music director of the Russian Church in Geneva came to Diaghilev's Villa Belle Rive to teach Byzantine chants[3] to the singers for *Liturgie*. Stravinsky must have been aware of these rehearsals through his close friend, the Russian choral director Vassily Kibalchich, and would certainly have attended some of them.

Born in a village close to Tolstoy's Yasnaya Polyana, Goncharova came from a family of linen manufacturers on whom Peter the Great had bestowed nobility. She is still mistakenly referred to as the great-granddaughter of Pushkin but was actually his great-niece by marriage.[4] Since her mother was a professor of theology in Moscow, Natalia was familiar with the Orthodox services, and with censers, chalices, votive candles and the other paraphernalia used in religious celebrations. While studying at the Moscow School of Art she met and in 1900 married Mikhail Larionov, who in that year executed four portraits of her. Under his tutelage she successively mastered the techniques of drawing, pastel, watercolour, tempera and oil. In 1903

2   Natalia Sergeevna Goncharova (1881-1962).
3   The great scholar on Byzantine chant, Egon Wellesz, was a pupil of Schoenberg.
4   The poet wedded the beauty Natalia Nikolaevna Goncharova, the painter's great-aunt and namesake who, six years after their marriage, caused the duel that resulted in Pushkin's death (1831). The painter's grandfather was the brother of Pushkin's widow and in 1844 married one of the poet's closest friends.

the couple moved to the Crimea, where the vegetation, the Black Sea and the spectacularly vibrant colours of the Middle Eastern peasants' clothing attracted her.

Before the Revolution, Goncharova and Larionov escaped to Paris, where she became close to Diaghilev and in effect joined the Ballets Russes company. Influenced by Cubism, Futurism, Neo-Primitivism and Diaghilev's publication *Mir Iskusstva*, she and Larionov developed Rayonism. In the early part of the war, from May to December 1915, the couple had lived at Belle Rive, where they were Stravinsky's neighbours and saw him frequently. Later Goncharova moved with the Ballets Russes to San Sebastián at the invitation of Diaghilev's patron, King Alfonso XIII. In 1919 the two artists settled permanently in the atelier in Paris in which Racine had opened the first French theatre. News of Goncharova's death reached Stravinsky while he was in Assisi in 1962 and deeply upset him.

The impossibility of staging *Liturgie* would have been in the vocal domain; Diaghilev's first letters to Stravinsky about the piece suggest that a choral part would have to be based on Gregorian chant.[5] But the lingering Byzantine theme of *Liturgie* carried over into *Noces*, converting the character of the Second Tableau from secular to sacred. Church bells are sounded on off-beats throughout the scene, which builds to a majestic climax. After *Liturgie* was abandoned, Stravinsky employed ecclesiastical chant in the lines sung by the two archimandrites who perform the marriage ceremony in *Noces*. He gave up on the experimental ensembles of his early versions and in 1922 rewrote the work for a percussion ensemble of seventeen instruments and four pianos. The stroke of genius in the piano combination modernises a work that would have been a mere curiosity in the 1919 pianola score with its combination of harmonium and cimbaloms. Stravinsky specified pianos 'with tensile strength and a very light, clear sound, above all, not velvety'. Alastair Macaulay has written more panoptically about *Noces* than any music critic:

---

5   Stravinsky had had recourse to chanting in *Zvyezdoliki* and later would employ it in his Russian Sacred Choruses and in the Credo of his Mass.

The correspondence of movement to music is enthralling, moment by moment in a way that we too seldom encounter in performances of the pre-1914 ballets. Thrillingly bleak in its pounding power, *Les Noces* remains among the most uncompromising of all Modernist works of art. Nobody can miss the pathos of the central couple getting married, the two most passive people in the ballet. But the most unsettling aspect of *Noces* is that the same pathos, the same bound body language and forlorn helplessness, also characterize the whole peasant society to which they belong.[6]

Without the influence of *Liturgie* and the Futuristi, *Les Noces* would have been a very different piece. The spirit of the work was transformed by Byzantium and the aborted *Liturgie*; the architecture became geometric, the artistic approach mathematical. Underlying *Noces* is the philosophy of Gregory of Nyssa, whose belief in universal salvation and the transcendent power of Beauty made him the most beloved of the early Russian theologians for both Catherine and Igor Stravinsky: 'Every desire ceases with the possession of its object except the desire for Beauty. It is Beauty alone that the insolence of satiety cannot touch.'

6   *TLS*, 28 May 2004.

CHAPTER 9

Dysfunctional Family

Dickens's children... would attract no opprobrium (and no attention) if they didn't have the Dickens name attached to them.

Robert Gottlieb in *Great Expectations: The Sons and Daughters of Charles Dickens*

My first impediment in attempting to profile Stravinsky's family was that I did not know his wife, Catherine, his first cousin and mother of his four children. Most of what I have learned about her has been deduced from her bi-weekly letters to him during his four-month concert tours in the Americas and extended excursions in Europe. Following a provision in Stravinsky's will, his side of the correspondence was destroyed, and the information about him that can be inferred from her letters is meagre. His health and religion are her primary concerns, even before the woes of their extensive family. Her tone is unrelievedly nagging – 'You have for so long been leading a vain life with your work, business and people, completely without the church' (27 March 1935) – and ranges from reminders of upcoming saints' days, and overdue contributions to churches and charities, to sheer fanaticism. On 9 December 1937 Catherine reports that 'Yesterday Father Vasilii was here, and I was able to confess longer than in church. I thank God that He considered me worthy to share my secrets with His priest.' Most of her letters are headed by drawings of the sign of the cross.

Attentiveness to Vera de Bosset, who did not accompany Stravinsky on his transatlantic tours, is also conspicuous in Catherine's letters to Igor in Europe in the 1930s. The writer regularly inquires about Vera's well-being and her social life, and reports on their visits together in Paris. His wife imagines Vera's happiness in receiving gifts from her husband – a new apartment, a new automobile – of which he insensitively keeps his wife informed. He had written to both women from the U.S. in January 1925 insisting that they meet, partly because he realised that the healthy, vigorous, younger woman could assist in ministering to his family[1] and in attending to business matters during his absences. Their first encounter took place on 1 March 1925, at the Stravinsky home in Nice. They jointly cabled him in Detroit: 'We are together today and embrace you. Vera and Catherine.'

But for Catherine the seismic event had already come in 1922, when Igor sent a confession of his double life with Vera. The ultimate humiliation for both women must have been manifest when the money for the family's household and medical expenses was regularly sent to Catherine through Vera, since postal service from the U.S. to Paris was more expedient than it would have been to Biarritz, Nice, Talloires, Voreppe or the sanatorium at Sancellemoz where Catherine was confined.[2] After the family's move from Voreppe to Paris in 1934, Catherine and Vera, living only a short distance from each other, shared his communications. Vera increasingly assisted Catherine and became a surrogate mother to the Stravinsky children during their illnesses. Vera did not conceal her partiality to Mika, taking care of her while Stravinsky was abroad in 1937.

Some of Catherine's letters reprimand Igor for his sartorial self-indulgence, in particular his budget-breaking expenditures on the best of Bond Street: coats, suits, jackets, shirts, neckties, scarves,

---

1   'Vera has been helping the children diligently,' Catherine writes on 31 January 1935.
2   Catherine would live there for six months in 1935.

vests and spats. Indeed, almost every interview with him mentions the snazzy colour combinations of his wardrobe and the items that constitute his *endimanché* appearance. The modesty of Catherine's own wardrobe is revealed in pathetic contrast, as when she expresses her doubt that he would wear anything so drab as the sweater she is knitting for him.

Concerning Stravinsky's public statements en route, Catherine's advice proves to have been more astute than her husband's. She correctly predicts that his candidacy for admission to the Académie des Beaux-Arts would oblige him to appeal for votes from artists of much lower stature.[3] As she had foreseen, the outcome was a terrible trouncing. He garnered less than a handful of ballots (only six), while his chief opponent, Florent Schmitt, was grandly victorious.[4] (Eric Satie once said to Stravinsky: 'Il s'appelle Schmitt pour nous épater.')

Not all of Igor's letters to Catherine are combative. He invited her to Brussels in 1930 for the premiere of Symphony of Psalms, the first and last experience of this kind she would have. He treated her with great kindness during the visit and reverted to his earliest affectionate name for her, Katik.

But after 1935 a sharp change of tone occurs in the letters. She abandons her attempts to conceal her resentment, and communications between them become increasingly hostile. Unable to pay a doctor's bill, she wrote to Igor in Buenos Aires on 13 March 1936, 'Please send money. Some day [soon] I'll free you from payment of all these large bills.' Stravinsky's visits home became shorter and less frequent, his concert tours more numerous. Photographs taken of him with his wife reveal the distance separating them; nearly always he looks like a man desperate to be elsewhere. He seldom looks at her, and not because she is mortally ill. Squeezing more than 200 words on a postcard to him on 28 November 1938, in Turin, she

---

3   One of the electors was the organist Charles-Marie Widor, whose treatise on instrumentation Stravinsky employed from as early as *The Rite of Spring* to as late as *Ebony Concerto*.

4   Stravinsky and Schmitt remained friends after the vote. He had been the most prominent promoter of *The Rite of Spring* before its premiere, and Stravinsky always enjoyed Schmitt's malicious criticisms. After writing to Diaghilev of his desire to play Schmitt's *La Tragédie de Salomé* 'endlessly and madly from start to finish', Stravinsky wrote again that 'the music is terrible'.

writes that no more letters will be sent for fear that 'you'll scold me for wasting stamps'.[5] The message continues:

> Today Mikusha[6] is doing somewhat better, but it's true that this is the result of the morphine injections. [She died two days later.] Her temperature is 37.2 [99˚F], her pulse 120, and her breathing 24. She wanted a piece of pastry for tea. I went to see her but not for long because I didn't want her to talk too much and also because Yura [her husband] was with her. He spent the night in your study.[7] My temperature is 38.2 [100.8˚F]; the compresses have a soothing effect on my coughing and dry up some of the phlegm at night. I hope to have a letter from you tomorrow. I hope you receive this postcard on the day of your concert. God grant that it may go well. Keep well. I embrace you both [Soulima was with him] with all my heart and soul. Christ be with you. Katya

Catherine reports the children's slightest mishaps and shortcomings, and she is more protective of her husband than of her children. In the wake of Igor's performances with Soulima, the letters are mostly concerned with possible damage to the father: 'Did Soulima play out of phase? Did he suffer memory lapses?' After one of his recitals, she reveals that he 'got a little lost in the Bach suite and in an Étude by Liszt'.[8] But his father never encouraged him and did not even attend his 1930 debut recital, obliging Vera to go instead.

Of Stravinsky's children, Milene Marion,[9] the youngest, was the one I knew best and the only one with whom I remained friendly. Since her Hollywood residence was little more than a mile from her father's, she visited him almost daily. We regularly dined at her house, where on special occasions she prepared *boeuf bourguignon*

---

5   The Stravinsky household in 1934 employed five servants, including a pastry chef.
6   Their elder daughter, Mika Liudmila Igorievna Stravinskaya Mandelstam (1908-1938).
7   This would have been a deliberate aggravation to Stravinsky.
8   A letter to Stravinsky from his sister-in-law, Liudmila Beliankina, reveals that his Kholodovsky mother, an excellent pianist and an iron-willed woman, tended 'to give severe criticisms of piano playing'.
9   Milene Igorievna Stravinskaya Marion (15 January 1914 - 12 February 2007).

en gelée, knowing that it was one of my favourite dishes. In my early days with Stravinsky, I drove her to Malibu Beach with friends visiting me from New York, and I sometimes accompanied her to movies with her husband. In the last years of her father's life in California, Milene came every fortnight to trim his hair and mine. She was good-natured, had a pleasing musical voice and was a talented designer, as the covers of some of her father's American-period music reveal. She had spent much of her life in the Sancellemoz sanatorium, hence her formal education was limited, which helps to account for her extreme shyness. Among the Stravinsky siblings and their spouses, she alone appreciated my work with her father, as is clear from her deposition in the 1974 lawsuit by the Stravinsky children against their stepmother. Further, Milene was the only deponent in that litigation who initially showed scruples about the embezzlement of their father's Swiss bank account.[10]

At first my relations with Andre Marion were convivial. Having been a purser on a Caribbean cruise ship, he spoke English more fluently than the rest of the family. No matter that he was aggressively uninterested in music, literature and the arts. In January 1952 Stravinsky commissioned Andre and me to translate Theodore's book about him. Every afternoon for about a month we collaborated on this project, sometimes collapsing in giggles at the hagiographical tone. After each of these sessions, the Marions would join us for dinner at the parents' home, to the obvious annoyance of the cook, Yevgenia Petrovna (Mrs Gates). The book translation was submitted to Anthony Gishford of Boosey & Hawkes, who found it so obsequious and dull that he flew to Amsterdam, where Stravinsky's seventieth birthday was being celebrated, to persuade me to convince him to withdraw the publication. At that date I did not feel that I knew him well enough to broach the matter. The translation duly appeared without fanfare or significant notice.

Andre had been Milene's closest friend during the war years in Sancellemoz, where both were patients. Milene was less subservient to her father than to her husband, who had reputedly inherited his

---

10   See the chapter 'The Last Two Summers'.

naturally brusque manner and occasional irascibility from his father, a judge in Lyon. Several times, alone with me, she confessed her belief that her father was responsible for her mother's death. In the early 1950s Andre accompanied his father-in-law on a train to Chicago for a concert; on their return, Stravinsky complained that Andre had read magazines continually, scarcely speaking.

At Stravinsky's request, I welcomed Soulima, his wife Françoise and infant son, John (born November 1945), at Idlewild Airport on their arrival from Paris in June 1948. I drove them around New York, helped install them in the Ambassador Hotel, and dined with Soulima at the popular 'Maria's' on East 52nd Street. I also accompanied the family to the station for their trip to California. Our next meeting was in July in Denver, where Soulima played his father's Capriccio at the Red Rocks outdoor theatre. At this time Soulima and I became companionable. A few weeks later in California, his father noticed that Françoise's *franglais* was on a par with mine, whereupon he entrusted us to work together translating his letters from Debussy for possible English publication. Françoise and I soon became close friends.

After a few weeks, I became aware that the father–son relationship had become strained. Soulima told me that when he played his own compositions for his father, he criticised them severely, freely deleting and rewriting. Soulima had brought his father's Breitkopf & Härtel Mozart with him from Paris, and had showed me unfinished Mozart fugues that his father had ingeniously completed. Meanwhile, Françoise had expressed her apprehension that the 'small tree cannot grow in the shade of the larger one'. That the Soulima family would soon relocate to New York was foreseeable, and by 1950 Stravinsky - through a friend, John Kuypers - had secured a teaching position for Soulima in the music department of the University of Illinois at Urbana.

In the autumn of 1948 Soulima returned to New York, where I escorted him to rehearsals of Mozart's Piano Concerto, K. 503 for a CBS broadcast. His next trip east was to conduct a ballet that he had stitched together from favourite pieces by Domenico Scarlatti and scored for strings. Disapproving of this venture, his father confided in me: 'It must be *composed*, like *Pulcinella*, and can't simply be orchestrated.' Soulima conducted the premiere at the Metropolitan Opera with choreography by Antonia Cobos, a dancer friend from Paris. Stravinsky wrote to me asking for my confidential opinion. The piece had not been a success, partly because Soulima was not a conductor and had difficulty keeping the orchestra together, but, sympathising with him, I restricted my reply to what I thought were a few miscalculations in the string balances.

In the summer of 1949 the Soulimas moved to Mendocino, where Darius Milhaud had arranged for him to teach piano at the Music Academy of the West. At Françoise's invitation I visited them on weekends, driven there by Stravinsky's personal physician, Max Edel. We strolled in the meadows and woods, talking about Sartre and Camus. Apart from this, my summer was spent at Soulima's Hollywood house on Holloway Drive, a seven-room, two-storey building with a concert recital stage in the main-floor living room.

I returned to New York in September 1949 for concerts and to find more patrons. Stravinsky approached Arthur Sachs[11] on my behalf, who responded with a cheque for $900 to rescue my Carnegie Hall performance of *Perséphone* with Vera Zorina.[12] The concert (which proved to be the most difficult I would ever attempt) bankrupted me, nevertheless. On the afternoon of the performance Toscanini[13] unexpectedly called a rehearsal in the hall for his NBC Symphony, a move in NBC's ongoing war against CBS's Goddard Lieberson, but a devastating one for me as it reduced my dress rehearsal on the same stage to one hour. I scarcely had time to start and stop each piece and to clarify a few complex sections. In *Pulcinella*, the first performance of the complete score in the U.S., and in *Perséphone*, I set the tempi in each number and did what I could with *Zvezdoliki*, which was also

---

11 See the chapter, 'The Hollywood Years'.
12 My long friendship with Vera Zorina (*née* Hartwig) began at this time, shortly after she divorced Balanchine and married Goddard Lieberson.
13 Ansermet had written to Stravinsky humorously describing Toscanini's growls provoked by the gnarling dissonances of the *Symphonies of Wind Instruments* while listening to rehearsals of it with the NBC Symphony in January 1948. (On 23 February 1916 Stravinsky wrote from Rome to his mother in Morges: 'In January in the Roman Augusteum *Petrushka* was performed twice under the direction of Toscanini [the great Italian conductor] in an overflowing 6000-seat hall... a colossal success.')

having its American premiere. Wystan Auden[14] came to my aid by reading poems to fill in the time for one of the pieces that could not be sufficiently prepared for even a scratch performance. I anticipated a cruel press, but in fact *The New York Times*'s Harold C. Schonberg praised the programming of such unknown and important music. The concert had had virtually no advertising, as the box-office receipts reflected. My revenge was to print a ream of flyers announcing treasures of Bartók and the Schoenberg school that would *not* be performed in my next six cancelled concerts. This was publicised and, indeed, made me famous.

With scarcely enough money for a snack at Horn & Hardart, I boarded a Greyhound bus back to Los Angeles, arriving with double pleurisy and pneumonia. The Stravinskys called Dr Edel, who confined me to bed for three weeks. Though the Soulimas were in California at the time, they departed for New York a few days after my arrival. Since Stravinsky had already paid the rent on their Holloway Drive residence for the first three months of 1950, I moved into the house where, in the spring of 1951, Stravinsky presented the first piano run-through of the newly completed *Rake's Progress* for a party of invited guests. Ingolf Dahl[15] accompanied singers from the USC Opera Department for the solo parts. Otto Klemperer was given a private audition to see if he would conduct it, but the subject did not appeal to him.

In the next few years we rarely saw the Soulimas, who spent their summers at Françoise's family home, 'La Clidelle', in the Auvergne. Françoise had written to her father-in-law asking for financial help

---

14 The year before, on 30 November 1948, Auden wrote to Kallman about one of my concerts: 'Went to the Yiddish Y yesterday to hear a concert performance of *Mavra,* which I thought a lovely work, all about a Huzzah [Hussar] in drag.'

15 At the time of my first arrival at the Stravinsky home in July 1948, this pianist and composer was Stravinsky's closest musician friend in California, together with the violinist Sol Babitz. Stravinsky entrusted Dahl to prepare piano reductions of some of his first American pieces, particularly *Scènes de Ballet.* Dahl conducted excellent performances of *Les Noces* as well as of *Pierrot Lunaire.* He also translated *Pierrot* to English in a version that Schoenberg approved. Dahl suffered severely from asthma and spent his summers in Switzerland. In the summer of 1970, shortly after the death of his wife from cancer, he committed suicide, just across the lake from Evian where Stravinsky was living temporarily. Years later Dahl's son published a disturbing memoir of him, revealing among other things that he was Jewish and homosexual.

in refurbishing the residence, which was given reluctantly and only through Vera's intervention.

In Venice in 1956 Stravinsky, composing *Agon*, cancelled a rendezvous with Soulima, sending in his stead a mutual acquaintance, Lawrence Morton. The composer advised him that Soulima was 'very stupid', which shocked Morton, though he left an inexpungible memo about it, now in the Morton Papers at UCLA. A few days later Stravinsky visited his son in Asolo, where he was staying in the summer home of the French Senator Henri Monnet, who had been managing concerts in Paris for Stravinsky since 1928 and who became his attorney and advisor in a family crisis in the 1960s.

When I conducted at the Domaine Musical in Paris in November 1956, Françoise invited me to dinner – Soulima was on a concert tour in Algiers – in the Montmartre apartment she had rented from the Milhauds. She was very friendly, but the evening turned tragic when a call informed us that Balanchine's wife, the ballerina Tanaquil LeClerq, had contracted polio and was hospitalised in Copenhagen.

In June 1957, when I conducted three Stravinsky seventy-fifth anniversary concerts on Boston Common with Soulima as soloist, I was struck by the resemblance of his stage manners to his father's. Soulima provided me with a sheet of cues that he feared might be needed in the Capriccio but were not. I liked him personally, and I still cherish the manuscript he copied as a gift for me of two passages from Mozart's C minor Mass.

The manuscript of Soulima's two-hand piano reduction of the Third Tableau in *Perséphone* resurfaced in the summer of 2010 and was sent to me for explication and evaluation by John Lubrano. The score, in Soulima's hand and in black ink, is annotated in red ink with a large number of corrections ranging from the filling-in of missing notes to mistakes in phrasings, articulations and dynamics. Since the composer would not have had time to dictate the corrections, we must assume that he had shown them to his son in the completed orchestra score. In at least two instances (in the bar before [241] and in two bars before [242]), small blank spaces appear on each side of the line connecting the bass and treble clefs. These empty spaces had been scraped clean by means of a small instrument of Stravinsky's invention: a razor-sharp metal tip attached to an ivory handle, designed for dislodging notes, as he did throughout the printed score of the 1919 *Firebird* while revising it for the 1945 version. The composer's imprecations when he saw Soulima's manuscript must have been explosive.

Stravinsky delighted in composing piano transcripts of his orchestral music, always recomposing in the process. In later life, when this task was assigned to editors, he rarely accepted their versions, which included as much of the orchestral music as possible for ten fingers. Stravinsky would inventively change accompaniment figurations and sacrifice secondary parts. His piano reductions were usually written to keep pace with his composition of the full score, and he worked long hours to rewrite the reductions of his editors, even those of Erwin Stein.

Stravinsky's friend Pierre Souvtchinsky always referred invidiously and cruelly to the composer's sons as 'Mufle' (Theodore) and 'Coupes St Jacques' (Soulima). Always critical of the brothers, Souvtchinsky temporarily vanished from Stravinsky's life when his family moved from Voreppe to Paris (1934). This old friend's advice to Stravinsky to discourage Soulima from pursuing a career in music was, nevertheless, compassionately intended. But in asking Souvtchinsky for help with Soulima's social troubles, the father explained his own position obdurately: 'From every point of view and in all circumstances, it is absolutely unacceptable that my grown-up children, who are financially dependent on me, disregard rights which belong to me and not to them.'

The rift between Stravinsky and his progeny originates neither with me nor his second wife, but with the composer himself. As early as 1916 Nijinsky recognised that Stravinsky was ill-suited for parenthood, confiding to a diary that 'Stravinsky treats his children like soldiers.' Others observed that the composer's imperious control continued even after the children had become adults. Letters from friends pleaded with him to be more patient and understanding with his sons. But the father's concert tours kept him away from his family most of the time, as did his wife's and children's confinements for extended periods in tuberculosis sanatoria. In short, while deeply attached to his progeny, he was critical and demanding of them. A letter from Igor to Theodore, then fifty-five, scolds him with an asperity more appropriate to a fractious adolescent: 'What thoughtlessness! Reply immediately and explain this stupid misunderstanding.' In June 1936 Theodore met and married Denise Guerzoni, who, like the entire Stravinsky family, was tubercular. Stravinsky saw her infrequently in the years before his departure for America, and after his twelve years abroad he rarely saw his elder son and his wife during European concert tours. Once, in the 1960s, Stravinsky actually concealed his presence in Europe from them.

In spite of having met Theodore only in the summer and autumn of 1951 and on rare occasions after that in Europe and New York, I saw him more often than I did Soulima in Stravinsky's later years. I admired Theodore's old-fashioned manners and his talents as painter, draftsman and thespian mimic in the tradition of his paternal grandfather. He alone of the Stravinsky children bowed to Vera at his father's funeral and, eleven years later, he was the only one who acknowledged Vera's own death with flowers. In gratitude I sent the family heirloom silver – a samovar, tableware and some icons – to him.

After Soulima's eighteen-year-old son John[16] and some friends attended his grandfather's concert at Ravinia in July 1964, the family chasm yawned still wider. The circumstances were not propitious: the city was sizzling; Vera the peacemaker was not there; Lillian Libman[17] *was* there; and a large open-air concert with airplane *obbligati* was not conducive to a performance of the quiet, intimate *Orpheus*. Stravinsky realised this but he nevertheless wanted the concert as a rehearsal for recording the piece. He was in a foul mood without Vera and instructed Libman not to allow any telephone calls to be put through to him, remaining mewed in his room. During the concert intermission, John came backstage expecting to greet his grandfather. Since no one but Vera was ever admitted to Stravinsky's dressing

16 John accompanied his parents to New York when he was two, still a child in rompers, and saw his grandfather scarcely a dozen times after that, in Chicago, Cleveland, Urbana and New York.

17 A representative of the S. Hurok Concerts, Inc.

room immediately before a performance, John saw his grandfather only from the audience. After the concert, he and his companions made their way toward the green room but found that the composer had already been whisked in a limo back to his Chicago hotel.[18]

Checking out the next day, John appended his and his friends' hotel bills to his grandfather's without permission. The composer became furibund and on his return to Hollywood he complained to John's mother about the incident and received a stinging reply that he never forgave. Henceforth, the always tenuous family relationship deteriorated further, ultimately culminating in the five-year lawsuit against Vera that erupted three years after the composer's death.

John's revenge came forty years later, when he scotched a plan to publish a crucially necessary variorum edition of his grandfather's collected works which the Sacher Foundation, Boosey & Hawkes, and the several other publishers of Stravinsky's music had already agreed to subsidise. The scores and players' parts are notoriously error-strewn. A corrected edition was the abiding wish of Stravinsky's late years, as well as that of the entire musical world. Let us hope that this decision will soon be rescinded.

Much of what I know about Stravinsky's domestic life in his European years came from Mina Svitalsky, his family's Polish governess from 1917, called 'Madubo' by the children. At his invitation, she came to the U.S. with the Marions in 1947, a move initiated by Vera, who worried about Stravinsky's care if something were to happen to her. But the then middle-aged children had no room for Madubo in their Hollywood homes, and Andre was so irritated by her that he secretly retained Stravinsky's attorney, Aaron Sapiro, to find legal justification to evict her. This seventy-year-old woman fled on her

---

18 To prepare for his Monday recording, the composer rested most of the day following the concert. On the way to the studio session, John McClure, the musically acute and understanding Columbia Records producer, told me that the Chicago Symphony would like to record the Brahms–Schoenberg, which I had performed on the first half of the Stravinsky concert, on condition that each movement be played straight through 'in one take'. We succeeded in this, and Stravinsky recorded *Orpheus* afterwards. He then flew to Los Angeles with McClure, while I flew to Albuquerque en route to Santa Fe. When George Balanchine heard the edited tape of the Chicago Symphony's electrifying Brahms–Schoenberg, he choreographed the piece for the New York City Ballet, where it has remained one of the most popular pieces in the repertoire.

own, walking the uphill mile to North Wetherly Drive where Igor and Vera sheltered her temporarily; but with only one bedroom they could not accommodate her in their even smaller home. With the arrival of Soulima and family the next year, Madubo was resettled with them to look after their young son, but this also ended in a debacle. She was finally given employment by the Aldous Huxleys.

Mlle Svitalsky, an intelligent woman, often prodded me for information about Stravinsky's strange new preoccupation with Schoenberg,[19] an indication that Stravinsky had voiced feelings of rivalry during his Swiss and French years. I was fond of Madubo and drove her to appointments and on errands in Hollywood; indeed, most of our conversations took place in the Stravinsky automobile. Finally, in 1953 Stravinsky wrote to Mina's brother in Bern, asking him to take her back and generously offering to support her financially during her retirement. In May 1955 I spent a pleasant afternoon with her in the Swiss capital.

Of all the writings about Stravinsky by family members, the most engrossing are the 1925-6 letters from his niece Tanya,[20] daughter of his elder brother, Yuri, who had visited the composer in Carantec in 1920. Then a very attractive twenty-one-year-old blonde, Tanya lived in her uncle Igor's large home at Mont Boron, near Nice, from February 1925 and spent sojourns near him in Paris, eventually returning to Leningrad in August 1926. The correspondence contributes to the history of East-West relations in the post-World War I decade and is of general interest beyond Stravinsky biography. The letters convey a fresh impression of the mid-1920s French scene as well as of the American, as relayed from her uncle's descriptions following his 1925 concert tour. The account of this young woman's first experience outside Russia, contrasting the life in her grim and impoverished homeland with life in lively, luxurious France, is vivid.

---

19 Mina was employed for a time in Hollywood as the governess to Barbara Zeisl, who later became Mrs Ronald Schoenberg. Barbara, the daughter of the composer Eric Zeisl, was my neighbour on Holloway Drive.
20 Tatiana Yurievna Stravinsky (1904-1957).

In her initial communication from Nice following a three-day stop in Paris, Tanya writes to her father in Leningrad of her surprise, after a ban of several years, at suddenly being permitted to correspond with people in foreign countries. The reader may indeed wonder why she was allowed to live abroad for as long as a year and a half. The answer is that Stravinsky's music was belatedly being performed in the new U.S.S.R. He had declined official invitations to conduct there himself, and Tanya had undoubtedly been entrusted with a mission to persuade him to change his mind. The new government's cultural policy was to promote performances of his music and to invite eminent conductors to present not only the early ballets but also later works. Schoenberg's friend Fritz Stiedry conducted *The Rite of Spring* in Leningrad, followed by Ernest Ansermet, who a little later, in 1932-3, also introduced other works, all of them significant events that would become part of the history of Russian music and the restoration of Stravinsky in his native land. Otto Klemperer presented *Pulcinella* to Russian audiences. All of these maestros assured Stravinsky that the Russian orchestras were capable of and enthusiastic about playing his music, but he remained intractable on the question of visiting the U.S.S.R. His continuing feud with the Rimsky-Korsakov clan was one obstacle, and a book of pseudo-philosophical comment about Stravinsky by the influential critic Asafiev was another. But the deciding factor was money. Stravinsky's American concert tour had netted nearly a million dollars for only two months of work, a sum that would have required at least three years of concertizing in Western Europe. The rouble was worthless beyond the country's borders, and he had already accepted engagements for European concerts in the next months. More importantly, he was impatient to resume composing.

Tanya had been living in the Stravinsky home in Nice for three weeks when 'Uncle Igor' finally returned to his wife and family. He had gone directly from his steamship in Le Havre to a reunion with Vera in Paris, three concerts in Barcelona, and two in Rome. He arrived in Nice on 10 April and the next day began to compose the Serenade in A. Tanya's first letters home describe the spaciousness, the floral paths, shrubberies, and gardens of her uncle's 'Villa des

Roses' as well as the seductive Mediterranean ambience, the beaches, the palm trees, the natural beauty of the South – the balmy Riviera *vs.* the frozen Neva – everything that might irritate a Soviet postal censor but would surely tantalise her father and sister Xenya. References to the atmosphere of religious rectitude in the Stravinsky home and the pervading ill health of its residents are carefully omitted from the correspondence. Then suddenly, in April 1925, Tanya's famous uncle appeared, and the young woman was instantly infatuated with his 'incredible vitality', although she would later confess that her first impression was of someone 'haughty' and 'inaccessible'. Clearly he took little notice of her during this brief meeting:

> He was very kind to me but I saw him only at the table for a few minutes each evening... [H]e was working all the time upstairs.[21] I was struck by how short he is [very slightly over five feet] and by the smartness of his clothing, silk handkerchiefs, knitted jackets – a different one each day and each a different colour – a large choice of cravats, and a monocle. He is unbelievably lively, exuding life and energy. At dinner he shares some of his liqueurs with me, though normally no one else is allowed to taste them. He also started to teach me how to smoke and he uses improper language in his conversation, though he warns me ahead not to listen. His mother was horrified by all of this and protested that I was being permanently spoiled. I admit that a lot of this shocked me but when he left for Rome [to see the Pirandello production of *L'Histoire du Soldat*] everything seemed so empty.

The letters also reveal that Tanya was impatient with the limitations of her cousins' spoken Russian, which she determined to expand and improve. Naturally Mika and Theodore, born in St Petersburg, spoke with more fluency and a more extensive vocabulary than the Swiss-born Soulima and Milene, who conversed in Russian only with

---

21 A little later in 1925 when Diaghilev was planning a revival of the *Nightingale* ballet, Henri Matisse, who produced the décor and curtain for the revival, addressed one of his letters to Stravinsky, 'l'infatigable travailleur'.

their parents. The four children spoke French with their governesses and schoolmates, of course, and Tanya repeatedly mentions her own difficulties with that language.

An early letter reports that 'Aunt Katya does not want any guests'. Only Alexander Eduardovich Nápravnik visited them twice a week to give the children music lessons, staying for dinner. Alexander, the eldest son of the one-time conductor of the Bolshoi Theatre in Moscow, is a problematic subject in Tchaikovsky biography. When Nápravnik's father, Stravinsky's next-door neighbour in St Petersburg, wrote to Tchaikovsky asking him to accept his twenty-four-year-old son as a pupil, Tchaikovsky replied that he would 'advise him as best I can. After all, he is essentially a good person, if somewhat strange and dull-witted.' Grigory Beliankin, the translator of Tanya's letters in the present book, adds that Tchaikovsky 'wanted to help the youth find mental equilibrium'. The younger Nápravnik was now playing piano duets with Tanya and flirting with her. On 14 May Tanya wrote to her family:

> The house is surrounded by orange trees all around the terrace in front, and the entire home itself is filled with the aroma of orange blossoms. The gardens are full of bright flowers, the walls are covered with pink garlands, the lane entwined in rose vines bursting into bloom. Best of all, Uncle has returned from Toulon. You cannot imagine how phenomenally active he is, taking good care of himself, and so well developed physically that he bulges with muscles. He is extremely strong and can lift one-and-a-half times his own weight with a single arm. Yesterday he played portions of his Concerto and new Sonata for us, and also *Mavra*. Everything he plays himself sounds different from anyone else's performance... [T]he music is uncommonly difficult, not only rhythmically but in terms of conveying what he wants to communicate... Last night he and I had a long conversation. He explained that there is no public capable of understanding pure essence... He says that when he approaches a piano he tries to forget all forms of composition, all methodology, so that the music he creates is just that, a

creation rather than a fabrication... After composing for two or three hours, he is exhausted. As for conducting, his goal is to satisfy himself, yet inevitably he emerges drenched in perspiration. He changes his shirt and dress coat during every intermission, and even when he plays for us he has to wipe his neck with a towel... Uncle disliked America and Americans, saying that nowhere had he encountered a more stupid and lethally boring people... Nevertheless, that was where he enjoyed his greatest success.

Tanya describes a banquet given by Steinway & Sons in New York in January 1925 as being in Stravinsky's honour, which is what he must have claimed rather than the truth: that the occasion was a birthday tribute to Steinway himself. A mammoth chocolate birthday cake, a full-size replica of a Steinway piano, was the centrepiece of the celebration, but we are not told whether any of it was consumed by the large aggregate of musician guests. She goes on to say that when 'Uncle' arrived in America:

He found that the firm had prepared eighteen pianos, all according to his specifications, but each slightly different from the others. In New York, staying in a seventeen-storey building, he noticed that another building across the street was in progress, and by the time he left it had reached the twenty-first floor. In Chicago he went to the famous stockyard where three thousand cattle are slaughtered every day. I don't know what made him go there.[22]

I listen to Uncle's stories and less frequently am allowed to hear him play, but I spend more time with Fedya... [P]lease don't say anything to Aunt Sonya but Uncle doesn't want Uncle Kotya [Nicolai Alexandrovich Yelachich] to have his Concerto or in fact any of his works. Uncle Igor is very fond of him but knows how he plays and does not want his music performed that way. Uncle himself has only one copy of each of his pieces

---

22 The enormous abattoir was one of the principal tourist attractions at the time.

and only very rarely lends anything, even to Svetik [Soulima].
I've grown extremely fond of Uncle, and he seems to like me
too. Today he told me that he is very warm with those he loves.

On 13 June 'Uncle' returned to Paris. Tanya explains to her family:

> He did not have time to send a photograph to you. He has
> given me one... Uncle is so busy in Paris that he can't rest for
> a moment. Liulya [Georgii Yelachich] is there right now. Uncle
> saw him at his big concert but was so beleaguered that Liulya
> only managed to have a few words with him. I doubt very much
> that Liulya had any opportunity to play his violin for Uncle, yet
> at times he will receive the most unexpected sort of visitors.

In a letter of 19 June she notes that

> Uncle shows all of his creases and wrinkles in the enclosed
> photograph and, as you can see, he has aged. He lives in
> excellent material circumstances, but his work saps his moral
> strength. The quantity of concerts he gives, conducting and
> playing the piano in a single evening - which he does now all
> the time - takes its toll, but physically he is very strong and
> developed.

A second letter sent the same day contains a *surpoint*:

> I want to move to Paris as soon as possible.... I will be much
> happier if I can find work and send some money, and of course
> I would see more of Uncle than I do here.... Aunt Katya has
> written to Uncle in Paris about it saying that if he would pay my
> way I might be able to go. It would be very hard for me to do
> everything in French, but that's not really important.

Still in Nice on 21 July, Tanya reveals that 'Uncle has agreed to pay my
tuition at the Puget School' and that

Uncle Igor [now back in Nice][23] would very much like to help you, but at present his affairs are hanging by a thread [?!] and, given all of his family expenses, he is unable to do so now... One recent evening after Milene had been put to bed, we - Theodore, Mika, Uncle, Katya and I - decided to go for a ride in the automobile... Auntie almost in Uncle's lap and I almost in Fedya's. We went like this to Monte Carlo. It's impossible to describe the beauty of that fairytale country at night, the black silhouette of the peninsula with its palace and mountains, the quantity of lights.

On 7 August Tanya mentions 'Uncle and Fedya' wearing dinner jackets while dining at a restaurant with 'some composer'. This was Ernst Krenek, who happily reminisced about the occasion with Stravinsky three decades later in California. Tanya writes:

Uncle arrived home reeking of alcohol, and very 'high'. It was a perfect scene from the *Abduction of the Seraglio*. His mother nearly fainted... Finally Uncle lifted me up and took me to my room, saying it was children's bedtime. I came right back, of course, and we carried on for a long time afterwards.

The Russian original has been deleted at this point, but clearly some amorous dalliance took place. Tanya, whose pictures show her as very attractive indeed, was in love with her uncle, and her mention of Mozart's opera hints that an inebriated Stravinsky went beyond mere canoodling. After complaining, 'It's a torment for [Aunt Katya] to play the role of hostess,' Tanya closes her next letter with the ecstatic thought: 'How happy I would be in her place. I would not avoid Uncle's friends and, on the contrary, I would go with him everywhere.'

Like the composer, the most famous of his coeval geniuses had a considerable reputation as a philanderer. Tanya's letter of 28 September tells us:

---

23   Stravinsky was actually living at this time with Vera at Le Levandou, a short distance west of Nice, where the two took many photographs of each other in the nude. Stravinsky preserved these in his archives, but they were removed before his death.

Recently I met Picasso, his wife, and little Picasso, who is four years old,[24] on one of our automobile excursions to Juan-les-Pins, where he lives. I also ran into him near the beach. Uncle wasn't with us but Picasso recognised the automobile and waved to us. We got out and I had a chat with him. He is quite short himself, thickset, and very interesting looking. After visiting Picasso last week, Uncle has now gone to Venice to play his Sonata.

A letter of 25 December 1925 describes Stravinsky's method of dealing with fan mail: 'Uncle recently returned to Paris from Copenhagen. He has received his driver's licence. Today he sent off twenty-two letters of greetings to America, composing a single sentence and writing all sorts of variations of it for each addressee.' Meanwhile, Theodore had fallen abjectly in love with Tanya (letter of 6 February 1926) and had actually proposed marriage. She 'told Aunt Katya everything so that she could tell Uncle'. Katya's next letter to Igor remarks that 'we already have enough incest in our family'.

To escape Fedya, Tanya abruptly returned to Paris, where 'Uncle' paid her living expenses. To Katya he promised that Tanya would return to Nice as soon as she finished her secretarial course. That she moved into a modest hotel in the Latin Quarter next door to Stravinsky's niece (Vera's closest friend), Ira Beliankina, surely was not a coincidence. Stravinsky apparently wanted Tanya both to be looked after and at the same time kept at a distance from Vera, even though Tanya mentions an automobile ride with 'Uncle and Vera Sudeykina'. Both Igor and Vera must have realised it was time for Tanya to return to Russia.

Seven letters survive from this last Paris period. At first Tanya saw her uncle frequently, albeit in the company of 'all kinds of people'. She already knew Cocteau and Picasso and was now introduced to many of Stravinsky's other famous friends, attending performances of Diaghilev ballets with them:

---

24 One of Vera's letters describes her and Igor's attendance at the baptism of Picasso's son Paulo.

> A few days ago Uncle took Ira and me [to the ballet] and we sat
> in loge seats. There were six of us in all, Count and Countess
> de Matharel, Vera Arturovna, Uncle himself, Ira, and me. Ira
> and Vera are a bit too beautiful and make me feel quite small.
> The whole theatre looks at them, but if I were a tall coquette, I
> wouldn't go around with them. (2 June 1926)

So Vera has now become a 'tall coquette', and a rival.

Though Tanya's last letters home express a desire to return, she remained in Paris for several more weeks. Her father had wisely advised her not to leave France, but by now she has decided to return to Russia, agreeing that: 'Everything you write is true; it is very nice to have such comforts, though later on it will be harder to do without them.'

Finally, she is disillusioned with 'Uncle', writing a few days later that he

> arrived in Paris yesterday, but I haven't been able to see him yet,
> I've only spoken to him on the telephone... He has come back
> all the way from Italy, where he spent two weeks. He wasn't at
> the ballet last night. It seems as if everyone in the world wants
> to talk to him right now, so I'm not going to pester him by
> calling him myself. He will call me when he has a chance.

He never did.

Soon after her return to Leningrad in August, Tanya married a doctor, Boris Mikhailovich Dobrotin. Their son, Roman, became a professor of chemistry. We dined with him in Leningrad in October 1962. Tatiana Yurievna Stravinskaya Dobrotin died of cancer in 1957, aged fifty-two.

CHAPTER 10
Family Tragedies

Sad cold days before Christmas. Work is one escape – indeed,
there is nothing but work. I pity those who do not have this refuge.

C.-A. Cingria to Stravinsky

December 1938

The period from the summer of 1938 until the move to America
in September 1939 was the most tragic in Stravinsky's life. He was
despondent over the deteriorating health of his wife and elder
daughter. Mika's doctors had informed him that the altitude at
Sancellemoz was having a deleterious effect on her, and on 21 March
1938, her father brought her back to Paris. Accompanying him to the
7 April Feast of the Annunciation service in the Russian Church, Vera
remarked on the deep depression afflicting him. In March and April
he withdrew from his usual social life, seeing only a few close friends,
notably Sergei and Lina Prokofiev for one dinner and Arthur Lourié
for five others. On 30 May Igor and Vera attended Manuel Rosenthal's
twenty-fifth-anniversary performance of *The Rite of Spring*, seating
themselves at a distance from his mother who, escorted by Samuel

Dushkin, was hearing the work for the first time.[1] The outlook brightened somewhat on 14 July, when Mika's condition seemed to stabilise, but on 3 October Stravinsky wrote to Willy Strecker: 'My wife and daughter Mika are both in bed, and I am taking care of them. My wife has had pneumonia for two weeks, and Mika is undergoing a crisis right now. My life this year is enough to drive anyone crazy.'

By early November, Mika was no longer bedridden and was able to talk on the telephone. On 5 November Lord Berners wrote: 'I hope that Mika's health is improving. The last time I was in Paris she seemed much better.' Milene left her sister's side to visit her friend Gadon, the daughter of C.-F. Ramuz, at their home in Lausanne. Igor and Vera resumed their normal social life, going to the cinema, strolling in the Bois de Boulogne, and dining with Victoria and Angelica Ocampo, Roland-Manuel and Cingria. Then on 21 November Mika suffered a relapse. Having contracted to conduct concerts in Rome and Turin, Igor and Soulima departed on the night train of the 22nd for Rome[2], staying at the Excelsior Hotel. No shocking turn for the worse is mentioned in Katya's letters to her husband on the 23rd, 24th, 25th and 26th, but her angry postcard of the 28th reveals a sudden dramatic decline in their daughter's condition, a communication intended to reach Igor shortly before his next concert in Turin for which Katya includes her blessings.

Even though the inevitability of Mika's imminent death was clear, Stravinsky may have been judged too severely for abandoning the scene. The family had become accustomed to living with these fluctuations and thus could have viewed this as another episode from which Mika would recover, as she had many times before. Still, the programmes in both Rome and Turin could have been cancelled. The events of the 28th are unknown except that Stravinsky did not check out of the Excelsior until the 29th, and for him to have remained idle there for a day would have been uncharacteristic.[3] Father and son

---

1   Dushkin said to her, 'I hope you won't whistle', alluding to the audience riot at the 1913 performance. 'I won't,' she responded, 'if only because I don't know how to "whithle".' (She could not pronounce the word. Igor also could not whistle.)

2   Denise Stravinsky mistakenly gives the date as the 28th.

3   He gave a semi-private performance that Sunday of the Two-Piano Concerto, according to the Stravinsky biographer Roman Vlad.

entrained for Turin on the 29th, where a telegram awaited him from Theodore in Paris saying that the situation had 'suddenly become grave' and begging his father to return. Igor telephoned Vera, who confirmed that 'Mika's condition is beyond hope.'

Stravinsky was met at Turin station by Ada Finzi, one of his concert agents. Theodore telegraphed on the 30th that Mika had died at 5 a.m., but since Stravinsky had gone directly from the train to a rehearsal of the Turin Orchestra, he did not receive the news until later in the day. When I met Signora Ada Finzi in Genoa in November 1960, she described his tearful, out-of-control anguish on reading Theodore's telegram. She helped the composer to write a statement (drafted at '5 p.m.') cancelling the Turin concert of 2 December 'per improvvise gravi ragioni famigliari' ('for sudden grave family reasons'). By 1960 Signora Finzi had been awarded the General Directorship of the Genoa Opera, an honour bestowed in memory of her husband, a Jewish partisan killed by the Partisan brigands in the last days of the Second World War. Stravinsky accepted the 1960 Genoa engagement at less than his usual cachet in gratitude for Signora Finzi's help and human understanding in 1938.

A few minutes before Mika's death, Vera contacted a priest to administer the last rites. She promised to meet Igor's train in Paris at 10.25 p.m., and her diary records that she drove him to the apartment of his long-time friend Gabriel Paichadze, the Éditions Russes de Musique publisher, where they spent the night of the 30th.

In a note to the composer on Mika's twenty-year *Panikhida* memorial, 30 November 1958, Nadia Boulanger recalls the heartbreaking scene at the Stravinsky home a day or so before the young woman's death: 'Mika motionless, Katya praying on her knees, Kitty[4] calling "Mama".' On 1 December, the day after the death, Stravinsky returned to his family home at 25, rue du Faubourg Saint-Honoré, but in his overwrought emotional state could not be subject to public exposure. He also did not, could not bear to, attend her funeral on 2 December in the Russian church at 32, rue Boileau; Vera de Bosset went in his place. Her diary for 3 December contains only

---

4   Mika's daughter, Catherine ('Kitty') Mandelstam.

four words: 'All day sad, alone.' Igor did not appear, and she did not see him again until the evening of the 4th, when they dined at the home of his niece Ira Belline.

Immediately following the death, Stravinsky engaged Mina Svitalsky to be the guardian of Mika's baby in a sanatorium in Leysin for the next seven years, under the care of Dr Vera Nossenko.[5] Denise Stravinsky remained with them for the first two years. At age eight Kitty was adopted by Theodore and Denise, though not legally until 1952.

Twelve weeks after Mika's passing, in the afternoon of 1 March 1939, Catherine's doctor called Stravinsky to warn him of the certainty of her death within the next twenty-four hours. Vera drove him to see his dying wife. Catherine begged him to stay with her in whispered words heard only by Stravinsky (contrary to Denise Stravinsky's account in her *Au cœur du Foyer*[6]). But in truth Igor refused and returned with Vera to her apartment at 41, rue de l'Assomption, telephoning his mother from there to ask her to go to Catherine's bedside in his place and remain with her to the end. His mother, who was also Catherine's aunt, was closer to her than he had been for many years. Denise's version places the composer by his wife's side before and after her death. This is in contradiction to what I learned from Igor and Vera twenty years later. Since he could not drive and was dependent on Vera to chauffeur him, Vera awaited him in their car. Denise also asserts that at the time of the death, 'we all stood by the bed', and when Igor noticed that his mother was not there, he asked Milene to find her. Denise continues: 'At two o'clock the death rattle began. Catherine collapsed into my arms and suddenly felt leaden... The body was taken into the salon, where *longtemps debout, longtemps, Igor regarde Catherine.*' The rhetoric in the extra 'longtemps' increases the reader's scepticism. Vera's letters affirm that following the death she spent the afternoon with Igor struggling to convince him to attend his wife's funeral, if only to avoid the universal opprobrium and the charges of utter heartlessness. Vera

---

5   Vera Dmitrievna Nossenko was Catherine's cousin.
6   Éditions Aug. Zurfluh, Bourg-la-Reine, France, 1998.

finally succeeded in this, and they went to the 10 a.m. service, again in the rue Boileau Orthodox Church. But nothing would induce him to continue to the Cimetière de Liers in Sainte-Geneviève-des-Bois for the burial next to the grave of his so recently deceased daughter. After the funeral Vera went to the cemetery accompanied by her friend, Olga Ilishina Sallard.

The third and least painful death in the series was that of Stravinsky's eighty-five-year-old mother on 7 June 1939. Stravinsky attended the funeral with Samuel Dushkin, one of the few of the composer's friends to win his mother's affection. In his book *Themes and Episodes*, Stravinsky falsifies the chronicle. Writing on the day of his mother's death to René Auberjonois, who was always sternly critical of the composer's bigamous life, Stravinsky claims, 'For the third time in half a year, I endured the long Russian requiem service for one of my own family, walked through a field to the cemetery of Sainte-Geneviève-des-Bois, and dropped a handful of dirt in an open grave.'

Some of the inconsistencies in the reporting of events surrounding the family tragedies surface in Tony Palmer's film portrait of Stravinsky, *Once, At A Border...* (1982). This inadvertently repeats errors in Milene Marion's interview in which she recounts her father's agonies after the death of her mother. Milene's implication that he was with his wife when she died is mistaken: 'It was one o'clock in the afternoon, I recall, and the night had been very bad... [T]he nurse who was looking after my mother called us saying, "It's the end," and I remember my father was just absolutely shaking with emotion and tears, and I never saw him like that. It was terrible to see.' In fact, Stravinsky was not present at the time of the death. Milene used the identical description of her father, 'shaking with emotion and tears', regarding the death of Mika, not Catherine, in recalling the scene to me in Hollywood. Milene was prone to confusion,[7] heightened by the fact that this film interview took place thirty-two years after these two

---

7   Catherine Stravinsky's letters to Igor describe Milene as a 'problem child'. In a letter of 11 June 1935 we read that 'The poor thing has a presentiment that you want to take her away from [her current boyfriend]. Oh, what a difficult child we have!'

traumatic events which occurred only three months apart. At some point Stravinsky went to the children on hearing of their mother's death, but he detested all of her other relatives who were already there and whom he would certainly have refused to meet under these circumstances.

My failure to question Mina Svitalsky, the only full-time observer present during Mika's death, seems inexcusable, except that Stravinsky himself mentioned the subject only once. Mina had described to me his reactions to the 1917 deaths of his nurse Bertha Essert and his brother Gury as intense and prolonged. Stravinsky composed memorial music for Rimsky-Korsakov, Debussy, Dylan Thomas and T. S. Eliot, but curiously not for any members of his family. I believe, nevertheless, that the *Larghetto* in the Symphony in C,[8] begun on 21 April 1939, is an elegy for Catherine. The final bar says 'adieu' almost verbally in this most subtle, tender and inauspicious closing in the whole of symphonic music. Played by only two instruments, the three-note, off-the-beat, rising figure separated by rests achieves a powerful effect simply by doubling the length of the third rest and placing the final notes on the beat.

A lifelong thanatophobe, Stravinsky could not have endured a death watch for Mika or Catherine. Funerals and cemeteries horrified him to the extent that he would cross himself when passing them on a road. Igor and Vera were photographed in 1931 in a gondola bearing flower bouquets for Diaghilev's tomb in San Michele cemetery, but Vera was the one who placed the flowers on the grave. Stravinsky continually refused to visit this site, though the burial had taken place more than two decades earlier (August 1929). In fact, Stravinsky never entered the cemetery until 15 April 1971.

Though seriously ill with tuberculosis himself, Stravinsky continued to work throughout his last six months in Europe. Shortly after Catherine's death, while his Paris apartment was being fumigated, he was ordered by his doctors to return to Sancellemoz until August. A letter from Nadia Boulanger indicates that the composer had suffered a pulmonary lesion similar to the one that he had experienced in

---

8   The sketch-score was completed by 19 July.

America two years before, in 1937. Stravinsky's medically mandated confinement was almost immediately disregarded. On 4 May he was in Milan to rehearse for a concert[9] on the 11th and to deliver the completed score of the first movement of the Symphony in C to his publisher, Willy Strecker. On 12 May Stravinsky travelled to Florence to conduct two strenuous works at the Maggio Fiorentino; *Perséphone* with Victoria Ocampo, and on 21 May the complete *Petrushka* performed by the Ballets de Monte-Carlo. On the 22nd he returned to Sancellemoz exhausted, but nevertheless received an unbroken succession of visitors, including Pierre Souvtchinsky.[10] An unexpected guest was Serge Koussevitzky, who had come to express his condolences and to discuss Stravinsky's forthcoming concerts in Boston. The composer was deeply grateful to see him and had long since forgotten their contretemps when Stravinsky flew into a rage having come to play the Symphony of Psalms, describing the piano as 'an old casserole in B flat'. They remained on good terms for the rest of Koussevitzky's life (he died in 1951). Roland-Manuel had come to work on the Harvard Lectures, but this was interrupted after only six days by the death of Stravinsky's mother on 7 June. He attended the funeral on 11 June in Paris and returned to Sancellemoz, this time with Vera, an astounding schedule for a man critically ill with tuberculosis!

The second movement of the Symphony in C was begun in late March in Sancellemoz and completed there in August, though work on it was interrupted from the 6th to the 27th of May for his concert tours in Florence and Milan. The work in the Italian cities was extremely strenuous, with two rehearsals on three successive days. The La Scala programme on 11 May comprised Cherubini's Overture to *Anacreon*, Tchaikovsky's Second Symphony and Stravinsky's Divertimento and *Jeu de cartes*. The Milanese public was very enthusiastic, partly in reaction to the unfavourable receptions that Stravinsky was receiving from Parisian audiences at this time. He stayed with Victoria Ocampo

---

9   Milanese reviews blamed the alleged decline of his later music on 'the influence of Paris', but noted that he 'still commands a large and devoted public in Milan'.

10   While in Sancellemoz, Stravinsky read Jean-Paul Sartre's *La Nausée*, a gift from Souvtchinsky.

in the Excelsior Hotel in Florence. The first performance of *Perséphone* took place on the 13th at the Maggio Fiorentino and the second on the 21st on a double bill with *Petrushka* performed by the Ballets de Monte-Carlo.

On his return to Sancellemoz, Stravinsky wrote to his secretary in America, Dr Alexis Kall, saying in part: 'I plan to spend the first week of September in Venice and to be in Paris after 7 September.' Another letter to Kall, dated 11 July, tells him to reply by airmail since 'the clippers fly regularly now from New York to Marseilles... It would be good if Steinway would send a piano to you in Boston without charge, as they do for Dagmar Godowsky... (unless she lied to me, as she does about everything, this dear Dagmar).' In still another note to Kall, Stravinsky says that 'Koussevitzky came to see me here. He has a beautiful property near Aix-les-Bains.' The conductor told him the difficulties of finding 'a suitable servant' and Stravinsky complained about the 'increased costs of help in your charming country'. On 19 July Stravinsky completed the sketch score of the Symphony's second movement. The beginning of World War II changed all of Stravinsky's travel plans, of course, and Stravinsky arrived in New York from Bordeaux on the SS *Manhattan*. Toscanini was on board with him, but the two musicians did not meet. Stravinsky was installed in his habitual Sulgrave Hotel at 60 East 67th Street.

Stravinsky's first commitment at Harvard was to deliver his inaugural Charles Eliot Norton lecture on 1 November. He returned to New York immediately afterward for a few days at the Navarro Hotel and wrote to Robert Murphy at the American Embassy in Paris asking for help in securing a visa for 'ma meilleure amie, mais de longue date, Madame Vera Soudeykina'. Stravinsky and Vera had returned to Paris from Sancellemoz just ahead of World War II. Fearful of a German bombing raid, they moved on 5 September to the home of Nadia Boulanger at Gargenville, north-west of the city, where Stravinsky had several meetings with Paul Valéry (who described them in a letter to André Gide). On 21 September he travelled by train to Bordeaux to board the *Manhattan*, which was scheduled to sail on 25 September, five days before its actual departure on the 30th. The immigration authorities in New York asked if he wanted to change his name, and when Stravinsky laughed, they responded, 'Well, most of them do.'

While still in Sancellemoz, Stravinsky had received a visit from Theodore and Denise, but a quarrel broke out over Vera de Bosset,[11] seen as a rival in the distribution of his legacy. The composer angrily sent his son and daughter-in-law away, but Vera persuaded Stravinsky to forgive them. Souvtchinsky wrote to her on 16 August: 'I am glad that the conflict with Fedya and Denise has been resolved satisfactorily.' On his last day in Paris, Stravinsky opened a new bank account and deposited all of his money in it, limiting access to Vera, Theodore, Denise and – to care for his granddaughter – Mina Svitalsky.

On 28 October, Vera wrote to Igor in Boston:

> I am obliged to tell you about a very disagreeable surprise. Fedya and Denise came here yesterday from Le Mans. They have drawn out all of the money from the Paris bank and transferred it to Le Mans. Fedya's visit was to tell me that he cancelled my and Mlle Svitalsky's access to the account and that from now on if I need money, I will have to request it from him or, if he is conscripted, from Denise (!!!). The same is true for Soulima, who must be outraged, since the matter was not even discussed with him. Fedya manipulated this because he had heard a rumour that our bank might fail, but I do not see why trustworthy banks should exist only in Le Mans. He could have left the whole arrangement just as it was and – if he were really worried about our Paris bank – transferred the money to the Banque de France. Fedya said that as the eldest child, entitlement to decide such things resides with him, and that 'Papa would have approved of my action'.
>
> Not being a member of the family, I kept quiet. Also, I did not want to say that the whole thing was manipulated by Denise so that she could control the money and everyone would be

---

11 The quarrel appears to have been sparked when Denise informed Stravinsky that Vera had had an affair with Arthur Lourié in Russia before the Revolution and perhaps more recently in Paris. This resulted in Stravinsky's otherwise unexplained refusal to have any further contact with the gossiping Lourié during the years they both lived in California. The name was never mentioned in the Stravinsky home in my period, and Lourié's death drew no comment.

beholden to her. I hope that they will not do anything foolish, and that the money under their 'management' will not be lost. Nothing can be done now, the money having been deposited in their names in Le Mans, nor can any of us go there to find out if their bank is reliable. Money questions are always delicate, more so among friends; and now this very unpleasant thing has happened, the worst part of which would be to have to receive money from Denise, especially after all that she has done to me. Her animated and self-satisfied behaviour yesterday confirmed that this manoeuvre was a great success for her...

Forgive me, dearest, for having written this unpleasant letter, and believe me that I am not spiteful and have already forgiven Denise for her actions, though I cannot help being aware of her desire to dominate and to play a role. Fedya has nothing to do with all of this; if he had acted alone, he would have done so more tactfully, so that no one would have suspected him of manipulating. I wanted to say to him, 'First ask your father's permission' – after all, the money is yours, and you alone can dispose of it – but I decided to say nothing. I do not understand why they did not say to me: 'Take out your share of the money that is coming to you in May,[12] and put it wherever you choose; we will take our share to Le Mans.' But enough.

I embrace you fervently and once more ask you to forgive me for this disturbing letter. But maybe all will end well. I love you with all my heart and embrace you tenderly.

Your Vera.

On 6 November Stravinsky cabled to Vera that he had transferred 'three-quarters of my money to your name from Le Mans to Paris'. Meanwhile, he had written to Fedya in a rage, enclosing this letter in one to Vera for her to send to him. Ever in pursuit of harmony, Vera did not forward the letter, replying instead to Igor: 'What you wrote to Theodore is so harsh that I took pity on him... I do not want Fedya

---

12 Stravinsky had a return ticket to Europe in May. His Harvard lectures and concerts in American cities required that he remain in America until then.

to be upset once again... If something were to happen to any of us, a bitter feeling would be left for life.' (23 November 1939)

This action by Theodore and Denise marked the beginning of the long battle of Stravinsky's children against Vera, and the rupture in the Stravinsky family became overt.

CHAPTER 11
Vera

We had, as I had hoped, come to see much more of
Stravinsky and his wife, a thoroughgoing Belle Russe, that
is to say an example of that specifically Russian beauty
that radiates the most likable of human qualities.

Thomas Mann, *Diaries*, 1943

Vera Arturovna de Bosset was born in St Petersburg to a French father and Swedish mother, neither with any Russian blood. Publicly she gave her birth date as Christmas Day 1888 (7 January 1889, New Style). After Stravinsky's death in 1971, however, she stunned me with a confession. We were returning to our hotel in Venice after an emotionally and physically exhausting day visiting Igor's dirt-covered grave. Vera abruptly announced that she could not keep up, and that she was four years older than the dates on her passport. This was the only reference she had ever made to this secret.

Reared in a wealthy family, Vera as a child travelled between her city home and country villa in a private railway car with her favourite *milch* cow, 'La Générale'. One of her father's ancestors was mayor of Paris under Napoleon, and her paternal uncle Theodore was Tsar Nicholas II's admiral and one of the few heroes in the war of

1905 against Japan. Vera was educated in mathematics, history, the sciences and languages by live-in tutors from Paris and Berlin. When the de Bossets moved to Moscow, the thirteen-year-old Vera entered a boarding school and was trained in ballet at the Nelidova School. In 1907 she was enrolled in the University of Berlin, where she was courted by Baron Fred Osten-Sacken.

Many young men were charmed by this beautiful and gifted young woman, most notably the painter Serge Yurievich Sudeykin (1882–1946); in March 1913, she eloped with him toward Paris where, ironically, he had been engaged by Diaghilev as a scene painter for the forthcoming premiere of *The Rite of Spring*. Vera did not accompany Sudeykin all the way but stayed with Russian friends in their château near Antwerp. One wonders whether Sudeykin, a former lover of Diaghilev, was protecting that relationship, or did the painter, like Diaghilev, react to premonitions of the danger in introducing Vera to Stravinsky?

When Diaghilev visited the Nelidova School to conduct auditions for his Ballets Russes in the autumn of 1914, Vera was chosen to escort him. She soon became both a stage and cinema actress, appearing in plays by Chekhov and others but most famously in the role of Helen in the first film of *War and Peace*. She also starred in the Moscow French Theatre, where she met both Sarah Bernhardt and Eleonora Duse.

Moving from Moscow to St Petersburg ('Petrograd' from the beginning of the war with Germany), Vera and Sudeykin were active in the city's cultural life in 1916 and early 1917. He introduced her to the denizens of the popular Stray Dog cabaret, decorated with his murals, and where she attracted the attention of Vsevolod Meyerhold as well as many Symbolist poets and painters. She became a protégée of Anna Akhmatova, who painted the young woman's head in silhouette, and a friend of the leading painter Lev Bakst, whose 1922 full portrait of Vera was reproduced on the first issue of Yugoslavian paper currency. Vera kept a salon album[1] of paintings, manuscript poems and music dedicated to her by Osip Mandelstam,

1   Published in facsimile by Princeton University Press, 1995.

Kuzmin, Balmont, Blok, Pasternak, Gorodetsky, Remizov and, in Paris in 1921, Igor Stravinsky. In pre-revolutionary St Petersburg and in Paris afterwards, Vera was an intimate of Marina Tsvetayeva and a favourite chess partner of Sergei Prokofiev.

During the Russian Revolution, Vera and Sudeykin fled to the Crimea, first to Yalta and then to Tiflis, from the Black to the Caspian Seas. In the early spring of 1920 Vera sold her family jewels to purchase passage on a French steamer to Constantinople and Marseilles. Arriving in Paris on 20 May, on the day of the canonisation of Jeanne d'Arc, Vera and Sudeykin were unable to find a hotel room but found friends in the city's large community of White Russian refugees, one of whom was Boris Kochno,[2] the seventeen-year-old poet Vera had befriended in the Crimea. Kochno idolised Diaghilev and sought Vera's help in obtaining an introduction to him, which she arranged for Sunday 20 February 1921. Paris barber shops being closed on Sundays, Kochno knocked on Vera's door unexpectedly that morning asking her to shave him.[3] Whether she or Sudeykin did the barbering, the Diaghilev *rencontre* took place, resulting in Kochno's immediate engagement as the impresario's secretary.

According to Vera, the following morning Diaghilev telephoned, inviting her – without Sudeykin – to dine in a Montmartre restaurant that evening, saying, 'Stravinsky will be there. He is moody, so please be nice to him.' The meeting was a *coup-de-foudre* for the composer, whose behaviour she described as outrageously flirtatious. The Stravinskys told me that their conversation that evening began with Vera asking about Igor's early recollections as piano accompanist to her uncle, the Swedish cellist Eugene Malmgren. The day after the meeting Stravinsky called for her at her apartment building and sent a message upstairs: 'I am waiting for you in a car in the street below.'[4]

During my period with the Stravinskys, they celebrated the

---

2   1903-1990.

3   The shaving scene in Stravinsky's *Mavra* the following year was suggested by this incident.

4   This is in the Paul Sacher Stiftung, Basel, catalogued on page 173 of the Vera Stravinsky Correspondence, and is also reproduced in facsimile in my *Igor and Vera* (Thames and Hudson, London, 1982).

anniversary of their meeting[5] on 21 February, which would seem to indicate that they met at the Théâtre de la Chauve-Souris, since a newspaper notice reports that Stravinsky, Diaghilev, the Sudeykins, Boris Kochno and others attended the presentations by this company on that date. Of course it may be that Igor and Vera did not meet then, but perchance on the evening of the 20th or the 22nd; any earlier date is impossible since he was in Rome.

If Stravinsky did in fact attend the Chauve-Souris performance, his reason would have been a rendezvous with the 'voluptuous' dancer, Zhenya Nikitina, known as Katinka. In a 1921 review in *The Westminster Gazette*, Aldous Huxley wrote, 'The best thing at the Chauve-Souris is Katinka dancing the polka', to one of Stravinsky's Eight Easy Pieces for piano four-hands.[6] That Stravinsky continued to see 'the Sudeykins' in early March has been established, even after his attentions had abruptly switched from Katinka to 'Mme Sudeykina'. On one occasion the composer invited Diaghilev, Kochno, 'the Sudeykins' and Katinka to dinner at Fouquet's. Stravinsky's affair with Vera, after all, was not consummated until 14 July 1921[7] (Bastille Day), a date the couple commemorated all of their lives, including their final year together in 1970 celebrated in Evian.

In actuality, Vera and Sudeykin were never married because he had been unable to obtain a divorce from his wife, Olga; he had received a church dissolution but a caveat of the secular courts did not recognise this. A letter of 10 October 1939 from Vera in Paris written in Olga's presence (by the mid-1920s the two women were close friends) to Igor in Cambridge, Massachusetts, states this unequivocally. In order for Igor and Vera to be legally married, the judge required proof of her divorce from Sudeykin. On Stravinsky's instructions she invented a plausible date and place (May 1918, Tbilisi) for a divorce, and

---

5   It is possible that Igor's and Vera's paths may have crossed during the first decade of the twentieth century in St Petersburg, where they lived on opposite sides of the Neva River. (The Stravinsky Kryukov Canal apartment and the Mariinsky Theatre are in the Kazansky District. Vera lived near the Finland Station on the opposite side.)

6   The Polka was not orchestrated until August 1921, but Stravinsky had sketched the instrumentation.

7   Surprisingly, this date is confirmed in Catherine's letter to him in July 1935: 'How I long for the 14th of July to be over and then you'll come and, if possible, stay for two whole days.'

Stravinsky forged a document to that effect which survives. Prior to their marriage in New Bedford, Massachusetts, on 7 March 1940, Vera's lack of documentation – she had neither a French nor even a Nansen passport but only a Georgian visa – presented an obstacle in all of their pre-marital travels together.

Returning to 1921, shortly after the beginning of the Stravinsky affair, Vera was chosen by Diaghilev for the role of the Queen in his London revival of *Sleeping Beauty*.[8] This was partly because she was the tallest woman he could find to partner the towering Leonid Treer as the Tsar, but Diaghilev's ulterior motive was to lure Stravinsky into orchestrating two movements of the ballet that had been deleted by Tsar Alexander III during the dress rehearsal of the premiere in 1890.[9] Kochno became the liaison between the composer in Paris and Vera in London, a clandestine system having been set up by Stravinsky, whose letters to Vera were enclosed in envelopes addressed to Kochno. Stravinsky's name did not appear on the envelopes but only the pseudonym 'M. d'Anjou' (after the address of his music publisher, 22 rue d'Anjou, Paris). More than fifty of these letters to her via Kochno survive.[10]

As Vera's involvement with Stravinsky's family grew in the 1920s and 1930s, the contrast between her artistic–aristocratic upbringing and his intellectual, independent bohemian lifestyle (as distinguished from the petit-bourgeois mores of his family) became clear. But even the earliest Igor–Vera correspondence refers to their mutual wish not

---

8   In the early 1950s in Los Angeles, I sat next to the Stravinskys at two performances of *Sleeping Beauty* by the touring Royal Ballet. Not having seen the ballet since the beginning of their love affair thirty years earlier, they were profoundly moved; Vera wept at the end, and Stravinsky was on the verge of doing the same.

9   The Tsar and Tchaikovsky were sitting together at the dress rehearsal when, during the entr'acte, the Tsar remarked that 'This is getting rather boring, Tchaikovsky.' The entr'acte and another number were promptly withdrawn and never republished in the orchestra score. Here it must be explained that the Tsar himself, homosexual and a long-time intimate of the composer, shared his finest physicians and aided him in other circumstances. Poznansky's essay, *Tchaikovsky's Suicide: Myth and Reality*, provides a thorough history of homosexuality in the Russian artistic and intellectual world in the last decades of the nineteenth century, but fails to bring this to a critical peak in the world of Diaghilev. Nor does he convince the reader that Tchaikovsky did in fact commit suicide. Certainly he did not die of cholera, as Rimsky-Korsakov's visit to his rival's deathbed confirms. Victims of the disease were strictly quarantined.

10 Overstepping his function as go-between, Kochno warned Vera that 'Stravinsky can be fickle.'

to hurt others, offering solid evidence that both she and Igor were always deeply troubled by his bigamous situation. With her strong maternal instincts, Vera felt genuinely sympathetic to Stravinsky's tubercular children as well as to their modest mother. (In contrast, Vera was far from indulgent toward Igor's mid-life illnesses, nicknaming him 'Bubushkin' for his tendency to exaggerate the smallest bruise and the slightest sniffle, while he affectionately called her his little doggie, 'Vera Sobachkina'.) Only much later, writing to my sister in 1955 to congratulate her on her pregnancy, did Vera reveal her unhappiness in not having had her own child with Stravinsky (which prompted my sister Phyllis to give her second daughter the middle name 'Vera').

Although the Revolution had left Vera penniless, she never repined. Partly because the composer urged her to develop her own source of income, in addition to designing costumes for the Ballets Russes, she opened a shop in Paris with a summer branch in Deauville, where she made and sold artificial flowers and small *objets d'art*. Alfonso XIII of Spain was her first patron and later in London became her friend, as he had been Stravinsky's since 1916. That she coped with greater forbearance than her husband during their impecunious early years in Los Angeles can be attributed in part to the hardships she had suffered during the Russian Revolution as well as to her inherent equanimity. Her utter indifference to money, a lifelong characteristic, left her unprepared for the financial wrangling and hostility from her husband's children, particularly during his last illnesses and after his death. She felt, in T. S. Eliot's words, that the fact 'That money is always forthcoming for the purpose of making more money, whilst it is so difficult to obtain for purposes of exchange, and for the needs of the most needy, is disturbing for those who are not economists.'

During the twenty-three years of my life with Stravinsky, he always played his new compositions to Vera before anyone else and depended on her opinion as to which pieces should be performed to which audiences. Aware of an adversarial spirit in Paris in May 1952, for example, she beseeched him not to programme *Scènes de Ballet* as a curtain-raiser for Symphony in Three Movements, recalling that the ballet had detracted from this same symphony at its premiere in New

York in 1946. 'Champagne tastes less good in celebrating a *succès d'estime*,' she said. Stravinsky ignored her advice and conducted the Symphony; hence the paradiddle for two bassoons in the finale went unnoticed as well as its connection to the fugal piano-trombone exposition near the end of the movement. The reception in Paris was indeed more tepid than might have been the case without *Scènes de Ballet*. At her husband's concerts, Vera usually remained backstage helping him. He perspired profusely and required changes of clothes during intermission as well as at the end. Despite the monotony of the process, she also attended most of his recording sessions.

No one understood the apparent contradictions in Stravinsky's complex character more profoundly than Vera. In 1963, aboard the SS *Bremen* en route to Germany, the director of the Canadian film crew accompanying us asked her, 'Is Stravinsky difficult to live with?' She thought for a moment, then answered in a deeply serious tone, 'He is difficult with himself because he does not want to show that he has emotions.' This is the most insightful comment about Stravinsky's character ever recorded.

Religion was no less essential to Vera than to her husband but, unlike him, she was diligent in her religious observances. In Venice she attended daily Vespers which he never did, and it was Vera who remembered the *Panikhida* services for his wife and daughter, quietly made gifts to the poor, and remembered the fasts, feasts and namedays of the Russian saints. In New York, on days before long flights to Europe or California, she would walk to St Patrick's Cathedral, light three candles, and kneel to pray. When the time came, she made the painful decision not to have a priest administer last rites to Stravinsky, knowing that it would terrify him. He was fully conscious and had followed a score of Beethoven's First 'Rasumovsky' Quartet on the previous day.

Vera and Igor walking together reminded me of the famous drawing of Cosima and Richard Wagner entering the Palazzo Vendramin-Calergi. Like Vera, Cosima appeared to be almost twice as tall as her husband. Because of Vera's height and ample figure, her clothes had to be handmade; her wardrobe was original but not extravagant. She preferred her own simple creations to designer clothes, costume jewelry to diamonds. A serious painter in her own right, Vera had been a pupil of Sudeykin and by 1917 was already an accomplished artist. One of her paintings, *Flower Bouquet*, was included in an exhibit in Yalta in 1918 – alongside one by Elena Nicolayevna, the wife of Stravinsky's brother Yuri, showing the view from the Stravinsky apartment on the Kryukov Canal and the dome of the nearby synagogue. After a long hiatus, Vera's artistic imagination was rejuvenated in October 1951 in Baden-Baden – a more inspiring landscape than Sunset Boulevard, though many people preferred her pictures of the latter. After returning to California she painted for several hours every morning, as she continued to do in New York. In her later years she presented successful exhibitions in London, Paris, New York, Tokyo, Venice, Milan, Rome, Los Angeles and Santa Fe. Her art is happy but after Stravinsky's death becomes darker in mood and colour and increasingly drawn to a cemetery in the Venetian lagoon.

The French writer Charles Maray[11] published a description of Vera visiting her husband's grave in the 1970s:

> A Legendary Couple
>
> Each year since 1971, as the first days of spring come to Venice, a distinguished lady is seen disembarking; no sooner does she set foot on the quayside than she makes her way to San Michele... In the pathways, beneath the cypresses, a beautiful legend perpetuates itself. This extraordinary couple has found an oasis, a haven of peace beneath the sky of an otherworldly Venice.

Vera lived through Balanchine's Stravinsky centenary celebration, then took to her bed and refused to eat. After receiving extreme unction by an Orthodox priest, she died on 17 September 1982, shortly before her nameday (30 September), Vera Nadezhda Lyubov (Faith, Hope, Love). At her memorial service in New York the Princeton University choir sang two of Stravinsky's Russian Sacred Choruses.

---

11 Charles D. Maray, San Michele: *Le cimetière flottant de Venise*, Paris: private publication, 1979, p. 77.

After her funeral in San Giorgio dei Greci in Venice, Vera Stravinsky was interred beside her husband on San Michele.

All who knew Vera would agree with Christopher Isherwood's tribute (which, sadly, she never read): 'There seems absolutely nothing bad about Vera Stravinsky. She is sweet-tempered, funny, silly, kind, intelligent, and very industrious.' (24 July 1959)

After Stravinsky recuperated from his stroke in Berlin in October 1956, and the subsequent hospital treatments and return trip from London to New York, he enlisted the help of Lucia Davidova[12] to go with him to Tiffany and help him design for his wife a bracelet of eight letters in solid gold: 'I LOVE YOU'. He gave it to her on her birthday, 25 December 1957. She wore it every day thereafter, and it is buried with her.

---

12 One of Stravinsky's closest friends in America, though she had known Vera de Bosset in Moscow earlier, was Mme Lucia Davidova (1900-1993). A remarkably intelligent and accomplished *grande dame*, Lucia had made a fortune in the stock market and was one of the first women to fly the Atlantic solo in Lindberg's path, having been taught aviation in Connecticut by Igor Sikorsky. The widow Vera Stravinsky entrusted the translation of her Russian diaries into English to Lucia, a task that took many months and which was accomplished in the mansion where Lucia wintered in Palm Beach, the home of her old friend Alicia De Lamar. I worked there with Lucia two or three times a week, checking the English versions. I suspect that she bowdlerised some of the narrative, but she fulfilled the agreement with the writer that the originals be burned.

CHAPTER 12
Amorous Augmentations

If I cannot help you with my music, what can I help you
with? Despite my admiration for my male member,
I am not willing to offer you consolation with it.

Stravinsky to Diaghilev, 22 February 1922

An exploration of this subject is long overdue, yet during the composer's life and before the death of his widow eleven years afterwards, this could not have been openly considered. It will come as a surprise to most people that in the early Diaghilev period Stravinsky was exclusively in an ambisexual phase while writing *Petrushka* and *The Rite of Spring*. When he met Diaghilev, Nijinsky was the impresario's great love, though his homosexual friendships with Valechka Nouvel and Prince Argutinsky[1] were ongoing. The force of Diaghilev's feelings for Nijinsky became apparent in August 1913 when the great dancer married – less for love, it seems, than for

---

1   Prince Vladimir Nikolaevich Argutinsky-Dolgorukov (1872-1941), an art collector and member of the Russian foreign ministry who had known Stravinsky since 1910. In Rome in 1917 Argutinsky joined Maxim Gorky, Lev Bakst and Alexander Benois in encouraging Stravinsky to orchestrate the 'Song of the Volga Boatmen' as the new Russian national anthem.

honour, as was first explained to me by Adolphe Bolm, the best man at the Montevideo wedding of Nijinsky to Romola Pulszky, who had seduced him during the voyage that brought the Ballets Russes from Europe to South America. Receiving news of the marriage, a shattered Diaghilev dismissed the star of his company and fled to Stravinsky in Switzerland where, after days of struggling, the composer and his wife managed to restrain the impresario from suicide.

After the premieres of *The Firebird*, *Petrushka* and *The Rite of Spring* the composer's fame surpassed Diaghilev's, and by 1917 the Russian Revolution depleted Diaghilev's Russian income and also terminated Stravinsky's more modest one (from his vodka distilleries in the Ukraine). By the end of the year Diaghilev informed Stravinsky that the collapse of Imperial Russia had invalidated some of their royalty agreements. A hiatus of several months resulted in which the two friends ceased to communicate directly. Stravinsky persuaded Ernest Ansermet to represent him with Diaghilev in the matter of recouping fees for past and present performances of ballets no longer protected by copyright, the composer now being a 'stateless' person. The breach did not end until 1919 with the new project for *Pulcinella*. But relations between the composer and impresario were not fully restored, Stravinsky's musical direction having changed from ballet to concert music. In 1928 the old friendship returned briefly with the success of *Apollo*. The severance soon ended cruelly in the summer of 1929, when the two men passed each other without speaking in the aisle of a Paris-to-London train. Three weeks later, in Venice, Diaghilev died.[2]

Stravinsky had enraptured French society and become world-renowned overnight. The French audience responded to the new colours and rhythms seemingly without recognising that Stravinsky's delineation of gender was achieved, at least in outline, by traditional means. Thus the Firebird's initial solo dance, the first absolutely new piece in the

---

2   This has been contested with the argument attributed to Prokofiev, that when Diaghilev (with Igor Markevitch) saw Stravinsky in the Paris waiting room, he approached him and placed his hand on his shoulder saying, 'We have much to talk about.' But Vera de Bosset was with Stravinsky and maintained that the silent passing in the aisle of the train is the truth.

ballet, modernises a classic 6/8 metre by syncopation and emphasising off-beats, and through glittering new instrumentation. *The Firebird* was reviewed on the front page of the *New York Herald Tribune*, a rare accolade for any work of art a century ago. Claude Debussy embraced the composer on stage afterwards and invited him to dinner. Ravel also congratulated Stravinsky and introduced him to the Belgian composer Maurice Delage. The success of *The Firebird* was not without a bitter disappointment: the absence of its dedicatee, Stravinsky's closest friend, Andrey Rimsky-Korsakov, elder son of the composer.

In Stravinsky's own words, he was in love with Andrey, a University of St Petersburg classmate and music critic. Andrey had promised to attend the premiere but did not. Three days afterwards, on 28 June 1910, Stravinsky entrained for Ustilug to bring his family to the supplementary performance of the work by popular request (7 July). During the change of trains in Warsaw, Stravinsky wrote to Andrey in St Petersburg, expressing disappointment at his failure to attend and urging him to try to hear at least one performance. Andrey complied, but in Paris avoided Stravinsky, withholding even the slightest compliment and openly criticising the staging of the Kastchei scene. Four months later Stravinsky, still not understanding that the Rimsky-Korsakov family and its clan were seething with jealousy, wrote:

> While the whole of Paris is going wild over *Firebird*, St Petersburg, where only the Suite has been played,[3] has shown no enthusiasm for the music. I am enraged that there is no news from you… I waited, waited, and lost patience. To tell you the truth, I had a right to expect a letter from you… No one writes anything, from which I conclude that my *Firebird* made either little impression or a negative one. My soul is much oppressed.

Stravinsky wrote again asking Andrey to send copies of Russian folk tunes for inclusion in his new ballet, *Petrushka*. The request so

---

3   By Alexander Ziloti, on 23 October 1910. He wanted to make a large cut, but Stravinsky's friend Maximilian Steinberg stopped him.

infuriated Andrey that he openly attacked Stravinsky in the press. Although this must have been deeply hurtful, Stravinsky limited his rebuttal (20 January 1911) to a personal comment: 'You know after all that I have been in love with you a long time, and, if you were a woman, I don't guarantee what I would do to you.'

Stravinsky's next letter to Andrey in the summer of 1911 boasts of the even greater triumph of *Petrushka* and characterises their antagonistic musical philosophies:

> What can be better and more beautiful than the development of existing art forms? Certainly one thing, the creation of new forms. You hold to the first, I to the second not only with words and mind, of which no one ever has as much as he needs, but with feelings that each possesses to the degree he needs them.

Following the worldwide acclaim of *Petrushka*, Andrey published a scathing rejection of all of Stravinsky's music. Igor ignored this for two years, but the intensity of his feelings about this former intimate finally prompted the composer to send a note: 'Neither your poisonous, thunderous writings about my works nor your protest against my un-artistic behaviour should change our warm and friendly relationship.' With this the connection ended. The last communications are a congratulatory note to Andrey on his marriage in 1920, and, in 1932, a letter from Andrey which opens with 'Cher Maître' and goes on, *tutoyer*, as if nothing had happened, requesting a copy of his father's letters and a contribution to 'A book of tributes to my father by his pupils... Recalling the profound impression that his death made on you at the time, I believe that you will be inclined to associate yourself with a manifestation of this kind.' The silence of Rimsky's most celebrated pupil rendered the enterprise ridiculous.

Ravel's close friend Charles Maurice Delage had a major influence on Stravinsky's music at this time. The Belgian composer was immersed in Oriental and in particular Japanese music and, on his return from a two-month visit in Japan, inspired Stravinsky to compose the *Three Japanese Lyrics*. The moment was apt: Part 1 of *The Rite of Spring* had just been completed, and Stravinsky wished to compose something different as a respite before beginning the second half of the ballet (just as, the year before, he had written *Zvezdoliki* between *Petrushka* and the *Rite*). Stravinsky set the texts of the three *Lyrics* in the waka or tanka form of thirty-one syllables distributed in five lines. Unfortunately, he used the Russian translation of A. Brandt, displacing the tonic accent to offbeats instead of setting the Japanese syllables in an uninflected line. The titles of the first two are the names of their poets: 'Akahito' (Akahito Yamanobe), a court poet of the Nara period (eighth century); and 'Mazatsumi' (*sic*) (Masazumi Miyamoto). The third song comes from the earliest (late ninth-century) collection (Number 59) of Waka poems.

To return to 1910 and *Firebird*, the principal figure in Stravinsky's life throughout the period of *The Rite of Spring* was Delage. No correspondence with him exists until 1911 but the one communication that has been retrieved from that year indicates that both men had been very closely involved during and following *Petrushka*. In the spring of 1911 Stravinsky had spent a three-week vacation at Delage's gay agapemone near Paris, not alone but with the notoriously homosexual Prince Argutinsky[4] whose letters are still in private hands. A Russian gentleman who has read this correspondence told me a few months after Stravinsky's death that Argutinsky's letters are 'very compromising to Stravinsky biography'. In the late summer of 1911 Stravinsky sent to Delage from Ustilug a photograph of himself in the nude with a prominent upwardly mobile nozzle.

Already at this point a digression becomes necessary, to correct the myth of the influence of *Pierrot Lunaire* on 'Mazatsumi', the second of Stravinsky's *Three Japanese Lyrics*. In fact the first two *Lyrics* were composed before Stravinsky had heard *Pierrot*, while the post-*Pierrot* third *Lyric*, concluding in a perfect triad, is devoid of any Schoenberg influence. A detached sketch for the *Rite* dated 1 November 1912 also contains sketches for the two concluding bars of 'Mazatsumi', followed by a poem in Stravinsky's hand beginning with

---

4   He was one of Tchaikovsky's lovers (see the photograph of them together in Moscow in 1890).

the word 'Vesna' (Spring), directly linking the *Lyrics* to the *Rite*, whose original title was *Vesna Svyashchennaya* ('Sacred Spring'):

Spring is the subject of all three *Lyrics*. In 1914 Romain Rolland, Stravinsky's fellow refugee in Switzerland, wrote to a friend: 'Stravinsky is very intelligent... [E]verything he says is original and carefully thought out. In art, as in everything, Stravinsky loves only Spring, new life.'

The music of 'Akahito', dedicated to Delage, who had introduced Stravinsky to the haiku, evokes images of falling snow during spring using a slow, steady quaver rhythm, the time value of the entire opus. The first half of 'Mazatsumi' is purely instrumental, the singer entering only at the mid-point of the piece with four tempo-breaking, exclamatory, sustained notes – the principal motive of the song; the same four notes are repeated beguilingly by the piccolo six bars later. The piece sustains a D sharp played *ponticello* by the second violin throughout the first half. The central accompaniment features a rapid figure in the clarinet, sounded five times. The final song, 'Tsaraiuki', dedicated to Ravel, consists of three iterations of a five-note embellishment figure in the clarinets and ends with a recapitulation in the piccolo of the quaver melody in faster note values. The vocal line is confined to quavers, and the accompaniment is largely limited to two parts. The final chord is the first inversion of a perfect F major triad.

On 14 October 1912 Stravinsky sent a startling letter from Ustilug to Delage in Paris:

> I sit before your letter with that familiar and very dear signature, 'Maurice'... and those four words, '3 rue de Civry': I can't express to you how precious they are to me! Oh, I have such a desire to come to your house to spend a few autumn days with you again in that little pavilion which silently guards the memories of our compatible life of a year ago.[5] Far from the brouhaha of the high season of the Ballets Russes, [we were] calm and intimate there in that little pavilion with its little rooms, which I do so wish to see again. My old friend, we absolutely must see each other soon! Is it impossible to hear some word of what you have done and undergone during our separation of nearly five months? Paris is two cities: one of them gives me glory and money – the temptation gnaws relentlessly at my entrails – and the other is Maurice, 3 rue de Civry, who, without being aware of it, takes away all of the filth of the Grand Saison des Ballets Russes. Forever, your Igor.

---

5   This sentence is underlined by Delage, who has written in the margin, 'Oh, if only this were true.'

Part of the bombshell of this love letter is the discovery that Stravinsky's principal bisexual experience occurred during *The Rite of Spring*, widely regarded as the epitome of masculinity in music, comparable to Wagner. Delage was living with the Stravinskys in Switzerland when Diaghilev required the composer to attend performances of *The Firebird* in Budapest and of *Petrushka* in Vienna in January 1913. The composer entrusted his children to Delage's care during these absences. Delage wrote from Clarens to Stravinsky at the Hotel Hungaria on 4 January 1913: 'Mon cher petit, what are these desolate thoughts that disappear before Oscar Wilde? I hope that you have regained your good humour in the arms of that horrible fiend Diaghilev. Kisses from your Maurice.' The reference to Diaghilev was apparently intended literally.

Of the twenty-eight letters from Delage in the Stravinsky archives, all except the last few date from the *Sacre* period. Stravinsky saw this friend only once after the Great War. In 1961 his widow wrote to Stravinsky in Hollywood informing him of her husband's death. As I recall, Stravinsky betrayed no emotion on reading the letter.

In April 1913 Delage's close friend Ravel, accompanied as usual by his mother, came to Clarens to work with Stravinsky in recomposing and orchestrating parts of Musorgsky's *Khovanshchina*. During the visit Stravinsky played his *Japanese Lyrics* for the French composer, who promptly composed his *Trois Poèmes de Stéphane Mallarmé* using the same nine instruments. Even more importantly for music history, Ravel convinced Stravinsky to add new percussion instruments to the *Sacre*, in the polyrhythmic dance for full orchestra before the silence ending with the 'Dance of the Earth'. The most prominent of these was the Cuban güiro,[6] a hollowed gourd that produces the loudest imaginable insect-like stridulations. None of these noisemakers was originally employed in the Part One that Pierre Monteux had already rehearsed, and Ravel's suggestion of using the colossal ratcheting of the güiro remains one of the great thrills of the work.

---

6   The score calls for a 'rape güiro', perhaps because neither Stravinsky nor Ravel was familiar with the spelling of the Spanish word for 'calabash'.

One day Stravinsky and Ravel travelled from Clarens to the nearby village of Varese to purchase paper from a connoisseur dealer. Unable to find hotel rooms, they were obliged to share a single bed at an inn. Routinely questioned on this subject – 'How was it?' – Stravinsky would reply, 'You will have to ask Ravel.' Stravinsky maintained that Ravel (not Debussy) was the only musician who in 1913 understood *The Rite of Spring.*

Ravel and Stravinsky were, of all artists, the most successful in concealing their sexuality. The two were time-to-time lovers in the early Diaghilev years and it is conceivable that Stravinsky attended more than one of the infamous parties by the all-male group called the 'Apaches', since he recalled that Ravel had dressed as a ballerina complete with tutu and falsies. It was here that Stravinsky had made the acquaintance of Franc-Nohain, Ravel's librettist for *L'Heure espagnole*, a man of prodigious wit. Stravinsky's recollections of him revived during my rehearsals in Washington D.C. in 1961 of Ravel's opera, which Stravinsky admired and enjoyed immensely. The relations between the very small – scarcely five feet – composers warrants much more space and thought than the few remarks I can devote to them here. Most important was that now famous walk together in Monte Carlo in the spring of 1912 after a rehearsal of *Daphnis and Chloé,* which Diaghilev was preparing for performance in Paris in June. Suddenly the younger composer was seized by a musical idea and the two men sat down at a table in the Taverne Parisienne, where Stravinsky sketched on two staves the rhythm of the beginning of the 'Danse sacrale'.

A year later, on 19 April, Ravel and his mother arrived in a hotel near Stravinsky's Châtelard Hotel in Clarens to collaborate on editing Musorgsky's *Khovanshchina*, a commission from Diaghilev for his revival of the opera. Ravel's task was mainly to improve and fill in the orchestration, whereas Stravinsky actually composed a 100-measure final choral piece on a theme by the opera's composer. Ravel and his mother returned to Paris at the beginning of May and Ravel wrote to Stravinsky on the 5th, saying that he had found a hotel room nearby where Stravinsky could live thoughout the rehearsals and premiere of *The Rite of Spring.*

A decade later, when the Stravinsky family had moved to Biarritz, Igor visited Ravel in his nearby home in St-Jean-de-Luz to patch up an unhappy break in their friendship. In 1920 Diaghilev had obliged Stravinsky to pass judgement on Ravel's *La Valse* as a ballet. Diaghilev had called the work a masterpiece but not a ballet. After hearing it played by Ravel and a second pianist, Marcelle Meyer, Stravinsky had left the room without saying a single word. The old friendship was restored, however. In 1923 Ravel sent a very complimentary note to Stravinsky after hearing *Les Noces* and on 18 October 1928 Stravinsky and Ravel were conductors of the inaugural concert for the restored Salle Pleyel, leading respectively *La Valse* and *The Firebird Suite*.

A cataclysmic change in Stravinsky's life occurred in January 1914 with the flare-up of his wife's tuberculosis accompanied by pleurisy after the birth of their fourth child. Striving to finish his opera *The Nightingale*, Stravinsky began a liaison with Ruzhana Vlastimova Khvoshchinskya, whose husband Vassili, an attaché at the Russian Embassy in Rome, was an amateur musician and founder of a string quartet. His letters to Stravinsky do not mention her, but criticise him for complaining about too many German-named employees during his visit to the embassy in 1915. Vassili's first letter to Stravinsky in Morges seems unduly vexatious over his unspecified behaviour in Rome, thereby suggesting that the real cause may have been suspicion of Stravinsky's attentions to Ruzhana. Her letters to the composer are most affectionate. A tender note from her survives from February 1915, and the next month she wrote to him from Capri: 'The sun is splendidly bright and warm and there are millions of flowers. I hope to see you soon. My husband has already left Russia.' By the beginning of 1916 Ruzhana had rejoined her spouse in Rome. Her first letter to Igor from there begins, 'I have not had any news from you in a long time and I have been missing you. I hope you will not have forgotten me. I hope that you will write... I press your hand.' The letter mentions a Russian review of Prokofiev's ballet, *Alla and Lolly*, which Diaghilev had demeaned as a crude imitation of the *Sacre*. It also reports that Stravinsky's fame has multiplied in the Italian capital (partly due to performances of *The Firebird* conducted with great success by Thomas Beecham). She adds that Beecham informed her

that he had 'sent 10,000 francs to you via Diaghilev'. She also refers
to a secret rendezvous with Stravinsky in Paris. A letter of 11 February
1916 describes Toscanini's sold-out repeat concert of *Petrushka* (in
a programme with Beethoven's 'Pastoral' and pieces by Sibelius and
Elgar). But this raises a question, since Stravinsky was present at one
of Toscanini's Rome concerts, as the composer's exit visa, stamped by
Khvoshchinsky himself, verifies. How could Ruzhana not have been
aware of this from newspapers and friends?

After the two highly publicised performances of Stravinsky's Three
Pieces for String Quartet in Paris in November 1916, Ruzhana wrote
asking him to send the music to her in Rome, but he did not respond.
Léon Bakst wrote to him, describing the audience's excitement at the
premiere as well as at a second performance in the Salle d'Antin,
a historical occasion in that this gallery was currently exhibiting
Picasso's *Les Demoiselles d'Avignon*, together with paintings by
Matisse, Chirico, Derain, Léger, Modigliani and Rouault. The quartet
players included Arthur Honegger and Darius Milhaud, newcomers on
the Paris music scene. Ruzhana wrote again in January 1917, asking
Stravinsky to send the parts for a performance with her husband's
Rome quartet, but again the request was ignored. The advaunterer
had moved on.

With the abdication of the Tsar in the spring of 1917 and the
closing of the Rome Embassy, the Khvoshchinskys returned to
Switzerland and the Grand Hotel in Leysin, which was not far from
Stravinsky's temporary domicile in Diablerets. At the beginning of
August, Vassili wrote to the composer proposing a return to their
former good friendship, but Stravinsky bluntly rejected the offer,
saying that he could not 'negotiate with someone who retreats behind
a double nature'. Stravinsky's morose mood can be attributed to the
traumatising birth of his second daughter, Milene, and the serious
acceleration of his wife's life-endangering tuberculosis. A break
with Diaghilev, owing to the freezing of his Russian assets, thereby
disrupted all of Stravinsky's plans. Shortly after the birth, he received
an undesired visit from Jean Cocteau and his new lover, Paul Thévenaz,
an American painter hoping to make a portrait of the composer (now in
the present writer's collection). Stravinsky was deeply immersed with

the completion of his opera when Cocteau asked him to compose a ballet on the subject of the Biblical David. Not on very good terms with Cocteau since *Sacre*, Stravinsky did not welcome him and advised him to stay in the Hotel Leysin: 'Vieux maniaque: You will be comfortable there and for comparatively modest rates you will find everything you need: rooms, hot and cold water; lukewarm women, boys aged 8 to 13.' *David* became *Parade*, but in spite of music by Satie and décors by Picasso, the piece was a box-office and critical failure. Stravinsky attended the Paris premiere but did not speak to its creators. Cocteau wisely ignored the snub and later wrote to Stravinsky: 'I do not recall ever having approached the annex of your hotel without experiencing Nietzsche's emotion at the entrance to Triebschen.'

Something should be said about Stravinsky's psycho-sexual features before discussing his subsequent amorous adventures, especially of his protectiveness and partiality toward his numerous *tyotka* (homosexual) friends. He talked openly about the homosexuality of his younger brother Gury, with whom he had shared a room during their childhood and adolescent years. His gentleness toward this favourite sibling extended to friendships in his artistic world: Diaghilev – whom Cocteau described as a Moloch whose Ganymede was Nijinsky – Kochno, Satie, Öberg, Gerald Heard, Berman, Poulenc, Henze, Balthus, François-Michel,[7] Copland, Cingria, Berners, Tchelichev, Auden, Kallman, Isherwood, Bachardy, Spender, Edward James, Gide, Virgil Thomson, Nicolas Kopeykin (Balanchine's rehearsal pianist), Hugues Cuénod,[8] *e tutti quanti.*

---

7   François-Michel was Pierre Boulez's long-time 'housemate', as a recent biographer refers to him. François-Michel would become one of Stravinsky's most loyal French friends between 1956 and 1970. He drove to meet the composer's steamships at Le Havre and convey him and, in a second car, his baggage (eighteen heavy pieces) to and from Paris. A noted gourmet, he regularly invited the Stravinskys with Pierre Souvtchinsky to little-known restaurants of the highest quality. He compiled the *Encyclopédie Fasquelle* and was employed by De Gaulle's Minister of Culture, André Malraux, to edit books. François-Michel was the last person to see Stravinsky in Europe, having accompanied him to Zurich airport in August 1970.

8   Hugues Cuénod sang the part of Sellem in the original *Rake's Progress*, as well as the tenor solo in Stravinsky's Cantata in Hollywood and New York in 1952. Cuénod's influence on Stravinsky precedes these engagements in a way not heretofore acknowledged. In 1950 Cuénod gave copies of his recordings of François Couperin's *Leçons de ténèbres* to Stravinsky, who had discovered the beauties of this composer from Ravel and continued to play Couperin's keyboard works religiously.

Meanwhile, Stravinsky's engagements with women turned to the Diaghilev ballerina Lydia Lopukhova, as the composer freely admitted. Photographs show him alone with her in Bordeaux on her return from New York on 8 September 1916, and also with her in Anglet in 1921 and in Biarritz in 1922. He also assisted her in presenting a performance of *L'Histoire du Soldat* in London in 1928. Backstage after his concert in the Royal Festival Hall in the spring of 1965, I witnessed a moving scene between a weeping 'Lopushka', then the widow of John Maynard Keynes, and a perspiring but dry-eyed Stravinsky.

The more abbreviated and less publicised fling with Juanita Gandarillas took place in London in 1919-21. She was the wife of Tony Gandarillas, a nephew of Eugenia Errázuriz, the Chilean patroness of both Stravinsky and Picasso. All I remember Stravinsky saying about Juanita is that she gave a pair of sapphire and diamond cufflinks to him. Virginia Woolf described her as 'very stupid but also so incredibly beautiful that one forgives it all'. Lytton Strachey gossiped that 'she had the finest underwear in Europe' and that Clive Bell had 'fallen madly in love with her'.

Next in line was the beautiful Russian-speaking Brazilian soprano and violinist Vera Janacopoulos,[9] for whom Stravinsky orchestrated two of his songs. With the help of her uncle, the Brazilian Minister of War, she had emigrated from her mother's home in Brussels to Switzerland at the outbreak of World War I. She met Stravinsky there shortly after he had completed *Pribaoutki* (1914) and he gave the original manuscript to her. She had learned Russian from the poet Jacov Polonsky, a relative of Stravinsky.[10] Heitor Villa-Lobos copied the piece for her and she performed it in New York in 1919

---

9   Born in Brazil of a Brazilian mother and a Greek father, Vera Janacopoulos was a violin pupil of Enescu and a well-trained musician. Stravinsky was in correspondence with her and as late as 1950 sent an autographed picture to her in Brazil. She had been proposed for the part of Anne Trulove in *The Rake's Progress* in 1951 but Auden had heard gossip about her affair with the composer and, thinking this could be embarrassing for Vera de Bosset, proposed Elisabeth Schwarzkopf instead. Janacopoulos died in Brazil in 1955.

10   Stravinsky's first cousin, Nicolai Yelachich, married Natalie Polonsky, daughter of the poet who died in Auschwitz; he is probably best known today for his recognition of the genius of Isaac Babel.

Stravinsky's parents, Fyodor Ignatievich Stravinsky and Anna Kirillovna Kholodovskaya. They had been married six months and seventeen days.

Stravinsky's great-great-grandfather, Ivan Ivanovich Skorohodov (1766–1877), on his 111th birthday. He was born when Mozart was ten years old and died when Schoenberg was three. A Polish document mentions that he became a royal Lithuanian chamberlain in 1778.

Portrait of Stravinsky's maternal grandparents, Kirill Grigorievich Kholodovsky (1806–1855) and Maria Romanovna Kholodovskaya (1822–1880). The photo is dated St Petersburg, 23 June 1872.

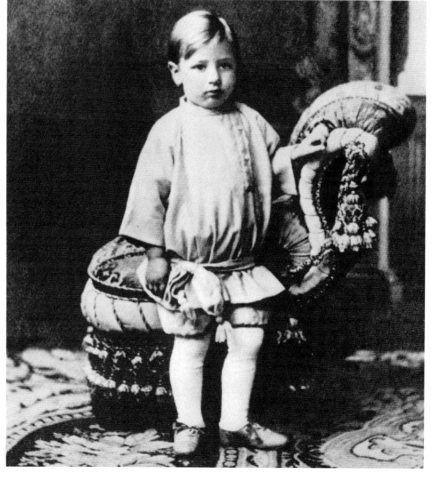

Top: Medallion portrait on wood of Stravinsky's great-grandfather, Roman Furman, who acquired the family's greatest wealth and distributed it liberally.

Bottom: Portrait of the artist as a child.

Portrait of the artist as a young man.

Crossing the Nevsky Prospect, St Petersburg, spring 1910, shortly before departure to Paris and the premiere of *The Firebird*.

Following the premiere of *The Rite of Spring*, Neuilly, June 1913.

Top: Maurice Delage, Maurice Ravel and Alexis Roland-Manuel, summer of 1911, in Delage's garden behind his home in the sixteenth arrondissement (Paris). Roland-Manuel became the writer in 1939 of Stravinsky's *Poétique musicale*, his Harvard lectures.

Bottom: Photo of Maurice Ravel taken by Stravinsky in April 1913 at the Hôtel des Crêtes, Clarens.

Top: With Maurice Ravel, Clarens, April 1913.

Bottom: Vaslav Nijinsky and his sister Bronislava Nijinska with Maurice Ravel. Photo by Stravinsky, May 1913.

Tempera painting from the cycle *Winter* by M. K. Čiurlionis, 1907.

Manuscript of the first page of *The Rite of Spring*, copied by Stravinsky for his Berlin publisher in 1920 to show the phrasings of the bassoon and English horn parts.

Stravinsky's revision of two measures in Part One of *The Rite of Spring* in a miniature score in the early 1920s.

Coloured panel by Natalia Goncharova (1881–1962) for the unrealised ballet *Liturgie*, inscribed to Stravinsky in 1915 in Morges.

Pencil sketch by Stravinsky of his first wife, Ekaterina Gavrilovna Nossenko, during a rehearsal of *Les Noces* in Monte Carlo, 1923.

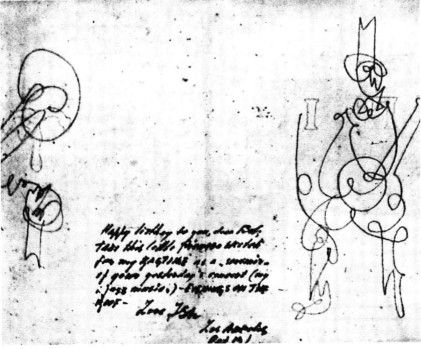

Picasso's one-line drawing for the cover of Stravinsky's *Ragtime*, inscribed to the author: 'Happy Birthday to you, dear Bob, take this little Picasso sketch from my *Ragtime* as a "souvenir" of your yesterday's concert (my "jazz music") – Evenings on the Roof – Love, IStr Los Angeles, Oct 19/53.' Resemblances have been noted between this drawing and the 'extravagant erection' in *Hypnerotomachia Poliphili*, the erotic poem printed in Venice in 1499, now at the University of Virginia.

*Moi, Sert, Missia et
Coco Chanel 1920*

In Stravinsky's hand: 'Moi, [José-Maria] Sert, Missia [*sic*], et Coco Chanel 1920.' The composer and Chanel lived together in her Bel Respiro home in Garches for a time in 1921. Misia and Sert had been living together since 1909 and finally married in 1920. At about the date of this picture, Sert had acquired a mistress, the famous beauty Roussy, the Princess Mdivani. Misia was aware of this relationship, but when she finally saw Roussy she also fell madly in love with her and brought her into their home. The *ménage à trois* survived for several years until Sert divorced Misia, the tubercular Roussy died, and Sert reinstated himself with Misia, then moved to New York.

Tanya Yurievna Stravinsky, 1925. This twenty-year-old niece of the composer made her home with him and his family for a year and a half in Nice, during which she spent periods in Paris near her uncle.

Arnold Schoenberg, Berlin, 1920s.

Anton Webern, Vienna, 1930s.

DIE GLÜCKLICHE HAND

DRAMA MIT MUSIK

VON

ARNOLD SCHÖNBERG

OP.18.

UNIVERSAL-EDITION A.G.
WIEN   LEIPZIG.

COPYRIGHT 1916 BY UNIVERSAL-EDITION

U.E. Nr. 5670.

To Mr. Robert Craft
cordially
Arnold Schoenberg
July 6, 1951

Score for *Die glückliche Hand* by Schoenberg. During my last visit to the composer he was unable to come to the bottom of the stairs, but talked to me from the top. He also inscribed this score to me, the last ever. He died a week later.

Prince Argutinsky-Dolgorukov with Tchaikovsky, Moscow, c. 1890; and with Stravinsky in Paris, 1923. Stravinsky had been the prince's intimate friend since 1910.

Top: With Charles Chaplin, Hollywood, 1937.

Bottom: May 1938, Paris. Left to right: Jacques Février, Serge Lifar, the Vicomtesse de Noailles, Stravinsky, Vera de Bosset, Coco Chanel. Février had played the two-piano version of Stravinsky's Capriccio at the Princess Polignac's salon before the public premiere in Paris. Lifar had published Diaghilev's letters derogating Stravinsky's *Le Baiser de la fée*, which helps to account for Stravinsky's annoyed expression. Février, Lifar and Chanel were three of the most prominent Collaborationists during World War II. The Vicomtesse de Noailles was a descendant of the Marquis de Sade and a remote descendant of Petrarca.

At home in 1948, photo by Vera Stravinsky.

Top: The author with Stravinsky on the deck of the S.S. *Bremen*, April 1963, on a voyage from New York.

Bottom: Claudio Spies and the author in the control room of Stravinsky's recording session of Symphony of Psalms, Toronto, 1963. Spies, a long-time Harvard, Princeton and Juilliard professor, was a close friend of Stravinsky's from the early 1940s. The composer entrusted him with the vetting of all of his serial-period music and greatly valued his opinion in most musical matters. In 1960 Stravinsky was a guest at the Spies family home in Santiago, Chile.

Top: With Nicolas Nabokov in Stravinsky's room in the Hotel Kempinski, Hamburg, May 1963, from a Canadian film.

Bottom: With Milton Babbitt listening to a rehearsal of *Threni* in The Metropolitan Museum of Art, New York, 1958.

Top: Stravinsky and Balanchine listening to the Requiem Canticles, New York, 1966. The composer thought that Balanchine understood his later music more fully than any of his musician friends, and after seeing *Movements* in 1963 said that the choreography actually added to the music.

Bottom: The recessional from Stravinsky's funeral service, Venice. Right to left: the author, Nicolas Nabokov (white hair), the widow, Vittorio Rieti.

Top: Alva and Robert Craft at home. Photo by Barbara Haas.

Bottom: Elliott Carter arriving at the Craft apartment, New York, New Year's Eve, 1999.

Stravinsky conducting in St Petersburg, October 1962.

Portrait by René Bouché, Washington, D.C., January 1962.

Stravinsky with Mme Furtseva, the Minister of Culture, and Dmitri Shostakovich, Moscow 1962.

'"Happy Birthday" to Robert Craft converted in music by Igor Stravinsky', 1966. The music with words identifies the first melody, after the introduction, of *The Rite of Spring*; the other music excerpts are motifs from the instrumental accompaniment. The staves are drawn by Stravinsky's styluses.

Stravinsky and the author in the library at 1218 North Wetherly Drive, Hollywood, December 1968.

under Prokofiev,[11] who sent an amusing note to Stravinsky about the music and spoke glowingly of her performance. Stravinsky's acknowledgement was terse: 'I know her very well.' When Janacopoulos returned the manuscript to its composer in Switzerland in 1920 he warmly inscribed a printed copy for her. In later years he gifted the manuscripts of his 1924 orchestrations of 'Tilimbom' and *Pastorale* to her, which she bequeathed to the Biblioteca Central de Universidade Federal do Estado in Rio de Janeiro. On the tenth anniversary of *The Rite of Spring*, 29 May 1923, Stravinsky attended a concert in the Salle des Agriculteurs, ostensibly to hear songs by Manuel de Falla but actually to hear her sing the *Japanese Lyrics*, *Pribaoutki* and the premiere of 'Sektanskaya', this last with newly added flute obbligato copied by the composer for the virtuoso Marcel Moyse. Shortly after this she married Alexis Staal, a former official in the Kerensky government,[12] but remained on close terms with Stravinsky and performed in concerts with him even during his early years with Vera de Bosset.[13] In 1928, while Stravinsky was concert-touring in London, he attended a gala performance of Falla's *El retablo de maese Pedro* featuring the singer. Stravinsky attended the concert with his friend King Alfonso XIII.

During the Ballets Russes season in Madrid in April 1921, Stravinsky and Robert Delaunay, who painted the composer's portrait at this time, became the clients of a woman in a bordello and for unimaginable reasons brought her to meet Diaghilev. A day later Diaghilev, Kochno and Stravinsky went to Seville for *Semana Santa* and to plan their new project about the mini-opera *Mavra*. Diaghilev had convinced Stravinsky not only to accept Kochno as librettist of this work but also to orchestrate the two numbers from *Sleeping Beauty* (that Tchaikovsky had excised after a hint by Tsar Alexander III) for the forthcoming London revival of the ballet.

11 She was Prokofiev's co-librettist for *The Love of Three Oranges*.
12 In 1917 Stravinsky declared that 'Kerensky is a man of great moral strength and intelligence who is also thoroughly reliable, about the only one still in power who can restrain the extremists.'
13 A letter, Stravinsky to Vera Staal, 24 August 1924, was sold under the Christie gavel in November 1995.

On 21 June 1920 Stravinsky moved from Morges to a home in Carantec[14] (Finistère) made available to him by Misia Sert. On 25 June[15] his family joined him there while he worked on revisions and additions to *L'Histoire du Soldat* and completed the three-instrument arrangement of five of its movements, notably replacing the percussion part with piano, giving exact pitches. The composer also finished a chorale in piano score[16] for *La Revue Musicale*'s Debussy memorial album. On 23 August Stravinsky wrote to C.-F. Ramuz saying, 'I just spent ten days apartment hunting in Paris but returned empty-handed to Carantec where I suffered an attack of oyster indigestion.'

Meanwhile, in mid-June 1920, seeking financial help for Diaghilev whose entire fortune had been confiscated by the new Russia, Misia persuaded Gabrielle Chanel to join her on a visit to him in Venice. At lunch they encountered the impresario with the Princess Royal Maria Pavlovna, one of his first St Petersburg patrons, and joined them. Diaghilev explained to this new guest that the future of his company depended on the revival of *The Rite of Spring*, scheduled for 15 December.[17] A large sum was needed, which Chanel, having succumbed to the impresario's charm, decided then and there to donate. Later in Paris, during her affair with Stravinsky, she presented Diaghilev with a cheque for 300,000 francs.

Chanel always claimed to have fallen in love with Stravinsky on the night of the 1913 premiere of the *Rite*. While it is not certain when and where Igor actually met Coco,[18] most likely they were introduced

---

14 The residence was the property of Misia Sert, whose niece continued to live in the house throughout Stravinsky's occupancy. That she may have been another candidate for inclusion in this chapter is inferable from her letter to Stravinsky shortly before his departure for America in 1939.

15 On 26 June 1920 Stravinsky wrote from Carantec to his Geneva publisher, O. M. Kling, acknowledging the receipt of proofs of the score of his instrumentation of the 'Song of the Volga Boatmen'.

16 The chorale became the concluding section of the *Symphonies of Wind Instruments*.

17 A letter from Nicolas Roerich in London to Stravinsky in Morges, 21 November 1919, confirms that Diaghilev had already decided to revive the *Rite* with Roerich's original sets and costumes.

18 The composer and the couturière may have met at the rehearsals for the 1920 premiere of *Pulcinella* or the midnight party afterwards. No meaningful encounter could have taken place with Stravinsky at the last of these, since the wildly inebriated composer was busy upstairs throwing pillows over the balcony to the dance floor below.

through their close mutual friend Misia, to whom Stravinsky had presented a copy (No. 41) of the four-hand score of the *Rite* on the day after the premiere, inscribing it 'à notre chère Missia [sic], notre chère et fidèle en tout affection Igor Stravinsky Paris 30/v/1913'.

Though Chanel was not Igor's preferred *zaftik* physiological type, they began a deep affair. She had purchased Bel Respiro in the Paris suburb of Garches in March 1920, but refurbishing was necessary before she could move there. The couturière solved Stravinsky's housing problem by inviting him with his family and Beliankin relatives to live at Bel Respiro beginning 15 September. She was currently living in Biarritz with the exiled Duke Dmitri Pavlovich, son of Grand Duke Paul and Alexandra of Greece.[19] When Chanel first met Dmitri at the Paris Yacht Club, he described Rasputin's gruesome murder to her. No doubt she magnified the details for repetition to Stravinsky who, as a college friend of Prince Felix Yusupov, the principal accomplice in the crime, would have been fascinated.

Picasso, who saw Stravinsky frequently during this period, could have contributed details about the Chanel affair. His portrait of Stravinsky is dated 24 May 1920, Paris. Stravinsky sent one of his *Pulcinella* sketch scores in return for the portrait, which Picasso acknowledged in a note postmarked 'Morges, June 26'. The famous coloured drawing of the violin and guitar *Pulcinella*-type figures was gifted to Stravinsky by the painter in September 1919, which confirms an earlier date for the artist's agreement to collaborate on the ballet.

On 22 September 1920, Stravinsky wrote to Ansermet from Bel Respiro: 'I am in the middle of finishing the Concertino for string quartet... Debussy [*Symphonies of Wind Instruments*] later.' Stravinsky completed the Concertino on 4 October and finished the *Symphonies* in mid-November. During the same period he corrected the proofs of the score and orchestra parts of *The Rite of Spring*. The Ballets Russes was in London at the time, and a letter to Stravinsky from Lord Berners reveals that Chanel was there as late as 7 December, while

---

19   Dmitri's mother died at his birth and his father, the Grand Duke, died in St Petersburg when the boy was eleven. Dmitri had been expelled from Russia for an offence to his first cousin, Tsar Nicholas II.

her Paris studio was completing the costumes for the *Rite* revival. By this date Stravinsky was in Paris supervising rehearsals and working with Léonide Massine, whose choreography was replacing Nijinsky's. Richard Buckle's *Diaghilev* quotes Ansermet's account of Stravinsky at an orchestra rehearsal 'prancing up and down the central aisle in a terrifying manner', something I also witnessed when he was preparing the *Renard* revival in New York in 1947.

In the December Paris performance of *Sacre*, the part of *l'Élue* was danced by Lydia Sokolova, Diaghilev's stage name for Hilda Munnings, his English prima ballerina. She concluded the piece lying on her arched back, legs parted, hips raised and groin thrust forward like the woman in Courbet's *L'Origine du monde.* Stravinsky rushed on to the stage afterwards and embraced the young woman before a cheering audience that included his current lover, Chanel. Afterward at the Hotel Continental supper party, Diaghilev was seated at one end of the table and Stravinsky at the other, with Sokolova to his right. All descriptions confirm that the composer passionately caressed the Sacrificial Virgin's bare arm.

Chanel went back to Biarritz before the Stravinsky family arrived at Bel Respiro but she returned on 12 January. Diaghilev's correspondence with the composer at that time confirms Stravinsky's address, as does his letter of 11 February to Ansermet: 'I will do my concert with Chanel alone. Nobody else, for reasons too long to explain.' The reference is to a projected chamber music soirée in Paris introducing *L'Histoire du Soldat*, but this did not take place. Bel Respiro continued to be the Stravinsky family's address until 19 February 1921, when they moved to Anglet and soon after to Les Rochers on rue de la Frégate in Biarritz, where they stayed until relocating to Nice in 1924.

Ten days after Chanel left Paris, Stravinsky met Vera de Bosset, but between these events he was involved in a steamy affair with the Chauve-Souris dancer Zhenya Nikitina. He enhanced her performance of his Polka by adding her theme song to his score. The adventure ended abruptly when he met Vera. Chanel then resumed her career as a demirep, becoming the mistress of the Duke of Westminster, reputedly the richest man in Europe, with whom she remained for five years.

To her Argentine friend Victoria Ocampo, Chanel confessed a dislike of 'sexual relations with any man more than two or three times'. But obviously Stravinsky engaged in many more *rencontres* with the couturière. A brief estrangement occurred in March and April 1927, a result of her evasiveness about underwriting the premiere of *Oedipus Rex*. Stravinsky wrote to Cocteau on 11 April: 'Chanel wanted to see me "as soon as possible", but she answered my telegram only last Friday saying she was going to Spain... She did not have the slightest inclination to make decisions that were of great urgency for us... I have had to surrender the production to Diaghilev.'[20] In August 1929 at Diaghilev's funeral in Venice, Chanel shared the first gondola in a cortège to the island cemetery of San Michele with the Baroness d'Erlanger, Misia Sert, Kochno and Serge Lifar.

Chanel contributed to Stravinsky's support during the Depression years[21] and also employed his elder daughter in her rue Cambon boutique. Eventually Gabrielle and Vera became close friends. Vera's diary informs us that Igor dined alone with Coco at the Ritz as late as 28 March 1938. In fact the Igor–Coco friendship continued until the end of their lives.[22] Chanel dined with the Stravinskys and myself at Maria's on East Fifty-Second Street, New York, in 1958. She was still among the quick when Stravinsky was staying at the Paris Ritz in November 1968 but they did not meet. She died three months before him. The icon he had given to her after his 1925 conversion stood by her bedside until her death.

Victoria Ocampo,[23] best known as the patroness of Jorge Luis Borges and for her biography of Lawrence of Arabia, had been present

---

20 *Oedipus Rex* was composed as a surprise for Diaghilev to honour the twentieth anniversary of the Ballets Russes but, unable to finance a stage production, Stravinsky's first performance of it was in concert form and sponsored by the Princesse de Polignac.

21 On 6 February 1933 Stravinsky wrote to Misia asking her to intercede with Chanel on his behalf: 'Chanel has not sent us anything since the first, and so we are with only a radish to live on this month. I ask you to be kind enough to mention it to her.' This suggests that he was receiving a monthly stipend.

22 One of Chanel's biographers quotes her: 'Stravinsky courted me. "But you are married, Igor. When Catherine finds out..." Here Stravinsky broke in with: "She already knows. To whom, if not to one's wife, does one confide something so important?"'

23 I first heard her name from Stravinsky in New York on 20 April 1948. Her picture was on the front pages of newspapers because of a scandal brewing in the House of Commons over the extravagance of her ⊓3,000 hotel bill charged to the government in connection with her visit to a writers' congress.

at the first *Rite of Spring* and remained captivated by Stravinsky for the rest of her life. Her name first appears with his when she introduced him to Aldous Huxley in London in 1934. The next year she acquired the Spanish publication rights for Stravinsky's autobiography and at that time also invited him to conduct in Buenos Aires. He responded by inviting her to undertake the *Récitante* role in the Argentine and Brazilian performances of *Perséphone* in 1936. Three weeks later, she shared a suite with Stravinsky on a steamship to Rio de Janeiro where she then met Dagmar Godowsky who, unbeknown to Victoria, had been his mistress a year earlier. In Rio, Victoria witnessed Stravinsky's contretemps with the pianist Josef Hofmann: a long-time enemy and even more inebriated than usual, Hofmann attacked Stravinsky's music during a dinner in the Hotel Gloria.

Stravinsky's affair with Victoria was pursued in her mansion above the Rio de la Plata, where he lived during his stay in Argentina, and continued until May 1939 when she performed *Perséphone* with him in Florence. Tall and somewhat plump, she resembled the gracefully buxom Vera; both exuded the promise of 'pneumatic bliss' and the *morbidezza* reputedly sought by small men. The two women became close friends in the years after Stravinsky's death. Victoria visited the Stravinskys in Hollywood in the early 1940s, bringing as a house gift a dappled Pampas cowskin rug, garishly ill-suited to their other furnishings but still there when I arrived in 1948. She was the only person I knew to whom Stravinsky kowtowed. During the Perón era, her family fortune was impounded and she was jailed for several weeks until Nicolas Nabokov rallied some of the world's most prestigious artists to help procure her release.

The affair with Dagmar Godowsky was the only one to become tabloid grist,[24] partly for the reason that this daughter of the famed pianist Leopold Godowsky had been a silent-film partner of Rudolph Valentino. She re-entered Stravinsky's life as his concert agent at the end of 1936. He arrived in New York on the SS *Normandie* on

---

24 I was present in 1958 when Stravinsky received a copy of Dagmar's memoir, *First Person Plural*, and watched him angrily underscore lines and paragraphs and fill margins with exclamation marks. The book reveals that he crossed himself before making love to her.

Christmas Eve and, feeling ill, retired to his hotel. The next night Dagmar persuaded him to escort her to the New Amsterdam Theater for the premiere of Menotti's *Amelia Goes to the Ball*, which provoked derisory comments from Stravinsky. On 3 January he caught the train for Toronto and, following his concert there, returned to New York for two weeks of conducting the Philharmonic. After giving an interview to *Musical America*, he stopped for concerts in Cleveland, where he informed the press that he was planning to write a new symphony. He continued to the West Coast, returned to New York, and left quickly for Europe. Dagmar followed him to Le Havre as a stowaway on the SS *Britannia*, arriving in Paris with only her pocketbook for baggage. Stravinsky, conducting in Brussels, avoided seeing her but answered a letter from her in a brutal manner accusing her of 'interfering with his life'. From Belgium he passed the problem on to Vera in Paris, asking her to 'take kefir to Dagmar and meet with her regarding money matters', presumably to pay for her passage back to the U.S. Another assignment for Vera on the same day was to escort Stravinsky's wife, Catherine, from a Paris hospital to their rue du Faubourg St-Honoré home.

A year later all was forgiven, and Dagmar resumed her role as Stravinsky's American concert manager. Once again Vera bore the brunt of the negotiations. Stravinsky asked her to telephone Dagmar and, since she spoke no French, to translate into German several pages answering her queries. Between October 1939 in Boston and Vera's arrival in New York three months later, Dagmar was Stravinsky's companion. Alexei Haieff described Stravinsky to me as entering an ultra-proper Boston hotel and in his resounding voice asking a dumbstruck receptionist if it was permitted to bring a woman to his room. During his Harvard lectures and music teaching he spent some weekends with Dagmar at the now demolished Navarro Hotel on 59th Street, New York, where, just before Vera's ship docked, he informed Dagmar that he planned to marry Vera as soon as their papers were in order. But he did not formally introduce the two women until the newlyweds were living in California. At first Vera refused to meet Dagmar, reminding Igor that they had already encountered each other in Paris. The collision finally occurred in Hollywood, where the two women spent an afternoon together in the Stravinsky home during the composer's convenient absence.

As late as October 1944 Vera's diary reveals that on the 2nd of the month they had dined at Dagmar's with Greta Garbo, Gayelord Hauser and the Artur Rubinsteins. The following week the Stravinskys attended a party at the Rubinsteins' with Ronald Colman, Jascha Heifetz, Erich Maria Remarque and Dagmar. Two days later Vera's diary says that Dagmar had phoned to say that she and Remarque had been on a binge and that Remarque had confided, 'he loves *you* very much'.[25]

Stravinsky remained libidinous well into his eighties, as I realised sitting with him after midnight in a Tahitian nightclub where he leered at young hula dancers, lusting to grope them beneath their grass skirts. Unconcerned about this tropical temptation, Vera was already in bed asleep. More than any other woman he had known, she understood not only the ritualised love in *Les Noces* but also the sexual dynamism of *The Rite of Spring*. Stravinsky had in abundance what Bertrand Russell described as 'the crude, insistent passion that one must have in order to achieve anything'.

Though Vera's own connection with Stravinsky began as an extramarital augmentation, she was his lifetime love; on tour without her he nevertheless required what Elizabethans called 'ease flesh'. Vera suffered from this but somehow tolerated it, and in the late 1930s, she also continued to see, and sometimes to cohabit with, her old companion the Baron Fred Osten-Sacken.[26] In fact she spent the summers of 1936 and 1937 with him in Germany while Igor, in Paris and Monthoux, composed respectively *Jeu de cartes* and *Dumbarton Oaks* Concerto. On the 1937 occasion, Vera was two weeks late rejoining Igor in Paris, whereupon he left for Italy with Victoria

---

25 See the chapter 'The Hollywood Years'.
26 The Baron (1888-1974) had met Vera in 1908 when the two enrolled in the University of Berlin. He lived in Mexico during World War II and afterwards became a racehorse breeder in Lexington, Kentucky. He continued to visit Vera during my period in Hollywood, and I met his flights from Mexico and drove him to the Roosevelt Hotel on Hollywood Boulevard. It seems unlikely that he could have reasserted himself amorously at that late date. All of his last letters to Vera conclude with 'Ne quitte pas ce monde avant moi.' He died with a photograph of her by his bedside, framed in a beautifully carved cherry-wood triptych taken when she played Helen in the 1915 Moscow film *War and Peace*.

Ocampo who always seemed to be available. Vera followed him to Rome and continued to Naples en route to Positano.

Stravinsky's love for Vera is distinguished from his casual encounters by a *tendresse* most beautifully expressed in *Perséphone*, the piece she inspired, and especially in 'Sur ce lit elle repose'. He composed this *berceuse* for her in August 1933 while he was visiting his family in Voreppe and sent the manuscript to her in Paris together with a poem:[27]

> In memory of a summer of oppressive summer weeks
>
> when my dear Perséphone
>
> behind a shutter seeking cool and calm
>
> hiding from a crowd of friends, and humidity –
>
> and from the unavoidable, that she cannot hide from,
>
> rings of the phone –
>
> from morning on for the whole day
>
> snuggled in bed.

In spite of his extraneous amours, Stravinsky's love for Vera was abiding and continued to mature throughout their last years together.

———

The film *Coco Chanel & Igor Stravinsky* requires suspensions of disbelief, since no one could enact the part of the composer with any degree of verisimilitude. Jan Kounen, the director, chose an actor who physically and temperamentally was antithetical to the real person. Stravinsky's music on the soundtrack, the only reminder of the living man, has been intelligently related to the script, at least in the sense of being limited to the period of the film (1913–1921). The opening scene of *The Rite of Spring* premiere offers more of the score than expected and familiarises the viewer with passages such as the opening bassoon melody, which becomes a theme song associated

---

27 The original is in Russian.

with romantic moments throughout the film. Further, the chromatic harmonies of the quiet beginning of Part Two are recalled in the composer's mind again and again after he and Coco have recognised that they are in love. The violence of the music of the 'Glorification of the Chosen One' and the savagery of the 'Danse sacrale' accompanying the immolation scene broadly suggest the conflict in Stravinsky's private life. The only other music used extensively is from the piano duets that Stravinsky wrote for his children in 1917, intending to teach them to play through actual pieces of music rather than scales and fingering exercises.

By choosing *Les Cinq Doigts* (completed 18 February 1921) Kounen has unwittingly contributed to musicology. This opus was actually written at Bel Respiro when Coco and Igor were there together and was intended as piano lessons for her while he was rethinking the art of composing from the most elementary level. He could not dictate the opus to her, of course, but she was clearly the inspiration for this simple and lovely album piece, which forty years later he would arrange for fifteen instruments under the title *Eight Miniatures*. The simplicity of most of the melodies is childlike and may well have been designed for Coco to hum to herself. A musician may have perceived this, or perhaps its selection, or was it the work of the god of coincidence?

Kounen employs these pieces while Stravinsky gives his inamorata a piano lesson, showing her how to play the accompaniment part and softly playing the other part himself. This fits the scenario since the composer's young children have just been shown arriving at Bel Respiro. Here the piano itself becomes the principal fixture of the film but we are introduced to it by an inconceivable episode in which Chanel bursts into Stravinsky's studio while he is composing at the keyboard. Always the aggressor, she straddles him as if he were a horse and his lap the saddle, unbuttons his trousers and reaches for the pommel. Grunts and groans replace the now silent piano, but the lovers' positions are so awkward and precarious that the scene is not in the least erotic. Kounen's miscalculation is that the film *doppelgängers* are tall and big-boned, whereas the actual people were sufficiently diminutive and slender to have fit cosily into this position.

To a small extent, Kounen overcomes the obstacle of historical accuracy by ignoring it. The movie audience does not know that in reality the Stravinsky family was not received at Bel Respiro by the doyenne in September 1920. They moved there only after Chanel's departure for Biarritz with her Grand Duke Dmitri, who does not appear as a character in the film. Chanel cohabited at Bel Respiro with Stravinsky during their mutual acceptance of his family and relatives there beginning in January 1921. The film misattributes the exodus of the Stravinsky family to the Basque country to a decision by Stravinsky's wife, who was totally dependent on her husband and incapable of such combative stances. Her portrayal is the film's most egregious mistake: the audience learns near the start that she is suffering from tuberculosis but a little later on she is shown brazenly asking Chanel whether she feels any guilt. This last word is so remote from Coco's vocabulary that she replies with a simple 'No'. Later Catherine asks her husband if he has made love to Chanel and, perfectly in character, he says nothing, which shows at least some directorial insight.

Kounen has carefully observed certain details of Stravinsky's daily routine but has missed the fact, for instance, that at this date he wore a pince-nez, not spectacles. Mads Mikkelsen's Stravinsky is languorous, even indolent, totally unlike Stravinsky the man. The disruption of the original 1913 *Rite of Spring* fails to enrage the impersonator. The real Stravinsky's electrically quick physical and mental movements, hypersensitive facial expressions and piercingly intelligent eyes are nowhere evoked by the phlegmatic actor.

In spite of the bassoon solo being phrased in the wrong places, the film can be recommended for its photography, beautiful colours, and the escape it offers to a more gracious, earlier era.

CHAPTER 13
The Hollywood Years 1940–1969

Que devient-t-il, ce cher Ygor Feodorovitch,
égaré dans cette Amérique puérile?

René Auberjonois, Lausanne, January 1941

We hope that the stupidity of this country will not kill you.

Jane Heap (*The Little Review*)
Telegram to Stravinsky on his arrival in the United States,
6 January 1925

Helmut Dantine[1] to Nicolas Nabokov, 1951:

Who is that man? His face looks so familiar.
N. N.: *Stravinsky.*
H. D.: *That's what I thought, but what is he doing in Hollywood?*

In the early 1940s the city in which Stravinsky would reside longer
than in St Petersburg was famously described by Thomas Mann as

---

1   The German-born actor is best known for his film roles in *Casablanca* and *Mission to Moscow.*

possessing a more interesting cultural and intellectual life than either Munich or Paris in the 1920s, thanks to the influx of refugee writers, artists and musicians. He may have been referring to himself and his brother Heinrich, but also to Theodor Adorno, Bertolt Brecht, Franz Werfel, Alfred Döblin, Lion Feuchtwanger and Emil Ludwig; to the Bauhaus architects Richard Neutra and Rudolph Schindler; to film makers and actors too numerous to name; and especially to Schoenberg and Stravinsky.

The Stravinskys had boarded the SS *Seminole* in New York bound for Galveston with stops in Miami and New Orleans. Vera's diary: 'At Miami we taxied around the city, the beach, the Seminole Village, and an alligator farm.' When the Stravinskys took me to these same sites on our return from Havana years later, what most impressed the composer was a caption's claim that the oldest of the alligators was born during Dante's lifetime. A letter from Vera concludes: 'The Gulf of Mexico is an unforgettable blue, and the night breeze is soft and perfumed.' Stravinsky describes the boat as 'bad' and the ocean as 'choppy'.

When the Texas port turned out not in any way to resemble the French Riviera the Stravinskys had imagined, they fled to the City of Angels, reaching it on 23 May 1940. They were met by Dr Alexis Kall, a Stravinsky classmate at the University of St Petersburg. Kall had been the composer's secretary and translator in Boston until 13 January 1940, when Vera de Bosset, the composer's fiancée, arrived in New York from Genoa. In Los Angeles they lived in Kall's home at 143 South Grammercy until moving on 6 June to a rented house at 124 South Swall Drive, near the Thomas Manns on North Swall Drive.

Within a few days Russian refugees began to call on the Stravinskys, but their first dinner guest was Otto Klemperer, the conductor of the Los Angeles Philharmonic who had been with them in Boston only weeks before. Next to appear were the Adolphe Bolms, who became their *ciceroni*, driving them to Big Sur, the Monterey peninsula, San Francisco, the nearby redwood forests and Yosemite National Park. Stravinsky had known 'Adya' Bolm since 1910 when he created the role of Kastchei in *The Firebird*, and his wife Beata since 1916 when she escorted Nijinsky from Bern across wartime France and on to a steamship for New York, where the Ballets Russes awaited its star dancer to launch its American tour. Beata, a petite Swedish woman raised in Persia, proved to be a rich source for Diaghilev history. She became the Stravinskys' secretary shortly after they moved into their Wetherly Drive home, remaining for six years until her husband's death in 1951. She was also a frequent luncheon guest to whom the Stravinskys continued their hospitality for the remainder of her life.

By the end of May Stravinsky received test pressings of *The Rite of Spring* with the New York Philharmonic, recorded a few weeks earlier. In her acknowledgement of the arrival of the discs from the Columbia Records producer Moses Smith, Vera complained that the orchestral players had insulted her husband during the recording sessions, mocking the dissonances and the difficulties of the changing metres, an indication of the backward state of American culture at the time. Goddard Lieberson, the producer of the record, described this disruptive behaviour to me,[2] as did William Vacchiano, a member of the orchestra and my Juilliard teacher. Lieberson would become a close friend of Igor and Vera and at one time was named, along with me, as a co-trustee of their estate.

On 7 June the Stravinskys dined at the home of the actor Edward G. Robinson, an old friend of the composer who became the principal witness at his U.S. citizenship ceremony in 1945, during which it was discovered that Robinson himself was not a citizen, having jumped a Russian ship in New York during World War I. The other dinner guests were Marlene Dietrich, also a friend from the European past, and Erich Maria Remarque, author of *All Quiet on the Western Front*, who fell in love with Vera at first sight and saw her often thereafter. When I finally met Remarque in Berlin in the 1960s with his then wife Paulette Goddard, formerly Mrs Charlie Chaplin, embers of the romance with Vera were still evident.

On Igor's birthday, 18 June, he and Vera attended a service in the Russian Orthodox Church on Micheltorena Street facing the home of Peter Yates, whose Neutra-designed roof would become the venue for the renowned concert series 'Evenings on the Roof'. The Stravinskys

---

2   I had met him years before meeting Stravinsky.

were escorted to the church by the popular actor Vladimir Sokolov and his wife Lisa who lived only a few blocks from the Stravinskys' future home at 1260 North Wetherly Drive. Lisa and Vera co-founded the La Boutique gallery on nearby La Cienega Boulevard, featuring Surrealist and pre-Columbian art. The couples saw each other frequently until Lisa's sudden death in June 1948 from hepatitis, which she had contracted in Mexico while travelling there with the Stravinskys. When the widower, typecast as a Mexican outlaw in countless westerns, began to inject some of his cinema persona into his private life, their friendship dissolved.

The fall of France to Germany in June 1940 cast a pall over the summer. Igor and Vera went daily to newsreel theatres, emerging with grim faces, Vera tearful at the scenes of families fleeing Paris on foot (as Irène Némirovsky so poignantly describes in *Suite Française*). Vera soon purchased a 'goose-turd green' jalopy, in Aldous Huxley's words; she passed her driving test on 28 June. The same 1930s automobile was still in use at the beginning of my incursion (1948), followed by other vehicles of which I remember only a maroon Buick and a black Jaguar.

The restaurants most frequented by the Stravinskys in the early Los Angeles period were The Brown Derby, Mike Romanoff's in Beverly Hills, Mischa Auer's Russian café and Bit of Sweden, the latter two on Sunset Boulevard quite close to the Stravinsky house. When I lived with them, we dined most often at Melody Lane, a modest establishment that lacked a liquor licence; the composer brought in thermos bottles of Bordeaux ('*grap* juice', he explained truthfully to the suspicious waiters). In a later period the Stravinskys dined at least once a week at Steve Crane's (Mr Lana Turner's) Polynesian restaurant, Luau, in Beverly Hills.

Igor, Vera and Max Reinhardt were invited to dinner at the home of the composer Erich Korngold and at Eddie Robinson's a few days later with Dietrich, Remarque and the leading film composer Max Steiner. Igor had met him in 1935 at a reception by Louis B. Mayer where the composer was less than warmly received thanks to his much publicised remark referring to film music as 'wallpaper'. During this early period the Stravinskys often saw the Baron de Meyer, famed for his photo portraits of Nijinsky. After Pearl Harbor they were horrified to learn that Meyer, whose baronial title, bestowed by the King of Saxony at the request of his cousin Edward VII of England, had been deported as an enemy alien.

In the first half of July, Stravinsky worked on the last movement of his Symphony in C. Vera's Bastille Day letter to Ira Belline[3] informs her of the turmoil of her uncle's life:

> I am writing this in a lawyer's office. We have spent an entire month sitting in the same place, making several visits each week, each lasting half a day. We are trying to get permits to remain in this country and visas to go to Mexico and return to the U.S. on the Mexican quota. Regulations are very strict now and all sorts of permits are necessary for exits and re-entries, but we are also fearful of being stuck in Mexico. We will not go by airplane since it takes fifteen hours. The train takes four days and will give us an opportunity to rest from all the visits, the parties, the chauffeuring, and the telephone calls. Distances in Los Angeles are enormous, and I drive as much as 150 kilometers a day. Igor is very nervous, always waiting for news from France and reading newspapers.

The Stravinskys left by train for Mexico City on 18 July and arrived on the 22nd, four days before his first concert there. Vera noted on 20 July 1940:

> After a long wait at El Paso, the train creaks across the Rio Grande bridge and stops at a miserable station, where Mexicans with guitars, babies, and bundles crowd on board. Next to the station is a café, the Caballero, and in front of it, in the middle of the street, a dead cow. A gendarme tells Igor that he does not have all the necessary papers and sends him to the

---

3   Ira Beliankina (Belline) moved from France to Tangier at the end of World War II. She became famous through Baron de Meyer's photograph of her 'supreme beauty' used by Elizabeth Arden in advertising her cosmetic products. Ira remained in Tangier for several years as an antique dealer, then moved to a villa outside Marrakesh, a gift from her good friend Barbara Hutton.

Immigration Office. I go along since I will not stay in the train alone - it could suddenly leave. Finally everything is in order and we depart, stopping at even the smallest village, where Indians come to the windows of the train to sell things and to beg. An endless desert. Once, three horsemen with braided hair and solferino pink shirts ride up alongside us trailing clouds of dust. Every hour or so all night long, the train stops, then, after a long time, jerks and rattles ahead.

On their return Vera describes the trip more fully in a letter to Ira:

No one told us that reading was impossible on that terrible train because of constant and violent shaking, and that the food in the restaurant car would be inedible. After the frontier, the hot, airless train filled up with families of shrieking Mexican children. It was not possible to lie down, and scarcely possible even to sit on the bench-like wooden seats. But the sights were unforgettable: the Indians on mules riding in a dry river-bed; the terrible poverty of the villages; the big buzzards with white necks sitting on crooked telephone poles; the old cars filled with women and naked children: there are so many children in this country! At the stations, instead of the expected small villages, we saw only one or two huts in open fields with cactus. The names of most stations were barely legible on rough boards covered with white paint. We rode through deserts all day and the first few small stations appeared only toward evening. In spite of the terrible heat, we left the train at many of the stations. We saw people sitting at tables in darkness, except for candles, eating bread and drinking tequila. At some stations merchandise was piled up and at all of them dirty children in tatters were selling fruit, drinks, and chickens. We bought mangoes, which I ate for the first time. Igor was enticed by the bananas, which really tasted much better than any we ever had in Europe. If we hadn't heard that we shouldn't drink tap water here, or eat raw fruit, I would have bought everything that I saw at those stations. When the train started up again no

warning was given, so we remained close to the steps. During
the daytime stops, horsemen came near the train. They wore
pink shirts, green or brown trousers, big sombreros, spurs on
their boots, and some of them had lassoes in their hands. What
we saw was real life and not something prepared for export.
On the third day we arrived in Guadalajara, a fragrant city full
of flowers; perfumes are made here. Since the train stops there
for one and a half hours, we took a taxi to see the city and the
cathedral. The air was wonderfully sweet, in spite of the dirt
and dust. At the Mexico City station we were met by Ricardo
Ortega, the orchestra manager, by Carlos Chávez and his
wife, and by a crowd of photographers. At the Hotel Reforma,
photographers and interviewers invaded us all morning.[4]

Stravinsky told an interviewer:

The Mexican people have a musical heritage; I had proof of it
this afternoon, rehearsing the Orquesta Sinfónica. Paul Valéry
explained everything biologically. He said that the writers,
musicians, or painters who made his glands work were the
people who really produce the sensations of those arts, and so
these Mexican musicians put my glands to work.

Turning to Alfonso Reyes,[5] Stravinsky said that his book *Visión
de Anáhuac* taught him more about Mexico than all the histories
because the ideas were expressed with such harmony. 'That is the
great difficulty in all art, to put ideas in their necessary order.' Vera's
letter to Ira continues:

Mexico City itself does not make a great impression, but the view
around it, the mountains, the air and the sun are extraordinary.
We were warned about food, water, and the altitude, but were

---

4   During his first days in Mexico, Stravinsky met Silvestre Revueltas. The encounter was
     clandestine because Chávez was jealous of him. Revueltas died only three months later,
     and Stravinsky did not hear *Sensemayá* until Leonard Bernstein conducted it with *The Rite
     of Spring* on the opening programme in June 1966 at the New York Stravinsky festival.
5   One of the leading Spanish–American writers of his time, 1889–1959.

not affected by them. The next day we went to see the cathedral
and the museum, where we were repelled by the characteristic
expression of the Aztec sculpture.[6] In the nineteenth-century
section a guard asked me to sit on a stool and put my fingers
on a harpsichord. We then went to Chapultepec Park with its
old trees. How much history they have witnessed! We also
visited Maximilian's Palace, but toward evening felt tired.
Reyes arrived and took us to his house for café-au-lait and an
omelette. Mexicans do not eat a heavy meal in the evening. It
is said that Reyes abducted his wife on a horse, supposedly a
custom here.

In a subsequent letter to Ira, Vera says that on re-entering the U.S.
they were detained at the border for three hours, filling in forms and
submitting to medical examinations. Back home in a frazzled state,
they spent their first morning hiring a cook, Bessie Nebraska, as well
as completing applications for American citizenship. Ten days later
they were horrified to read of the pickaxe murder of Leon Trotsky in
the same part of the Mexico City they had so recently left.

The Stravinskys soon began to attend concerts at Hollywood Bowl
where, on 30 August, Igor conducted a semi-staged performance
of *The Firebird* choreographed by Bolm. A telegram from Michel
Fokine in New York contested anyone's right to use choreography
other than the one he had established for Diaghilev in 1910. The
composer answered in character: 'This is my music and I'll do with
it as I please.' But when Fokine died a few months later, Stravinsky
telegraphed to his widow: 'Accept my heartfelt condolences in your
great grief. Am shocked and mourning my collaborator who gave the
world unforgettable visions.'

In still another letter to Ira, Vera conveys her first impressions of
Hollywood life:

---

6   This indicates that the Stravinskys had not seen Aztec and other pre-Columbian art in
     Europe.

> I like California for its beautiful landscapes, the sea, the
> mountains, the orange groves, and the cactus desert. But the
> taste of food is questionable. Everything that grows is irrigated.
> By now I am accustomed to the tastelessness of the vegetables
> and fruit. Americans serve their food decorated, cutting up
> fruit into little squares and balls. I spend much of my time
> fighting off invitations; we have several each day.

At the beginning of September, Igor and Vera enjoyed a holiday at
Eddie Robinson's ranch. On the last day of the month Vera's Russian
nameday was celebrated with her compatriots, the Remizovs,
the Bolms, the Sokolovs, the Bertensons, the Akim Tamiroffs and
Bronislava Nijinska. Sergei Bertenson had been Tchaikovsky's
physician on his deathbed and had written a biography of Musorgsky.[7]
As Sergei Rachmaninov's doctor in Hollywood, Bertenson arranged a
reconciliatory meeting between this fellow refugee and Stravinsky. In
his late teens, Stravinsky had told his Pavlovka uncle, Nicolai Yelachich,
that he would 'do better to hear and get to know Rachmaninov's piano
concerto than my sonata'. But Stravinsky's admiration for the author
of the famous Prelude came to an end in 1914 after Rachmaninov
happened to see the score of *The Rite of Spring* at the Berlin office
of the Éditions Russes de Musique, the publisher of both composers.
Sergei Vasilievich suggested rightly (in my opinion) that the last two
bars of the ballet could be improved upon, which enraged Stravinsky.

In 1942 Rachmaninov told Bertenson, 'I know how much Igor
Fyodorovich has always disliked my compositions... I'm not sure I
can invite him and his wife to my house, which I would love to do,
because I don't know how he would receive my invitation. Would you
be so kind as to send out a feeler?' Bertenson reported that he called
Vera Arturovna, whose immediate response was, 'Delighted'. Pleased
to have the old barrier broken, the composers chatted all evening

---

7   Stravinsky was naturally interested in the controversy of *Tchaikovsky's Suicide: Myth and
Reality*. He would have been fascinated by Alexander Poznansky's brilliant analysis of the
subject, having been present at the great composer's funeral as well as at the first two
performances of his *Pathétique* Symphony. He was close to Tchaikovsky's brother Modest
but did not like him. Stravinsky's opinions of the Bertenson brothers were also ambivalent.

about managers, concert bureaus and ASCAP royalties; music was not discussed. When Stravinsky returned the invitation, he incidentally mentioned his fondness for honey, and within a few days Sergei Vasilievich purchased a very fine jar of the nectar and personally delivered it, climbing up the two flights of stone stairs from the street and leaving it at the Stravinsky door during the middle of the night (they heard him). On 17 and 18 July Rachmaninov played at Hollywood Bowl and on the next day dined with the Stravinskys and Artur Rubinstein. Vera reported that Madame Rachmaninov tried to pry some of Stravinsky's thoughts about life in America from him. After learning that he showered daily, she said to her husband, 'You see, Sergei, Stravinsky showers every day, so why don't you?'

An important digression here is required since Artur Rubinstein was not only very close to Stravinsky but was his longest-time friend in Los Angeles. Legendary or not, an anecdote marks the beginning of this connection. Responding to a plea from Diaghilev to attend the June 1914 *Nightingale* in London, Stravinsky went to the Drury Lane Theatre in a taxi. Deposited at the stage door and forgetting about the high step to the street, he stumbled and fell on the pavement from which he was helped to his feet by that greatest of music critics, Corno di Bassetto (George Bernard Shaw).

At the conclusion of the *Nightingale* performance Rubinstein and his Polish compatriots - the violinist Paul Kochanski and Karol Szymanowski - made their way backstage to congratulate the composer. In high spirits, because of the triumphant reception of the opera and because they all spoke Russian, they went off to dine together, ending in the early morning hours as a most convivial quartet. Igor and Artur continued to enjoy each other's company during Stravinsky's Anglet-Bayonne-Biarritz period (1921-4), and especially during a June 1921 visit to London for the premiere of *Symphonies of Wind Instruments* where photographs show them frolicking with Ballets Russes ballerinas on English lawns.

In 1919 and 1921 Stravinsky composed two pieces for Rubinstein and in 1925 a transcript from *Pulcinella* of excerpts for Kochanski, precursory of a whole genre of piano-violin duos created by the composer for his concert tours with Sam Dushkin in the 1930s.

(Stravinsky also played the piano at the premiere of the Kochanski piece.) After Kochanski's untimely death in 1934 his widow, Zosia, remained an intimate of Stravinsky's Russian circles in Paris and America, and Rubinstein continued to support her financially.

In September 1925 Stravinsky joined Rubinstein at the Venice Biennale and dined with him at the Palazzo Contarini dal Zaffo, home of the Princesse de Polignac (*née* Winaretta Singer) and former residence of the notorious Lord Beauchamp (the model for the Laurence Olivier part in the *Brideshead Revisited* film). Since Igor had last seen Artur in Paris in the 1930s, the pianist had acquired a Beverly Hills estate. I met him there in June 1949 when the Stravinskys took me to one of his Sunday afternoon concert extravaganzas. A platform had been erected on the garden lawn on which he played a Mozart concerto with a small orchestra for an audience comprised almost exclusively of movie stars recognisable even without their makeup.

In June 1919 Stravinsky dedicated his Piano-Rag-Music to Rubinstein. This brief but richly innovative piece – with tone-clusters, jazz rhythms, an improvisatory style and the partial dispensing with bar lines[8] – puzzled the pianist, and he never played it. Perhaps to compensate for this failure he commissioned the piano arrangement of Three Movements from *Petrushka* and rewarded Stravinsky with the most magnanimous cachet he would ever receive: $5,000 (in 1921). Rubinstein attempted to play Stravinsky's Three Movements in public only once, at a concert in the 1930s in what would become Elvis Presley's hometown: Memphis, Tennessee.[9] In September 1956 the Stravinskys saw Artur almost daily in Venice, walking with him to a Segovia concert and attending movies at the film festival on the Lido. Celebs were seated hierarchically, with the Rubinsteins behind

---

8   No publication in Stravinsky musicology would have pleased the composer more than the Practical Performing Edition of the Piano-Rag-Music by Mark DeVoto that appeared in May 2010. DeVoto adds bar lines throughout, adjusts balkins and provides courtesy accidentals. This new version facilitates performance and makes the piece available to pianists who, like Rubinstein, have found Stravinsky's original score difficult to decipher.

9   The Three Movements has become a required piece in piano competitions throughout the world. While composing it, Stravinsky had interrupted his work in the third movement at the end of a page of the manuscript and on resuming work forgot to provide the sequence of the motive before the page turn; the music was published in that amputated condition and has still not been corrected in 2013.

Maria Callas, Callas behind the Stravinskys and me, Gina Lollobrigida in front of us, and a photo of her naked gluteus medius from her famous film about a hundred yards beyond the audience. Perhaps Rubinstein's balmiest years were during the period of Vladimir Horowitz's[10] seclusion in the 1950s and 1960s. After his comeback I remember Goddard saying, 'Artur isn't so happy anymore.' I still prefer Rubinstein's Chopin to that of any other pianist and I liked the man, his panache, and even his gargantuan ego. Of the Hollywood performer tycoons – Heifetz, Szigeti,[11] Josef Hofmann, Piatigorsky, Rubinstein and Rachmaninov – the last name will endure the longest because he was also a major composer.

In October 1940 Vera began taking English lessons from Anita Loos (*Gentleman Prefer Blondes*) and giving Russian lessons to Benny Goodman in preparation for a government-sponsored goodwill trip to Moscow. In the meantime, Igor visited film studios, starting with Disney. After seeing *Fantasia* for the first and last time on 12 October Vera wrote, 'Igor is horrified by the bad taste. Deems Taylor talks nonsense, and Stokowski cavorts up and down a staircase bathed in red light.' On the 14th Igor and Vera reaffirmed their marital vows in a Russian church wedding – crowns held overhead – and dined afterward with the priest. A few days later they attended a performance by the Fokine Ballet Company, and on the 22nd they dined with Italo Montemezzi, whose *L'amore dei tre re* was in the repertoire at the Metropolitan Opera and had been nationally broadcast.

---

10 It is not generally known that Horowitz, who had known Stravinsky in Paris, made a private recording of the Three Movements in the U.S. and sent it to the composer asking if it could be released. The answer was a polite 'No'.

11 During World War II Josef Szigeti, probably the closest friend of Béla Bartók in America, kept Stravinsky informed about the Hungarian composer. Stravinsky was particularly grateful when his friend Germain Prévost, the violist, played the *Élégie* (1944) for Bartók in his New York apartment, and to hear from Szigeti that the Hungarian composer had liked the piece very much. Fritz Reiner, also close to Bartók, wrote to Stravinsky on 17 January 1943 that Bartók had attended his performance a few days earlier of the *Chant du rossignol* and declared it the best performance he had ever heard. It was the first performance I ever heard and the only time that I saw Bartók, though he was said often to be seen eating at the Horn and Hardart on West 57th Street. Wanda Szigeti and Vera Stravinsky had been close friends in Europe. We occasionally dined with the Szigetis at their ocean-front home in Palos Verdes. The violinist was a cultivated man whose room displayed fine paintings and intriguing artefacts including letters to him from Rilke. Stravinsky once remarked that Szigeti was the only violinist who could play in a telephone booth.

Stravinsky conducted the premiere of his Symphony in C on 7 November in Chicago. The difference between the first two movements of the Symphony, written in Europe, and the last two, written in the U.S., was criticised as killing the concinnity and altering the mood between the two halves. The subtlety at the beginning of the third movement is in reusing the rhythm and figuration at the end of the second movement: a masterstroke.

Stravinsky's social life in Chicago proved to be hectic, a result in part of his long-time friendship with the composer John Alden Carpenter.[12] Vera and Igor frequented the Chicago Art Museum to see *La Grande Jatte* but they retreated quickly from Massenet's *Manon* at the Lyric Opera. On the 17th they took the train to Cincinnati and more performances of the Symphony in C. In New York they met Brigitta Hartwig (a.k.a. Vera Zorina, Mrs George Balanchine and in succession Mrs Goddard Lieberson) with whom they 'went to Harlem to hear swing bands'. Stravinsky also accepted a commission from Lucia Chase to reorchestrate dances from *The Sleeping Beauty* for a miniature ballet, *Bluebird.* Before Christmas the vagabond composer and his wife returned to Minneapolis for concerts. A newspaper interview with Vera preserves their favourable impressions of the city and its orchestra, rehearsed by the great Dimitri Mitropoulos. On the return to New York, Stravinsky and Balanchine worked on their forthcoming ballet *Balustrade* (Stravinsky's Violin Concerto). Arthur Sachs escorted them to a New Year's Eve party, and on New Year's Day they dined in the St Regis Hotel at a table next to Igor's good friend Charlie Chaplin.

Early in January 1941 the Stravinskys were in Boston, where Igor conducted three concerts featuring the Symphony in C and discovered numerous copyists' errors in the orchestra parts that Nadia Boulanger helped him to correct at the Gerry's Landing home of the Edward Forbes family. On the return to New York, Stravinsky conducted the

---

12 On 12 February 1950, during the Stravinskys' automobile trip to New York via Key West, Igor – having miscalculated the costs in travellers' cheques – was obliged to hire a boat to take him to visit Carpenter on Sanibel Island in order to borrow money from him. The Stravinskys were short of the same substance again on the road north but were able to cash a cheque in Palm Beach. Here they disliked the faux-Mediterranean architecture but admired the beautiful hedges and the shittimwood (sapodilla) trees.

premiere and two subsequent performances of *Balustrade* and, at a reception afterwards, saw his friend Nicolas Nabokov for the first time in America. Meanwhile, Vera and Serge Sudeykin met for the last time while Igor completed his orchestration of the four *Sleeping Beauty* excerpts. At the end of the month he played a new Tango for the duo-pianists Babin and Vronsky, who became close Stravinsky friends. Igor entrusted Victor to arrange the piece for two pianos.

Vera describes their return to Los Angeles:

> After San Bernardino, we see mimosa, orange groves, lemon trees, all in bloom, and small houses drowning in roses. At the Château Marmont, 8221 Sunset Boulevard, we have nice rooms – cosy, in good taste – and are very pleased. Igor slept badly, and today he has to conduct two rehearsals with the Los Angeles Orchestra.

The programme included Capriccio, *The Firebird*, *Jeu de cartes* and Symphony in C, but this last was dropped from the San Diego concert. On the 21st they moved from the Château Marmont to the Hollywood home of Earnest Andersson, who became Stravinsky's pupil for the next two years. After introducing himself to Stravinsky at New York's Café des Artistes as an inventor and would-be composer, this prospective pupil asked Sol Hurok to draw up a contract for lessons at $25 each. The first of these took place on 27 January 1941, at Andersson's home where the Stravinskys were temporarily staying. Subsequent lessons took place in Stravinsky's studio, no fewer than 134 of them in 1941, more than that in 1942, and in 1943 until Andersson's death that June. Since foreign royalties were blocked by the war and guest-conducting in America had nearly ceased to exist, Andersson was Stravinsky's only source of income. Stravinsky's friends attributed his change of parlance from Francophone to Anglophone to Andersson. The music of his Stravinsky-edited symphony, now in the UCLA library, is disappointing.

In early February the Stravinskys found 'a small white house on a hill at 1260 N. Wetherly Drive'. On 2 March, the beginning of Lent, they gave a second *Panikhida* service for the composer's first wife in the Russian church. Shortly after moving they discovered that a mansion on the same hill 200 yards below theirs was the residence of the Baroness Catherine d'Erlanger whom they had last seen in her Hamilton House in Green Park, London – Lord Byron's former home. She, not Chanel, had paid for Diaghilev's funeral service in Venice and burial in the Reparto Greco on San Michele Island. The Stravinskys had not been close to her in Europe, but as Hollywood neighbours they saw her almost daily, dining frequently in each other's homes. Since Stravinsky could not be left alone for fear of interruptions from telephone and doorbell, this former lady-in-waiting to Queen Victoria often replaced Vera as his answering service and babysitter.

Movie stars frequented the Baroness's home, many of them for her midnight pool parties. Cole Porter was a regular visitor, as he had been years earlier at her Venetian palazzo where Stravinsky had first met him. His wife, Linda, wanting Cole to become a 'serious' composer, asked Stravinsky to accept him as a pupil, but this did not happen. The 1919 marriage of the popular songwriter had quickly revealed that the partners were sexually incompatible, though they remained together for thirty-four years. The Stravinskys knew that Porter had been the lover of Boris Kochno, the librettist of *Mavra*.[13] A 1925 letter from Cole to Boris says, 'I love you so much that I think only of you – I see only you, and I dream only of the moment when we will be reunited.' Gavin Lambert's biography of Porter tells us that a pillow in his New York Waldorf Towers apartment was embroidered with the Baroness's motto, 'Never Explain – Never Complain.'

On 1 November the Stravinskys gave a house-warming party for the Baroness, the Robinsons, the Max Reinhardts, the Basil

---

13   Stravinsky had been especially close to Kochno in the autumn of 1921 when he became the composer's messenger to Vera in London during the rehearsals for Diaghilev's *Sleeping Beauty* revival. In 1922 Stravinsky became even closer to Kochno when they worked together on *Mavra* in a *pension* in Biarritz. Encountering Stravinsky in New York during his 1937 tour, Kochno told him that he was living with Sudeykin, who later visited Stravinsky in the Sulgrave Hotel. Pleading destitution, Sudeykin received a generous sum from Stravinsky. By then the painter had married the Metropolitan Opera soprano Jeanne Palmer and the pair lived part-time in Woodstock, New York, at first with the Diaghilev dancer Alexis Kozlov. Long after Sudeykin's death in 1946 his widow visited Vera Stravinsky several times in New York, hoping to sell art works by Sudeykin to her. (See *Dearest Bubushkin*, Thames and Hudson, 1984, and Sotheby's *Collection Boris Kochno*, October 1991, Monaco.)

Rathbones, the Arthur Sachses, the Man Rays, Richard Hammond[14] and his companion George Martin, Sir Charles Mendl (the British consul in Los Angeles) and Elizabeth Arden, who brought news of Ira Belline. The menu in Vera's hand survives: cold borscht with piroshki, cold duck with cranberries and salad, sorbets in a pineapple, Turkish coffee and cognacs, eight bottles of champagne.

A composition pupil of Boulanger, Dick Hammond sponsored special events for the League of Composers in New York, notably Stokowski's productions of *Die glückliche Hand* and *The Rite of Spring*. Dick and George, who lived next door to Stokowski, a block away on a higher hill from the Stravinskys, became their closest friends in Venice in the summers of the 1950s, dining with them regularly.[15] A few days following the housewarming party, Igor and Vera drove to the Sachs home in Mendocino. Stravinsky had been composing *Danses concertantes* in the intervening months and wanted uninterrupted time to complete it.

In April 1941 Stravinsky finally heard from his children in France and Switzerland, followed by a succession of cables from his elder son requesting money; Stravinsky wrote to Werner Reinhart for help in paying the $3,000 bond required by the Swiss government for every refugee entering the country. A deeply upsetting letter from a friend in Paris informed the composer that Soulima had given a successful concert in the Salle Gaveau in December 1940, thereby branding himself as a Collaborator. Further, on 19 January 1943, he accompanied the singer Georgette Denys on a programme of 'contemporary German music from Reger to Orff and Egk'.

On the morning of 7 December 1941 the Stravinskys' gardener, Dmitri Stepanovich Mirov, called to discuss flowers for the garden, adding, just before recradling his phone: 'By the way, the Japanese bombed Pearl Harbor this morning.' From this day until August 1945, Vera's diaries follow the war closely and Igor drew maps that he attached to walls with pins marking the veering positions of the

---

14 Hammond was introduced to Stravinsky by Rudolph Ganz in 1922 in the composer's Pleyel Studio at 22, rue de Rochechouart, Paris.
15 'The Hammonds' attended the pre-memorial service for Stravinsky in New York on the evening of his death, 6 April 1971.

opposing armies and navies. He also purchased an American flag, which he hoisted in front of his home on national holidays throughout the war.

A roster of the Stravinskys' movie-star friends and neighbours in Hollywood could begin with Natalie Wood (the actress and former ward of Orson Welles, who introduced her when she was six years old to Stravinsky, at the time he was composing music intended for Welles's film *Jane Eyre*). Ms Wood enjoyed speaking Russian with the Stravinskys during teatime visits in the 1960s. Cinema royalty were regularly on exhibit at Artur Rubinstein's lawn parties. On the day after their arrival from France in June 1948, the composer's younger son and wife were taken to one of these splurges 'so that they could see real live movie stars', who turned out to be Clark Gable, Nelson Eddy and Cole Porter. Balanchine's friendship with Fred Astaire[16] and Ginger Rogers soon brought them into the Stravinsky circle. Having known Greta Garbo in Paris, Vera was sought after for introductions to the reclusive star by her numerous sororal admirers, but the health-food fanatic, with the appropriate appellation Gayelord Hauser, the 'uncrowned queen of Taormina', monopolised her attention. The Stravinskys dined alone with Garbo in their home from time to time, but Stravinsky's principal friends in moviedom were Alfred Hitchcock, Ernst Lubitsch, Preston Sturges, Max Reinhardt and, above all, Jean Renoir (*La Grande Illusion*), a friend from Paris days with whom they dined at least once a month. Dinnertime regulars included Sir Charles Mendl[17] and his wife, Elsie de Wolfe,[18] Man Ray, Fernand Léger and Eugene Berman.

In 1942 the Stravinskys became friendly with the novelist Emil Ludwig, who fell in love with Vera and sent affectionately inscribed

---

16 I knew his daughter, Ava, in the 1960s through her friend and our next-door neighbour, Cynthia Conroy. At that time Astaire, infatuated with Kim Novak and staying with her in Carmel during the filming of Hitchcock's *Vertigo*, compensated Ava for his long absence with a gift of a new Brit convertible in which she took Cynthia and me for outings on Mulholland Drive.

17 Sir Charles Mendl had been press attaché at the British Embassy in Paris. In 1926 he married the American interior decorator, Elsie de Wolfe, and after her death married Yvonne Reilly, a ravishing young woman when I met her with him in Paris in May 1952.

18 Anita Loos describes Lady Mendl as 'a sort of eighteenth-century cockatoo with a voice to match'.

copies of his books to her together with a crate of parrots for Igor; one of the flock flew to freedom when the housekeeper unpacked them. Parrots had intrigued Stravinsky during his visits to Mexico. Vera visited floral nurseries at least once a week, and on discovering that a species of pale pink geranium was named 'Igor Stravinsky' she purchased two or three plants to place around the parrot coop, whose inhabitants had propagated to forty by the time of my arrival. Stravinsky's favourite, Popka, was often given dining-table privileges, perching on Stravinsky's left shoulder and feeding directly from his extruded tongue. The parrot period came to an end in the early 1950s and was replaced by an obsession with hummingbirds. Stravinsky became fascinated by the tiny, gentle creatures beating their wings like helicopters not moving outside his window. He had somehow trained them to eat honey from his hands.

During this period Igor composed the *Elephant Polka*. In February Vera read Vladimir Nabokov's *The Luzhin Defense* to her husband. But the event of the month was the composer's registration for defence work. In March (1942) Léonide Massine petitioned Stravinsky to compose a Donizetti ballet. He purchased a score of *Lucia di Lammermoor* and listened to a Met Opera broadcast. A sheaf of sketches for this soon-abandoned project survives. Later, during my period, Lily Pons, who had sung the title role, took coaching lessons from Stravinsky for European performances in the title role of his *Nightingale*. Vera's diary records that Stravinsky was repeatedly invited to compose music for films and once spent four hours dickering with Louis B. Mayer over a commission.

June 1942 was more active. After a vacation with the Bolms at Arrowhead Lake, Igor retained lawyer Aaron Sapiro to contest a pop arrangement of the *Berceuse* from *The Firebird*. Stravinsky lost the case in court when a musicologist demonstrated that the original was a Russian folk tune. The attachment to Sapiro continued for eighteen years of ongoing legal battles with publishers, tax collectors and accountants, Stravinsky being litigious by nature. Sapiro defended him selflessly, accepting money only if the verdict was in the composer's favour. During my first decade in Hollywood, the attorney and his accountant congregated at the Stravinsky home at least once every fortnight. Sapiro, in his seventies, was crusty and contentious, partly because of constant pain from rheumatoid arthritis that had gnarled his fingers and knuckles. His provincial manners belied his celebrity status: he was known nationwide as the lawyer who had won an historic case against Henry Ford for anti-Semitic remarks in his book *The International Jew*, forcing a public apology.

When Stravinsky routinely sent *The Rake's Progress* libretto to Sapiro, he trenchantly noted the flaws and weaknesses and was the only advance reader to have understood the double entendre in Shadow's line in the stones-to-bread scene: 'Does your machine look anything like this?' (an Auden joke greeted with guffaws by his and Chester Kallman's pals). When Sapiro explained that Baba the Turk was a homoerotic travesty, Stravinsky was so offended that he stopped composing, developed a bleeding peptic ulcer, and escaped to Palm Springs for several days of reflection that ended with the decision that he had already written too much of the opera to abandon it. At this juncture Andre Marion began to undermine his father-in-law's relationship with Sapiro and in 1959 succeeded in severing the connection altogether, replacing the honest lawyer with a dishonest one, Marion's intimate friend William Montapert.[19]

On 10 July 1942 the Stravinskys were again en route to Mexico, this time apparently on a less bumpy train since they were able to read Anna Akhmatova's and Alexander Blok's poems as well as *Eugene Onegin*. Vera also read her first book in English, Bertita Harding's history of the execution of the Emperor Maximilian, which made an indelible impression on her, as Manet's painting of the firing squad scene still does on most viewers. Igor recorded for RCA in Mexico, a musicians' union strike having made this industry impossible in the U.S., and undertook excursions to Cuernavaca and Taxco.

On the Stravinskys' return, Rubinstein and Remarque came for dinner, followed a few days later by Janet Flanner, who had published a worthy and well-written profile of the composer in a 1935 *New Yorker*. In the same month Balanchine and Zorina flew in from Buenos Aires after a Central and South American tour in

---

19 See the chapter 14 'The Last Two Summers'.

which they gave twenty-five performances of *Apollo* in nineteen cities, an exhausting zigzag route with many stops and changes of planes. Balanchine proclaimed that this had been the most beautiful staging of the ballet ever. Stravinsky tried in vain to obtain the set by Tchelichev for a forthcoming revival in New York. Between times, Stravinsky completed *Norwegian Melodies*,[20] read Leskov's *Journey with Nihilists* and heard as much as he could endure of a broadcast of Shostakovich's 'Leningrad' Symphony.

Early in 1943 Stravinsky met with Sam Goldwyn, whom 'Igor likes very much', Vera noted, 'but he spent the evening reading a film script which he curses as a *Schlafmittel*'. He quickly declined the offer to provide music for the film. At the beginning of February, Stokowski began to study Stravinsky's Symphony in C with him but the conductor's highly praised but slipshod broadcast performance provoked irksome congratulatory telegrams to the composer, one from Sam Dushkin who should have known better.

In March 1943 the U.S. Office of War Information induced Stravinsky to record a talk for a French Voice of America broadcast on the twenty-fifth anniversary of Debussy's death. The Stravinskys left for New York and, when changing trains in Chicago, were saddened to read the newspaper headlines of Rachmaninov's death. In New York in April Stravinsky conducted a revival of Balanchine's *Apollo*, after which they dined at the Russian Tea Room. On the 28th the composer conducted *Petrushka* for Lucia Chase's Ballet Theatre. The next day Koussevitzky came to commission the *Ode* in memory of his recently deceased wife, the former *grande* proprietress of the Russian tea industry who had been closer to Igor than he was to Koussevitzky himself. After another visit from Koussevitzky and a dinner with André Maurois,[21] the Stravinskys departed for Hollywood. A brood of fifteen chickens and a rooster awaited them on their return but

---

20 General De Gaulle heard the premiere in Lewisohn Stadium in New York and sent a 'eulogious' (Stravinsky's word) telegram.

21 In New York during World War II Stravinsky met with several refugee French writers, most notably St-Exupéry (who had lived for a time on Central Park South) and Claude Lévi-Strauss (author of *Tristes Tropiques*), on 17 February 1945. They lunched together with the son-in-law of Marc Chagall at the time the artist was preparing décors for a new production of *The Firebird*. Vera meanwhile had made the acquaintance of Simone de Beauvoir in California.

their early morning crowing obliged the owners to divest themselves of the raucous avians. (Stravinsky composed a requiem for the chicks which, perhaps fortunately, has not survived.) After his birthday communion, he organised a memorial service honouring his father's centenary. Igor and Vera were in the Hollywood Bowl on the 22nd for a Russian Day concert with Stokowski conducting *Petrushka*, which its composer said 'he did very well'. The film *Hôtel du nord* filled them with nostalgia since they had been close friends with Louis Jouvet, the movie's star and Ira Belline's lover.

When the Stravinskys arrived in Boston for concerts in early 1944 they began to count the days until their return home. They lunched at the Amalfi restaurant (near Symphony Hall) with Balanchine and on another day with Aaron Copland. On the way back west, Stravinsky conducted *L'Histoire du Soldat* at the University of Chicago and Vera went to see Velázquez's *Kitchen Maid* at the Art Institute. On the evening of the 20th Stravinsky lectured at the University and dined afterward with Artur Rubinstein and Jacques Maritain. This same trio had last dined together in Cologne on 20 December 1931.

Stravinsky first attended an Evenings on the Roof concert in March 1944 and during the same month wrote a centenary memoir of Rimsky-Korsakov at the request of the Office of War Information. Gas rationing had by then become an obstacle and Stravinsky was required to fill in forms on which he wrote, after the word 'Occupation': 'A music composer and conductor, I drive to and from work. I have irregular hours and in my type of work it is not possible to take other people with me. I have to carry my music, and I work very late hours. I average 460 miles monthly.'

Stravinsky's 'type of work' did not exempt him from a hearing by the 'rationing board', but in fact he never drove in the U.S. and, until my arrival, Vera was his chauffeur.

In the autumn of 1944 the Stravinskys joined Isabelle Papineau-Couture, a young Canadian Boulanger pupil at the Longy School in Cambridge, accompanied by her husband, the composer Jean Papineau-Couture, at the Featherhill Ranch (Montecito), home of Arthur and Georges Sachs. Another house guest from Montreal, the Abbé Fortier, became intensely interested in Stravinsky and encouraged him to complete his Mass. The three Canadians dined with the Stravinskys and the Sachses every evening, with Isabelle seated at the composer's right. Stravinsky busied himself correcting the score of *Scènes de Ballet* and the 'Danse sacrale'[22] and playing the music four-hands with Nadia Boulanger. Isabelle's diary records the intensity of Stravinsky's concentration as she turned pages for the pair at the piano (he 'literally focused his head on the score'), adding that his partner read the music with an amazing facility: 'Stravinsky reached out to a note beyond the register of their four hands with an incredible speed.' The diary mentions previous encounters with Stravinsky in 1942-3 in Boston and New York where Isabelle saw him conduct *Apollo*. His gestures, she wrote, though angular and precise, were supple in indicating nuances and phrasings. She also noted that he addressed the players 'with great courtesy and showed his exactitude in explaining his intentions', adding: 'This rigor of thought was also very noticeable in his conversation, in which there was also a certain humor. This was obvious in his very severe judgment of a world-famous conductor as "un saint homme, mais il n'a pas de goût".' At this point Vera started to tell a *loufoque* story; despite her husband's protests ('Véra, je t'en prie'), she continued to recount the anecdote of Koussevitzky's premiere of the *Ode* with the trumpet in the wrong key.[23]

---

22 Stravinsky gave a part of the manuscript of the 1943 *Sacre* to Boulanger, a part to Alma Mahler (who in compensation gave him a painting by Paul Klee that he had originally gifted to Rilke when the two artists had shared an apartment in Munich in 1919), and a part to the Los Angeles dentist Dr Kestenbaum in settlement of a bill. I helped him to arrange the last because I was a close friend of his daughter, the famous violist Myra Kestenbaum.

23 Trumpets in B flat were preferred in the manuscript but the Boston Symphony favoured trumpets in C. The part was wrongly marked at the premiere, which was broadcast, and the *saint homme*, Koussevitzky, did not recognise the error. When Stravinsky explained this to him the reply was: 'I prefer the first version.' Stravinsky was personally very fond of Koussevitzky, less so after his second marriage to Olga (the niece of his first wife, Natalie), referred to by the composer as a 'plaster saint'. I was present when the conductor came to consult Stravinsky about the problem of the heir apparent of the conductor of the Boston Symphony, Leonard Bernstein. When the term 'homosexuality' came up, Stravinsky's answer was, 'All the better.' Koussevitzky gave a wedding party in his Boston home for the marriage of Igor and Vera in March 1940. The only guest was the always-amusing Gregor Piatigorsky. Stravinsky's own choice would have been Boaz Piller, the contrabassoonist of the Boston Symphony. They had sipped tea together every autumn afternoon in 1939 at Stravinsky's apartment, but of course Boaz, as a lowly orchestra player, could hardly be invited to dine at the conductor's table.

The memoirist remarks that Stravinsky could be capricious and childlike and that he delighted in browsing in antique shops and bookstores, proud of his own taste: 'J'ai le goût, moi, de faire les boutiques.' While at Featherhill, Stravinsky attended a Santa Barbara concert by Andrés Segovia, mainly because Arthur Sachs had organised a reception for him. Disturbed by the liberties taken in the guitarist's transcriptions of Bach in the programme, Stravinsky 'fell into a desultory mood and even Nadia could not animate his conversation'. He did not speak to Segovia, and the reception was brief. Igor and Vera had become acquainted with him during a channel crossing from Ostend to London in 1928. In the 1950s we saw him several times at the Luau in Beverly Hills and attended his concerts at the Teatro Argentina (Rome) and the Conservatorio Benedetto Marcello (Venice). At about this time I approached the guitarist to play in my first recording of Schoenberg's Serenade, but Segovia would only agree on condition that he be allowed to make changes in the part. I had to explain that absolutely nothing could be changed in any Schoenberg work.

The Papineau-Couture memoir ends with comments about Stravinsky's Russian 'atavism' and 'mysticism... radiating a profound intelligence and a powerful will, but his presence was a power in itself'.

———

After my March 1949 New York Town Hall concert in which Stravinsky conducted his Mass for the first time, he invited me to California to work with him during the summer months. He wanted me to sort and catalogue his music manuscripts, sketchbooks, scores, and indeed his entire archives, which had only recently arrived from Paris. I would live in his home, sleeping on the couch in the small den adjoining the library, where Auden had bunked. Stravinsky stressed that the invitation was not a business proposition, but I would have no expenses and he would be immensely grateful for my work, as well as for the opportunity to expand his English. To respect the Stravinskys' privacy in these cramped quarters he asked me to promise not to learn Russian.

I arrived at 1260 North Wetherly Drive on 1 June and began the work of identifying loose sketch pages, which required spreading out complete manuscript scores on the living-room table and creating a filing system for everything else. But Stravinsky showed little interest in his archives and only glanced at bits of music when I needed enlightenment. I soon found myself assisting him in his studio at the piano. He began by explaining the contents of his studio: the plywood board attached to his piano rack for composing, the tilted desk for orchestration, the small table containing stopwatches, rulers, razors, knives, inks of several colours, glasses of pens and pencils, several styluses, stacks of music paper and implements used in composing and writing. One of Stravinsky's ingenious inventions, perhaps the most remarkable, was an instrument the size of a butter knife with a metal, razor-sharp, arrow-shaped tip attached to an ivory handle for delicately carving out unwanted notes from a manuscript. He also showed me a pickle jar containing thirty or forty erasers of many different sizes and tints, saying, 'On compose la musique avec la gomme.'[24] While in the initial stage of composing, he was always alone in his studio with three soundproofed doors separating it from the rest of the house so that no outside sound or intrusion could interrupt his concentration. But soon I found myself assisting Stravinsky in his inner sanctum, helping him at the piano while he was trying out new combinations and passages. These keyboard sessions with him, playing notes he could not reach in widely spaced harmonic structures, were more thrilling than anything that had happened in my life.

After a few days Vera Stravinsky informed me that I should comment on his work, which I would never have dreamed of doing. 'He is deeply interested in your reactions, even dependent on them. Whatever you think, tell him briefly, because he interprets silence as disapproval.' I proceeded cautiously, enduring the strain of

---

24 Twenty-three years later, on our return to New York after the funeral in Venice, Mrs Stravinsky and I found my sisters and niece preparing the apartment for the widow. They had uncovered the mirrors and Stravinsky's piano and work table in his studio. My sister Patricia had gathered all of his erasers into a large jar thinking that I would cherish this. Instead I burst into tears.

these challenging sessions two or three times a week at first, and then as a daily routine. The simple part of this procedure was in making suggestions about the settings of words, proper speed, appropriateness of register, and clarity. Stravinsky over-respected Auden's *Rake* libretto, wanting every syllable in every part to be audible and sometimes sacrificing the ensemble textures, breaking rhythmic unisons by changing the rhythm of one part, the better to hear a syllable in another. While composing, Stravinsky sang all of the vocal parts in turn at an octave or two below the written pitches; even some of Shadow's music was too high for Stravinsky's *basso profundo*. Initially he asked me to recite the verses and even the recitatives at different tempi in order to determine which one best suited the dramatic situation. At the keyboard he always played the bass part, groaning throughout and leaving the treble to me. The act of creation was so strenuous that he immediately began to perspire and, discarding his shirt, continually mopped his head and neck with towels. His facial expressions during struggles with harmonic combinations could be painful to watch, but when he had found one that satisfied him, he smiled radiantly. Intensive work would continue for an hour or more, and during rest periods he remained silent. This most impatient man in extra-musical matters was capable of mental wrestling for two or three days in deciding whether or not to retain a perhaps extraneous note in an aggregation of them. As he said in a filmed interview: 'I can wait as an insect can wait.'

During my first month in their home, both Igor and Vera coached me on idiosyncrasies of the other. Competition for my attention had developed between them. My relationship with him quickly deepened through music, crossing an invisible barrier, and we became closer than I would ever have thought possible. He criticised his wife to me for the deviations of her upper-class behaviour, while she tried to explain his many quirks before I experienced them myself. One curiosity is that he enjoyed correcting her English pronunciations, always checking them with me first, which was also a way of informing me that I was not to make corrections directly, as I would not have had the audacity to do anyway.

At this early stage I was less close to Vera than to her husband.[25] Only gradually did we all come to understand and respect each other's diverse backgrounds. Now, in retrospect, I marvel at the bridging over the chasms in our cultures and ages. The household upheld distinct social divisions: Vera, the anti-*nouveau-riche* bohemian aristocrat; myself, the absolute middle of middle-class America; Yevgenia Petrovna (Mrs Gates), the stern, unsmiling Russian *moujik* housekeeper and cook; and Stravinsky himself, the usually tender tyrant and the opposite of Adorno's 'authoritarian personality', of indefinable social denomination but always set apart by his genius.

The Stravinskys took me under their wings and protected me as only parents would, insisting that I receive the same medical care as themselves, including the twice-weekly vitamin B12 and vitamin C *piqûre* boosters and the veronal drops for anxiety attacks. On airplanes, Stravinsky in first class always shared his meals and whiskys with me, bringing them himself to my economy seat. Occasionally on long flights, he would ask his wife to exchange seats with me for an hour or two of conversation, mostly about American history. He soon memorised the names and capital cities of all the states and the chronology of all the presidents.

In September 1949 I returned to New York to organise and conduct three concerts, one of them including Berg's Chamber Concerto with violinist Isidore Cohen and pianist Robert Cornman, Falla's Harpsichord Concerto with Sylvia Marlowe and Stravinsky's *Renard*. A second concert included *Mavra*[26] with Phyllis Curtin as Parasha, Robert Harmon as the Hussar, and Sandra Warfield as the Mother. Although I had promised to return to Hollywood quickly, I could not do so until the beginning of December. I had earned no

---

25 Christopher Isherwood's diary for 6 April 1957 describes an incident reminiscent of my early days there: 'We invited Gerald Heard, the Stravinskys, and Bob Craft... The Stravinskys were nearly three-quarters of an hour late - they hadn't been able to find the way - and Bob was sick with a terrible headache in the car... Igor and Vera were both greatly upset by this - he more than she - one sees how deeply they love him. Vera wanted to know didn't we have some Miltown or something? So Don [Bachardy] fetched some Equinal... Quite soon Bob had apparently recovered and was with us at the table, laughing... At one point Igor said to Gerald, "I am not sure I am creative, only inventive," then a little later, "Yes, I am thinking, but am I thinking well?" He was so sweet and touching.'

26 *Mavra* and *Renard* were recorded by Dial Records.

money all summer and found myself sharing a Hell's Kitchen cold-water flat with two other out-of-pocket musicians on the far west side of mid-town. After my luxurious months with the Stravinskys, the adjustment was difficult but my own musical life resumed and I developed new friendships, particularly with Auden, who told me which books to read, from Panofsky to Kierkegaard. I also acquired two new girlfriends, Arlene Carmin, the mezzo-soprano with whom I recorded *Pribaoutki* and *Berceuses du chat*, and the contralto Sandra W.

Thinking back on Hollywood at that time, I recall Stravinsky beginning his day with his Hungarian exercises on the porch outside his studio, removing his white terrycloth bathrobe and wearing only pyjama bottoms to practise his calisthenics, the grand finale of which was a five-minute headstand, feet against the wall. He would then shower and breakfast on a *demi-tasse* of espresso and two raw eggs. Just over five feet tall, he pointed out that he was the same height as Bach, Mozart, Wagner, Schubert and Chopin. Lacking brawn, the 120-pound Stravinsky was all sinew, with especially developed abdominal muscles. At house parties he would occasionally lie supine and invite hefty guests to stand on his stomach. Stravinsky was lithe, cat-like, bandy-legged and, when I first knew him, walked very fast, ahead of his wife. His own stride was abbreviated but always energetic, the opposite of the leisurely saunter of his taller friends. There was impatience about it as there was in everything he did, except composing. His hair, though much thinned at this date, was a light ginger that never whitened, always a surprise to concert audiences who had pictured him from photographs as dark-haired. Since his 'haars', as he would say, were too sparse to be combed, he carried a leather case containing two ivory-backed hairbrushes.

An intent topiarist, Stravinsky regularly trimmed the shrubbery that nearly secluded his house. He would also cut fresh flowers from his private garden every morning and fill a vase with them in his studio. Then after prayers to the thaumaturgic icon ('An icon is a signpost to God'), he would devote the rest of the morning to composing. This began with the limbering of the musical mind and fingers in a Bach fugue. Lunch was announced by his wife with two handclaps if his studio doors were open but his acute olfactory sense usually rendered this unnecessary. If ready he would respond with the same signal and, if not, with just one clap. If a kitchen odour leaked through the house to his studio, he could not compose. His favourite scents were leather, tobacco and freshly ground coffee. He asked for the tin to be opened in his presence to savour the first whiffs.

At the noon meal, Vera sipped and Stravinsky quaffed a carafe of white wine (California's Livermore), then napped for a half-hour on his studio couch. Between then and teatime his creative mind was in high gear. *Chai* – actually a tisane – was an inalienable ritual sipped in the living room with his wife. During this break they sometimes played cards or Chinese checkers which she was careful to let him win or, if a musical idea was gestating, solitaire.[27] Evenings were for orchestration or for me to read English translations of Russian classics to him – *Oblomov*, Tolstoy, Shchedrin, *Dead Souls* (in 1934 Stravinsky himself began a French translation of a volume of Gogol). He did not like Turgenev.

Movies were an escape, preferably films in which good and evil were explicit – gangsters, westerns and mysteries. Stravinsky disliked animated cartoons, especially those ending with 'That's all, folks!' ('I am not a folk,' he would protest.) For movie outings he wore blue jeans and a U.S. Navy pea jacket purchased at an Army & Navy store with the assistance of Isherwood's friend Bill Caskey, in contrast to

---

27 Stravinsky seemed to be able to play cards mechanically while thinking about composing. He was said to be a good chess player but was not in the same class as Vera. What he most enjoyed playing was poker. During his American concert tours in 1935-7-9 he found a perfect partner in New York in, of all people, the kosher wine tycoon Manischewitz, to whom he was introduced by Severin Kavenoki. The two men became great friends. Oddly, no Stravinsky biography mentions this as leading to the composition in 1936 of *Jeu de cartes*. Since Balanchine did not like the subject and wanted something in the fairytale line, Stravinsky had to coach the choreographer through the ballet at rehearsals in the spring of 1937 before the New York premiere. For the first time, Balanchine was obliged to follow the composer's ideas on the sequence of dances and the positions. Finally there was an *entente cordiale* and there are photographs of Stravinsky playing poker with Balanchine during rehearsal breaks on the Metropolitan Opera stage. Most important for Stravinsky was the introduction of the Joker. Certainly Stravinsky saw him in a diabolical role, which connects back to the part of the Devil in *L'Histoire du Soldat*. It should also be mentioned that the music becomes increasingly dissonant at the end of *Jeu de cartes* like the triumphant Devil at the end of *L'Histoire du Soldat*.

dapper suits, ascots fastened with a pin, and bow ties. His shirts were monogrammed on the pocket 'I.S.: 1, 2, 3' to distinguish them from mine in the laundry, needless as this was since his dress collars stretched only halfway around my neck. He also had my socks embroidered at the top in red thread, 'Bob's sock' and 'Bob's other sock', hosiery being regularly lost in the wash.

Stravinsky shared his rich dream life with me at breakfast along with, occasionally, a résumé of his 'disarranged digestive system'. If costive he had recourse to a syringe (his 'poire') or, if the contrary, a dose of the same electuary that Mozart had administered to his wife. This earthiness seemed incongruous to the ultra-refinement, tidiness and fanatical hygiene (he often carried a bar of pumice, a habit acquired from Erik Satie). His medicine cabinet was stocked with French pharmaceuticals, some of them purchased during the 1950s by Virgil Thomson at Stravinsky's request; the New York critic travelled to and from his Île de France apartment frequently. I should add that Stravinsky believed in the Greek classification of temperaments:[28] the *hepar* as the primary affective organ and the bowels as the source of emotion. He insisted, 'There is no music of the heart.'

Superstitions surfaced during evening meals: if someone spilled wine, he or she was required to dab two fingers in it and touch both sides of the neck, then cast a pinch of salt over the left shoulder. Among the composer's culinary foibles was that water and wine should not be allowed on the table together, another that to remove a bottle of wine before it reached the dregs was a venal sin. Stravinsky swallowed capsules of charcoal as an antacid (it isn't) with champagne and to avert what he called 'gazz'; he never twirled a silver swizzle stick in the palms of his hands as some of his friends did. Though cocktails were unknown in the house, he drank glasses of pure Dutch gin from terracotta bottles. (To Auden's dismay, Stravinsky did not like martinis.) His *cave*, though very modest, was outside the kitchen door, but he delighted in showing his magnums of Latour Margaux to visitors and his few precious bottles of port, his preferred emollient. His wife chided him on the quantity of his intakes, but he defended

---

28   See Panofsky's *Saturn and Melancholy.*

himself with the proverb that 'there are more old drunkards than old doctors'. Vera was acknowledged as the superior arbiter of clarets and he always deferred to her; after the evening meal he often drank a grappa, a marc or, depending on seasons, a 'tot of rum' (for its thermostatic properties). On long automobile rides he carried a hip flask of Armagnac and, while I was driving, I would suddenly detect a tantalising insufflation of this great brandy from the back seat, followed by a convivial turn in his conversation.

Dining out with Stravinsky often included embarrassing moments. On being seated he would summon a waiter to bring an empty glass in which to park his spectacles, simultaneously instructing him not to bring water. Stravinsky would then unfold his napkin and loudly blow his nose in it. Borscht and shchi were noisily slurped *à la russe*, which embarrassed his wife, who warned him that this could destroy his very sensitive palate. He was primarily carnivorous but would have subsisted on oysters, *écrevisses*, lobster, scampi, periwinkles, smoked salmon,[29] *loup de mer* and, supremely, *omble chevalier* (found at great depths in Lake Geneva). After finishing a dish he would call for its immediate removal or push the plate aside and, if not retrieved in a few moments, place it on an empty neighbouring table. I remember a dinner at the Baroness's when he shoved his plate in front of her, which she promptly pushed back. With this exception, his etiquette in the presence of aristocracy was impeccable.

Stravinsky experimented with diets during most of his mature years. In July 1931 he had been put on a strict regime because of liver and gall bladder attacks and severe migraines. At the beginning of April 1933, Ida Rubinstein telegraphed a dinner invitation to him together with Debussy's widow, saying, 'We will all dine according to your diet.' In October of that year a Paris newspaper reported that his digestion had improved and that 'snails and grills were now permitted since his inspiration required vitamin Z'. Stravinsky had been seen 'returning home at 3 a.m., a foulard wrapped around his throat and carrying four bottles of champagne'.

---

29 See Samuel Beckett's description of his lunches with Stravinsky where he ordered several straight scotches and smoked salmon for both hors d'œuvres and the main course.

Since Stravinsky has never been described at a typical Hollywood party, a single brief example should be permitted. I recall one at the director George Cukor's, who lived near the composer on Doheny Hill. Several tables were already full when we arrived, seating arranged by celebrity status. On finding myself separated from the Stravinskys and placed between Bette Davis and Groucho Marx in a galaxy of scantily clad starlets, I wanted to bolt but hung on, the food and vintages being epicurean. I ate and imbibed but said nothing, stupefied by Ms Davis's scatological chatter and Groucho's instantaneous and equally scabrous wit. Katharine Hepburn arrived alone near the end of the dinner, offering a transparent apology for 'Spence's absence due to a bad cold' (hangover). Having come only to see the Stravinskys, she followed her host to their sequestered corner table in the living room. Casually attired in a trouser suit and kerchief with no cosmetic attempt to conceal freckles, she talked about filming on location in Africa. Cukor made certain that no others joined the Stravinskys' circle but the composer wanted to return to his work and made a polite early departure. As he was leaving, Groucho called out to him: 'Maestro, give my regards to Beethoven.'[30]

The return of the Stravinskys to Europe in 1951 left an impression transatlantically that they had become American patriots critical of European class structures. Although they themselves did not vote, they praised what was then known as American democracy (which became the military-industrial catastrophe followed by the corporatocracy that rules the country in 2013). I still recall Vera declining a dinner invitation from the Queen of Belgium and the affronted wife of the Brussels musician Paul Collaer reproving her: 'On ne refuse pas à une reine,' to which Vera responded, 'Mais je suis Américaine, Madame.'

In spite of the Stravinskys' newfound nationalism, when we sipped tea with the Princess Royal Maria Pavlovna at the Villa Malcontenta, the Baroness d'Erlanger's Palladian digs[31] on the south

---

30 Groucho's mother's maiden name was Schoenberg.
31 As we approached the villa, Stravinsky remarked on the architect's genius in designing aulic domestic structures in comparison to his grandiose Veneto masterpieces, which impose a Roman classical style not always compatible with the Venetian vernacular.

bank of the Brenta River, I was astonished by their transformation
in the presence of Romanoff royalty. By this time the princess was
an unknown and impoverished exile, yet the Stravinskys conducted
themselves in a subservient manner that I would never have thought
possible. Igor bowed deeply, Vera curtsied, and neither spoke until
spoken to by the Princess Maria, to whom they listened attentively.
They had been staunch monarchists and at home they occasionally
talked about the good deeds of the liberal Tsar Alexander II, but
never mentioned Nicholas II. On hearing of his abdication in 1917
Stravinsky had telegraphed his family and friends in St Petersburg
to share the 'joyous news' that Russia was now 'free'. Yet on learning
of the Tsar's assassination on 17 July 1918 Stravinsky mourned the
death and, incredibly, in Hollywood in 1945 he and Vera attended a
thirty-year *Panikhida* service for the Romanoff dynasty. (*Panikhida*
means 'service for those Fallen Asleep'. The Orthodox Church text is
sung by a chorus in alternating two- and three-part harmony, chant-
like melody, and in a very limited range. Vera acquired an American
edition of this booklet in preparation for a service observing the first
anniversary of her husband's death.) On the Brenta that afternoon
in September 1951, they appeared awestruck in the presence of the
Princess Royal Maria Pavlovna, and the drive back to Venice, with the
young composer Baron Raffaello de Banfield Tripcovich as chauffeur,
was silent.[32]

Throughout this 1951 return trip to Europe Stravinsky lauded
the superiority of American over European orchestras, even to the
players themselves. When he first conducted in Germany I recall him
rehearsing a string section in Baden-Baden, then shocking everyone
by remarking, 'You lack tone quality because you killed your Jews.'
(This was received with stony-faced silence, which I interpreted to
mean, 'That was not our fault.') A reversal on aesthetic grounds
occurred immediately back in the U.S. during the drive from the New
York airport to central Manhattan, when the Stravinskys expressed
an urgent desire to return to Europe. This was satisfied only three

---

32 His mother's tutor in German was Rilke, and in English, James Joyce.

months later, and almost every year thereafter until the ends of their lives they spent as much time as possible in Europe.

Already in the mid-1950s Stravinsky wanted to extend his Hollywood house over the southern terrace to increase storage space for his ever-enlarging library as well as a nook for guests. Mary Vartikian Harris had met Vera Stravinsky in 1954 at a New Year's Eve party at the Bel Aire mansion of the Hormel family, and thereafter became her art instructor and friend. We dined periodically at the Harris home on Sunday nights and they at ours. They recommended young architects Perry Neuschatz and his wife, whose hobby was playing recorders. (Even before proposing house designs, they insisted that the only remuneration they would accept was a page of music manuscript.) Stravinsky's curiosity about recorders was aroused, and he transcribed the voice-and-two-flute lullaby from the *Rake* as a voiceless duet for treble and alto recorder, an ingenious adaptation that includes the music of the choral responses by reducing the three- and four-part harmony to two-part harmony. Though pleased with his arrangement, he never heard it played. When the new room was completed, the Stravinskys gave a champagne party there on 15 May 1960. [33]

My own circumstances in Hollywood did not change until January 1963 when my encroachment began in this new library, which in 1965 became my abode in the Stravinsky house. At first the only furnishings were a chair, a cot and stacks of books. I began to work there after midnight, writing a memoir of our Soviet tour of the previous autumn. After installing an electric heater, I laboured there every night for about three weeks, trying to forge a coherent narrative of our experiences in the U.S.S.R. Our Persian cat, Celeste, joined me, nestling down at my feet and purring as loudly as the hum of the heater. Meanwhile, Stravinsky, in his adjoining studio often as late as 2 a.m., could be heard through the wall testing combinations

---

33   Lawrence Morton's dates for the construction of this porch and the composition of the 'Lullaby for two flutes, for George and Mary Harris... Christmas Eve 1955' are mistaken. Stravinsky was in New York at that time recovering from a 23 December dinner with Auden and composing *Vom Himmel hoch* for me. The transcription Stravinsky made for two recorders coincided with the completion of the new room in 1960.

on his muted piano. Again and again he would repeat a chord, trying to decide whether to remove or retain a note in a harmonic structure, fearful of destroying balance and allure.

Stravinsky liked to type and until his last years used the Russian machine that Diaghilev had given him in 1924, having it updated to include the new letters added by the U.S.S.R. and to subtract a few others. Stravinsky actually typed much of our *Conversations* books himself and was eager to do the same with my new essay, impatient to read my impressions of him in his native land. Fearing that he would revise what I had written, I could only elude his invigilation by continuing to work long after his bedtime. I wanted the essay to convey my thoughts exclusively, and I managed to dodge the composer until Stephen Spender sent the proofs for its first publication in *Encounter*. Seeing it, a greatly relieved Stravinsky congratulated me and offered minor corrections concerning people and places but said nothing critical about the tone of the piece or about my narrative of his Dostoyevskyan confession scene at his dinner with Shostakovich and other Soviet composers.

On publication, telegrams and letters began to arrive from everywhere, and awkward situations arose at meetings with people who believed that Stravinsky had written the memoir himself. As the unique account of Shostakovich and Stravinsky together, and for a sympathetic personal portrait of Khrushchev on our private meeting with him, the article generated wide interest. The first telegram, from Goddard Lieberson, kindly informed me that the essay had been enthusiastically reviewed in *The New York Times* by Joseph Wood Krutch, then the paper's prepotent critic. But when T. S. Eliot told Stravinsky of reading the article 'with great interest' the thought paralysed me. Spender felt that my candour sometimes bordered on indiscretion but he praised the piece and deemed it worthy of worldwide attention. Recalling the period, I still see Celeste pawing and purring on the carpet and hear my baby-talk to her – 'puddy cat'– which in my falsetto sounded like Schoenberg's string harmonics, or so Stravinsky said.

Stravinsky would enjoy the new room for less than five years. His 1956 stroke had made it difficult for him to negotiate the steep staircase from the street. When the Baroness was moved to her son's estate near Paris, the Stravinskys decided to purchase her very much larger three-storey house on flat land at 1218 North Wetherly. This increased the number of bathrooms from two to seven and allowed Vera to have a studio in the same house as Igor. The actual move did not take place until 1965, by which time the adjustment was emotionally disturbing for him and nightlights had to be left on in his bedroom and bathroom. I eventually moved into the new basement and transformed it into a music room and library. For a time I slept in one of the Baroness's bathhouses next to her pool, and when her property was divided and sold I moved to a gatekeeper's cottage on the other end of her estate where an entrance from another street was a convenience for our neighbours, Mirandi Masacco and Dorothy Parker. On 15 September 1969 the Stravinskys left Hollywood permanently for New York because of family feuds[34] and the larger city's superior medical resources.

Stravinsky was ill throughout his life. He was born tubercular. X-rays taken in his last year show lingering intestinal scars, the likely cause of his later-life afflictions with peristaltic functions, collywobbles and colitis. In the spring of 1939 he had been confined for five months to the sanitarium at Sancellemoz in the French Alps. Because he was always vulnerable to pneumonia, bronchitis, colds and pulmonary infections, his parents had not allowed him to swim. He swathed himself in scarves and towels, wore a gray fedora or a woollen cap outdoors regardless of season, and a beret to bed at night. (His heavily fur-lined *shuba* – Russian overcoat – made for him by Chanel is now displayed in the Paris Conservatoire.) At the age of thirty he contracted typhoid fever from an unculled *Ostrea edulis*[35] (classified by Aristotle and Seneca as an aphrodisiac); his and Cocteau's friend Raymond Radiguet died of the same disease in 1923. But Stravinsky never overcame his addiction to briny Belons, and throughout World War I iced packets of them were sent by overnight

---

34 See the chapter 14 'The Last Two Summers'.
35 After Stravinsky's post-*Rite of Spring* typhoid fever he wrote to Maximilian Steinberg, Rimsky-Korsakov's son-in-law: 'Neuilly 3rd July 1913. Dear Max, I am gradually recovering from this hellish disease – I am walking like a fly on two legs. If everything goes as it is now, I'll leave Friday for Ustilug.'

trains to his Swiss residences. Several of his first wife's letters from the 1930s warned him about the oyster peril, recalling his painful regurgitations from them, particularly in Brittany.

In Switzerland in 1916 Stravinsky was hospitalised with intracostal neuralgia from nicotine poisoning but it did not break his cigarette addiction. At home in Hollywood he smoked at least two packs of cigarettes a day until his stroke in Berlin in October 1956. I used to admire his deftness in spreading tobacco on thin strips of paper (procured from an Armenian merchant in Bakersfield) and liked to watch him processing them in his rolling machine – those large hands with such sensitive, tapering fingers!

When Stravinsky's Éditions Russes representative and friend Ernest Oeberg suffered an appendicitis attack during a 1925 Christmas dinner in Paris, the composer remained in the hospital with him for two days until his death from peritonitis. Nine years later, after seeing his elder son suffer from a burst appendix, Stravinsky had his own appendix removed and compelled his whole family, including Vera de Bosset, to do the same, thus pre-empting the danger. In a letter to his father in March 1937 Soulima describes his appendectomy as requiring five days in hospital. He lamented, 'Now no one in our family has an appendix anymore.'

A surgical procedure that Stravinsky should have undergone would have repaired an inguinal hernia, the consequence of lifting a piece of baggage from an overhead compartment on an airplane. He wore a truss thereafter but never found one that fit, a cruel encumbrance in his last decade. His other surgical experiences included three facelifts (in early Hollywood years) and in his seventy-first year a prostatectomy, a harrowing experience due to an inept injection of a spinal anaesthetic that left him with a limp and a slower walking pace. But his most dangerous and protracted surgical experience took place in New York Hospital on 2 and 3 May 1969, when he underwent two eleven-inch embolectomies on successive days, both in his left leg, and spent seven weeks in hospital recovering.

Stravinsky's allergies, too many for enumeration here, were aggravated in California by smog, and the scorching desert wind and heat that he referred to as the *Föhn* which melted his dining-room candles. In July 1949 he suffered from a bleeding ulcer, medically attributed to the excessive intake of alcohol but blamed by the victim on his crushing anxieties about the role of the freak Baba the Turk in the *Rake*. Doctors placed the patient on a strict diet but also increased his dosages of the contraindicated vitamin B12, which accelerated the production of red corpuscles and elevated his blood pressure. This haematological imbalance continued for seven years and on 2 October 1956 resulted in a basilar stenosis in Berlin while he was conducting the end of the first movement of his Symphony in C. At the end of that year he was diagnosed as polycythaemic and phlebotomised every week for the next two years. In late spring of 1958 his recurrent peptic ulcer resulted in the overnight loss of nearly half of his blood. He was quickly restored to a normal haematocrit level at Cedars of Lebanon Hospital, Los Angeles.

Since venesectomies were debilitating and offered no hope of a cure, the only other treatment option was radioactive phosphorus, then in an experimental stage. Fully aware of the mortal risk, he nevertheless watched a man in a spacesuit drop a pill into a glass of water, which he swallowed. When the liquid fizzled, he exclaimed, 'Now I will light up like a firefly.' Fortunately no ill effects followed, and Stravinsky soon adapted to the weekly blood tests to determine his prothrombin level and Coumadin schedule. Miraculously, much of *Agon*, that youthful masterpiece, had been composed during the initial phlebotomy period in 1957.

In October 1961 Stravinsky flew from Belgrade to Zurich to conduct his *Soldat* at the Opera. He was interested in Dr Paul Niehans's longevity experiments in implanting cells from sheep placentae and sought an entrée to the doctor through a mutual friend, Paul Sacher, conductor of the Basel Chamber Orchestra, who headed Niehans's roster of exclusive patients. An appointment was arranged in Zurich but it ended when Stravinsky refused to abstain from alcohol during the treatment. Much relieved, both Stravinskys regaled themselves with champagne that night, Vera ecstatic at being able to return to New York.

Dr Maurice Gilbert of Geneva, medical director of the International Red Cross and physician of the Theodore Stravinsky family for many years, had been especially attentive to the composer's tubercular granddaughter Kitty. In October 1951 the doctor had been our guide on visits to Stravinsky's World War I Swiss residences. Dr Gilbert flew to Munich in October 1956 to consult with the composer's German physician in the Rote Kreuz Hospital, where Stravinsky was recovering from his Berlin thrombosis. In blatant disregard of doctors' orders, not to mention hospital rules, photographs feature the composer defiantly smoking cigarettes in his hospital bed.

I happened to be in Lausanne at that time for a broadcast concert and had dined with Dr Gilbert the day before. Late that same night I drove with Theodore and Denise Stravinsky to Zurich and the next day on to Munich, arriving at the hospital at about eleven in the evening. Vera awaited me at the door of her husband's room and said, 'He wants to see you, but no one else.' Although sedated, Stravinsky was eager for news of what was foremost in his mind: the performances and the reception of his music in Lausanne.[36] (He knew that he would be seeing a lot of his son in the days following.) Against Gilbert's and the other doctors' advice, on discharge from the hospital three weeks later Stravinsky entrained for Rome to conduct the *Canticum Sacrum* in the Teatro Eliseo. Gilbert followed him there and in conference with an Italian physician finally allowed the patient to depart for Paris and London. Although the prospect of the Rome concert terrified Stravinsky, the performance helped to restore his confidence. (I assisted by giving cues behind a screen on stage left.)

On the night train to Paris, Stravinsky seemed to rest well and arrived there in good spirits, happy to see Pierre Souvtchinsky at the station in the early morning and embrace him after their sixteen-year estrangement. A dilemma awaited the composer at the street exit: members of his family had come in a large automobile to bring him to his hotel and Souvtchinsky had come with Pierre Boulez in a limousine for the same purpose. (Boulez, Stockhausen and Luigi Nono had visited Stravinsky in his Munich hospital only a few weeks before.) Stravinsky chose to go with Souvtchinsky and I had to go with them, since Boulez had come to take Stravinsky and me to produce my

---

36   He still had guilt feelings about his cancellation of his concert there in 1951.

recording sessions of the *Canticum Sacrum* and the Bach Variations. Vera was obliged to go along with the children. She checked our baggage at the Ritz Hotel and rested in the Arthur Sachs suite.

After six hours of concentrated listening, Stravinsky rejoined his wife at the Ritz and then went to a rendezvous with his old friends, both living in the same hotel, Pavlik Tchelichev and his long-time companion Charles-Henri Ford. Following a sumptuous dinner with the Sachses we boarded a night train to London for doctors' visits and a crowded schedule of rehearsals for me. A slow voyage to New York ensued (during which I won the boat's quiz, finishing slightly ahead of Janet Flanner).

Stravinsky's most traumatic illness struck in 1967, three months after his eighty-fifth birthday party, which was celebrated near San Diego in the Hotel del Coronado (where Henry James had resided in April 1905). The Marions drove from Los Angeles to be with Milene's father for a few hours. Family relations were taut and the depressed Stravinsky refused to venture a walk on the beach. On the third day we returned in a morose mood to the city often referred to then as the despoliation of the desert. In August I went to New York to overdub the vocal part of the orchestral soundtrack of *Abraham and Isaac* with Richard Frisch as soloist. During one of these recording sessions I received an alarming call from Vera telling me that her husband was in Mount Sinai Hospital having lost a large quantity of blood from the same ulcer. I flew to Hollywood and went directly to the hospital to see him. During his fourteen days there, Stravinsky lost eighteen pounds and, more importantly, his powerful will. His haematocrit level stood at only 35,000, but the platelets had shot up to 1,200,000, indicating that he was both anaemic and producing red corpuscles too rapidly. Confined to bed at home he refused to read or even to watch his favourite African animal programme, *Daktari*, saying, 'I only like to look at it in Vera's room.' He told me that he had seen his birth certificate in a dream and 'it was very yellow'. When Balanchine visited the following week he could not conceal a wince, but the great old man rallied and said, 'Like all Americans, I am reducing.' In the early afternoon of 8 October he complained of a chill and his temperature rose to 101 degrees. I packed his bag, carried him to the car, and drove him to the nearby Cedars of Lebanon Hospital. The fingers of his left hand were blackening, and one of the cardiologists mentioned the possibility of gangrene as well as the danger of pneumonia. It was nearly midnight when I drove Vera home, exhausted and frightened. She herself was ill with flu and scarcely able to walk.

The next three weeks were the most strenuous in my twenty-three years with Stravinsky. I was alone with him for eight to twelve hours every day. Mrs Stravinsky herself was confined to bed, and Milene Marion visited her father only once, while he was asleep. (Her husband did not come at all, nor did Stravinsky's sons.) The *concilia* with doctors totally unfamiliar with their patient and reluctant to take action were left to me. They also neglected to conceal their belief that he would not survive. I had to assume all responsibility, call nurses for him, talk to doctors and interns about his condition, and at the same time try to raise his spirits and think of encouraging things to say. I struggled to keep my own anxiety and native pessimism under control. Perhaps because he was so heavily medicated, he talked freely about his childhood and experiences in his early life that I had not heard before. He was very affectionate and grateful for everything I read and said to him. After four days the coagulated capillaries began to dilate and the blackness to disappear. He grew stronger, his determination returned, and he was home for Thanksgiving. We listened to recordings then and every day thereafter. Miraculously he recovered and lived for three and a half more years, which included many hours of musical enjoyment. None of his subsequent bad periods was quite so disturbing as this one had been.

Sadly, in mid-December I was committed to conduct in Toronto and in Ithaca. After my arrival in Canada, a blizzard cancelled all flights and I had to taxi from Toronto to the Finger Lakes town and then to New York. But the more painful burden was the constant worry about Stravinsky. His last words to me after begging me to cancel the engagements resounded in my brain. I had made a feeble attempt at an explanation: 'But I am playing your music.' He looked at me intensely and said: 'Je crache sur ma musique.'

CHAPTER 14
The Last Two Summers

On 18 August 1969 Soulima and Françoise Stravinsky, together with her son by her first husband, Jacques Bon, met with Milene and Andre Marion at their favourite motel in the resort town of Cambria, north of Santa Barbara, to plot the embezzlement of Igor Stravinsky's money from his Swiss bank. The next day Soulima and Françoise visited Stravinsky at his sickbed in Hollywood to judge the state of his health. I witnessed the scene from my apartment about thirty feet away from Stravinsky's bedroom window. Vera was not present and did not see them but remained in her room awaiting their call to join them. That this never came is not surprising, a standoff between them having been in effect for several months.

Later the same day the Soulimas signed a pact drawn up by William Montapert, Igor Stravinsky's duplicitous lawyer, to remove all monies from the composer's numbered account in Basel and divide it, half for Montapert and half for the Stravinsky family heirs. Three days earlier Laure Lourié[1]- one of Igor's and Vera's closest friends

---

1   Stravinsky had known her husband, the painter Eugene Lourié, in Paris since 1932 and in Hollywood recommended him to Jean Renoir, who employed him as art director in Rumer Godden's *The River*. Lourié spoke Russian exclusively with Stravinsky during the couple's bi-weekly visits. His much younger wife, who spoke English with me, had a scrappy temperament, even with the Baroness d'Erlanger, who once asked about her lineage and was told 'Je suis métèque, Madame.' The Louriés published a book about their Hollywood life that omits any mention of the Stravinsky connection because they thought it would be regarded as name-dropping.

for more than two decades as well as a time-to-time dinner guest of the Marions – had discovered that Montapert had been tapping her and Vera's telephones. For years the Louriés had been informing Vera that the ongoing dinner conversation at the Marion home was the distribution of Stravinsky's financial assets. Laure persuaded Igor and Vera to replace Montapert with their New York attorney, Arnold Weissberger, whom Igor called, asking him to come immediately to Los Angeles. The transfer of representation was effectuated the next day. The discovery that Montapert was scheming against them convinced the Stravinskys to leave California for the Plaza Hotel in New York. Their first visitor there, of all unwelcome surprises, was the ousted Montapert, who had somehow managed to finagle a meeting with Weissberger and the Stravinskys even though the New York lawyer had warned Montapert that he had no right to intrude on his former clients.

Montapert arrived at the Plaza well in advance of the appointed time and told the Stravinskys that their monies in the Basel Bank Verein would have to be removed, and that I would be obliged to act as their proxy and sign a stack of documents in Basel which would transfer Montapert's power-of-attorney to me. Privately I disclosed the existence of Stravinsky's numbered account to Weissberger, explaining to the Stravinskys that they could no longer conceal it from their new attorney. On 29 September I flew to Berlin to conduct a concert in the new Karajan Philharmonic Hall (2 October). Montapert, staying with Stravinsky's son Theodore in Geneva, called and fixed an hour to meet him near the entrance to the Basel bank the day after my concert. I flew to Munich during the night of 2–3 October, then to Zurich and, after hours of waiting, on to Basel where, feeling exhausted and extremely uneasy, I entered the bank with Montapert. He introduced me to a Monsieur Puenzieux, to whom Montapert had regularly been giving $10,000 perquisites from Stravinsky's account. Without any time to read the papers prepared for me, I signed them. Returning to the hotel, I called the Stravinskys to tell them that I would be in New York the next day. Vera alarmed me with the news that in my absence she had executed a two-year lease for a suite on the wrong side (Fifty-Eighth Street) of the Essex House, a less expensive but also much less pleasant accommodation for her husband than the Plaza.

In New York I immediately signed my power-of-attorney over to Weissberger, who proposed to repatriate Stravinsky's money in the form of bearer bonds. He entrusted this errand to a young lawyer with dual Swiss and American citizenship, Elwood Rickless. The bonds duly arrived at a Swiss bank on Wall Street, where Vera collected and straightaway deposited them in a vault at Bankers Trust, Fifty-Seventh Street and Park Avenue. Totally innocent of financial matters, she cashed the bonds, unbeknown to me, and placed the money in an ordinary interest-bearing account, thereby forfeiting the entire illegal $450,000 to the IRS. Weissberger also employed Andrew Foldi to bring Stravinsky's Picassos, Klees, Giacomettis and other valuable art from a Paris bank on the rue Cambon to New York. After her husband's death, desperate to pay debts, Vera sold the eleven Picassos for sums infinitely beneath their market value. I knew nothing of this or that she had come under the influence of an art dealer and old friend.

In the litigation against Vera initiated in 1974 by the Stravinsky family heirs, Martin Garbus, her new New York attorney, took the depositions of Milene and Andre Marion, which exposed their thefts and machinations. Garbus wrote:

> According to sworn, uncontested testimony, on August 18, 1969, Stravinsky's younger son, Soulima, and daughter, Milene, in collusion with the composer's California attorney, W. Montapert, signed an agreement to remove the composer's remaining monies from the Swiss Bank Verein, Basel, and divide them fifty percent for themselves and fifty percent for Montapert. It is uncontested that Montapert did remove the money but eventually returned it to avoid charges of defalcation.

During one of the depositions Milene obligingly produced the letter she had sent to her brother Theodore in September 1969 seeking his signature on the theft agreement:

> Montapert managed, through a great many acrobatics, to
> take out of the Basel account the money that was there... by
> combining his own power of attorney with that of Andre, who
> warns you to be very careful when using the above information.
> No one must be able to accuse Andre and Montapert to have
> plotted together, especially at the time when Montapert was
> the parents' attorney.

After five years of litigation, the ninety-year-old Vera Stravinsky prevailed upon Garbus to reach a settlement based on the principal terms of her husband's will. I was not privy to this, nor was I present at the court hearings. According to Garbus's summation in the 1979 agreement, 'The total amount the Marions had taken from Igor Stravinsky in the 1960s will never be known.'[2]

Apart from the Marion–Montapert collusion, another aspect of the court proceedings was a consequence of Stravinsky's gift to his wife of the full-score manuscript of *The Rite of Spring* as a nameday present (30 September 1968). This had been in Theodore's possession until he returned it to his father on his demand (11 October 1968), at the Dolder Hotel, Zurich.[3] I carried the cumbersome volume to my room across the corridor from Stravinsky's where the gifting[4] took place and witnessed the composer adding an *envoi* denouncing the first Paris audience for its insult to his masterpiece in 1913. Theodore and Denise (now on crutches as a result of her tuberculosis) remained in the living room with Rufina Ampenoff, a representative of Stravinsky's London publishers Boosey & Hawkes whom Denise had chauffeured from the airport. Ampenoff tried to prevent Stravinsky from adding the postscript, for which reason he signed it in my room and not in his

---

2   While the Stravinskys were in Europe, in a single day in October 1968 Marion wrote two
     cheques to himself totalling $30,000.
3   The remainder of the Stravinsky floor was rented by the Shah of Iran for his sister.
     Coincidentally, in 1979 the Shah himself would occupy Stravinsky's former room in New
     York Hospital, thanks to Henry Kissinger's connivings.
4   It has been postulated, 'Nobody saw Vera's husband give [the *Sacre* score] to her, not even
     Robert Craft, though he later described the scene as if he had been there.' But on the day of
     the event, as recorded in my published diary, I was there, as could have been traced to my
     registration in the hotel records - how else could I have described it, and who else could
     have carried the large, heavy volume to my room across the corridor from Stravinsky's? It
     is here that he wrote and signed the *envoi* and presented the manuscript to his wife.

own. This also accounts for Theodore's shambolic testimony during the 1970s litigation that French was the language of the envoi. It is Russian. Further, under oath, Theodore declared in his deposition that Pierre Souvtchinsky was also there, when in actuality he had returned to Paris the day before precisely to avoid Theodore. This declaration alone should have disqualified the latter as a witness. The account in my *Chronicle of a Friendship* of Stravinsky's presentation to his wife was accepted as legally binding evidence by the Supreme Court of the State of New York.

All of Stravinsky's wills, except the last, named Vera as his principal heir. But the final one drawn up by Montapert omits her altogether in favour of the children. During a business lunch at the Stravinskys' Hollywood home, Montapert had presented the fraudulent will under the pretence that it was a contract to purchase another citrus grove in Yuma, Arizona,[5] and Stravinsky trustingly signed it unread.

In the autumn of 1970 Stravinsky initiated a lawsuit for the return of his manuscripts held in a bank vault in Los Angeles under Marion's name. Ironically the news of this scandal was featured on international television while Theodore, on a visit to his father in the Essex House, silently watched the broadcast with him. Marion finally agreed to surrender the manuscripts only on the condition that he would not be prosecuted for monies he had diverted from his father-in-law's U.S. bank account into his own over the last several years. When eventually received in New York in December 1970, the manuscripts were superficially inventoried and appraised for tax purposes at a mere $200,000 by Sigmund Rothschild, a certified New York City art appraiser. Stravinsky's archives and most of his manuscripts had filled a large moving van and were lodged in a room in the Essex House.[6] Here the biographer Francis Steegmuller, who had rented a room near Stravinsky's, examined them with a view to writing a biography, a project to which Vera had given her blessing.

---

5   Montapert had invested hundreds of thousands of Stravinsky's dollars in citrus farms near Yuma for the Marions, who sold them after the composer's death.

6   It has been claimed that 'the rest of the archives arrived in New York in a consignment of large cartons and were stored away in the cupboard in Craft's bedroom'. In fact, Craft did not have a bedroom, let alone a cupboard, but only a chauffeur's closet (in which it was necessary for him to move crablike to a cot) and no other furnishings.

I have been accused of taking up 'arms' against my old 'legal adversaries', Stravinsky's children and grandchildren. But I was never an adversary, and my name does not appear in their 1974 lawsuit against Vera Stravinsky. Quite the contrary, I was and still am their greatest benefactor. When they accepted a $2,000,000 offer from the Paul Sacher Foundation for the purchase of Stravinsky's archives, I managed to increase the price of the sale to $5,250,000, though today they would be worth many times that. Moreover, the composer's granddaughter, Catherine, owed her inclusion in Stravinsky's will entirely to me. During a day alone with him in Philadelphia in 1966 between rehearsals for a concert – Vera was in New York lunching with her old friend Marcel Duchamp – I persuaded the composer to name his granddaughter and Mika's daughter, Catherine, as beneficiary for two-ninths of her grandfather's estate. Stravinsky's note regarding this survives, written in block letters, and the change was implemented immediately. Kitty came to Hollywood to thank Stravinsky as well as me. His sons and daughter are likewise indebted to me for helping Vera convince her husband to pay their taxes and to purchase houses and automobiles for them. Most important of all, my recordings and performances of Stravinsky's music, which was still far from popular at the time I met him, continue to provide royalty income that since his death has bestowed millionaire status on remote descendants.

In New York before the move to Evian, Elliott and Helen Carter were regular visitors to the Essex House. Elliott has published a memoir of listening to recordings and following scores there with Stravinsky. Nicolas and Dominique Nabokov were almost daily guests, and other frequent visitors included the Goddard Liebersons, the Dushkins, Paul Horgan, Virginia Rice (Stravinsky's literary agent) and Columbia University professor John Malmstad (researching Vera's archives about her association with the Russian poet Kuzmin), Lucia Davidova, Natasha Nabokov, Carlos Chávez, Alexander Schneider, Ahron Propes (director of the Festival of Israel), George Balanchine, Wystan Auden, Christopher Isherwood, Don Bachardy and Dr Maurice Gilbert.

In the summer of 1970 the scene changed to the Hôtel Royal at Evian-les-Bains where, on the recommendation of Sol Hurok, the Stravinskys spent two and a half months. Barely a week before our departure the composer had been hospitalised in New York, but his cardiologist, Dr Lax, found him fit to travel, comparing the salubrious Evian air to that of sweltering and polluted New York. We packed hastily and in two days left for Geneva with his nurse, Rita Christiansen. We were met in Europe by Theodore and Denise but the senior Stravinskys travelled the forty miles to the hotel not with them but in a limousine. The next afternoon Stravinsky expressed a desire to go outdoors: Ms Christiansen wheeled him to the nearby church at Neuvecelle, where he crossed himself with holy water from the baptismal font, then smoothed his hair with it. That evening and the next the composer dined on the outdoor terrace with Arnold Weissberger and his companion Milton Goldman.[7] Meanwhile, two nurses and a physical therapist, Danielle François, had been engaged. Among the first visitors were Stravinsky's granddaughter Catherine and her young daughter, Svetlana Marie. When Stravinsky asked the child's surname, the answer 'Stravinsky' came as a shock to him, as he was not aware that his granddaughter was unmarried.

Hurok's agent, L. Libman, was with us for a few days at the Hôtel Royal, having been brought along to fetch the Stravinskys' automobile from a steamship at Rennes; she lingered in Paris but returned to New York before Stravinsky's birthday. Theodore came infrequently, partly for the reason that his father was receiving almost daily treatment for his polycythaemia by the Geneva doctor Della Santa at a hospital in Thonon-les-Bains, a considerable drive from the hotel and a wearying experience for the patient. In addition Stravinsky was enjoying the company of other visitors. These included Miranda Levy and the Babitzes from Los Angeles; Stravinsky's niece Xenya from Russia; Rufina Ampenoff; the Robert Patersons; the photographer Lord Snowdon, with a friend from London; Natasha Nabokov (then living with the Vladimir Nabokovs in Ouchy across the lake from Stravinsky); Hugues Cuénod from La Tour-de-Peilz; the pianist Nikita

---

7   The Neuvecelle story can be verified by Ms Christiansen's diary, and the holy water toilette is so characteristic of Stravinsky that it cries out to be told. Further, the composer's own diary confirms that Weissberger and Goldman dined outdoors with Stravinsky the next day. Weissberger's photographs of the visit have been published in his book *Famous Faces*.

Magaloff and his wife (Joseph Szigeti's daughter); Pierre Souvtchinsky; and François Michel from Paris.

The Theodore-Denise letters to the Marions that summer avow that 'Papa's health steadily improved', and on 28 August, after seven blood transfusions, Dr Della Santa announced that the polycythaemia that had plagued the patient for twelve years had been a misdiagnosis.

During the Evian evenings we listened to recordings as did, through our wide-open windows, a captive dinner audience on the outdoor terrace below. At the time, Stravinsky was immersed in Beethoven, but whether the music by the colossus of Bonn annoyed the diners we never knew. Neither the hotel manager nor anyone else complained to us, perhaps because everyone was aware that it was Stravinsky listening.

Stravinsky's favourite composers were always Bach, Mozart and Schubert. Only after he stopped composing did he embrace Beethoven fully. The inadequacy of recorded performances of Beethoven's symphonies was always an obstacle for him. No conductor – not Toscanini, not Furtwängler, not Klemperer, not Reiner, certainly not Szell – performed any of them to Stravinsky's satisfaction. I remember him frowning throughout Furtwängler's dragging tempo in the second movement of the Fifth – though he also criticised the repetitiveness of the movement itself. He squirmed and groaned during the grossly exaggerated *ritards* ending the opening theme of the third movement (marked *poco rit.*), and he turned off the record player at the onset of the protracted finale.

When I first lived with Stravinsky he refused to listen to the start-and-stop last movement of the Ninth Symphony, disliking the bass instruments' recitative-style introduction and the interruptions repeating excerpts from the earlier movements, although he thought the return of the Scherzo in the middle of the finale of the Fifth was a stupendous inspiration. The quartets and sonatas claimed most of his time. I sometimes think about similarities between Stravinsky's state of mind and Beethoven's after composing his last quartets. As Milan Kundera wrote:

> The quartets are like nothing else; in the complexity of their construction they are far from classicism, yet do not come close to the facile spontaneity of the young Romantics. In the evolution of music he has gone off in a direction where no one has followed; without disciples, without successors, the work from his vesperal freedom is a miracle, an island.

Differences of stature and scope aside, so it must have been with Stravinsky, who was also cut off from public musical life, beholden to no tradition and expecting no successors. His late style is accessible only to those who have followed him through many years. Stravinsky's Jacob-and-the-Angel struggle against Beethoven in earlier years can be attributed in part to an antipathy for the heroic: 'There are too many marches,' Stravinsky said, even in the Op. 127 Quartet. How different it was in Evian, where he continually gasped with wonder. Did the fifty-bar, three-octave ostinato in the Scherzo of the last quartet (Op. 135) remind him of the unstoppable spirit he must have experienced in composing *The Rite of Spring*? Both composers possessed that inevitable force for the drive to the end, in those three-chord *forte* hammerings in the first movement of the 'Eroica' and in the repeated chords in the 'Danse des adolescentes' about which Diaghilev asked, 'How long will this go on?' and Stravinsky answered, 'Till the very end, my dear.'

PART THREE
Friends and Acquaintances

Giacomo Puccini

Puccini heard *Petrushka* at the Théâtre du Châtelet in Paris in June 1911, less than a month after Stravinsky had completed the score at the Albergo d'Italia, Rome, 'in a room overlooking the Barberini Gardens'. He had arrived in the city in April. Conceivably the paths of the two composers may have crossed in this vicinity in April–May of that year. Both had at different times resided in the hotel nearby at 54 Via Margutta. This narrow street – best known today as the set for *Roman Holiday* with Audrey Hepburn and Gregory Peck – runs parallel to a stretch of Via del Babuino through a neighbourhood favoured by artists since Rubens and Poussin. Today the Hôtel de Russie near the Piazza del Popolo is famed for its 'Stravinsky Bar'. That the younger composer influenced the older is certain: Puccini admitted having borrowed from *Petrushka* in *Il tabarro* and musicians agree that he did so again in *Gianni Schicchi*, from the tuba part in the ballet's scene of the dancing bear. Stravinsky would have been interested in the twenty-first-century discovery that Puccini had also borrowed the melody of *Shiba Mo* ('The Eighteen Touches') from a Swiss music box and used it in *Madama Butterfly*. This nineteenth-century musical apparatus had turned up in Rome into the hands of the composer's friend, Baron Alberto Fassini Camossi. Puccini knew that the principal tune was banned in China as pornographic, since the text celebrates, according to W. Anthony Sheppard, 'the eighteen parts of a woman's body in explicit detail, moving caress by caress from head to toe'. Musical box tunes are effectively employed in *Petrushka*.

Puccini's fascination with this ballet prompted him to attend one of the first Paris performances of *The Rite of Spring*, though surely not the rowdy premiere. He reported to Tito Ricordi, his publisher, that the music was 'sheer cacophony but strange and not without a certain talent'. On hearing that three days after the *Rite* Stravinsky had been hospitalised with typhoid fever and was recuperating at the Villa Borghese clinic in Neuilly, Puccini visited the patient there on 16 June. The two composers remained in touch thereafter through their mutual friend Serge Diaghilev. Stravinsky recalled that during his last dinner with Debussy in November 1916, Puccini was the subject of conversation: 'Debussy had a genuine esteem for Puccini and knew and liked many pages of his music... I had a genuine feeling for [him] too. He invited me to his home in Torre del Lago, but alas, he died before I could go.'

An interview with Diaghilev on the arrival of the Ballets Russes in New York in 1916 quotes him: 'Who do you have writing for opera now? Puccini, who hardly merits consideration musically?' (*The New York Post*, 24 January 1916).[1] The question pertains to a then current view that ballet, not opera, was the door to modernism. Whether or not this statement ever reached Puccini's ears, Stravinsky repeatedly vouched that Puccini was Diaghilev's favourite composer, and that he frequently sang to himself melodies from *Tosca* and *La Bohème*.

Nine years after the *Rite*, Puccini heard *Mavra* in Paris and, predictably, did not like it. Conveying his reactions to a lady friend on vacation in Rügen, he concluded: 'If Stravinsky wishes, the sun of Puccini has gone down, but *Turandot* still has modern intentions.' While composing the opera's third act, Puccini travelled from Milan to Florence to hear Schoenberg conduct *Pierrot Lunaire* (1 April 1924). The nineteen-year-old Luigi Dallapiccola, who was also present, noted that after the boos and catcalls of the Palazzi Pitti audience, Puccini was the only person to go backstage and congratulate the composer and spend a considerable amount of time discussing the piece. Puccini

---

1   Diaghilev spoke of the growing importance of ballet and the difficulties of presenting opera as music drama: '[T]he twenty-year-old Prokofiev, our future, is writing for the ballet, not to mention Debussy, Ravel, Stravinsky and even Strauss.' Richard Buckle condemned Diaghilev's betrayal of his hero, Puccini: The 'coq must have crowed thrice'.

commented that 'to enter such a musical world one must possess a nature quite different from what one has at present, but who can say whether Schoenberg may not be a point of departure for a goal in the distant future?'[2] Schoenberg acknowledged that 'I was indeed honoured that Puccini, not an expert judge but a practical expert, made a six-hour journey to hear the piece, and came backstage and said some very friendly things to me. That was good, strange though my music may have remained to him.' For Schoenberg, Puccini was a 'great man, superior to Verdi in technique'. By this time, having recently heard *Parsifal* in Vienna, Puccini was under the thrall of Wagner ('five hours of utmost bliss'). Only a few weeks before his own death, after playing the *Tristan* prelude on the piano, Puccini burst out with a denigration of Italian composers: 'We are mandolin players, amateurs. This music annihilates us and renders us unable to achieve anything.'

Surprisingly for Puccini admirers, Stravinsky did not hear *Tosca* until 5 February 1929, in Lyon, but soon after went out of his way to hear another performance in Lugano. Hearing it again on 4 August 1956, in the Campo San Angelo in Venice, he praised the music even in a miserable performance but criticised the conception of the libretto. He loved the music deeply, at least until the death of Scarpia.

> I think that Puccini identified with Cavaradossi as a handsome artist philanderer. Tosca recognises that the painter's portrait of her is actually a likeness of the Marchesa Attavanti, a very simple passing event in the opera that most of the audience does not understand. In Act II, when Tosca disobeys her lover's demand that she does not reveal Angelotti's hiding place to stop Scarpia from torturing her lover, Cavaradossi is furious with her. The turnabout in his fervours is not conveyed by the music, which becomes hollow, and, in spite of many beauties, declines all the way to the end of the opera. The orchestral

---

2   A few years later Schoenberg constructed the twelve-tone series of 'Von Heute auf Morgen' from Puccini's *Manon Lescaut*, and in 1947 Schoenberg seems to have borrowed the idea of the unison male chorus ending the first act of *Tosca* for the one that concludes *A Survivor from Warsaw*.

ending of Act II is very poor stuff, and the beginning of Act III sounds as if another composer had written it. The morning bells and chorus are inferior, mere filler, and the prison farewell is blatantly false. Ironically, the funeral music for Scarpia, perhaps the most memorable in the opera, is heard only in the strings – no voices – and its delicate eighteenth-century embellishments are hardly suitable for the police-chief villain.

In May 1965 Puccini's nephew Giulio Razzi, director of the Radiotelevisione Italiana (RAI) in Rome, telephoned Stravinsky in Warsaw, inviting him to a special concert in his honour at the Vatican. Travel and hotel expenses for the composer and his entourage, Paris to Rome to Los Angeles, would be provided by the Vatican, and CBS television would film the performance of Symphony of Psalms with Stravinsky sitting next to Pope Paul VI.[3] On the day of the concert Stravinsky lunched in the Hassler Hotel with his sculptor friend Giacomo Manzù but imbibed too much Scotch too close to the matinée concert. Genuflecting before the Pope after the Psalms performance, Stravinsky stumbled as he was about to kiss the Pontiff's ring, whereupon an elderly but alert gentleman in the front row of the audience rushed to the composer's support. This would-be rescuer turned out to be Giovacchino Forzano, the librettist of *Gianni Schicchi*, co-author with Mussolini of three plays, and the producer of the first *Turandot*.[4]

A formal dinner at the Hilton Hotel hosted by Signor Razzi followed the concert. Deeply moved by the Vatican reception, Stravinsky swallowed even more of his favourite liquid. At a round table for about twenty people, he was also unhappy to find himself flanked by two garrulous society ladies. Signora Adriana Panni, Stravinsky's self-appointed guardian in Rome, jockeyed for the chair on his left, but the lady occupying it was her social superior. He asked me to sit between him and the woman on his right, which Vera Stravinsky approved while imploring me to try to restore her husband to a degree

---

3   A close-up of the scene is included in Tony Palmer's film *Once at a Border...*
4   Puccini and Mussolini were on very good terms, but Toscanini's refusal to play the Fascist hymn at the premiere of *Turandot* compelled the dictator not to attend.

of sobriety. I failed in this, since he was satiated and then some, and by the end of the meal his head was resting on the table. Just as Signor Razzi, a tall, dignified figure, was approaching the peroration of his eloquent tribute from across the table, Vera left her seat next to him, crept up behind her husband, and whispered sternly in his ear that he absolutely must pull himself together and respond. Miraculously, the command reached his brain, and he programmed himself to stand and utter a single but clearly audible, 'G–R–A–Z–I–E.' At the end of the dinner, Signora Panni organised the retreat, locating a stretcher-like conveyance to transport the sleeping composer of *The Rite of Spring* to his limousine.

Nino Rota

The *New Grove Dictionary* introduces the prodigy Nino Rota simply by revealing his long friendship with Stravinsky. When the film director Federico Fellini questioned Rota about this, he replied that 'Stravinsky was always fun; his mind struck sparks. Age was no barrier.' Their ages at the time of their first meeting were twenty-one and fifty, but no matter: Rota was a self-assured young man who, when they were together in Milan and Torino in 1932–3, was already a successful composer. The most extraordinary aspect of the relationship is that Rota's music did not borrow from Stravinsky's, unlike that of the many Hollywood film composers who plagiarised his musical ideas, rhythmic patterns, instrumentation and much more. Rota concocted an idiom of his own and developed it in his own way. He began to compose as a child and at the age of eleven achieved a high degree of success with his oratorio *The Childhood of John the Baptist*, which was staged in Milan and Paris. I assume that this music and what followed is rooted in that of his teachers, Ildebrando Pizzetti and Alfredo Casella, a conservative and a modernist, both mediocre composers but well-grounded mentors. The most perceptive observer of Rota's gifts was Fellini, who called him 'the most precious collaborator I ever had':

> Between us, there was, immediately, a complete, total, harmony.
> He had a geometric imagination, a musical approach worthy of
> celestial spheres. He thus had no need to see images from my
> movies. When I asked him about the melodies he had in mind
> to accompany one sequence or another, I clearly realised he was
> not concerned with images at all. His world was inner, inside
> himself, and reality had no way to enter it.

This should be understood in a general way, since specific events and
emotional content in movies must be connected to music that exactly
fits them. Rota worked very closely with his directors, all of them men
of keen vision and sensitivity to the musical qualities. From the same
interview with Fellini, who collaborated with Rota on *8½*, *La Dolce Vita*
and *La Strada* (where his name in the credits precedes the director's),
Rota himself said:

> When composing at the piano I tend to feel happy; but - this
> raises the eternal dilemma - how can we be happy amid the
> unhappiness of others? I would do everything I could to give
> everyone a moment of happiness. That is what is at the heart
> of my music.

Fellini believed that his films achieved their cohesion through Rota's
music and that the film is partly directed by the music. The same
could be said by the composer's other filmmakers, Luchino Visconti
(*The Leopard*), Franco Zeffirelli (*Romeo and Juliet*) and Francis Ford
Coppola (*The Godfather*).

A biography of Rota is not needed here, books and films about him
being available, but it must be said that his career is one of the most
spectacular in twentieth-century music. In addition to more than 150
film scores, he composed prolifically in all of the traditional musical
forms, from solo piano pieces to large orchestral works. Of his ten
operas, the best known are *The Florentine Straw Hat*, which was
presented by the Santa Fe Opera in 1977, and *Aladdin and the Magical
Lamp*, performed by the Vienna State Opera and released on DVD. He
was also a gifted writer: the University of Milan awarded him a degree

in literature for his thesis on Gioseffo Zarlino. In the 1930s Toscanini encouraged Rota to move to America, which he did after winning a scholarship to the Curtis Institute in Philadelphia. As a student there of Fritz Reiner, Rota also became a proficient conductor, which led him to teaching. On his return to Italy shortly before World War II, he accepted the position of director of the Conservatory of Music in Bari where his most famous student was Riccardo Muti. I learned more about Rota from the renowned New York cellist Fred Sherry, who was a member of the orchestra in the 1968 Menotti production of Rota's opera *Napoli Milionaria!* in Spoleto.

The Stravinsky–Rota correspondence is small but affectionate. Vera Stravinsky made several photographs of him with her husband in Torino and Milan, and the great composer spoke generously about the technical skills in Rota's 'improvisatory movie-music'. He remains a dominant figure in the musico-cinematic world where millions have heard – and some wish they could forget – the *Godfather* theme music.

Sergei Prokofiev

Igor Stravinsky and Sergei Sergeyevich Prokofiev were good friends both publicly and privately, though their correspondence tends to conceal conflicting feelings about each other. Prokofiev was ten years younger than Stravinsky and a decade ahead of him in his musical career. Then, between 1910 and 1913, the year he turned thirty-one, Stravinsky's musical genius burst into the world in three successive ballets which established the modern music era and incidentally almost eradicated the career of his younger potential rival.

It is often asserted that Prokofiev cultivated Stravinsky's friendship chiefly because of his influence on Diaghilev, who had met the younger composer in London in 1914. Diaghilev invited him to the Hotel Continental in Milan in June 1915, forewarning Stravinsky that Prokofiev did not possess a great talent. Stravinsky came from Switzerland for the meeting with an ulterior motive. He knew that Prokofiev was en route to Petrograd and could be entrusted to deliver the scores and parts of *The Nightingale* to Vsevolod Meyerhold. This renowned director planned to produce the opera in 1918 at the Mariinsky Theatre. (Mme Khvoshchinsky, a close friend of Prokofiev, wrote to Stravinsky from Rome informing him that the materials had been safely delivered.)

In Milan in 1915, the two composers played the *The Rite of Spring* together four-hands and, for Diaghilev, the first two tableaux of *Les Noces*. Stravinsky was *bouleversé* by the younger man's musicianship and piano technique. Diaghilev had warned Stravinsky that Prokofiev's music was rough and showed little accomplishment, and told Igor that he would have to rewrite Prokofiev's ballet, a poor imitation of *Sacre*.

Prokofiev had lived in the Caucasus and composed some excellent music there, including the first Violin Concerto and the 'Classical' Symphony. But with the abdication of the Tsar in the spring of 1917 and the October Revolution that replaced him with Lenin, Prokofiev realised that he would have to escape to America, then back to Western Europe. He took the train to Vladivostok later in 1917 and went on to Japan. Stravinsky's next communication from him came from Nara in 1918 and subsequent letters followed from Hawaii, San Francisco, Tijuana and Chicago, where he composed the opera *The Love for Three Oranges* with Vera Janacopolous as co-librettist. He conducted Stravinsky's *Pribaoutki* with her in New York and wrote a jewel of an account of the piece to the composer.

Photographs of Stravinsky and Prokofiev together in Paris date from the summer of 1920 and others followed at important moments in their respective careers. All of them reveal a very short man looking downwards and grumpy, the tall one beaming. In reality Prokofiev churned with jealousy in Stravinsky's presence, though both men managed to conceal their feelings, whatever they were.

Stravinsky had a considerable fondness for the young man and a genuine desire to help him in his career, much as he generally denigrated the driving ambition of performing musicians. In 1928 at the Théâtre Sarah-Bernhardt, they actually appeared in a concert together, Stravinsky conducting *Renard* and Prokofiev his *Prodigal Son*, one of his finest works. By a chilling coincidence, Stravinsky was with Prokofiev, Souvtchinsky and Koussevitzky in August 1929 in the conductor's home in Aix-les-Bains when they received the news of Diaghilev's death in Venice, a cruel blow to the three musicians, profound to Stravinsky, worrisome to Prokofiev, and something of a relief to Koussevitzky.

Stravinsky knew little of Prokofiev's music before they shared a concert at the Paris Opéra in October 1923. Koussevitzky had invited Stravinsky to conduct his new Octet on a programme that included the 'Eroica' Symphony and Prokofiev's Violin Concerto. The Octet required a small three-sided booth in the centre of the huge stage for acoustical and logistical reasons (large orchestra *vs.* chamber music ensemble). But the Stravinsky piece was the only one that provoked any comment, most of it puzzled and negative. The little Octet was not recognised by the audience or the critics as marking a new direction in world music. Prokofiev's Violin Concerto, one of his best works and perhaps his only one on a level with Stravinsky, went unnoticed by the press and received only tepid audience reaction. But a pattern was established that day: Prokofiev realised that he would spend his entire life in Stravinsky's shadow. The younger man blamed his lack of success on this and adopted the view that in France, the rest of Europe and the United States in the 1920s and 1930s, his music was insufficiently appreciated. Five years after his return to France, he married the Spanish-born dancer Lina Llubera. He decided to turn to the Soviet Union in 1927, hoping that his Russian compatriots would value his music more highly.

Prokofiev was an aloof personality, whose only friends were musicians. He wrote a good many letters to his closest confidant, the Soviet symphony composer Miaskovsky; most of these contain rude comments on Stravinsky's latest compositions, though the letters usually conclude with redeeming observations as well. For example, in his comments on Stravinsky's Concerto for Two Pianos he admits that the music has greater depth than his own and perceives that it represents a continuing growth.

In Paris, Igor and Vera were especially close to the Prokofievs, especially to Lina. On the return from the 1927 Soviet experience, which had proved disappointing, the composer, his wife and two sons rented an apartment at 7, rue Frémiet, next door to the temporary residence of Vera de Bosset at number 5. The two families often dined together, attended operas and theatres, and Vera enjoyed playing chess with Sergei.

Throughout the 1930s, Stravinsky pleaded with the younger composer not to return to the U.S.S.R., predicting that conditions would become worse there and eventually intolerable. But Sergei Sergeyevich was obstinate as well as under the influence of the young and beautiful Stalinist devotee, Mira Mendelssohn. The Soviet government refused to allow him to divorce Lina and marry Mira, and all three resided under the same roof in Moscow.

In 1941 Sergei survived a severe heart attack; it was followed by milder ones that prevented this prolific composer from working, and much of his time was spent in hospitals. He nevertheless attempted a comeback and in his final years wrote music of a high quality, particularly in his last piano sonatas. But his late major works were inferior to anything he had ever attempted: the last film scores and the incomplete opera *War and Peace*, after about ten minutes of which Stravinsky crept out of the Bolshoi Theatre during his 1962 return to Moscow.

The overshadowing role in Sergei's fate did not change when he died on the same day as Josef Stalin, and news of the composer's death was suppressed for several days. Stravinsky was informed after it had happened by Nicolas Nabokov, who had an underground connection in the U.S.S.R. Stravinsky deeply mourned the loss and wrote a touching letter to Lina, unaware that she had been condemned to a concentration camp for eight years on a charge of espionage. She spoke perfect English and as wartime deprivations had become unendurable she begged for morsels of food at the British Embassy, because of which she was imprisoned on suspicion of being a spy. Lina was released to attend Stravinsky's Moscow concert in 1962, but she was never left alone with him or with her very close Paris friend, Vera de Bosset.[5]

At the time of the composer's death, *Peter and the Wolf* had become a popular piece in the U.S., but not in Europe or the U.S.S.R. In the

---

5   I had pleasant chats with Lina during Stravinsky's rehearsals and became very fond of her and one of her sons. I met the family in London in the late 1970s.

second decade of the twenty-first century, a Prokofiev revival began and good music was discovered in several pieces. Michael Tilson Thomas discovered some of it in the Third Symphony, for example, as I did in the Second Piano Concerto, which has replaced the Third and Fifth concertos in concert programmes. *Romeo and Juliet* became an established and popular theatre piece as well. Whether this activity increases or sputters along is difficult to predict, but at least one critic, Ned Rorem, has proclaimed Prokofiev - justly, I think - as a major composer.

Since very little of Prokofiev's correspondence has been published in the western world, here is an excerpt from one of his letters to Stravinsky in 1915. This morsel comes from one of the richest musical and artistic periods of the early twentieth century and was sent from Petrograd.

> Dear Igor Fyodorovich,
>
> Your kind postcard made me terribly happy, though it took just under a month to get to Petrograd. I received it on my return from hearing your symphony [in E flat], which was very handsomely played by Nikolai Malko. The second part especially pleased me [it contributed to his style, in fact], as did a lot of the finale. The public and the press gave it a splendid reception... In any case, I'll be in your sweet surroundings within a month. In the meantime, I am passionately engaged in writing the ballet, which is coming together easily, merrily, and speedily... Occasionally I meet Benois, Nouvel and the aging Nurok. I haven't played the draft of *Chout*, nor am I going to. Recently Karatygin and I performed *Spring* and *Petrushka* for four hands. During the latter, Alexander Nikolaevich Scriabin burst in ecstatically and shouted and waved his hands about, explaining to the guests what would be happening on the stage. For now I embrace you tenderly. My regards to Sergei Pavlovich [Diaghilev], Massine, and the Khvoshchinskys. If you're in touch with the publisher Jurgenson and are still kindly disposed toward me as before, please mention my name to his firm... I have a whole series of

manuscripts including the Second Concerto,[6] but he is wheeling and dealing, I know, and personally I find him downright repulsive. Keep well.

Yours, S. Prokof.

George Gershwin

Do it again... Ohhhh, do it again. I may say
no, no, no, no, no, but do it again.

Song by George Gershwin

George Gershwin came backstage to meet Stravinsky after Stravinsky's American debut conducting the New York Philharmonic in Carnegie Hall on 7 January 1925. This brief introduction was extended the next day at a private party for Stravinsky at the home of his friend Arthur Sachs, the banker, but conversation was impossible here because of the noise of the many guests in a long reception line. Stravinsky invited the young American composer to join him at his hotel, the Langdon, the following morning. To this meeting Gershwin brought Jascha Heifetz to help translate and he, in turn, brought Samuel Dushkin, explaining that the young man's Russian and English were more fluent than his own. George's brother, Ira, was also present. The Dushkin tagalong appearance becomes a considerable irony in that five years later, by commissioning and performing Stravinsky's Violin Concerto, Dushkin was branded as a proponent of modernism,[7] while Heifetz, who would denounce the concerto as 'unplayable from the first

---

6   I conducted this concerto in Seoul in the 1980s and enjoyed it very much, not knowing at the time that it was an early work, from 1912. In the early 1930s Stravinsky heard Dimitri Mitropoulos play and conduct the Third Concerto in Hollywood Bowl and spoke enthusiastically about it to me.

7   It should finally be acknowledged that Stravinsky's and my own dear friend Sam Dushkin was not a virtuoso violinist. Stravinsky's piano and violin arrangements for his earlier friend, Paul Kochanski, are technically more demanding than those composed for Dushkin. A handsome, modest, unassuming man with a sterling character, Dushkin in his later years began to develop real or imaginary problems with his fingers and did not perform with Stravinsky after January 1941. In that year, Dushkin commissioned William Schuman to write a concerto for him, but months after receiving the score was obliged to admit that he was unable to play it.

bar', acquired a reputation as a conservative and even a reactionary. Stravinsky told the press that he found the young Gershwin extremely sensitive, intelligent and 'possessing great nervous energy'; since Stravinsky himself was thus endowed, perhaps the implication for him was that Gershwin may have had the talents and temperament of a major composer. His music was obviously closer to Stravinsky's at this time than to that of any of their contemporaries, with the possible exception of Ravel's. Gershwin's sudden death in 1937 came as a great shock to Stravinsky when he heard the news in Paris. His cable of condolence to Gershwin's mother spells the name in Russian.

What happened during the *tête-à-tête* of 9 January 1925 has become a popular anecdote that Stravinsky preserved by affixing the following New York newspaper obit in his personal scrapbook:

> It is hard to believe that George Gershwin is dead. For years he has sailed so easily and successfully down the currents of existence, he has been so triumphantly the playboy of American music, even when he pretended to wear the tragic mask, that the national scene without his presence seems for the moment incredible. Gershwin's achievement was remarkable. He was the first to bring jazz out of Tin Pan Alley and make it not only fashionable but musically estimable. When the *Rhapsody in Blue* was first performed in New York a dozen years or so ago under the direction of Paul Whiteman, Mr. Gershwin woke up to discover from an almost unanimous chorus of critical praise that his true place was not in those halls where the saxophone is king, but in those halls where the symphony is king. Mr. Gershwin was invited by an unassailably dignified symphony society in New York to compose a concerto for piano and orchestra to be presented to the world by that organization. Mr. Gershwin did so, and the concerto was played at a concert in Carnegie Hall with Mr. Gershwin at the piano and Mr. Walter Damrosch conducting. Mr. Gershwin became the most popular composer in America. When he appeared with the Philharmonic Orchestra as soloist in an all-Gershwin program at the Lewisohn Stadium he drew a record crowd of almost 18,000 listeners

and a $10,000 gate. But not only was he the most popular of American composers, he was perhaps the only American composer whom Europeans took seriously. It is said that when Mr. Gershwin requested the great Stravinsky to give him some lessons in composition Mr. Stravinsky asked Mr. Gershwin what his yearly income was, and was told $100,000 or something of that sort. 'Oh,' said Mr. Stravinsky, 'then it is I who should take lessons from you.'

But in spite of the fact that Mr. Gershwin made a great deal of money by writing music, he was nevertheless a composer of skill, rare charm, and feeling. In his last important work, the opera *Porgy and Bess*, there were indications of growing mastery and power that might have yielded an even more important contribution to American music.

Milton Babbitt

The composer and Princeton professor Milton Babbitt was a cherished friend of Stravinsky. Babbitt's scintillating mind was involved both with combinatorics and lyrical poetry. Stravinsky strove to acquaint himself with both of these, but of Babbitt's music he preferred the songs *The Widow's Lament in Springtime* and *Philomel*. The senior composer first heard *Philomel* while standing on a stairway landing – no studio was available – in the CBS building on Seventh Avenue, with Bethany Beardslee in the role of Ovid's ravaged and speechless maiden transformed into a nightingale. In spite of these awkward circumstances, Stravinsky found the piece beautiful and moving. At this time and beyond, Milton was the nemesis of what he stigmatised as 'fun and games music'.

Milton accompanied Stravinsky during his New York visits to as many as possible of his rehearsals for recordings and concerts, the older composer trusting the younger one's perfect musical ear and clarion opinions as they sat together following scores. The two men resembled each other in height, head size and alopecia. Many photos indicate a mutual fondness. Their sense of humour was compatible, and they ridiculed the absurdities of every aspect of professional musical life, though Milton was a very private musical treasure and Stravinsky the most public one on the planet. Finally, it should be remembered that Babbitt forged the friendship between Stravinsky and Chicago's Maecenas, Paul Fromm.

Milton was with Stravinsky in London in 1954 when he conducted the Royal Philharmonic and received the orchestra's gold medal as well as the famous rosewood, silver-tipped baton legendarily presented to Joseph Haydn at his last London concert. In New York, Milton, one of the regulars of the Stravinsky Gladstone gang during the 1950s, relates a story of a typical incident there:

> In late December 1958 [Stravinsky] came to New York from London. He was to conduct the first performance of *Threni* but was working on a new composition, *Movements*. Mrs Stravinsky, Robert Craft and I were sitting in the living room of the Stravinsky suite waiting for Stravinsky to join us for dinner. He was in the bedroom, doing we knew not what, until he suddenly bolted out of the room in his robe, waving a page of manuscript paper, smiling broadly that pixy-like smile and shouting, 'I found a mistake and the right note [serially speaking] sounds so much better!'

I remember returning to the same hotel one day from a lunch with Auden at Schrafft's, complaining that the poet was overly addicted to generalisations. Milton responded with a laugh as he answered the door: 'And whose generalisations do you prefer?' – a question that started me on a road to intellectual maturity.

In the spring of 1972 I was invited to lecture at the University of Chicago, perhaps because a few people thought I was being unfairly subjected to a post-Stravinsky backlash in the press. After the distinguished Bach scholar Robert Marshall warmly introduced me to the audience, I followed him to the podium and on the approach caught a glimpse of Milton's bright eyes and shiny pate in the front row just beneath me. Near the open microphone I unintentionally blurted out my impulse to flee: 'I cannot speak in the presence of

Mr Babbitt, the disciple of John von Neumann' (the Game Theory mathematician). Milton good-humouredly stood up and said, 'If you really want me to go, I'll go' – which would have eliminated both his pain and my crippling self-consciousness. Those who overheard the exchange giggled, breaking the tension, and I began my talk by explaining that after Bertrand Russell, Milton was the most brilliant lecturer I had ever heard, and that his analysis of Schoenberg's Fourth Quartet had led me to consider changing my profession. I repeated to the audience Milton's leg-pulling comment about me: that Stravinsky's first decade in America could be described as B.C. (before Craft) and the second decade as A.D. (the abbreviation of Arnold Schoenberg's given name). Milton himself, of course, was deeply involved in Schoenberg's influence on Stravinsky.

That evening Milton, staying in the same hotel, knocked on my door at about 11 o'clock to invite me to a party for Saul Bellow and the modern-art critic Harold Rosenberg (*Art on the Edge*). I declined by opening the door a sliver, enabling him to hear a female voice. My visitor had come unexpectedly from Knoxville, where I had conducted and lectured that January, fulfilling Stravinsky's contract to appear there. In 1973, after a repeat concert in the same city, I persuaded the young woman, Donna Wright, a virtuoso flautist and pianist, to come to New York to study with Julius Baker, the principal flautist of the New York Philharmonic; a year later she became Vera Stravinsky's secretary.

Milton had a reputation of being very attractive to women, reportedly a characteristic of exceptionally intelligent men. Stravinsky was aware of this and wished to know the secret of what can only be called Milton's sex appeal. But Stravinsky also wanted Milton's opinion of my friend, the elegant Italian lady who at New Year's Eve 1961 was sharing my room next to the Stravinskys' in the St Regis Hotel, New York. He invited the Princeton composer to a house party with this purpose in mind. After the fireworks and the departure of the celebrants, Milton whispered 'open city' in Stravinsky's ear, knowing the composer to be a good friend of Roberto Rossellini and an admirer of his famous film about post-war Rome. In a very late-night confession, my *signora* told me that she found Milton the most sexually magnetic man that she had ever met. By the end of the week, I had sent her back to Rome.

Elliott Carter

In the late afternoon of 5 November 2012 my friend Fred Sherry called, saying, 'Elliott is gone.' Fred's wife, Carol, who had been alone with Elliott in his room, said that he had been asleep and suddenly stopped breathing. My wife Alva and I could not suppress tears, a response that might not be understood by anyone not close to him; the death of a man aged 103 would be considered natural. But at the next dawn the world seemed much emptier. Unlike most lives, his seemed to become richer and more fulfilled as he grew older. His discovery of his creative musical world did not really begin until he was in his fifties, during his isolation in the Arizona desert, when he first composed radically new and original works, ever accelerating explorations of new and different territories, from the Double Concerto to *Night Fantasies*, the Piano Concerto to the gigantic pieces for multiple ensembles. At age ninety he was dining with us and the art critic John Russell and his wife, Peggy, at La Caravelle, when he exuberantly revealed his plan to write an opera. At ninety? We couldn't help feeling a twinge of doubt, but Elliott was in high spirits and full of self-confidence. The opera *What Next?* was a major success at its premiere in Berlin and it led to a new decade of compositions that would include such orchestral masterpieces as *Soundings*.

I was a close friend of Elliott's for sixty-four years,[8] and though our friendship began through Stravinsky it continued after his death partly through of our memories of him. Countless afternoons and

---

8   I first met Elliott at a concert I conducted in May 1949 at Columbia University. He did not recall this, but I do because of an involvement with my soloist, Arlene Carmin, who sang Wolpe's *Palestinian Songs* on an ill-assorted programme that also included a batch of Cage's prepared piano pieces. I was interested in the Cage opus because I had met him at one of my rehearsals of *Les Noces* for a Town Hall concert a few weeks before. He was quite unlike anyone I had ever encountered but I found it difficult to sustain conversation with him. He was charming and witty but tried too insistently to indoctrinate me about the greatness of Erik Satie. No music by Elliott was performed at this concert but I recall him working like a stagehand to move chairs and music stands and help arrange the setup of the ensembles.

evenings, reminiscing about Stravinsky, occurred until the last few months. Elliott was always close to Stravinsky, whether in New York, Hollywood, Paris, Rome, London, Berlin, Dartington, or Carleton College (Minnesota), when Elliott was a guest professor there.

When Elliott's beloved wife Helen died we worried about him, but he rallied and composed with even greater intensity, and his creative career projected him to the peak of the musical world. The ovation that greeted him and his new concerto at the London Proms in August 2003 was followed by Andrew Porter's acclamation of him as 'the greatest living composer'.

On 15 July 1966 the Lincoln Center Stravinsky Festival presented a staged performance of L'Histoire du Soldat with Elliott as the Soldier, Aaron Copland as the Narrator, and - typecasting a bit - John Cage as the Devil.[9] Three days later Helen and Elliott dined with the Stravinskys at La Côte Basque. As always, the composers talked music, and so intently that neither of them saw the famous face, better known as 'the Voice', approaching their table. Helen, the first to identify the intruder, nudged Elliott. Stravinsky only noticed that a piece of paper and a pen had been placed next to him on the table - not a novel occurrence, but when he autographed the paper without bothering to look up, both Helen and Elliott were aghast. Frankie, unaccustomed to anonymity, retreated to his secluded table and rejoined Mia Farrow, who would fly to Las Vegas with him the following day and become the next Mrs Sinatra.

As their closest longtime friends in the American musical world, Elliott and Helen witnessed many curious incidents in their adventures with the Stravinskys, especially from 1952 and during the last years of the elder composer's life in New York. Vera Stravinsky's

---

9   After the performance Cage called on Stravinsky at the Pierre Hotel. By now each was interested in the other, though they had been at odds since 1960 in Venice, when Cage ridiculed Stravinsky's transportation by palanquin from the street to the uppermost floor in the Doge's Palace (which lacked an elevator). Stravinsky stalked out of Cage concerts in two instances in 1963: a Cage-Cunningham 'happening' at La Fenice, and in Zagreb after some Cage pseudo-musical shenanigans. At the Pierre he had come to ask Stravinsky for an autograph to be sold to raise money for a concert. When Stravinsky made a deprecatory remark about The Firebird, Cage responded by calling it 'one of the great masterpieces of the century'. Stravinsky admired Cage's poem: 'I have nothing to say and I am saying it / and that is poetry / as I need it' (from Lecture on Nothing, 1959).

diaries are the source of an extensive but far from complete agenda of visits, dinners, concerts, ballets and vernissages with Elliott and Helen. The Carters attended the private New York funeral service for Stravinsky on the day of his death.

'Call Helen' was Elliott's response when a difficulty of any kind arose, and often Alva and I did. When we were negotiating to rent an apartment in Venice, Helen brought us back to reality with the reminder: 'Just try to have a light bulb changed!' When the tenor chosen for my performance and recording of *The Rake's Progress* in New York[10] proved incapable of learning the rhythmically intricate passages and had to be replaced two days before the dress rehearsal, we turned to Helen in despair. 'Get Jon Garrison,' she said, knowing he was familiar with the role. We explained that he was vexed with us since we had cast him for the Shepherd's part in *Oedipus Rex*, instead of the title role. Helen volunteered to arrange the matter herself, and within a half hour we had an excellent as well as bonhomous 'Tom Rakewell, Esquire'. The next day our Anne Trulove succumbed to laryngitis. Again we called Helen. She proposed Lucy Shelton, who to our chagrin had a previous engagement, but we found a substitute who achieved a convincing performance. Later, Elliott wrote praising my recording of the opera:

> The Craft *Rake* is wonderful. It avoids the dragging gait of the Stravinsky recording, which hurts the Third Act especially... I had forgotten that pervasive melancholy that surrounds the whole in some strange way, but adds a beauty... Perhaps Bedlam is the artist's true place in capitalist society.

One day Alva was lamenting her difficulties in luring me out of the house for some exercise. She called Helen for advice and was told: 'That's simple. Just open the door and *push* him out. I do that every day with Elliott.' Helen's spunkiness was one of her most endearing qualities. During an evening at a Fifty-Eighth Street bistro, Elliott

---

10   The Carters attended an Avery Fisher Hall concert performance of the opera. My recording was re-released on the Naxos label in April 2009.

must have feared that Helen was on the verge of mentioning someone out of favour in our company, since she suddenly said to her beloved husband – *sotto voce*, but audibly – 'Don't you *dare* kick me under the table again.'

Shortly after Helen Carter's death on 17 May 2003, at the age of ninety-five, a memorial service was held for her. Elliott (knowing my fondness for her) asked me to deliver an obsequy. I knew her too long and loved her too much to read anything appropriate and borrowed two short passages from D. H. Lawrence that I had recently found in his letters, both addressed to newly widowed friends:

> I knew Sallie was turning to go. And what can one do. Only it hurts, the inevitable hurt... And if Sallie had to go to sleep, being really tired, having gone a long way... well, the rest of the journey she goes with us, but as a passenger now, instead of a traveller. Nevertheless, one uses words to cover up a crying inside one.

The second letter is addressed to Katherine Mansfield's husband: 'I had sent a new book I wanted Katherine to read. She'll know, though. The dead don't die. They look on and help.'

When I read these I realised the emotions were too personal and inappropriate for a crowded room. Then I remembered Elliott's dedication of his *Boston Concerto* to Helen, from William Carlos Williams: 'As the rain falls, so does your love / Bathe every open object of the world.'

In the absence of a worthy tribute to Elliott, I can only recount my failure to find one. I searched for suitable poetry to no avail. Browning's 'Bang-whang-whang goes the drum' attempts to express music in terms of the musician's art, and so does Tennyson's 'The moan of doves in immemorial elms', but onomatopoeic renderings of music in terms of another art are ludicrously inadequate. Keats's *Nightingale* suggested Milton, from whom the young poet had borrowed the expression 'plaintive anthem'. (D. H. Lawrence called it 'Caruso at his jauntiest'.) I then began to rummage in Milton himself and soon discovered that his driest prose tracts mention the essential seductiveness of music – 'And who shall silence all the airs and madrigals that whisper softness in chambers?' – but found that his 'music poetry' seemed confined to celestial choirs singing the 'music of the spheres' with angels plucking 'golden-wired harps' or playing organs with sweet stops. True, some of the poet's adjectives concerning performance styles survive, but in a newspaper notice of the latest keyboard *wunderkind*, wouldn't 'volant touch' sound fruity?

Elliott was buried next to Helen in the Green-Wood Cemetery, Brooklyn.

Paul Hindemith

Stravinsky met Hindemith in Weimar in September 1923 during the week of the German premiere of *L'Histoire du Soldat*. Stravinsky reported to Ansermet: 'In the concerts I heard interminable Lieder [*Das Marienleben*] by Hindemith.' The first photograph of Stravinsky with Hindemith was taken in Amsterdam in November 1924 with his colleagues in the Amar String Quartet.

Never attracted to Hindemith's music and unable to respond to the composer about it, Stravinsky was nevertheless fond of Hindemith the man and interested in his theoretical writings. One of his compositions that Stravinsky applauded was *The Four Temperaments*, but Balanchine's leaping choreography near the end may have been the principal cause of this positive reaction. I remember Stravinsky in Hollywood playing through Hindemith's *Ludus tonalis* and remarking that 'it has all the juice and flavour of cardboard'; when I recorded the same composer's setting of Mallarmé's *Hérodiade*, Stravinsky did not stay to the end. In New York in April 1948, he rearranged his social calendar to hear Hindemith play the viola d'amore in a performance of Bach's St John Passion, thereby obliging a distraught Auden to delay the hour for a dinner planned to introduce Chester Kallman to the Stravinskys.

Since I was not present during Stravinsky and Hindemith's meetings in Montreux in late September 1956 and in Santa Fe in 1961, I do not know whether they discussed the music and theories of Schoenberg and Webern. It is unlikely that Hindemith, knowing Schoenberg's *Satires*, would have mentioned them in the early 1920s when they first met (they met frequently in the 1930s and again after World War II). Conversely, in the late 1950s Hindemith was fully aware of Stravinsky's adaptation of Schoenberg's serial concept. It is hardly possible that Stravinsky would not have spoken to Hindemith about Webern, at least in Munich in 1957 (Stravinsky conducted a concert there while Hindemith's *Die Harmonie der Welt* was receiving its first performance in the same city). I myself was unaware of Hindemith's admiration for Webern and have only recently realised that when this composer became *à la mode* around 1959, an annoyed Hindemith told an interviewer: 'My God, we played Webern – the things that today are called new – we played them already in the early twenties. The question of Webern's greatness was decided then. What you have now is simply a rediscovery of his music.'

Indeed, Hindemith was familiar with Webern's music already in 1915, having made a copy of one of the movements in the violin and piano duets, Op. 7, and programming his String Trio as soon as it became available. The Amar Quartet, with Hindemith as violist, had performed Webern's Bagatelles in Paris as early as 28 December 1924, and, as a committee member for the 1924 Donaueschingen Festival, Hindemith (having enlisted the help of another colleague) managed to persuade Schoenberg to conduct his new Serenade:

> How is it with the Schoenberg Serenade? If you cannot get it, please try to obtain the new Wind Quintet. Leave nothing untried; we must definitely have something from him as well as from Webern. Schoenberg especially, you must get, whatever the circumstances. If you have these things in hand, Donaueschingen will stand morally high above all the other musical festivals this year.

In December of the same year in Frankfurt, Hindemith and his musician friends presented three performances of *Gurrelieder* and even sang in the chorus. Schoenberg wrote to Scherchen, who conducted, asking him to 'tell Hindemith that I am extremely pleased with him'. In fact Hindemith played in no fewer than thirty-two performances of Schoenberg's Second Quartet, one of them conducted by the composer.

Schoenberg was offended when Hindemith published a critical analysis of the older composer's Piano Piece, Op. 33a, and when the two were teaching in Berlin at the same time no meeting took place to repair the rupture. On one occasion Hindemith called on Schoenberg at his home but was not invited in. Nevertheless, Hindemith followed all of Schoenberg's theoretical writings, acquiring and learning his music even through the late American period. Hindemith's analyses of Schoenberg's last string quartets remain among the enlightening studies of these difficult pieces, especially of the Fourth Quartet in which the composer of *Mathis der Maler* discovered the expanding developments in Schoenberg's serial technique: that, for instance, a series may appear incomplete, and that it can move from part to part. As one critic put it, Hindemith 'continued to gravitate toward the nineteenth-century notion that harmony lies at the top of the hierarchy of musical materials, which was not Schoenberg's way'. When the younger composer visited Los Angeles in Schoenberg's late years, the older one still declined to see him. But by then Hindemith had become the presiding force in music departments of American universities.

I hope to be forgiven for my audacity in remarking that although I knew Hindemith only slightly, he seems, coincidentally, to have followed my path. The last of his University of Zurich lectures in the autumn of 1959 was devoted to Gesualdo, and the second to Schoenberg.

On 1 January 1953 Stravinsky gave the manuscript of the second movement of his Symphony in C to me, commemorating my 1948 performance of the work. I did not know at the time that he had already made and sold a copy of it to the Library of Congress. (My copy of the original is in pencil and the Library's copy is in ink.) Moreover, the title page does not bear the dedication to the Chicago Symphony, the commission not yet having been concluded to the composer's satisfaction. (He had hoped to be able to sell the premiere performance to another orchestra for a higher fee. On 13 April 1940

Stravinsky wrote to a friend that he had already sold a handwritten copy of his as yet incomplete manuscript of Symphony in C to the Library of Congress, which indicates how financially desperate he was.) Mildred Bliss of Dumbarton Oaks eventually commissioned the piece, but the reprinted score still does not mention her or even the Chicago Symphony. My original pencil score of the second movement remained in Mainz until Gertrud Hindemith somehow smuggled it out of Germany in 1942. But why her husband did not return it to Stravinsky until 1 January 1953, when Hindemith visited the bedridden composer in his Gladstone Hotel suite, remains a mystery.

Luigi Dallapiccola

Luigi Dallapiccola, Italy's best-known modern composer, was Anton Webern's first disciple in that country. Dallapiccola's visit to Webern in Vienna during the darkest days of World War II has become legendary. When lecturing at UCLA in the mid-1950s, Dallapiccola called Stravinsky to ask for an interview and in reply was invited to lunch at the Stravinsky home. The table talk began with Dallapiccola's retrospections of the British premiere of *Perséphone* in Stravinsky's 1935 BBC broadcast.[11] Our guest soon became impassioned on the subject of Schoenberg's 'protest music', citing *A Survivor from Warsaw* as the masterpiece in this category. After Dallapiccola's Los Angeles sojourn, the Monday Evening Concerts and the Ojai Festival performed several of his song cycles with instruments. Of these, the *Goethe Lieder* rehearsed in Stravinsky's home made a strong impression on him, as did other Dallapiccola song cycles of that genre which I conducted – at Ojai the *Due liriche di Anacreonte* with Magda László as soloist, and in Rome in 1955 the *Tre laudi* with the same singer. Stravinsky was disappointed on hearing Dallapiccola's opera *Il prigioniero* in Hamburg but continued to follow the composer's development, and when Dallapiccola joined the faculty of Queen's

---

11 Dallapiccola's diaries indicate that he borrowed the idea for a work of his own, turning Eumolpus, the Narrator (*Storico*) in *Perséphone*, into a radio-telegraph operator.

College in New York they became friends. My own relations with him continued through correspondence until he learned that I had recorded the *Le Marteau sans maître*, after which he sent a letter berating me for helping a composer who had 'dishonestly released a recording conducted by himself in which nearly every note of the vocal part is off-pitch'.

Luciano Berio

In Venice in 1956 Stravinsky met Berio and his wife, the American mezzo-soprano Cathy Berberian, and saw them after that in Rome, Paris, New York, Boston and California, where Stravinsky attended the UCLA performance of Berio's *Circles*, admiring both the piece and its staging. At a later period Stravinsky may have been less enchanted with the graftings of a section of his own 'Dance of the Earth' to one of Berio's orchestral collages, but nevertheless granted permission. No doubt Berio and his *Circles* reminded Stravinsky of his Futuristi friends of the Great War period, at least in spirit, for none of that amusing but amateurish group – Cangiullo, Pratella, Russolo – possessed an iota of Berio's technique. In 1960 Berio arranged a lunch in Rome for Stravinsky to meet Bruno Maderna at the time of the Italian premiere of *Movements*; Maderna contributed helpful comments on performing the piece. We spent pleasant days with the Berios in Milan in June 1963, when Stravinsky conducted *Oedipus Rex* at La Scala and I *The Flood*. On free days we dined with them in their apartment, and on performance days and dress-rehearsal nights at the Biffi Scala.

A few years later Luciano became a visiting lecturer at Mills College in Oakland. Divorced by this time, the personable and vivacious composer was surrounded by women. But when an enamoured female faculty member lost out to a young student and squealed on him, he was dismissed from the college; a police order compelled him to leave California, which he did by way of the Stravinsky Hollywood home. The composer gave him sanctuary, money, and ongoing asylum with friends in Santa Fe.

Benito Mussolini

After a late-night dinner in Milan in the summer of 1963 with Berio and his friend Umberto Eco, Luciano asked Stravinsky in a hushed voice to tell them something about his personal impressions of Mussolini. Stravinsky would never have discussed the subject, but his tongue was loose that night, and the two young men were determined to extract something from him. Their intent was not to convict him of crypto-fascist ideology, nor was he of that breed. The dictator cultivated famous artists, writers and, above all, musicians. Stravinsky was the most renowned in this last category, of course, and he was enamoured of everything Italian. He had chosen to live in Rome after World War I but was unable to find a suitable residence. Il Duce was guilty of artistic social climbing and Stravinsky found him helpful in the promotion of his concert touring. No one will believe this, of course, and Stravinsky's political obtuseness remains unfathomable, but nevertheless believable. Both men were opportunists. When Evelyn Waugh left Ethiopia in January 1936 and arrived in Rome, Mussolini was eager to have his civilian assessment of the situation in the country of his new conquest and granted him a long interview in the Palazzo Venezia. Waugh describes the long hallway-type office, which had to be hiked to reach Il Duce's desk at the end of the room, and which gave him time to study his visitors. Stravinsky had to tread this distance in the same way on every visit.

At that dinner in Milan, I was equally interested in what Stravinsky might say, since I had first stumbled upon his large file with the taboo name of Il Duce containing many photographs and letters to and from him. Ever since my arrival in Naples in 1951, I had been struck by the tone of mortification at the mention of the dictator's name. It was avoided but also whispered amongst friends and colleagues who were last seen wearing the Fascist uniform. Mario Labroca, one of Stravinsky's closest pre-war friends, had apparently held a position of some power in Italian musical affairs; this friendship was renewed in 1951, and in all of Stravinsky's Roman and Venetian visits until the end of his life. At his Venetian funeral on 15 April 1971 it was Labroca who helped to arrange for the orchestra and chorus to perform at the service in Santi Giovanni e Paolo.

The survival of a certain respect for the brutal murderer under whose rule everyone had suffered was puzzling. Many people in the early 1950s were ashamed by the savagery of his death, and most thought that he should have been brought to trial, if only in the name of history. Stravinsky's connection to him disturbs us because he was not an Italian and he withheld the facts of their relationship from his liberal friends, one of them the esteemed French statesman Eduard Herriot. Stravinsky met Il Duce in April 1925 and saw him many times during the next dozen years. The relationship came to an end in 1938 when Hitler coerced Mussolini into adopting Germany's anti-Semitic laws. Stravinsky had programmed Vittorio Rieti's Second Piano Concerto in a concert scheduled to take place in Milan, but the Fascist boss there demanded the removal of the Rieti piece from the programme. Rieti was one of Stravinsky's closest friends, and Stravinsky protested, cancelling the concert. But the music director in Milan appealed to Mussolini to solve the dilemma by arranging for another orchestra and conductor to perform the piece, and persuading Stravinsky to present a concert purely of his own music. Stravinsky was painfully disturbed by this solution, but he did conduct the concert.

Stravinsky was the least politically informed person I have ever encountered. In his college years he had been briefly jailed as a leftist radical. At the outbreak of the Russian Revolution in the spring of 1917 he had supported the movement, even agreeing to compose the new Russian National Anthem – but with an orchestration of the slave-like 'Song of the Volga Boatmen', that reminder of the long history of coffled peasants hauling the barges from the river banks. In December 1916 Stravinsky cheered the assassination of Rasputin led by Prince Yusupov, a fellow student at the University. But in 1918 the composer deplored the murders of the Tsar and his family. With all of his possessions confiscated by the Bolsheviks, the impecunious Stravinsky was supported by wealthy New Yorkers. When he moved to Paris in 1920, he cultivated New York society figures.

On 11 April 1925 Stravinsky began to compose a serenade for piano solo but interrupted the work to see Luigi Pirandello's production of

L'Histoire du Soldat in Rome in the Teatro Odescalchi.[12] The Italian translation was by Alberto Savinio, the brother of Stravinsky's friend Giorgio de Chirico. Since Pirandello was the most prestigious figure among Il Duce's supporters, Mussolini attended a performance seated next to the playwright and not far from Stravinsky. (Only two or three days previously, on the same stage, Pirandello had been introduced to the beautiful actress Marta Abba and fallen in love with her.) The next day in Rome Stravinsky received an invitation from Mussolini to call on him in the Palazzo Venezia. The Duce greeted the composer saying, 'Stravinsky, I know you well,' referring to his musical career. (The dictator was himself an amateur violinist and actually learned to play the *Duo concertant*.) In recounting this to Berio and Eco, Stravinsky exaggerated the dictator's heavily accented French and commanding gestures. No handshaking took place, Mussolini claiming that the custom was 'unhygienic', which he gave as his reason for instituting the Fascist salute in 1919. The most memorable of Stravinsky's impressions was that Mussolini was shorter than the composer expected and that he moved quickly. Stravinsky emphasised that the Duce's eyes were 'very cruel', the whites too large for the irises. Mussolini said that he had heard *Petrushka* in Rome in 1916 under Toscanini. Near the end of the visit 'the great dictator' summoned his mistress, Clara Petacci, whom Stravinsky described as 'incredibly beautiful'. Five months later Stravinsky returned to Italy to perform at the Biennale, a modern music festival whose patron happened to be Mussolini. Throughout the 1930s the composer was frequently in Italy and saw Mussolini several times. The two men corresponded until the late 1930s, and Stravinsky actually contributed to the Duce's fundraising for the war in Abyssinia.

One more incident must be told since it exposes Stravinsky's scarcely believable political naïvety. He had contracted to conduct the Biennale in the first week of September 1939, though the world was already aware

---

12 A friend of Mme Odescalchi since 1917, Stravinsky composed a melody for her in a copy of his Easy Pieces. She was a descendant of Prince Ladislao Odescalchi, the same who purchased *La Tentation de Saint-Antoine*, long misattributed to Pieter Brueghel the Younger – the picture that haunted Flaubert from 1845, when he first saw it in Genoa, until 1874, on the publication of his novel of the same title.

that the fuses had been lighted for the beginning of World War II. On 1 September, Stravinsky, still in Sancellemoz and packing his bags for the trip to Venice, received a telephone call from his Paris publisher, Gabriel Paichadze, saying that the Italian border had been closed and that he was unable to obtain a visa. A rankled Stravinsky instructed Paichadze to telephone Mussolini directly and ask that an exception be made. The call actually went through, and permission was granted, as confirmed in the Stravinsky–Paichadze correspondence. But this part of the history was not told to Berio and Eco that night in 1963.

Aaron Copland

When the young Aaron spotted Stravinsky walking in the Rue Saint-Honoré in the early 1920s, the budding American composer followed a few steps behind as if 'drawn by a magnet'. According to Vivian Perlis's monograph,[13] Copland met Stravinsky shortly afterward at a Nadia Boulanger Wednesday-afternoon class, but serious conversation between them first began when Stravinsky was established at Harvard in 1939. The two saw each other in California throughout the next three decades, regularly dining together during Copland's visits on film-music business. Stravinsky was both fond of and frank with Copland: 'Aaron, my dear, you are too political to tell me what you really think.' On 19 May 1957, during another visit to movieland, Copland told his diary[14] that Stravinsky picked him up on the way to dinner at the Bel-Air Hotel in Los Angeles 'with Madame Stravinsky, Robert Craft, and Lawrence Morton' and noted that Stravinsky was

> looking better than in N.Y.[15] – seems almost to have his old vitality back. Much talk of Boulez and Gesualdo, led by Craft.

---

13 *Copland: Since 1943*, Aaron Copland and Vivian Perlis, New York: St. Martin's Press, 1989.
14 Aaron Copland Collection (Box 244, Folder 13), edited by Vivian Perlis. Music Division, Library of Congress.
15 Stravinsky conducted *Petrushka* and *Perséphone* in Carnegie Hall in January 1957, his first major engagement since his stroke in Berlin in October 1956. After the concert Leonard Bernstein introduced him to Maria Callas, whom Stravinsky had seen every day in Venice in the summer of 1956 but never met.

> It is clear that I.S. reflects the enthusiasms of young Craft...
> [Stravinsky] will not swallow Messiaen, however, saying
> categorically that he does not like him. I.S. has been adding
> parts to a motet of Gesualdo. [Original parts missing.] I.S.
> showed old interest in good food and best wine.

I had first met Aaron in Tanglewood in 1946 when he was on a
solitary trek in the woods and encountered me there with the singer
Vera Kassman.

A few months after Stravinsky's death, Charles Schwartz, the
Gershwin biographer, organised a concert performance of *L'Histoire
du Soldat* in New York's Whitney Museum with Sessions and Copland
as Devil and Speaker respectively, Virgil Thomson as Narrator, and
myself as conductor.[16] During rehearsals I was keenly aware of
Thomson's officiousness, as well as his and Sessions's long-standing
enmity. Everyone laughed when it turned out that they had last met
in Paris nearly a half-century earlier. Virgil assigned stage positions
for the cast – himself out front, Sessions far to the rear, and Copland
almost hidden. Aaron's dementia was already quite advanced; he was
continually asking me, 'Did I just say that?' On 24 January 1974, in
Vera Stravinsky's 920 Fifth Avenue apartment, Aaron recorded his
memories of Stravinsky for the Canadian Broadcasting Company.

Roger Sessions

Both Aaron and Roger were on affectionate terms with Stravinsky.
In 1935 and 1937 Sessions followed him to Cleveland, to New
York, and to other U.S. cities, partly to learn how Tchaikovsky
(*The Nutcracker*, the Violin Concerto, the *Pathétique*) should
be played. In the late 1960s the multi-lingual Sessions[17] visited
Stravinsky regularly in the Pierre Hotel for Russian-language talk.

---

16 The Pulitzer Prize Committee in 1971 consisted of Copland, Thomson and myself. We
    awarded the prize to Mario Davidovsky.
17 His English translation of Berenson's *Italian Painters* has become a classic.

In August 1959 the Stravinskys drove from New York to Princeton, partly to visit his friend Robert Oppenheimer, but primarily, through Sessions, to extricate me from a three-week symposium, thereby enabling our earlier departure for London. Stravinsky obtained my release by delivering an extempore lecture himself. I was very proud of him and his talk. His off-the-cuff speech without hesitations impressed the students, who were lackadaisically sprawling on the floor when he entered the room. I complained about this later to Milton Babbitt who said that they never stood for anyone, to which I replied that this seemed to me an exceptional occasion. Stravinsky dwelled on practical issues, and the audience quickly perked up with his sparkling delivery. At the end everyone stood and applauded warmly. My friend Lawrence Moss reviewed the event in *Tempo*.

During the week I had spent at Princeton, Sessions had graciously lunched with me every day. On our return to New York I found an envelope containing a cheque and a note from him: 'Dear Bob, This is for bringing Stravinsky here at a tenth of what would have been his cachet.'

Lawrence Morton

I first met Lawrence Morton at Ingolf Dahl's, where we spent an evening arguing over the merits of *Pierrot Lunaire*, Dahl on my side, Morton intransigently opposed, as he was to all modern music except Stravinsky's. My next encounter with Lawrence came in 1953 when he asked for help in obtaining permission from Stravinsky to change an offending phrase in the 'Sacred History' movement of the 1952 Cantata ('The Jews on me they made great suit... because they lov'd darkness rather than light'). This had proved an obstacle to performing the work on a Monday Evening Concert, of which Morton was the newly appointed director. I told him that only Stravinsky could make an alteration, but that he would be reluctant, having just conducted the work in Town Hall, New York and recorded it there without any dissent, and that Auden had advised him against changing a 400-year-old classical English poem. I arranged for Morton to ask the maestro himself, thereby beginning a longstanding relationship. I also helped in providing the substitute words ('my enemies'), which, in spite of their jarring the musical rhythm, Stravinsky accepted. In truth I was as surprised by Morton's adamant stance as I was by Stravinsky's concession.[18]

That Stravinsky and Morton had never met before seemed odd, since they lived only a few blocks apart during the previous twelve years and Lawrence attended all of Stravinsky's concerts at the Los Angeles Philharmonic. One explanation may have been that in his capacity as a critic Lawrence had ridiculed *Scènes de Ballet* by inanely referring to the 'trumpet tune of almost incredible sentimentality... a solemnisation of Broadway, a halo for a chorus girl, a portrait of Mr. Rose as Diaghilev'. Stravinsky must have seen this portentous comment but evidently did not remember Morton as its author.

Lawrence's sudden connection to Stravinsky was an immeasurable benefit for the Monday Evening Concerts, primarily because they inspired him to compose several pieces for the organisation: *Three Songs from William Shakespeare*; *In Memoriam: Dylan Thomas*; the *Elegy for J.F.K.*; the Eliot *Introitus* dirge; the instrumental versions of the *Quatre Chants Russes*; the Russian Female Choruses with four horns; and the *Balmont Songs* for chamber ensemble. When it became known that Stravinsky himself attended the concerts, the audiences quadrupled, and the Stravinsky premieres gave the MEC international coverage. This success led to a wrangle in the press, most notably between Vladimir Dukelsky (Vernon Duke), who published a defamatory article, 'The Deification of Stravinsky', and Lawrence, who wrote a rebuttal under Stravinsky's name, with his approval and encouragement. Though Lawrence had long been feuding with Dukelsky, some soothsayers believed that I wrote the article. But I did not know Dukelsky, had never heard his music, classical or pop, and took no part in this scurrilous exchange except to contribute the title, 'A Cure for VD'. Lawrence had also ghostwritten Stravinsky's caustic letters to the *Los Angeles Times* reviewer, Albert Goldberg, and was an old hand at the game.

---

18 Stravinsky's re-recording of the piece in Hollywood in the 1960s reverts to the original text because the English tenor refused to tamper with the verse.

Lawrence was sharply intelligent in and out of music, and his critical writings and programme notes are of the highest quality. Though old-maidish and finicky by temperament, he had a bright sense of humour. He was a gourmet chef and often invited us to his modest apartment for delicious dinners. Both Stravinskys became fond of him and in July 1956 invited him to sail from New York to Venice with us.

After Ingolf Dahl had turned down an Oxford Press commission for a Stravinsky biography, Lawrence accepted it and took a sabbatical from the MEC, going to Paris for research. But when the Stravinsky *Conversations* books began to appear, the prospective biographer realised that comparatively little could be learned from the composer's few surviving Paris friends and abandoned the project. Later, seeing the opportunity for a Stravinsky biography written from another angle, Morton, back in California, courted Vera, inviting her to tea, taking her to bars, and pumping her for recollections and insights as source material for his book, which regrettably never came to fruition.

In November 1956 I instigated a connection between Morton and my then good friend Pierre Boulez, writing from Paris to suggest that Morton invite him to conduct *Marteau* at one of our concerts. I countered Morton's negative response that Boulez was latching onto Stravinsky entirely for self-promotion, only later realising that this was the reality. My answer at the time strongly contradicted him, and he only very reluctantly and gradually accepted my proposal, arranging for financial support from donors that included USC and UCLA. In recent years the French maestro has denied any intention of conducting at the Monday Evening Concerts, but his as yet unpublished correspondence with the present writer contradicts this.

When Boulez arrived, via San Francisco (where he had been visiting Hans Popper, the multi-millionaire patron of the Domaine Musical), Morton's former adversarial position quickly transformed into that of an acolyte. The irony of this turnabout is explained in part by his discovery of other compatibilities. They vacationed together, in tents in Yosemite and hotels in Mexico, and Morton not only aligned himself with the twenty-two-years-younger Frenchman but became an advocate of his musical partisanships. This naturally led to a strain in Morton's relations with Stravinsky, who disliked the post-*Marteau* music and, in his own words, 'greatly mistrusted' Boulez. On his next visit to Los Angeles, Boulez brought a new opus written for the MEC concerts. Morton had persuaded me to induce Stravinsky to attend a rehearsal, but he disliked what he heard, thereby causing a further deterioration in their relationship.

Lawrence did not visit Stravinsky during his long hospital siege in the autumn of 1967. As the composer's health continued to decline, Morton renewed his involvement in the composer's household, but primarily to assist Vera, with whom he had become very close. During the composer's last illnesses in California, Lawrence sometimes cooked for the Stravinskys and brought the meals to their house – by taxi, since he did not have a car.

My own relations with Lawrence were not affected during the Boulez break-up or afterward. It is sad to have to say that the last time I saw Lawrence was in Roosevelt Hospital in New York, where he had been taken after suffering a heart attack on a flight from Washington. I spoke to him daily by telephone during the final days of his life back in California and conducted a memorial concert for him in Ojai[19] shortly after his death in 1987.

Warren Zevon

The now canonised rock 'n' roll composer Warren Zevon is an unexpected personality in Stravinsky history. This young musician from Fresno, who bragged that he had the highest IQ ever tested there, wrote asking to become my pupil after hearing my 1957 Webern recordings. Lacking all teaching experience and not being *au courant* with what might be required, I despaired of the prospect but nevertheless fixed an appointment. Opening the Stravinsky front door

---

19 This inland valley about 100 miles north-west of Los Angeles sponsored the Ojai Music Festival. Founded in 1947, the festival was produced by Lawrence Morton from 1954. According to *The New York Times*, 13 June 2012: '[T]he music directors included Robert Craft, Stravinsky, Copland, Michael Tilson Thomas, and Pierre Boulez.'

one afternoon in the spring of 1960, I was surprised to see a bright-eyed, nervously energetic thirteen-year-old boy. We were listening to a recording of Stockhausen's *Gruppen* when suddenly Stravinsky appeared from his studio. Zevon retreated toward the door and the composer intervened, inviting him to stay for Scotch and zakousky. Zevon accepted, of course, and talked to Stravinsky with astonishing maturity. With the help of the anodyne – against the law at Zevon's age – the composer put the youth at ease. The contents of his glass quickly evanesced but were swiftly replenished by one of the creators of modern music himself.

Pop-music historians now tell us that this was the zenith of Zevon's early life. From the perspective of alcohol addiction it may also have been the beginning of the end. Obliged to leave for Europe, I was his teacher for only six lessons but learned some gems of pop language from him such as 'zapped', 'zilch' and the tmesis 'absofuckinglutely'. He never mentioned rock 'n' roll to me and was even dismissive of all but Stravinsky's classical modern music. When I saw him next, he had become a world-renowned rock star. The media presented him together with Stravinsky in cartoons, but Zevon's interviews always credited me for the connection. He died of cancer in 2003 at age fifty-six. Since he looked girlish, I was surprised to read in obituaries that he had been a compulsive womaniser before, during and after his eleven-year marriage. His own lyrics owe something to Dorothy Parker, and I recall that he was delighted to learn that she lived around the corner from the Stravinskys and was an occasional visitor. For me, Zevon's most memorable line is, 'If California slides into the ocean like the mystics and statistics say...' Zevon has since been immortalised in a poem by Paul Muldoon:

> ...That must have been your first brush
> with greatness, in Chicago, before the mean streets
> of LA where your Moses met with the bulrush
> of Stravinsky and every chord became a *cordon sanitaire*
> against the bum's rush
> that *Wanderjahre*
> with Stravinsky...

Michael Tilson Thomas

Of the Los Angeles musicians who can still provide valuable firsthand information about Stravinsky, foremost among them is the celebrated conductor Michael Tilson Thomas. As a student at the University of Southern California and a pupil of Ingolf Dahl, Thomas had more opportunities to observe Stravinsky than any other musician of the time, having attended all programmes at the Monday Evening Concerts when the master was in the audience. In fact, Stravinsky was introduced to him after Thomas had performed Beethoven's Opus 111 at the Monday Evening Concerts. Not wanting to appear in public, on this occasion Stravinsky sat backstage, followed a score, and found the performance electrifying. The next time he heard Thomas play was as the first pianist in a performance of *Les Noces* that I conducted. The audience greeted Stravinsky, who had just been released from hospital, with standing ovations to welcome him back to public concert life.

Stravinsky again saw Thomas play when I conducted Schütz's 'Christmas Oratorio' in which Michael skilfully improvised the cembalo part. A multi-talented, highly intelligent and in every way sympathetic musician, he can cite passages in *Agon* and other late Stravinsky works that reflect influences from Baroque composers. Moreover, Michael can recall Stravinsky's own symphony concerts, including one in Beverly Hills in 1967 in which the composer confused the programme order and began beating the slow 12/8 of *The Firebird* while the orchestra launched into the Fourth Tableau of *Petrushka*, resulting in a shemozzle. As the son of Boris and Bessie Thomashefsky, the directors of the Yiddish Art Theater, Thomas's impersonations bring Stravinsky to life appealingly and with verisimilitude. With the January 2011 opening of Frank Gehry's New World Symphony Concert Hall in Miami, built for Thomas, he became an international figure.

Gregg Smith

Between 1959 and 1966 this gifted choral conductor and composer prepared most of Stravinsky's vocal music for his concerts and recordings both in Los Angeles and New York. The Gregg Smith Singers performed eleven of Stravinsky's mostly late pieces under his direction, some of them several times. Gregg met Stravinsky at a rehearsal for a Monday Evening Concert that I conducted in which the chorus sang Bach's Cantata No. 4, *Christ lag in Todes Banden*, on a programme with the Berg Chamber Concerto. While waiting for me to finish the latter, Stravinsky, following the score in the hall, asked Gregg to sit by him and turn the pages. Thereafter the composer supervised dozens of Gregg's rehearsals of new Stravinsky pieces. In 1965 Gregg worked with Stravinsky on a translation of *Les Noces*, rehearsed the chorus and soloists for the Requiem Canticles premiere, and again for the composer's Venetian funeral. Gregg also conducted the three Russian Sacred Choruses at the composer's New York memorial service.

On the musician-to-musician level the man with the least exotic name in the present book was as close as anyone to the composer in his final American years. A year before, Gregg had left his position at Ithaca College and was teaching at the State University of New York at Stonybrook on Long Island. On 27 April 1969 he organised a concert entitled 'Homage to Stravinsky', which turned out to be the last one Stravinsky ever attended. At the back of the hall Gregg opened the concert by conducting his choir in Stravinsky's Three Sacred Russian Choruses. I followed with *Les Noces* and the Requiem Canticles on the stage at the opposite end of the hall, both pieces with Gregg's perfectly prepared chorus. His wife, Rosalind Rees, recalls that Stravinsky was seated in the front row centre, just behind the conductor's podium, invisible to the audience. Rosalind, who sang in the stage chorus, recollects that she had 'the best view in the house':

> In spite of singing some very difficult music (some in Russian)
> and having to watch both the music and the conductor like a

hawk, it was impossible to take our eyes off Stravinsky. At the
end of the concert, the audience was standing and cheering
and shouting 'Bravo', and Stravinsky began to struggle to rise
to his feet. It was difficult to watch. It seemed to take him a
long time. But he at last turned, stood, and took a bow. Only
at this moment did the audience know that Stravinsky was at
the concert, and the audience began to cheer him as well as the
performers.

Gregg remarked that Stravinsky 'seemed very moved by the
performance and very focused. The standing ovation went on and
on as Stravinsky stood and bowed very slowly and solemnly to the
audience, and also to Robert Craft and the performers on stage.'
Rosalind added that

> Stravinsky was keenly aware of how much time and preparation
> was needed to rehearse each work. Nothing, especially not
> Stravinsky's own precious time, was to be wasted. Gregg knew
> that he needed to rely on pre-rehearsals for a vital preparation.
> Without them the music would not be ready for Stravinsky or
> Robert Craft to step in and take over rehearsing.

Rosalind has left the only reliable memoir of Stravinsky's funerals (in
New York on 9 April 1971 and in Venice on 15 April) titled 'The Final
Performance - Invitation To A Funeral'. Gregg wrote:

> Igor Stravinsky died on 6 April 1971. While returning to New
> York that same day after being on tour, we heard the devastating
> news in the airport terminal. I found out that a public service for
> Stravinsky would be held at the Frank Campbell establishment
> on Madison Avenue. I cabled Lillian Libman and asked if some
> Russian music might be wanted at the public service. She
> agreed, and we were to perform the *Otche Nash* (*Pater Noster*)
> and the *Bogoroditse Devo* (*Ave Maria*).

In fact this music opened the New York service, bringing the reality
of the loss to me more strongly than the announcement of the event

itself. Shortly after the service, Eugene Berman called from Rome and, translating for Italian government officials, confirmed that the Venice funeral would take place in the Basilica dei Santi Giovanni e Paolo the following week (Holy Week). The service would be Greek Orthodox, presided over by Archimandrite Cherubim Malissianos, but a high Roman Catholic cleric would first have to 'deconsecrate' the church before the Orthodox service could take place. The Requiem Canticles would have to be performed, but the only available chorus and orchestra were those of the Teatro alla Fenice, which had no experience of music of this extreme difficulty, and only a tiny amount of rehearsal time could be made available. Gregg instructed his wife to fly immediately to Venice and 'find an orchestra and a choir. The music is already there, ready for rehearsing. You've just got to go out and get somebody to do it. Pay them double if you have to, and make sure the choir has between 16 and 24 singers.'

That same day Rosalind flew to Milan and quickly found a French-speaking priest at Santi Giovanni e Paolo who agreed to help her organise the performers. He accompanied her to the office of the Mayor of Venice and translated for her. But since Easter weekend was looming, meetings and rehearsals were difficult to arrange. Nevertheless, the Mayor introduced her to the General Manager of the Teatro alla Fenice, who promised to provide an orchestra. She recalls that

> when he found out that they were being requested to perform the twelve-tone Requiem Canticles, I almost lost them. The General Manager protested that the music was too difficult and there wasn't enough time to rehearse it. I replied that 'It's not as bad as you think. The Requiem Canticles is composed of nine very short movements, and the full orchestra does not play in most of them.'

The next hurdle was the chorus. Rosalind explains:

> The French priest contacted the Rome Radio Chorus, the most professional group in Italy, but its conductor was negative, even

> antagonistic. He said that the chorus would not be able to do
> the Canticles, but they could do Stravinsky's little Mass, with
> ten instruments and a small chorus, which was in the group's
> repertory. He also offered to do Scarlatti's Requiem Mass.

At this point Vera Stravinsky received a telephone call from Gregg in New York asking whether she would accept the little ten-minute Mass, but she refused, saying that her husband had wanted the Canticles.[20] Vera, Lillian Libman and I flew to Rome on Monday night, and from there the next morning to a Venice-bound plane which was called back from the runway to include us. I was met by Mario Labroca, who took me in a speedboat directly to the Teatro alla Fenice where I began rehearsing the orchestra in the foyer, since a rehearsal of *Carmen* was in progress on the stage. The music was totally alien to the players, some of whom never successfully grasped its rhythms. They were proud to have Stravinsky buried in their city, despite the fact that they griped about his music.

Meanwhile, the conductor of the Rome Radio Chorus had suddenly agreed to turn over his chorus to Gregg, who began rehearsing with the group on Tuesday night. Rosalind, a mezzo-soprano, was obliged to sing the alto solo, and Gregg himself, actually no singer at all, managed the tenor solo part. On Wednesday we had our first full orchestra and chorus rehearsal, and on Thursday night a 'dress rehearsal' took place in Santi Giovanni e Paolo, where the acoustics proved to be a great obstacle. Gregg found an 'acoustical halo' where the solo singers could stand in order to be heard at all, but at a distance from the other performers. When the other soloists heard Rosalind's part, they joined her in the 'halo' in the penultimate piece for four solo singers. She generously compliments me: 'Robert Craft was fabulous to sing with as a conductor. He gave me every cue.'

The service began with Alessandro Scarlatti's Requiem *Missa defunctorum* conducted by Nino Antonelli, which was followed by a statement by the Mayor of Venice, then Andrea Gabrieli's *Praeambulum quarti toni*, *Toccata del decimo tuono* and *Pass'e*

---

20   Vera said about Requiem Canticles, 'He knew that he was writing it for himself.'

mezzo antico (played by the organist Sandro Dalla Libera), and finally the Requiem Canticles. Rosalind's account continues:

> An hour of Greek chanted Liturgy for the Dead followed, beautifully and movingly intoned by the Archimandrite Malissianos. At the end of the long service the family was beckoned by him to kiss the coffin, and then Stravinsky made his last journey via gondola to San Michele. After the burial service there Gregg and I were right up front near the gravesite while the last chants were sung by this wonderful Greek cantor. The paparazzi were still coming over the wall of the cemetery, flash bulbs popping, paying no attention to this beautiful liturgy, so beautifully and movingly sung.

According to Stravinsky, Gregg Smith had the most perfect ear for pitch that he had ever encountered. I am personally indebted to Gregg for his preparation of the singers for many of my own recordings, especially Monteverdi's Vespers, a work that overwhelmed Stravinsky.

Lincoln Kirstein

> *For me it is wonderful to know that you*
> *exist, as an island of genius and integrity*
> *in this disastrous world.*
>
> Letter from Kirstein to Stravinsky,
> Christmas 1947

As a subscription member of Lincoln Kirstein's Ballet Society, I knew him in 1946, two years before I met Stravinsky. When my relationship to the composer had been generally accepted, Lincoln became very friendly to me, though I found him a terrifying figure in both his giant physical proportions and his intellectual intensity in face-to-face conversation. His mind was as swift as his bodily movements. Stravinsky was fond of him, and Lincoln regarded the composer as God. Lincoln's knowledge of the artistic and literary world was prodigious, and his generosity of spirit and money were real as well as legendary. He began to appeal to Stravinsky through me. I still remember him calling me in Hollywood almost every day in the spring of 1964, prodding me to urge Stravinsky to compose the *Fanfare for a New Theatre*. This forty-second-long testament to the composer's genius was finally written in an afternoon. The piece was intended to announce the ends of intermissions, like the brass-ensemble leitmotivs that recall the audience to the theatre in Bayreuth. In passing it should be said that this tiny opus for two trumpets provides a measure of Stravinsky's growth in old age by comparison to the greatly inferior 1953 fanfare sketch for the beginning of *Agon*. Stravinsky hoped *Fanfare* would melt Elie Nadelman's 'sculptures in yoghurt' which Lincoln had commissioned for the first upstairs lobby of the New York State Theater.

In the winter of 1968 Lincoln sponsored a Stravinsky concert in St Thomas Church on Fifth Avenue in New York that helped to stimulate interest in the later religious music. The composer received complimentary communications about the programme from Saint-John Perse, Balanchine, Elliott Carter and many others. The concert was followed by a dinner party for Auden and Kallman at Lincoln's downtown Manhattan residence, the real intent of which was to interest Stravinsky in a new theatre project. On the wall behind the table, Tchelichev's life-size portrait (6'4") of the host in the nude, except for boxing gloves, made me bilious.

Pierre Souvtchinsky

Pierre Souvtchinsky and Nicolas Nabokov, Russian refugees in Paris, were rivals for Stravinsky's trust and affection from the 1920s to the composer's death. Both influenced his intellectual life, but from widely divergent perspectives. Also, they were not good friends themselves, and their jealousy of each other was always evident.

Son-in-law of the philosopher Lev Karsavin, the enigmatic Pierre Souvtchinsky was one of Stravinsky's intimates in Paris from 1924 to 1939 and, being familiar with the musical scene in the U.S.S.R., ghosted Stravinsky's 1939 lecture on Russian music in *Poétique musicale*. According to Isaiah Berlin, a dossier was discovered in Washington during World War II that exposed Souvtchinsky as a Soviet spy. He kept his 1934 visit to the U.S.S.R. secret from Stravinsky but re-established his friendship with the composer on returning to Marseilles after a long absence.

Communication between Souvtchinsky and Stravinsky came to an end in 1939 and continued until December 1956. A staunch supporter of the composer Henri Sauguet and promoter of his opera *La Chartreuse de Parme*, Souvtchinsky turned full circle in 1944 and became a disciple of the young Boulez.

I met Souvtchinsky at the Opéra in Paris in May 1952 during intermission between the performances of *Oedipus Rex* and *Erwartung*, which were conducted by Hans Rosbaud. This makes clear that Souvtchinsky had deliberately avoided the first performance of *Oedipus* conducted by Stravinsky the previous night. At the repeat performance an audience protest erupted, ostensibly targeting Cocteau,[21] the Narrator, but this was understood to be directed against Stravinsky and his American-period music. In truth, all of *Oedipus*, that flagship of neoclassicism, was under attack. When the audience had settled, Cocteau shrewdly deflected the criticism by denouncing the interruption as an 'insult to Stravinsky', who had long since left his loge and returned to his hotel.

From 1957 until his death, Stravinsky was Souvtchinsky's principal provider. In the late 1960s and through 1970, Souvtchinsky was also the composer's closest companion and conversational partner in Paris, Donaueschingen, Zurich and Evian. Stravinsky intently discussed the Second Viennese School with him, though much Russian reminiscing took place as well. Souvtchinsky was also responsible for bringing the composer and Giacometti together in October 1957. The failure of

---

21 Cocteau had revised the texts of the Narrator's first speech to introduce a series of *tableaux vivants*. These contained some remarkably good ideas but the movements of the handsome young male actors were too effeminate for the tragic dignity of the work. On the second night, following the speech 'Maintenant ensuite l'Epilogue', hisses came from the gallery and the balcony, and a stentorian voice bellowed from a loge, 'Assez avec Cocteau', whereupon the entire house booed in agreement. Nevertheless, the beginning of his opening speech in *Oedipus* with the crackling syllables of 'Spectateurs' remains unforgettable.

this old friend to attend Stravinsky's Venetian funeral perplexes me, as it did most others, the more so because Souvtchinsky had been generously paid by Boosey & Hawkes for work never undertaken on the composer's archives.

Sanguine, irrepressible, but instantly likable, Souvtchinsky was my first *tutoyer* friend. I most vividly recall our evenings dining with him; he was always the first to order dinner and I the last, at which point he invariably switched his menu to duplicate mine. I still see him doing this at a large gathering at Le Clos des Lilas, which he did not frequent because of its predominantly American and British clientele. Souvtchinsky was an amateur, musically speaking, and his pleasing tenor voice did not really suit the part of Eumolpus in *Perséphone*. He nevertheless sang a private preview performance of the piece with Stravinsky at the piano in the salon of the Princess Polignac.

Nicolas Nabokov

Nicolas Nabokov, the most ubiquitous person in Stravinsky's American years, the cousin of the author of *Lolita*, entered the composer's life in Paris in 1927. The Stravinskys greatly looked forward to his visits in their Hollywood home, where, like Auden, he slept on the couch in the den. His height, measured and notched on the inside door of the closet there, was just below the marks for such other guests as Aldous H. and the poet Charles Olson.[22] Warm-hearted, witty, highly cultivated, Nicolas had taught Classics at St John's College in Annapolis. He was polylingual, cosmopolitan and nympholeptic (though Edward James, a believable source, has testified that Nicolas was also bisexual, or had been when with James on a steamer between Le Havre and New York in 1933). His linguistic range and historian's knowledge enhanced his value to the U.S. government in the divided Germany after World War II. As capable of conversing with Soviet, German, French and Italian politicians as with the poets and artists of these countries, he

---

22 On 13 September 1947 the Stravinskys' painter friend Corrado Cagli brought his companion, Charles Olson, to visit them.

became the culture nabob of Willy Brandt's walled Berlin. Regrettably, Nicolas was an inveterate gossip, even about Stravinsky, who did not withhold his annoyance on hearing rumours of Nabokov's mimicries of him, above all mockeries of his exaggerated parsimony. Otherwise Stravinsky enjoyed Nicolas's antics. Canadian television filmed him with Stravinsky in his Hamburg hotel in the spring of 1963 conversing in Russian, English, German and French in a brilliant half-hour of unrehearsed dialogue and lively banter, infinitely more illuminating than any recorded memoirs.

Early in 1948 Stravinsky asked Nabokov to interview me in New York and relay his impressions. Evidently they were favourable, as were mine of him, and we remained good friends until Stravinsky's music began to show the influence of Webern's 'constipated style', as Nicolas called it, referring to the second and third movements of the Concerto, Op. 24. Among many memorable adventures with him was a visit to a massage parlour in Kyoto in 1959 where, after stomping on our embrocated backs and abdomens, the masseuses unsuccessfully proposed 'to empty the gland' for only three more yen.

Nabokov's aspirations to be recognised as a serious composer sometimes strained his relationship with Stravinsky, but this was not true in Paris in the late 1920s when Nabokov played the score of his First Symphony for Stravinsky, who asked Ansermet to perform the piece. Stravinsky attended the premiere of Nabokov's Diaghilev ballet *Ode* in Paris in 1929, partly because the featured performer was Ira Belline. When *Symboli Chrestiani*, dedicated to Stravinsky, was presented in Venice in 1956 in the same month as his *Canticum Sacrum*, Stravinsky arranged his rehearsal schedule to avoid hearing it. Nicolas knew Stravinsky's friend Vera Janacopoulos and in 1933 composed some lovely Russian songs for her. Interestingly, when Nabokov played his opera *Rasputin* for the older composer in Paris in the mid-1960s, Stravinsky returned from the audition having enjoyed it.[23]

---

23 Stravinsky did not live to hear Nabokov's last opera, *Love's Labour's Lost*, with a libretto adapted from the play by Auden, who gave a draft of his text to me, referring to it as 'L's L's L'. Vera was invited by the Baroness Hansi Lambert to Brussels for the premiere but was unable to attend.

Nabokov is best remembered for producing flamboyant contemporary art festivals, in Paris in May 1952, in Rome in April 1954, and in Berlin in October 1964. I recall during the 1952 festival, above all, my unwarranted nerve-wrenching anticipation at meeting Jean Cocteau, whom I found to be modest, considerate and generous – in short, much the opposite of the glittering intellectual exhibitionist I had been dreading. On 5 May the Stravinskys, my sister Phyllis and I dined with Cocteau at Le Grand Véfour, where a private *chaise* bore his name on a brass plaque next to Fragonard's and near those of Balzac, Dumas, Hugo and Colette. Cocteau illustrated his new staging of *Oedipus Rex*,[24] drawing sketches as he talked. Stravinsky handed these *dessins* to me sheet by sheet under the table, and I noted that they were executed on Sennelier paper (Picasso's supplier). The next day Cocteau wrote to Stravinsky: 'You cannot imagine my perfect joy last night at the Véfour. It was like finding one's self again.' The press quoted Cocteau's remark about Stravinsky: 'As soon as you begin talking to this man, everything is numbers, and disorder ceases.'

I accompanied Stravinsky to a concert in which Olivier Messiaen and Pierre Boulez played the latter's *Structures Ia* for two pianos. Near the beginning, a young woman in the middle of the hall began laughing hysterically, thereby provoking a young man a few rows behind her to leap over the empty seats between and slap her face. Guards, forewarned, ejected both of them. The pianists continued as if nothing had happened, and Stravinsky whispered to me, 'Now I know I'm in Paris.' The incident was not reported in the papers, and the surprising sensation of the festival was Jerome Robbins's misogynist and risqué *The Cage*, based on Stravinsky's String Concerto. Scandalised by the 'nude' ballerinas in praying mantis positions, stinging their prone male victims, the audience forgot to object that the score was shockingly tonal–neoclassic. Stravinsky had been amused by the ballet in New York, but in Paris it detracted from *Orpheus*, in which the beautiful 'Pas de deux' and 'Apotheosis' were,

---

24 Cocteau wrote in his *Journal*: 'In most of the masks the eyes were protruding from their sockets, and in the finale popped like ping-pong balls painted red, what is called *semble-sang* in the Midi.'

as always, disadvantaged by the preceding cancan dances.

The Vienna State Opera's quarter-of-a-century-belated Paris premiere of *Wozzeck*[25] was the crowning event of the week, greatly outshining Monteux's Boston Symphony performance of the overly familiar *Rite of Spring*. The previous evening Stravinsky had suffered through a second-rate, under-rehearsed production of his *Rake's Progress* in Geneva, which had exposed the too-thin textures of some of the music and the several weaknesses of the libretto, including the inheritance from a non-existent rich uncle and the stones-into-bread machine. In Paris, he was overcome by *Wozzeck*'s orchestral richness, the dramatic tensions, and the perfect co-ordination of music and stage action in this greatest of modern operas. The French music world was transformed overnight.

Otherwise, the main Paris Festival attraction was literary. André Malraux chaired a symposium, after a warning that if the lionised novelist William Faulkner failed to appear and speak, the event would be cancelled. Faulkner had been billeted in the same hotel with the Harlem Ballet, which compelled the author of *Sanctuary* to inure himself in gin. My friend and Faulkner's, the young Jean Stein, finally managed to sober him up to a presentable state and see that he delivered his brief address to the spellbound, if uncomprehending, French audience. Nabokov kept us informed about every development in the Faulkner housing problem. Otherwise he spent most of his time with Stravinsky, escorting him through lavish lunches, multi-course dinners, and bibulous late-night receptions. The Stravinskys and I enjoyed Nabokov's Rome Festival much more than the one in Paris. Arriving a week before the concerts, we were provided with a car and driver for daily excursions to the cities and cemeteries of Etruria. The Romans were friendlier than the Parisians, and feuds among artist cliques less apparent. We were also surrounded by people we

---

25 We sat in Nabokov's loge behind and above the one occupied by Alban Berg's widow, Helene, with her escort Arthur Honegger, who introduced Stravinsky to her. After the performance we dined at the Plaza Athénée with Albert Camus and his beautiful wife. The writer spoke glowingly to me about Melville but dismissed Henry James as 'an insufferable American pederast'.

knew, many of them, like the Carters, from the American Academy.[26] I had the instructive experience of watching Hermann Scherchen rehearse new music, especially that of Luigi Nono. He was joined by Mrs Arnold Schoenberg and her daughter Nuria, his fiancée, who had come directly from the *Moses und Aron* Hamburg premiere and were staying in our hotel, where we saw them frequently.

Hans Werner Henze's opera *Boulevard Solitude* was the sensation of the Rome Festival. Stravinsky heard the second performance,[27] sitting next to his and Henze's publisher Willy Strecker, who induced the older musician to inscribe a score of the opera with an uncharacteristically extravagant compliment. But he was genuinely taken by the piece and particularly loved the voice of the opera's *prima donna*, Magda László, as well as her artistry and her personal beauty; henceforth he engaged her in concerts in California, Venice and Rome. Stravinsky treasured her performances of Bach's 'Wedding' Cantata (BWV 202) and the soprano arias in the St Matthew Passion (both conducted by Scherchen) more perhaps than any other recordings in his library.

When I introduced Stravinsky's Septet in the Teatro Eliseo,[28] he came on stage to bow with me, partly to show his approval of the performance and partly to create some excitement for this puzzling new work. Stravinsky's own concert at the Foro Italico with the Rome Radio Orchestra was enthusiastically received, for which reason he appeared at what was supposed to be an intimate reception. The Carters drove him there, but on entering a ballroom and seeing a crowd of about 500, Stravinsky turned to Elliott and asked, 'Where did you park your car?' That same week Elliott's String Quartet No. 1, played at the Accademia Santa Cecilia, placed him at the head of a new avant-garde. After Stravinsky publicly presented a composer's

---

26 One of them, Samuel Barber, launched the *bon mot* of the Festival by inquiring of Vera Stravinsky whether she liked California. Her answer: 'No. There is no one to talk to there,' was repeated at dinner parties.

27 I accompanied him to the first performance without a tuxedo and was not admitted. Stravinsky, also not wearing a tuxedo, was admitted but declined to enter on my account and he left the theatre with me. Meanwhile, Nabokov had socked the ticket-taker on the jaw, causing a ruckus that was described the next day on the front page of *The New York Times*. The mayor of Rome came to the Hassler Hotel to apologise.

28 Not in the Foro Italico, as some biographies state.

prize to Mario Peragallo for his Violin Concerto, we dined at Ostia with him and his attractive, flirtatious wife. Stravinsky also attended a concert at the Foro Italico to hear a piano concerto by his friend Karl Amadeus Hartmann. Just before the piece began Stravinsky passed a note to his neighbour, Stephen Spender: 'Fasten your seatbelt.'

Stravinsky entered only one Roman church during our visit, San Luigi dei Francesi, to see Caravaggio's St Matthew masterpieces. The composer spent most of his time in the city with old friends, including Princess Marguerite di Bassiano[29] and her husband, Roffredo Caetani, seventeenth Duke of Sermoneta (the family is mentioned in Dante) and the Prince of Bassiano. He was also an illegitimate son of Liszt, or so Diaghilev had told Stravinsky, and the physical resemblance was indeed remarkable. We enjoyed pleasant hours with the Contessa Anna Letizia Pecci-Blunt (*née* Levy), the musically sophisticated niece of Pope Pius XI, who sponsored sophisticated chamber music concerts in her Palazzo Pecci near the Campidoglio.[30] I still remember her description of a party for the newly installed American ambassador to Italy, who 'went about slapping people on the back like a Wyoming lodge-keeper'. We dined frequently in Trastevere with our new friends, the Pannis (the administrators of the Filarmonica Romana); in the Hassler with my friend from Lucca, the pianist Loredana Franceschini; and with the Roman Vlads, he a gifted composer and Italy's leading Stravinsky scholar, she a beautiful, elegant Ferrarese and the director of the Istituto Restauro who was then restoring Duccio's *Maestà* and Antonello's *Ecce Homo* and extending hours of private access to the masterpieces to us.

Stravinsky had an unpostponable concert in Turin (*Perséphone* and the Violin Concerto) but Vera, confined to bed for several days with flu, could not accompany him. He departed from Rome by train with his son-in-law, Andre Marion (whom Stravinsky had invited to accompany us precisely for this eventuality), nearly a week before

---

29 *Née* Chapin, born in Connecticut. Her nephew, Schuyler Chapin, was the newly appointed director of Columbia Records' Classical Masterworks Division. When introduced to him, Stravinsky famously, but without getting the joke, identified himself as a member of this category: 'I am a "Classical Masterwork".'

30 Countess Mimi's daughter married Alberico Ludovisi-Buoncompagni, the Duke of Venosa (the city of Horace and, 1,500 years later, Prince Carlo Gesualdo).

Vera, Milene and I could follow. In the interim Milene and I spent a day in the Abruzzi searching for the Sacro Speco in the Convento di San Benedetto, where a spiral staircase leads to an ilex grove and the chapel of St Gregory, famed for its portrait of Francis of Assisi without a halo (1210). The next day a fully recovered Vera travelled with us to Orvieto, Siena, Pisa, Florence and Arezzo, joining Stravinsky and Milene's husband in Milan a few days later.

Nabokov's Berlin Festival was more efficiently organised than those in Paris and Rome. The main event was Fischer-Dieskau singing the German premiere of *Abraham and Isaac* in Hebrew, a language the renowned baritone, after months of tutoring, had come to love.[31] Photographs of the dress rehearsal show Elliott Carter sitting in the front row turning pages of the score for Stravinsky, who wanted to supervise the rehearsal and be as close as possible to me on the podium at the edge of the stage immediately above him. He interrupted me in nearly every bar, which was exasperating because my intent was to give the players an overall impression of the continuity of the piece in a run-through. At one point I muttered the thought under my breath and out of range of the orchestra, 'Sit down and shut up.' This was overheard only by Fischer-Dieskau standing inches from me, but the singer's recounting of the story in his autobiography implies that the entire hall resounded with my whisper. No matter; the piece went smoothly at the concert and was warmly received. I had worked on rhythms and pitches with the soloist in his apartment. His performance was rhythmically exact, but his intonation, particularly on large intervallic leaps, was only approximate. However, the voice was mellow, stirringly dramatic, and the audience cheered.

We dined several times with Wystan Auden, then residing in Berlin on a Ford Foundation grant. He seemed less irritable than usual, with one exception. During the official post-concert dinner, the seating cards had not been assigned to his liking, and he was

---

31 The lengthy obituary for the great singer in *The New York Times* (20 May 2012) makes no mention of this German premiere of *Abraham and Isaac* or of the singer's tutoring in Hebrew, which smacks of censorship.

loudly disgruntled to find that, while he was relegated to preside over the second table, Nadia Boulanger was seated at Stravinsky's right at the first. The *Observer* music critic Peter Heyworth, who worshipped Auden but had never met him, was even unhappier at the third table. When the two were introduced the day after we left Berlin, a deep friendship developed between them. A day or two later, when Auden was arrested on a charge of public intoxication, Peter came to his rescue, explaining to a young judge – whom Auden found 'very cute' – that the apprehended chap was the most famous living poet after T. S. Eliot and perfectly harmless. Auden's next book is almost too lovingly dedicated to Heyworth.

In Hamburg more than a year earlier, Nicolas had introduced me to his secretary Dagmar Hader, a *sehr hübsch* young lady as well as a gifted painter and set designer for the West Berlin Opera. At that time the pair was inseparable but in Berlin we found them scarcely civil to each other. He had asked her to look after me, of all dangerous people, ostensibly to guarantee that I arrived at rehearsals on time. During Stravinsky's rehearsals, the East Berlin Opera invited him to attend its production of *L'Histoire du Soldat*, but as the main attraction of the West Berlin Festival he obviously could not accept. As was by now common practice, I had to become Stravinsky's plenipotentiary, escorted by Heyworth and Dagmar. After the barricades and the ordeal of clearing 'Checkpoint Charlie', we were not admitted to the *Soldat* and had to return to West Berlin. Re-entering the parking lot of our hotel we encountered Nicolas, morphed into a madman, waiting for Dagmar; she jumped out of the car while it was still moving, and, faster on her feet than her employer, eluded him.

After our West Berlin concert I went back to my room in order to change clothes, but found Frl. Hader in my bed. When I returned to the scene of the dinner, Auden regarded me closely and barked, 'You look terribly pale.' Following the dinner I found the occupant asleep in my bed. At 2 a.m. the telephone rang. She dashed to answer it ahead of me, knowing that the voice would be Nicolas's. Obviously she wanted him to know where she was, since she had hoped to escape to New York with me. The next morning Nicolas seized 'Daggie' in the Kempinski lobby and beat her with a folded newspaper until restrained by the guards and porters. He fled to the Stravinsky room, feigning a heart attack, and was met by Nadia Boulanger who calmed him. That same day Nicolas drove the Stravinskys to the airport while Dagmar drove me. Some forty-five years later, now a Roman *signora*, she came to a concert of mine in that city and sent a white rose backstage, but we did not meet.

Two years earlier Nabokov had engineered the Stravinsky White House invitation through Jacqueline Kennedy and Arthur Schlesinger, unbeknown to the guest of honour. A letter from Mrs Kennedy invited Stravinsky to a dinner at the White House on his eightieth birthday in June, to which he responded that he had prior concert engagements during the entire month. Schlesinger informed Nicolas that the refusal was unsatisfactory and had greatly disappointed the First Lady. Nicolas begged Stravinsky to propose another time; he came up with one in mid-January that suited the calendars of all parties.

For their loving care and fidelity to Stravinsky in New York during the last two years of his life, I am grateful to Nicolas and his intelligent new wife, the photographer Dominique Cibiel, who visited Stravinsky almost daily at the Essex House. I am even more grateful to Nicolas for his chivalry in standing between the divided Stravinsky family at the Venetian funeral, with Vera to his right and Theodore to his left, our only friend still on speaking terms with both the widow and the Stravinsky children. Nabokov died seven years to the day after Stravinsky, and Dominique continued as a regular visitor to Vera at 920 Fifth Avenue until her death in 1982.

Eugene Berman

Genia Emilianovich Berman was born into a St Petersburg banking family and educated privately in France and Germany. After fleeing the Bolsheviks in 1919 he settled in Paris, until moving in 1935 to the U.S., where he found patrician patrons in San Antonio's Robert Tobin and the Metropolitan Opera's Rudolf Bing. Berman was a necrophiliac in his art (*Andromeda, Natura Morta, Perpetuum Immobile*) but his real-life sexual preference was for epicene young men. In 1955, after the suicide of his wife, the actress Ona Munson (*Gone with the Wind*), he moved to an apartment in the Palazzo Doria-Pamphilj in Rome, which he converted into a gallery for his priceless collection of Etruscan and other art.

Berman was my closest friend among the Stravinsky old guard. I first met him in Hollywood in July 1948 in an Italian restaurant famous for its zabaglione. In 1963, feeling responsible for having introduced me to a sophisticated and alluring Roman lady with whom I would become involved, Genia flew from Rome to Zurich and sat up all night persuading me not to leave the Stravinskys: 'They are utterly dependent on you.' But I had never considered leaving them.

Berman was Stravinsky's first choice as costume and set designer for *The Rake's Progress*,[32] but Auden vetoed this proposal and insisted on Pavlik Tchelichev, Genia's archrival. When Tchelichev refused because of ill health, Kirstein suggested Balthus, which delighted Stravinsky but outraged his son Theodore, who had known the painter in Geneva and wrote to warn his father against this 'dangerous atheist and sexual pervert'. The eventual choice of Gianni Ratto resulted in a *Rake* whose rich Italian colours could hardly have been further from English eighteenth-century gardens, townhouse interiors, bordellos and cemeteries.

Genia was with the Stravinskys every summer in Venice and became our docent on visits to Palladian villas. He was a learned and perceptive cicerone in all regions of Italy and its islands. Leaving the Stravinskys to repose in Palermo and Catania, I accompanied Genia over Sicily's bumpiest terrains and enjoyed the experience as much as any in my lifetime travels. The only fretful hours were the two we spent with the widow of Prince Lampedusa, who was overbearing and monotonous on the subject of her spouse. (She spoke Russian with Genia and Vera Stravinsky and upper-class English with me.) In the summer of 1958 Genia guided us through the Po Delta's recently discovered Etruscan tombs, from which artefacts can now be seen

---

32 It has been asserted that Stravinsky preferred Berman 'because of his penchant for neo-baroque curlicues', which are exactly what the composer abominated in Berman's art – together with flounced dresses and deckle-edged patterns – and which had caused a serious conflict over his too-crowded designs for *Danses concertantes*.

in a Ferrara museum. In the late 1950s Genia and I undertook to follow the path of Virgil and Horace during their 38 BC journey with Maecenas to Athens for his negotiations with Mark Anthony. This adventure led from Porta San Sebastiano (Rome) along the Appian Way to Brindisi; but we had to complete the expedition in stages, which allowed us to linger in the rich area around Capua. Genia was with me only on the stretch from Benevento, a war-flattened city except for its great WWII-bullet-battered Roman arch. I finally finished the segment to Bari and saw Brindisi only by boat from Greece, years after struggling through Hermann Broch's *Death of Virgil.*

Vera Stravinsky and I last saw Genia in 1972 in New York, where he had come to design the sets and costumes for Balanchine's *Pulcinella* in the Stravinsky centennial festival – also the last time I saw Balanchine dance in one of his ballets. Genia had been traumatised on his arrival, having been robbed when he emerged from his hotel. I sat with him during lighting rehearsals for the ballet. Not long after his return to Rome, the ultimate catastrophe befell him when he dropped dead in a diabetic coma on a pavement. This cruel ending came just prior to a general revival of interest in his neo-romantic paintings and the publication of a handsome monograph of his work. His loyal housekeeper sold his entire collection to art thieves for a pittance.[33]

Alexei Haieff

Next to Balanchine, Stravinsky's closest Russian-American friend in the 1940s, Alyosha (Alexei) Haieff, had lived with the composer on more intimate terms than anyone since Samuel Dushkin in the 1930s. Born in Siberia in 1914, Haieff moved with his parents to Harbin (China) during the Russian Revolution and in 1932 immigrated with them to the United States. After studying composition at

---

33   Fortunately, his designs for *Renard* and his portraits of Stravinsky were not stolen. Berman had gifted these to me in 1968.

Juilliard he moved to Boston as a pupil of Nadia Boulanger. He met Stravinsky during the months of his Harvard lectures and served as an early warning system by telling him in Russian which faculty members and students were 'sticky' or 'pas très commode'. Alexei translated for the Stravinskys on some of their U.S. World War II concert tours, accompanying them and sleeping on the floors of their compartments on overcrowded transcontinental trains. He also conducted *Ebony Concerto* (1946) on a tour with the Woody Herman Band. One of Nadia's most gifted students, Haieff was a buoyant companion, though he smoked and drank too much and giggled too long at Stravinsky's jokes. Alexei loved the Stravinskys, as they did him, and his own music is naturally much indebted to Stravinsky's. When Haieff's Divertimento (1947), choreographed by Balanchine, was successfully revived by the Suzanne Farrell Ballet Company in 2010, Alastair Macaulay cleverly described it as 'attractively [using] several characteristics of Stravinsky's lighter music from the 1930s'. In 1947 Alexei and Eleanor Clark[34] stayed in the Hollywood home that Vera Stravinsky had selected and Stravinsky purchased for the Andre Marions in anticipation of their arrival from France. During my April 1948 rehearsals of the Symphony in C in the presence of its composer, Alexei's support was invaluable to me. We became close friends during a Canadian Rockies automobile tour with the Stravinskys in June 1952. Later in the 1950s Alexei married the Countess Bronte and lived in her Roman palazzo and Sicilian villa[35] until his death in 1994. After being introduced to the countess in Venice in 1957, Stravinsky rarely saw the couple. In 1969 Alexei left Italy temporarily and accepted a guest-teaching appointment at the University of Utah, spending weekends with the Stravinskys in Hollywood. After Stravinsky's death, I saw Alexei in Rome from time to time, and he attended my 1990s concerts there even when quite frail.

---

34 Eleanor Clark, the author of *Rome and a Villa*, was the love of Louis MacNeice's life and the future wife of Robert Penn Warren. In 1964 she published a book perhaps intended for Stravinsky, *The Oysters of Locmariaquer*.

35 This had been inherited from her ancestor Lord Nelson, who received it from the people of Naples in gratitude for his defence of the city during the Napoleonic wars.

M. K. Čiurlionis

Of the great individuals of the new epoch,
Čiurlionis must be given a foremost place.

Bernard Berenson, 1949

Readers of Stravinsky's *Expositions and Developments* are inevitably intrigued in the first chapter by the author's highest praise of the Lithuanian painter Mikalojus Konstantinas Čiurlionis:

> ...the most talented member of the Russian School at the beginning of the twentieth century... I myself bought a handsome picture by him in 1908, partly at the prompting of Alexander Benois. It depicted a row of pyramids, of a pale, nacreous tint, in flight towards a horizon, but in *crescendo*, not in the *diminuendo* of orthodox perspective. The picture was, in fact, part of my life, and I remember it very distinctly still, though it has been lost these fifty years in Ustilug. I recall talks with Romain Rolland, who, in 1914 in Switzerland, was also passionately interested in Čiurlionis.

Stravinsky seems to have met Čiurlionis at an exhibition of the artist's pictures in St Petersburg in the last months of 1909 when both Nicolas Roerich, who wrote an enlightening essay on the artist, and Alexander Benois convinced the young composer of the painter's power and originality. The picture that Stravinsky purchased was the *Sonata of the Pyramids*. The titles of all of Čiurlionis's paintings are borrowed from musical forms. Čiurlionis - Stravinsky pronounced it 'TSCHIU' - was a musician before he began to paint, a child prodigy composer who also played several instruments. In 1902 he was graduated from the Conservatory at Leipzig and went on to the Warsaw Academy of Fine Arts, remaining there only long enough to realise that what he wanted was to 'paint music', and that he would not learn to do it here. Čiurlionis continued to compose throughout his short life

(1875-1911), producing about 300 paintings and eighty pieces of music. Since he came from a desperately impoverished background, the quality of the tempera employed in all his work was so poor that it has now faded; hence much of the force of his art has been lost since the time when Stravinsky first saw it. Čiurlionis was creating abstract pictures a decade before Kandinsky, whose expressionism and aesthetics are remote from the art of the younger man. Čiurlionis disdained amorphous splotches of colour and opted for Euclidian spheres, circles, ellipses, spirals, triangles and the upward thrust of objects. The movement, rhythm and vitality of the pictures are what overwhelmed the composer.

Čiurlionis had intuitively understood a relationship between concept and form, between a principle and its visible expression. His art is visionary, not illusionary but a confession of 'spiritual emotions', or what Dante called 'spiriti del viso', which is also the feeling of the skyward movement that inspired Stravinsky. Čiurlionis's attempt to synthesise painting and music remains an idea, obviously, since no art can exceed its natural limits; the kinetic nature of music discloses itself in time, and that of painting only in space. The two can confront each other only as a harmony of spheres, singing colours and shining sounds. Čiurlionis's *Sonata of the Sea* erupts and rumbles like passages in *The Rite of Spring* (the volcano erupting before the 11/4 bar). *The Pyramid Sonata*, a picture of a very different kind, delineates portions of space, thus creating new shapes.[36]

Stravinsky's correspondence with his wife in December 1934 and 1937 during his concert tour in the Baltic Provinces indicates that he might have stopped at the Kaunas Museum between conducting concerts in Tallinn and Riga. Although he did not in the end do this, his fascination with Čiurlionis was lifelong.

Historians tell us that the peasants of this fascinating little country (Lithuania), not liking machines or machine-made articles,

---

36 It is a great pity that Benoît Mandelbrot's *The Fractal Geometry of Nature* was not published until a century after Čiurlionis's death. The great mathematician's study of computer-generated and irregular shapes would have mesmerised Picasso, particularly of the *Ragtime* single-line drawing period. (See Mandelbrot's illustrations of the motion of a colloidal particle.) Hokusai's famous cresting wave and Čiurlionis's *Water* cycle are examples of Mandelbrot's gallery of fractal images.

believed in the harmony of forms of nature and liked to handle earth-grown materials, which they did with their eyes and minds fixed on the ever-present cosmic background.[37]

Salvador Dalí

Dalí had a time-to-time role in Stravinsky's political and artistic life throughout both his European and American years. The artists first met when they travelled in the same train compartment from Madrid to Barcelona in 1921 and afterward saw each other and dined together on many occasions in Paris. An interview published in *La Noche* (Barcelona, 12 March 1936) entitled 'Igor Stravinsky and Surrealism' must have invoked fulminations from Dalí when he discovered that most of the text was a tribute to Picasso: 'I am a great friend of Picasso, and I admire him in all of his tendencies: he is always and consistently a great artist.' Presumably the lesser artist's envy was swallowed, since Vera's diary mentions many dinners with Dalí in the 1930s, including one with Chanel on 18 June 1938, Stravinsky's fifty-sixth birthday.

In the summer of 1952 the composer became friendly with Edward James, an illegitimate son of King Edward VII, and Dalí's wealthiest patron. In the 1950s James gave several Dalí paintings, as well as a ranch near Taos, New Mexico, to the Stravinskys. In New York James invited them to lunches with the Dalís, at one of which I sat between the painter and his wife, Gala, an occasion I still remember vividly. To remove one's eyes from Dalí's sometimes drooping handlebar moustaches was difficult, but talking to him was an ordeal, his French being heavily accented and his English exceedingly laborious, though he claimed to read the language at high speed. While his egotism was palpable, it was evident that his wife dominated their relationship. His parsimony, at least with James, embarrassed his guests. James had told Stravinsky that the lunch was at Dalí's invitation, but when

---

37   Stravinsky wrote to his St Petersburg friend Findeyzen: 'I want the whole of my work to give the feeling of the closeness between the lives of man and the soil, and I sought to do this through a lapidary rhythm.'

the painter received *l'addition* and glanced at the total he rapidly passed it to Edward.

A recent biography alleges that when Stravinsky was living in the St Regis Hotel in January 1961 he 'ran into Salvador Dalí, who... would ostentatiously emerge when the Stravinskys came along the corridor, ringing a little bell... to attract attention to his long, waxed moustaches'. Stravinsky, of course, had become accustomed to this tonsorial attraction forty years earlier. Moreover, Dalí was a part-time resident at the St Regis in a suite more remote from the main corridor than the Stravinskys'. The composer was irritated not by a silver bell but by Dalí's routine of whistling *Frère Jacques* on his return to his room, signalling his wife to unlock the door. This could be as late as dinner time, after he had held court in the main lobby with his two pet ocelots. He had an idea for a theatrical collaboration with Stravinsky and later presented the composer with a drawing, whether to pique his interest or annoy him I cannot say.

In recent years Dalí's status as an artist and talented writer has grown considerably with the re-evaluation of his later work. The 2010 exhibition at Atlanta marked a reappraisal by even the most high-minded critics of his earlier activities, both personal and pictorial. His *Portrait of Juan de Pareja, Assistant to Velázquez* is now commercially valued on a par with the best of Tanguy, the acknowledged master of *grisaille*, who admitted to Dalí's influence on him. Dalí's portrait of his wife as the Virgin Mary is also admired today, and the *Debris of an Automobile Giving Birth to a Blind Horse Biting a Telephone* is recognised as a clever parody of Picasso's *Guernica*.

Alexei von Jawlensky

Another eminent painter friend in Stravinsky's Swiss years was the Russian Alexei von Jawlensky, who visited the composer, his neighbour near Morges, several times in 1916 and later in Zurich. I knew little of this connection until 1958, when we dined at Lucie Lambert's Hietzing (Vienna) home, where the rich colours of the Jawlensky canvases on her walls revived Stravinsky's memory. At the outbreak of World War I, the artist, by then a German citizen, was forced to leave his home on the Italian Riviera, whence he moved to the Vaudois village of Saint-Prex. One of Jawlensky's letters describes the incident:

> We could bring only what we were able to carry ourselves, and were not even allowed to keep our poor cat. At Lindau we were forced to walk a hundred paces from the station to the steamer surrounded by soldiers with rifles, while the crowds lining the streets swore and spat at us.

Jawlensky knew Schoenberg through their mutual friend Ferruccio Busoni, and Stravinsky was increasingly curious about the composer of *Pierrot Lunaire*. In the late teens Stravinsky and the painter also shared an interest in Dada, the artistic movement centred in Zurich. In 1920 he joined the roster of the Dada magazine's vice presidents and gave the manuscript of *Chanson pour compter* for publication in facsimile therein. He became a good friend of the Dadaists Tristan Tzara, Marcel Duchamp, and Francis Picabia in Paris in 1922. One of Jawlensky's close friends in Munich had been Emmy Scheyer; the painter induced her to change her first name to Galka.[38] In my early years with the Stravinskys in California, we enjoyed visiting the Scheyer home in Pasadena to see her famous art collection, which included a hundred paintings by Jawlensky and at least as many by Klee. After her death and the subsequent legal wrangles concerning ownership of the artworks, the entire collection was purchased by the U.S. industrialist Norton Simon, who eventually donated it to the Pasadena Gallery, therewith renamed the Norton Simon Museum. Mr Simon later became the principal patron of the Monday Evening Concerts in West Hollywood.

---

38 In July 1946 Schoenberg wrote to Oskar Kokoschka: 'You had a great friend here who died some time ago: Frau Galka Scheyer. But I am afraid it was a bit of a similar case to that of my adherents who all rank Hindemith, Stravinsky, and Bartók, if not above me, at least as on a par with me: she had *too many gods*: Klee, Kandinsky, *et al*. But thou shalt have one God, and for all I care, leave me out; I'm not a modern...'

Henry Moore

One pleasant evening in May 1963 Stephen Spender took the Stravinskys and me to dine with Henry Moore at the Garrick Club. The sculptor was immediately likable; he delivered his opinions interspersed with an appealing, debonair giggle. At one point the talk drifted towards the quagmires of 'taste'. I.S.: 'Taste is for pederasts. For other people it is simply a matter of familiarity.' Moore supervened: 'But there is something much grander than taste, and that is the sense of terrible importance.' I asked which sculptors had this sense, and he came down with finality on each of the names I proposed: Rodin was 'a sculptor', Brâncuşi was 'only and totally a sculptor', Matisse was 'a sculptor', Picasso was 'a great sculptor', Wotruba was 'a sculptor', Giacometti was 'a great artist', Marini was 'a bit of a sculptor', and Manzù was 'a real sculptor, but a bad one'. Describing a Cycladic vase that Moore had just acquired, words failed him, whereupon he took a pen and drew the object for us with a few swift strokes, saying: 'Well, as you can see, that's not a ceramic at all but a sculpture.'

Stravinsky did not comment on these evaluations because he was in agreement and thought them astutely observed. He knew personally all of the artists mentioned except Wotruba, whose work the composer did not like. Wotruba was the art teacher in Vienna of Stravinsky's Dr Max Edel, who in 1965 sculpted Stravinsky's head in a heavy, academic style, much too large but preserving the features. This bronze was purchased by Goddard Lieberson at an exhibition at the Wildenstein Gallery in New York. The opening was preceded by a dinner at a private home in Sutton Place, where we were seated with Leonard Bernstein. Stravinsky greatly admired but did not love Rodin's work in the way that he loved Degas's. Of the others Stravinsky was most attracted to the art of his friend Brâncuşi. Of Picasso's sculptures the composer preferred the late-period owls, and he agreed with Moore's judgment on Giacometti, preferring his paintings and drawings to his sculpture, which Jean-Paul Sartre had described as 'taking the fat off space'.

The Moore connection did not end with the Garrick dinner. Later the same evening he decided to make a gift to Stravinsky of one of his finest paintings, of people sleeping in a London tube during the wartime bombings. Spender owned the picture that Moore wanted to give to the composer; he reimbursed Spender with another picture of equal value.

Months later, on 21 November, Moore sent a handwritten note:

> Dear Igor Stravinsky, I want to tell you how absolutely delighted I was to get the page of music of *Abraham and Isaac* in your own hand, which you so kindly inscribed to me. It is very beautiful and Stephen Spender had it handsomely framed before bringing it to me, and from a few feet away it looks like, and gets mistaken for, a Paul Klee. With warmest regards to both you and your wife and with sincerest admiration for all you have given to the world.
> Yours ever, Henry Moore.

After his death Vera Stravinsky donated the picture to the Henry Moore Foundation.

Sir Isaiah Berlin

Sir Isaiah's role in the creation of Stravinsky's *Abraham and Isaac* (dedicated 'to the People of Israel') was to secure its commission, to translate the Hebrew text into Russian as a crib for the composer, and to organise the performances in Jerusalem. I was much interested in Isaiah's discussions of the problems peculiar to translating Hebrew, which he called 'a diffuse language'. He cited as an example of a neologism a sentence in *Judges* which says in Hebrew, 'And Samson went down to Thamnatha, and he noticed a girl,' whereas in the Ronald Knox version this becomes 'Samson paid a visit to Thamnatha and there was a woman there... that took his eye.' I prefer Knox's rendition.

Isaiah wrote to Stravinsky through me, knowing that the composer could not take the time for personal correspondence. In London on 15 October 1998 I was warmly introduced by Tony Fell, before reading Isaiah's witty communiqués, ostensibly to me, to an audience at the Royal Philharmonic Society. Lady Berlin, accompanied by Lady Spender, sat almost directly in front of me in the second row. As I left the rostrum, Lady Berlin, whom I had known for many years, approached me saying, 'These must be published; they reveal another side of Isaiah and are like no others in his correspondence.' At the time I was completing a volume of memoirs, *An Improbable Life*, and realised that the letters would be an important addition to my book. When Isaiah's executors and literary agents withheld permission, I appealed to my good friend Stanley Baron of Thames & Hudson, who volunteered to raise the matter with one of Lady Berlin's sons, a friend of his. Accompanied by Lady Grace Dudley and Robert Silvers, Aline Berlin herself came to my New York apartment a short time later to encourage me to proceed with publication of the letters, which she continued to feel would be a significant contribution to her husband's legacy. She gave me her word that there would be no further difficulties with intermediaries.

I doubt that Isaiah's scandalous Dictaphoned letters released posthumously will contain any acid-tipped barbs aimed at Stravinsky, though I anticipate several of them for me because of my own opinions, expressed during a 1964 press conference in Jerusalem, concerning the banning of Wagner in Israel. I supported the Daniel Barenboim–Edward Said position and mentioned that Chopin's anti-Semitism was on a par with Wagner's. Stravinsky's deft sidestepping of the incendiary Wagner question drew vigorous applause.

Isaiah himself genuinely loved Stravinsky's music, *Oedipus Rex* and Symphony of Psalms above all, and was always protective of the composer. His luncheons for Stravinsky at Headington House, Oxford, were limited to such top culture figures as Robert Graves and A. J. Ayer, and to reliable familiars such as Stephen Spender, John Sparrow, Maurice Bowra and Lord David Cecil. (After all, Isaiah coined the word 'homintern', though he never explained his own early attachment to and transatlantic voyage with Guy Burgess.) Table talk at these Oxford *déjeuners* sparkled with 'quiptifications', to borrow Samuel Beckett's word, but in Stravinsky's presence Isaiah himself said little beyond explaining in unhurried Russian some of the rapid-fire English discussions. T. S. Eliot had once warned us that he had not understood a single word when he shared a train compartment from London to Oxford with Isaiah: 'They went by so quickly.' The only conversation I remember from Berlin's luncheons was one with Robert Graves concerning 'moral philosophy' and the arts. After Stravinsky had endeavoured to explain the abstract side of diddling with serial sets, Graves bravely announced that poetry was 'far more closely involved with moral issues than that'.

In London, Isaiah's solicitude extended to procuring theatre tickets, restaurant reservations, private access to art galleries and exhibitions, and otherwise unobtainable seats in Covent Garden loges. I remember one of these last shared with Lord Bob Boothby, for which a private bar and full dinner service in several courses was prepared in the corridor for consumption course by course at intermissions. For the premiere of a new production of *Figaro*, Isaiah had secured orchestra seats to enable Stravinsky to leave after the first act and rush to the Albert Hall for Part Two of Monteux's fiftieth-anniversary performance of *The Rite of Spring*. But when the second act of *Figaro* followed the first without intermission, Isaiah had to extricate the Stravinskys from a fully occupied front row and hustle them off to hear the *Sacre*. The departing composer apologised to his neighbours in a stage whisper, 'Excuse us but we all have diarrhoea.' Isaiah only later realised that Stravinsky had come to Covent Garden purposely to avoid hearing the *Sacre*,[39] dreading the ovation that he would inevitably have to endure following the piece.

---

39 Stephen Spender reported in *The New York Times*, 7 October 1963: '[A] special pleasure for the Eliots was the visit of the Igor Stravinskys at the end of the evening in which Stravinsky managed to hear half of the performance of *Figaro* at Covent Garden, and the second half of a gala performance, conducted by Pierre Monteux, of his own work at the Albert Hall.' It was on the day after this visit with the Eliots that Spender revealed his story of the poet Emanuel Litvinoff's reading of his poem *To T. S. Eliot* at the Institute of Contemporary Arts in London. It seemed that Eliot himself had entered the hall just before the reading began, and that the audience was aware of his presence. At the conclusion Stephen stood up and denounced Litvinoff for insulting Eliot, whereupon the entire hall shouted in agreement ('hear, hear!'). When the tumult ended, a single voice from the back of the hall protested. It was Eliot himself who was heard to say: 'It's a good poem. It is a very good poem.' Eliot included it in his 1948 anthology, *Selected Poems*.

A few years later I was at a luncheon with Sir Harold Nicolson, Isaiah and Stravinsky at the Connaught. A year after that we enjoyed a New Year's dinner with Isaiah and Alan Pryce-Jones in the Berlin suite at the Carlyle Hotel in New York. I remember Isaiah on a visit to Stravinsky in Paris in 1963, but we saw him most often in Venice in 1958. He had not come for the premiere of *Threni* but for a culture congress presented by the Cini Foundation. Similarly, he spent an afternoon with Stravinsky in New York a day or two after the premiere of Requiem Canticles in 1966 but missed the performance at Princeton.

Long before the Stravinskys first met Isaiah – through Nabokov in the Savoy Hotel in December 1956 – Vera Stravinsky and Isaiah had two mutual Russian friends,[40] Anna Akhmatova and the Princess Andronica (*née* Salomeya Halpern). Vera and I had visited Salomeya in her London home, but I knew little about her until a year or so later when an unsigned obit for Akhmatova, presumably by Isaiah, appeared in *The Times*. Akhmatova was allowed to leave the U.S.S.R. during her last years, and, on a visit to Isaiah at Oxford, entrusted him with a profile portrait of Vera that the poet herself had painted in 1916, with a caption in Russian on the obverse identifying the subject as a 'naughty girl'. (Sudeykin had jilted Akhmatova for Vera.)

On 7 April 1971, the day after Stravinsky's death, Isaiah wrote to me:

> Dear Bob: There is absolutely nothing one can say when really fateful events occur and one's life is altered for good... But when it actually happens, it is always much worse. Nothing will ever be the same... The tiny part I played in *Abraham and Isaac* is literally the proudest recollection of my life... I shall not write to Mme Stravinsky. I would much rather see her when she is ready.

---

40 A friend I shared with Isaiah was Mary Jane Benton Sherwig, his amanuensis at Lowell House, Harvard, when he lectured there for several months until being called back to England during his father's illness.

We did see him again, in London for luncheons at the Ritz and, for the last time, in September 1981 in Vera's rooms at the Dorchester.

Stark Young

Arthur Sachs introduced Stravinsky to Stark Young, the popular novelist (*So Red the Rose*), when he was the drama critic of *The New York Times*. One of Stravinsky's first American-born friends, he was also one of the most sympathetic and gifted. Stravinsky introduced me to him after our Town Hall concert on 11 April 1948. I was greatly impressed by his note to Stravinsky the next day referring to the premiere of his revised *Symphonies of Wind Instruments*:

> I am wondering - as happens to me very rarely in art - how these incredible patterns of form and tone appear to any soul, how can the wonder and beauty of what you say come to us like that... all the miracles of the ancient barbaric, passionate world are there, and all the human heart is there.

I still cannot read this without hearing Stark repeat those words in his mossy southern accent. When I joined the Stravinskys in Denver two months later, Stark was a house guest of Charles Bayly, a descendant of Marie-Henri Beyle (Stendhal), with whom we enjoyed many lunches and soirées. In the spring of 1950 we saw Stark frequently in New York, dining at his home there with his lifetime companion, Bill Bowman, and accompanying them to the theatre and to movies. The Stravinskys also visited Stark at his summer home in Waccabuc, New York. After an excursion there, he wrote to the composer apropos his choice of designer for the forthcoming Metropolitan Opera production of *The Rake's Progress*:

> When you spoke of Horace Armistead[41] and the scenery for your opera I could not bring any image to mind of a setting

---

41   He was Lincoln Kirstein's choice of designer, imposed on Stravinsky via Balanchine.

of his. Then I remembered it for Menotti's *The Consul*.[42] There the play indicated a chance for a very effective setting, but Mr. Armistead missed it very badly. This, of course, does not mean that he would do it every time or often. Just the same, I wanted to tell you so that you could keep a sharp eye on what he does.

Charles-Albert Cingria[43]

This bicycling companion during Stravinsky's Swiss years – they pedaled to the Vaudois vineyards during the harvesting of the new grapes – remained close to him in Paris in the 1930s despite Cingria's hatred of Mussolini, who had jailed his brother for two months. A medievalist and Latin scholar, Cingria strongly influenced Stravinsky's philosophical thinking. Additionally, Cingria's study of medieval music, *La Civilisation de Saint-Gall* (1929), influenced Stravinsky in its thesis that 'music always precedes language, and more precisely'. Cingria was an ailurophile – he gave walk-on roles to cats in his plays – as was the composer of *Berceuses du chat*, but he was principally interested in Charles-Albert's discussions of music and mathematics. Cingria introduced Stravinsky to Amedeo Modigliani and arranged for the artist to paint the composer's portrait. The titles of the movements of *Duo concertant* derive in part from the association with Cingria.[44]

Stravinsky's interest in the St Gall library had been kindled by Charles-Albert Cingria, a scholar on questions of medieval musical notations, especially the Gothic (Lorraine style), the Aquitanian

42 Stravinsky envied Menotti's Broadway successes with *The Consul*, *The Medium* and *The Telephone*. (I was present when the composers met at a party at Virgil Thomson's.) In later years Stravinsky roughly criticised Menotti's *The Last Savage*, mistaking himself as the target of this naïve satire of avant-garde music. Menotti did not respond, but he gladly accepted Rolf Liebermann's invitation to stage the *Rake* in Hamburg, a masterful production, we were told. Some time later when Menotti asked Stravinsky to send a self-portrait for an auction to raise money for Spoleto, he promptly obliged.
43 His *Correspondence avec Igor Strawinsky* was first published in Lausanne in 2001.
44 Some of the titles, such as 'Dithyramb', seem askew, the piece being ethereal and almost motionless. Alastair Macaulay's discussion of Balanchine's choreography for *Duo concertant* illuminatingly emphasises the parts of the piece that are not danced and should be heard for the music alone.

and the Byzantine. The collection contained many Benedictine parchments widely acknowledged as the world's most beautiful. The oldest item in the collection was a tenth-century *Cantatorium* which was taken out of its case for Stravinsky to examine; he removed his glasses and squinted at the manuscript for a half-hour. In most of this music rhythm is conveyed by the distance of the breaks between neumes. The notation of musical motion interested him most, and he was always suspicious of rhythmic interpretations. This library is best known for its secular Latin songbook *Carmina Burana* (Bavaria, thirteenth century). I left the building resolving to study the subject, if possible with Nadia Boulanger, whose knowledge of it was vast. She had tutored Stravinsky in it and continued throughout her life to send copies of ancient manuscripts to him. St Gall's own notational system had at one time prevailed throughout Central Europe.

I was with Charles-Albert and Stravinsky together only twice, when Cingria had biked to Venice from Geneva for the premiere of *The Rake* (and one or two Baron Corvo-type rendezvous). When we left Paris for Brussels in May 1952, he accompanied us through the Gare du Nord to our compartment on the train. He always referred to Stravinsky as 'le maître d'Oranienbaum'. Stravinsky's affection for Cingria was abiding. On hearing of his death, the composer wept.

Charles-Ferdinand Ramuz

C.-F. Ramuz is best known as Stravinsky's collaborator on the libretto of *L'Histoire du Soldat*. The creation of this play and of the friendship between the two men during the latter part of World War I was more personal than the composer's work with Gide on *Perséphone* or with Auden on *The Rake*. Furthermore, Ramuz's book about Stravinsky has become a classic and is still in print. Unhappily the following paragraphs are devoted to the deterioration of the relationship.

The anti-Calvinist Stravinsky was more intimate with the Roman Catholic Cingria than with the Protestant C.-F. Ramuz. When Diaghilev revived *Renard* in the late 1920s, Ramuz claimed a third of the author's rights for the use of his translation of the text. Stravinsky countered this by banning Ramuz's French translation of *Les Noces* and by recording the work in London in English.[45] It has been claimed that the relationship between Stravinsky and Ramuz 'had been slowly drifting apart for years... their friendship constantly undermined by the painful question of *Soldier's Tale* royalties and by growing artistic differences'. But the royalty issue was not of prime importance, and since no further collaborations materialised, there could be no 'growing artistic differences'. In truth Stravinsky intensely disliked all of Ramuz's French translations: *Renard*, *Les Noce*s and the Russian song texts. Too many of the music rhythms had to be readjusted to accommodate the translated words.

Stravinsky received 250 Swiss francs per performance as his author's rights to the *Soldat*, the same amount as Ramuz and the scene painter, Auberjonois. Ansermet's fee as conductor was considerably higher, and the other performance costs – actors, a narrator, a dancer (the Princess), music and costume rentals – amounted to 4,000 Swiss francs. As it happened, the Spanish influenza closed most European theatres after the premiere, although the music continued to be played as a concert suite, most importantly in London in July 1920, for which Stravinsky extended the final movement (from the 3/16 bar). The most celebrated of all fully staged performances was in Weimar in 1923, an event of international interest because it marked the first major stage production of the Weimar Republic after World War I, and because Stravinsky himself and Vera de Bosset were present. A critic wrote that 'some of the great figures of the modern movement' attended the Weimar *Soldat*, 'including Paul Klee and Vasily Kandinsky, as well as Walter Gropius and perhaps László Moholy-Nagy'. But this statement is ambiguous: was Moholy-Nagy a great figure or simply 'perhaps' present at the concert?

Ramuz's misrepresentation of the *Soldat* collaboration offended the composer. The original story and most of the episodes of the piece were incontestably Stravinsky's 'intellectual property', though

---

45 I remember Leonard Bernstein at a lunch with Stravinsky in the Four Seasons restaurant in New York singing passages of this by heart, amusingly emphasising the quaintness of the Brit translation.

of course the survival of the work at all is due entirely to the music.[46] That Ramuz did not acknowledge the composer's contribution to the play on the credits page of the proofs is baffling in that its subject, taken from Russian folklore, was proposed by Stravinsky and the exposition follows his outline. In 1920 the composer wrote to Ramuz concerning 'the omission of the ultimate collaboration between us on your and my *Soldat*'.

A crisis occurred in 1925 in Rome backstage after a performance of Pirandello's production of *Soldat* when the librettist and the composer quarrelled. But a deeper dispute was ignited by the 1927 publication of Ramuz's *Souvenirs sur Igor Strawinsky*. Though Ramuz had sent drafts of his book chapter by chapter, Stravinsky did not read them, and Ramuz had not formally sought the composer's permission; when the book appeared, Stravinsky was riled by what he considered an invasion of privacy and breach of trust. He did not respond until Ramuz wrote asking for comments which were, in part: 'Of course I have reactions, my dear Ramuz, but when I am asked to formulate them into commentaries, as you have just done, I recoil like a snail into its shell, fearing to expose my nakedness.' After Ramuz's death, on 23 May 1947, Stravinsky refused an editor's request to write an obituary note: 'These things must be done in cold blood, otherwise one risks altering one's memories and being unfair to the past. Facts reconstructed by memory are deformed if invoked during a state of grief.'

Though I had not yet met Stravinsky at the time of Ramuz's death, I sent an obit from a London newspaper to the composer, which he acknowledged by saying that this was the first time he had received the news. I was surprised by this note, since I had assumed that the news would have been cabled to him by his son Theodore.

---

46 One critic has denied that Stravinsky's original intention was to limit the music to a solo violin, though both Ramuz and Ansermet have confirmed this, and the score shows that the other six instruments were added one by one as the work progressed. The same critic also doubts that Stravinsky could have written a musically and dramatically viable *Soldat* with only a violin, even though this instrument is the subject of the work, which in its final form features solo violin music. The criticism reveals a sorry incomprehension of the extent of Stravinsky's powers as a composer.

On the sixtieth anniversary of Ramuz's death, his work was awarded the accolade of publication in the Éditions Gallimard's Pléiade collection; he was the first French-Swiss writer to receive this honour, though he had always indignantly claimed independence from Parisian influences in his local Vaudois novels.

Thomas Mann

Stravinsky had first dined with the Thomas Manns in Zurich in the 1920s, then again at their home in Munich on 29 January 1933, the day before Hitler forced Hindenburg to sign a decree suspending the German Constitution. The Nobel novelist attended the Stravinsky-Dushkin concert in Munich on 2 February and then left the city for Holland on the 11th.

On 28 January 1943 the Manns, then living in Pacific Palisades, dined with the Stravinskys at the home of the Werfels (the novelist and his wife Alma Mahler). Stravinsky looked forward to his every meeting with Mann, as well as with his in-laws, the Pringsheims, one of whom had been a Berlin music critic; Katja Mann's brother Hans translated for Stravinsky during his 1959 concert tour in Japan. Stravinsky was also on good terms with two of Mann's other sons, Klaus and Michael. When in an army training camp in Missouri, Klaus had corresponded with the composer, and Michael, a violist, was the first to play Stravinsky's *Élégie*, in the composer's studio.

Thomas Mann's diary for November 1942 notes that he 'read the Memoirs of Igor Stravinsky, underlining passages for rereading'. A month later, passing through San Francisco, Mann added that he remembered Stravinsky confessing to him in Zurich years before that he admired Tchaikovsky. Mann's agenda for 1943 refers to planned meetings with Stravinsky and Schoenberg which confirms that (unlike most Angeleno 'intellectuals') Mann was on good terms with both composers. He also notes 'a nice soirée at the Werfels' with Stravinsky. Talked about Schoenberg.' Mann's notebook for *Dr Faustus* says that:

> Talking with [Stravinsky] at an evening gathering at our home,
> I was struck by things he said - with Gide as a starting point,[47]
> and speaking alternately in German, English, and French -
> concerning confession as the product of various cultural
> spheres: the Greek Orthodox, the Roman Catholic and the
> Protestant. In his opinion, Tolstoy was essentially German and
> Protestant.[48]

The post-war political turn to the right in America alarmed the author of *The Magic Mountain*, who soon fled back to Switzerland. Surprisingly, Stravinsky himself became involved in the U.S. politics of the time, though perhaps more for musical than ideological reasons. He became a good friend of the refugee composers Ernst Toch and Mario Castelnuovo-Tedesco and wrote to Hanns Eisler complimenting him on his incidental music for Brecht's *Galileo*, which opened at the Coronet Theater in West Hollywood on 7 July 1947. When the U.S. began proceedings to deport Eisler as a communist, Mann wrote to a friend: 'I hear that Stravinsky (a White Russian!) means to start a demonstration in [Eisler's] favour.'[49]

Christopher Isherwood, closer to Mann than any other English writer in America, wrote sympathetically and perceptively about him during the period of Mann's Hollywood friendship with the composer. Isherwood describes Mann at a lunch in his home as

> urbane as ever, looking wonderfully young - perhaps because,
> as a boy, he was elderly and staid - with careful, deliberate
> gestures he chooses a cigar, examines a cognac bottle, opens a
> furniture catalogue, giving each object his full serious attention.
> Yet he isn't in the least pompous. He has great natural dignity.
> He is a true scholar, a gentlemanly householder, a gracefully
> ironic pillar of society - solid right through. He would be
> magnificent at his own trial.

---

47 Stravinsky remarked that in fact this was Roger Martin du Gard, and the composer's archives include several photos of Stravinsky dining with the du Gards.
48 Tolstoy had been excommunicated from the Russian Orthodox Church.
49 Stravinsky signed a letter protesting at Eisler's extradition.

On hearing of Mann's death in 1955, Isherwood observed that: 'He died tidily, as he did everything. There was a greatness in his dry neatness... I think of him with real love... [H]e was kind, he was genuinely interested in other people, he kept cheerful, and he was brave.'

During Stravinsky's 1956 hospitalisation in Munich, I met the novelist's widow, Katja, and daughter Erika (Mrs W. H. Auden)[50] almost daily, since we lived on the same floor of the Kempinski Hotel.

Sir Kenneth Clark[51]

On 31 May 1963 Stephen Spender drove the Stravinskys and myself to Canterbury, then to Saltwood Castle for lunch with Sir Kenneth and Lady Clark. The Kentish woods were carpeted with bluebells, and pink hydrangeas were blooming in country gardens. The hop fields near Canterbury were honey-coloured like the newly scrubbed sandstones of the cathedral itself.

To drive from Canterbury Cathedral to Saltwood is to travel back from the scene of Thomas à Becket's murder to the site of the hatching of the plot, Saltwood having been the appointed place for Henry II's conspiring knights to make their pledge, extinguishing their candles afterwards to avoid each other's eyes – or so Tennyson wrote, imbuing the murderers with consciences they seem unlikely to have possessed. Turning to more recent Saltwoodiana, Stephen said that a prospective caller had once 'knocked at the portcullis' but was turned away with the explanation that 'Lady Clark is busy weeding the battlements'. In another Spender anecdote, the chatelaine once reproved a serving wench for 'fingering the tulips just before the Kents came to dinner'. But the best of this Firbankian anthology is a story about some gentlewomen at a court ball complaining to each

---

50 Aldous Huxley had arranged for the marriages by proxy of Auden to Erika Mann, and of a young gay Englishman, Terry Bedford, to Sybille von Schönebeck, to effect their escape from Nazi Germany to England.
51 This section was published in the U.S. in my *Chronicle of a Friendship*.

other about the nuisance of having to send to the bank once or twice a year to fetch their tiaras from the vaults; Lady Clark remarked that her tiara had become terribly worn. But to visit Saltwood is to see that indeed the battlements would need weeding.

At table, I wanted to ask the great Leonardo authority what he thought about T. S. Eliot's word 'simper' for the Mona Lisa's smile and his detection of a touch of anger in her eyes, but I thought better of it and, as I recall, did not venture a single word at the meal. For Stravinsky's sake, Sir K. put forth the notion that

> instead of trying to suppress modern painting, the Russians might reasonably have claimed to be its discoverers, what with Jawlensky, Malevich, Gabo, Archipenko, Soutine, Chagall, El Lissitzky, Tatlin, Kandinsky, de Staël, Poliakov, Goncharova, Larionov, Berman, Tchelichev. The difficulty for the Soviet Union was that every one of these artists became a refugee. Kandinsky's case is the most curious because he was potentially, if not in fact, a great painter, at least up to his return to Russia, where he became a commissar. I'm sure he liked that, for a time anyway, but after his experience in politics, his sense of reality went underground and he painted only squares, circles, abstractions, all very dead. This may be a clue to modern art.

I recall only one other remark by Sir K. during lunch: 'Real gourmets always take red wine with salmon,' and in rapid succession I thought of myself as an unreal gourmet, no gourmet at all, and an anti-gourmet. Having shown the highest appreciation of Sir K.'s Scotch, a private stock, Stravinsky was given a bottle of it. Seeing this, Lady C. gasped 'Oh, no!' to which Sir K. archly replied: 'Don't worry, dear, there is enough left for you.'[52]

---

52 Sir K. sent us a copy of his catalogue *The Romantic Movement*, organised and introduced by him. It is inscribed in his hand 'Souvenirs de Henry Moore!' and in Stephen Spender's 'To Robert Craft with affection and gratitude May '63'.

Eugenio Montale

A half-century of listening to the Rake *has*
rendered most of us pretty well 'uncritical'
about it - maybe still questioning a word
or two, here and there, but never a note.

Andrew Porter

Stravinsky never knew what a friend he had in this great poet. In
truth they were only acquaintances, but the 1975 Nobel Prize winner
was a percipient champion of Stravinsky's music. As a one-time opera
critic, Montale naturally attended the premiere of *The Rake's Progress*
in Venice in September 1951. An additional motive for the trip was
his admiration for W. H. Auden, whom Montale had never met. On
one of their first evenings in the city the two poets dined together,
joined by Stephen Spender and Louis MacNeice, in a restaurant in the
Frezzeria. It is regrettable that the only remark preserved by Montale
from the conversation on this occasion was that Auden was, as he
would say, 'in his cups'. Clearly Montale was fascinated by Auden,
describing him as

> the kind of personality who excites the air that surrounds
> him... [H]e knows every secret of technique... [H]is poetry
> is sweet like Spenser's, ironic and witty like Pope's, dry and
> discursive like Eliot's. He jumps from the old to the new with
> perfect nonchalance and enjambs his stanzas like the best of
> *Don Juan.*

Montale's essay *On the Trail of Stravinsky*[53] begins with a
description of the atmosphere in the Serenissima two days before
the opera's premiere. Montale had found a room on the Riva degli
Schiavoni 'with a view like a Canaletto' and had retired there to study
a copy of the English libretto. The poet had wanted to be present 'at

---

53   In the *Corriere della sera*, Milan, 19 September 1951.

the birth of a presumed masterpiece, or rather to spy on its baptism from the wings, from the back of the shop. But God only knows whether I'll be able to get near Stravinsky, who has arrived with his entire *suite* (wife, son, personal physician[54]).'

Montale abandoned his plan of a 'direct approach' after having read descriptions of the composer's arrival in Naples. The 'Maestro, it seems, is rather *arancino*, as Florentine journalists say, meaning a bitter orange'. On debarking in Naples, Stravinsky had indeed been set upon by journalists, whose description of the composer as 'the great violinist'[55] induces chuckles from Montale and inspires him to quote from a satire by Juvenal, 'inde irae', the Latin plural of 'whence the wrath'.

After perusing the libretto, Montale acclaims the book of the new opera 'a jewel of its genre' that 'may contain Auden's most beautiful verse', while also noting that 'the libretto is not functional, as Auden perhaps thinks'. Wondering about the kind of music that will be able to underscore many lines, Montale imaginatively attributes the opening monologue of Baba the Turk to the style of the *Mikado*. This indebtedness to Gilbert and Sullivan refers to Baba's patter in the alternating three- and two-metre introduction to the breakfast scene, the first of the Rake's married life. Montale quotes one of Nick Shadow's pre-nuptial inducements to his bachelor victim:

> What deed could be as great
> As with this Gorgon to mate?
> All the world shall admire
> Tom Rakewell Esquire.

Doubting that much of the text can be successfully set to music, Montale amuses himself by humming a tune of his own invention to this quatrain, adding: 'I do not envy the translator, who must preserve the sense and the rhythm, here and in many other difficult passages…

---

54   Dottore Musella, who had accompanied the composer from Naples, attended him for most of a week in Milan and followed along to Venice.

55   On 18 March 1955, the Stravinskys, en route from Lisbon to Seville, were stopped at the border in Badajoz by an immigration official who was heard informing his assistant that Stravinsky was '*Un famoso violinista. No me gusta.*'

and I have the impression that this text... will always gain from being read and sung in its original language.'[56] Further, and more seriously, the poet fears 'an imbalance between Auden's highly ramified and allusive intelligence and the naked, almost abstract intelligence of late Stravinsky'. But Montale rejects Stravinsky's 'distinction between opera and musical drama', even though predicting that 'a new generation of barbarians will continue to write tedious music dramas, not operas constructed like chamber sonatas'.

After the dress rehearsal and, on the same evening, the premiere, Montale shares some of his thoughts:

> I don't presume to make a judgment on Stravinsky's new work, but I cannot fail to note with satisfaction the reappearance, after so many years, of an opera with parts for the singers. Another welcome innovation is the abolition of the large orchestra with its symphonic padding. Here the Devil is accompanied by piano and it is enough. On the day that a theatrical composer will believe in the expressive power of music (Stravinsky is a rationalist who hates expression and wants to reduce music to pure Platonic idea) this score will be able to suggest a great deal to him.

The day following the gala, Montale was present, he writes, at

> a vermouth [toast] in the composer's honour given by the city of Venice. Stravinsky arrived at the Imbarcadero near the Rialto and was greeted by the applause of a hundred peasants in worn-out shoes, wearing open shirts over messy trousers. I am told these are not peasants at all, but the very cream of the fashionable intelligentsia. They speak Anglo-Roman (*Il Progresso del Racchio* instead of *La Carriera del Libertino*) and they all know each other.

The troupe of beatniks then moved to a room in the City Hall, crowding around the mayor, who made a well-received speech

---

56 The chorus at the first performance sang in unintelligible English, even after many hours of tutoring by the librettists.

mentioning Aeschylus, Hugo and Arrigo Boito. Stravinsky, who was seated, took this beating and expressed his thanks, bowing in the Russian manner from the waist as if about to dive. Here Montale finally met the composer, but the poet reveals only that

> I managed to exchange a few words with him and was not surprised to find him so simple and humanly solitary. Fame, Hollywood, and dollars have not marred in the slightest his personality, which is that of a small *barine* who is afraid of the devil and would like his whole life to be a beautiful opera, closer to Tchaikowsky than Wagner.

Montale and Auden departed from the Treviso airport at almost the same time, before the second performance. Since the Italian poet's flight to Milan took off after the English-American poet's flight to Naples, Montale was able to watch Auden bounding aboard the airplane 'like a Roebuck'.

Montale did not attend the premiere of *Canticum Sacrum* in the Basilica di San Marco five years later but in the intervening years followed the musical scene closely and was aware of a swerve away from the *Rake* and toward the avant-garde and John Cage. But the poet was present at the premiere of *Threni* in the Scuola Grande di San Rocco on 24 September 1958, despite a gondoliers' strike. His diary for that date is more illuminating about the new piece than any other commentary known to me:

> One cannot help but be moved year after year by the sight of the elderly Stravinsky mounting the conductor's podium to present the latest product of his study to the city of Venice (a city that now considers him an adopted son) and the habitués of the Festival. The seventy-six-year-old Maestro embodies fifty years of musical experience, and this imbues each of his reappearances with a warmth of feeling that overrides any purely critical consideration. No one, in fact, would have wanted to see him replaced yesterday evening by a conductor more expert than he is in the interpretation of his music,

even though in the dress rehearsal given yesterday afternoon for journalists, the frequent interruptions showed that the good preparatory work done by the young Craft in pulling it all together was thrown to the winds by the still younger Stravinsky, always unsure, always in search of himself.

Of the five Elegies making up the *Lamentations of Jeremiah*, Stravinsky has set to music fragments of the first, third, and fifth in the Latin. There are six soloists: soprano, alto, two tenors, a bass, and a basso profundo. The makeup of the orchestra is complex and rich in little-used instruments. The first fragment is divided into five groups, each of them designated by Hebrew letters which are syllabized by the chorus. The chorus recites the whole text *sotto voce*, and it is then taken up by the tenor with counterpoint by the women's voices. And so it continues by groups or subgroups, for each of which the Hebrew letter is repeated. It would be too long and dry and confusing to list all the devices that make up the structure of the work. This was explained here yesterday by maestro Roman Vlad, who is as competent as they come. Vlad follows the fundamental twelve-tone constellation of the work through all of its changes and bringing out the various songs to be found in it, the monody of the bass and all the architectonic symmetry to the final perfect consonants in which every motion of the soul is resolved.

Needless to say, here, as in the *Cantos* of Pound and the *Ulysses* of Joyce, the intelligence of the schema is of little assistance to one who listens as the work should be listened to, with a kind of mental virginity. And the ingenious impression left by *Threni* is true: that Stravinsky has not been suffocated by the technique and the format he has imposed on himself, for the score bears the stamps of his own personality, and he comes particularly alive whenever the undercurrent of normal tonality breaks in as if by a miracle through the forest of discordant voices – which happens in many places with the chorus and in a few phrases with the soprano and alto. We would not attempt to deny that from the complex of the sober and yet highly intricate score there emanates an afflatus of religious inspiration. Why should we deny to an intellect that has known all experience the right to a conversation with the Divine?

The *Threni* performance took place in Venice during a congress of philosophers and writers that included Auden, Montale and E. M. Forster. We were with Auden every day but did not see Montale. One evening when we were dining at the Martini, Auden came rushing in from a *calle* to the Campo S. Fantin and, passing our table, offered news from nowhere: 'I have just discovered that Leopardi wasn't born in the South.' The next day we learned that he had to wire a word change to the publisher of the forthcoming poem *Good-Bye to the Mezzogiorno*. The line contains the names of five meridian-born artists: Vico, Verga, Pirandello, Bernini and Bellini. Surely Pirandello was the substitution, since four syllables were needed; Auden did not particularly extol him but loved Leopardi. To me the change was unnecessary: whatever the Mercator projection indicates, Recanati is a typical southern Italian town, only a short hike downhill from Loreto, where Richard Crashaw is buried and where Orlando di Lasso made his pilgrimage. Moreover, most of Leopardi's poetry was composed in Naples, his *Ginestra* in a vineyard on one of the slopes of Vesuvius.

Proust, Joyce, Picasso, Stravinsky

We may come... from atoms
and ifs but we're presurely destined
to be odd's without ends.

Finnegans Wake

When Stravinsky and Diaghilev entered a Paris hotel on the night of 18 May 1922, for a gala dinner party after the premiere of the ballet *Renard*, they noticed that two chairs were unoccupied but did not remark on the names on the place cards: 'James Joyce' and 'Marcel

Proust'. The fête had been organised by Sydney and Violet Schiff with the help of their friend T. S. Eliot, who once said that 'the great point in the Schiffs' favour was bringing very diverse people together and making them combine well'. The Schiffs were notorious lionisers, and Sydney had been a persistent friend of Proust, as well as a translator of *Le Temps retrouvé*. Sydney's abiding ambition was to gather the 'four greatest living artists: Stravinsky, Picasso, Joyce and Proust'. The *Renard* premiere offered an opportunity to assemble this incongruous foursome in either the Hotel Majestic or the Ritz.[57] While Stravinsky and Diaghilev could have been relied upon to bring Picasso, only Eliot could have induced Joyce to attend an affair of this sort, particularly when the publicity surrounding the billowing reception of *Ulysses* was only weeks behind him.

A few mere mortals were also invited, above all the Princesse de Polignac, who had commissioned the ballet and underwritten its production, as well as the *Renard* performers: Bronislava Nijinska, the choreographer who also enacted the title role; Mikhail Larionov, the scene and costume designer; the vocalists impersonating the animal cast; the actual dancers; and the conductor Ernest Ansermet. The guest list included Eliot, Marinetti, Edith Sitwell, Katherine Mansfield, Clive Bell and Frederick Delius, this last a Stravinsky friend since 1913, when he carried the cumbersome score of *The Rite of Spring* for the composer to the second dress rehearsal.

The festivities began at about 10.30 but Joyce, spifflicated, arrived an hour late. Schiff ushered him to a seat near his own where Joyce's head sank into his arms on the table. For the next two hours he slept in this posture, perhaps dreaming about Bloomers, but when he began to snore sonorously Clive Bell and others indignantly departed. The perfectly groomed Proust made his entrance after that, stopping to converse with Stravinsky; the two men already knew each other through their mutual friend, the Venezuelan-born

---

57 Richard Davenport-Hines's memoir names the Hotel Majestic (the future headquarters of the Gestapo) as the venue for the party but it has been confirmed that Proust was present at the ballet and went from the Opéra to the Ritz, which makes nonsense of the claim that he made his first appearance at 2 a.m. and rode with Joyce in a taxi.

composer Reynaldo Hahn. Proust sought to engage Stravinsky in a discussion about late Beethoven quartets, but the composer, himself marinated in alcohol, was annoyed, and a tiff seemed likely to ensue. This embarrassed Diaghilev, especially because *À la recherche* refers to Stravinsky as the one real genius of the Ballets Russes. But Schiff intervened and, following his original intention, seated Proust next to Joyce. As sobriety gradually returned to the latter, he is reported to have listened to Proust's eloquence with fascination. When the party dispersed, Proust returned to his hotel to continue writing, while Schiff found a taxi, helped Joyce into it, and directed the driver to deposit him at his residence. Stravinsky had been pleased by the *Renard* production but the press was unanimously unfavourable. Thereafter, gossips contended that Proust spent the last six months of his life avoiding the Schiffs, and Stravinsky refused to accompany Diaghilev to the great writer's funeral in November.

Stravinsky and Joyce had several Parisian friends in common, most notably George Antheil, who had latched on to the composer in Berlin in the autumn of 1922 while he waited six weeks in Stettin for his mother's émigré-crowded steamship from St Petersburg. Antheil had proposed a collaboration with Joyce on an opera about Byron, which, of course, was never begun. From 1930 until Joyce's death from a perforated ulcer in 1941, he and Stravinsky were kept informed about each other through Paul Léon, Joyce's factotum and business manager. Léon's sister Henrietta (later Hirschman) had been a Stravinsky girlfriend in 1905 in St Petersburg. In the U.S. in the late 1950s she became Koussevitzky's secretary at the Boston Symphony and in this capacity often visited the Stravinskys in New York. When Charles Munch performed the *Canticum Sacrum*, Henrietta was helpful to both Stravinsky and this new conductor. I knew and liked her, as did my friend Claudio Spies.

In Dublin for a concert in 1963, Stravinsky spent his first day on visits to the Martello Tower and to the birthplace of James Joyce.

Pablo Picasso

*The uglier my paintings become, the more
people want to buy them!*

In conversation with James Lord

By the second decade of the twentieth century, the linking of
the names Picasso and Stravinsky became both automatic and
synonymous with modernism. Although the two *enfants terribles*
did not meet in person until 1917, they simultaneously shattered all
conventional notions of the arts to which they were born, reflecting
each other in the changing stages of their respective developments.
Les Demoiselles d'Avignon (actually the denizens of a brothel in
Barcelona's Carrer d'Avinyó) was a revolution in form, just as the
combining of chords of adjacent but remote tonalities in *The Rite of
Spring* demolished existing concepts of harmony. And Picasso's sad,
épuisés voltiguers and saltimbanques are mirrored in the puppets of
Petrushka. The two trajectories merge briefly in the *Ragtime* era, and
again in 1920 with the *Pulcinella* collaboration. The parallels between
cubism and polytonality are intangible but discernible in the layered
compositional perspectives and common evolutionary elements that
they share.

From 1916 to 1919 the wealthy Chilean expatriate Eugenia
Errázuriz sent a stipend of 1,000 francs a month to Stravinsky. At the
beginning of 1917 she wrote to him from her WWI home in Biarritz: 'I
have a strong desire for you to make Picasso's acquaintance because
someday you must collaborate with him. What a genius! As great as you
are, cher maître.' Stravinsky had already discovered Picasso's genius
in 1912 and purchased paintings by him. The actual meeting came
about in Rome on 12 April 1917, after Stravinsky had conducted the
Ballets Russes performances of *The Firebird*, *Fireworks* and excerpts
of *Petrushka* in the Teatro Costanzi. At a gala reception that followed
in the Hôtel de Russie, where the Via del Babuino meets the Piazza
del Popolo, Diaghilev introduced the painter to the composer. Olga
Khokhlova, with whom Picasso had become infatuated when he saw

her dance in *Les Femmes de bonne humeur* (and whom he married in Paris the next year), was also present that night.

On 16 April Picasso drew the first of three portraits of Stravinsky, in the painter's studio located at 54 Via Margutta (the palace built by the Marquis Francesco of Patrizi for the use of artists). The next day they were joined by Diaghilev and Massine on a sightseeing trip to Pompeii and Vesuvio. Stravinsky photographed Picasso and Massine in a natural cubist arrangement of some ruins in the excavated city. The composer and painter spent time exploring Naples, where they were arrested one evening for urinating against a wall. (That the same two instruments had already been employed in this bordello district is more than likely.) The culprits asked the police to take them to the opera house – the Teatro di San Carlo – and were released with apologies when the theatre staff addressed them both as 'Maestro'. The two men were attracted by Neapolitan gouache paintings of the bay area, several of which Stravinsky purchased and continued to collect for the rest of his life, using them to decorate the walls of his California bedroom. Composer and painter attended performances at a local theatre of a *commedia dell'arte* which, including the masks, became the inspiration for their next major work, *Pulcinella*. Back in Rome they visited more ruins together and discovered the palimpsests of styles: the broken brick wall of an early church hidden behind a baroque façade. When Diaghilev asked him why he spent so much time looking at lesser artists, Picasso replied: 'I am studying it carefully to learn how not to paint.' One imagines the painter and the composer with their bursting energy scrambling through the streets and alleys of Rome and talking together afterward in a taverna. Of their conversations only a single line survives in a Stravinsky diary: a statement of his astonishment concerning Picasso's newly lowered appraisal of Cézanne.

Stravinsky departed Rome for Switzerland on 24 April but he was again detained by Italian police, this time at the border town of Chiasso. Picasso's portrait of Stravinsky, which the authorities suspected of being a coded map of fortifications, was summarily confiscated. The composer argued to no avail that 'the picture *is* a map, but of my face'. He was obliged to spend the night in Chiasso, but succeeded in having the picture sent to the Russian Embassy in Rome where Gerald Tyrwhitt (Lord Berners) forwarded it on to Picasso in Paris via the diplomatic post bag. For fifteen months it remained there until Stravinsky's friend the writer Blaise Cendrars managed to return it to the painter. It arrived on 10 July 1918, two days before the wedding of Pablo Picasso and Olga Khokhlova.

In the year between the meeting of the two masters in Rome and the artist's marriage, he and the composer saw each other in Paris at a performance of the Diaghilev-Satie-Cocteau-Picasso ballet *Parade*, a concoction negatively received by both popular and critical audiences. When Stravinsky said little about it, his silence caused a rift with Cocteau, who retaliated by publishing some jibes at Stravinsky in the widely read *The Coq and the Harlequin*. Stravinsky and Cocteau nevertheless dined together in April 1919 in the regal home of Jean Hugo, after which the inebriated Stravinsky played his *Ragtime* for Diaghilev, Picasso, Cocteau, Poulenc and Auric. A collaboration with Picasso resulted, and when the composer revealed his intention to dedicate the piece to Mme Errázuriz the artist offered to contribute a cover drawing for the publication. He sent his first version of this to Les Éditions de la Sirène, but withdrew it, as he did five subsequent others. On 20 February 1919 Cocteau wrote to Stravinsky: 'Yesterday I took your *Ragtime* to the *graveuse*; the work will begin immediately.' It did not, and on 24 May the publisher, Paul Laffitte, informed Stravinsky that Picasso had promised to deliver the cover that evening. But this also did not happen, and when Stravinsky finally received the printed score with cover in December he telegraphed to Laffitte that an appalling mistake had been made in the spelling of Mme Errázuriz's name which would have to be corrected in a new edition. The only explanation for Picasso's delay was his current obsession with one-line-drawing. The one version that both the composer and the artist really liked had such a grotesquely inflated, obscene phallus that it was considered unprintable.

As any prescient observer would have realised, the marriage to Olga was a major mistake. Picasso's bohemian character and lifestyle were unacceptable to the strait-laced and bourgeois former ballerina. Nevertheless, Picasso's full portraits of her capture the woman's beauty. The marriage lasted until 1935 but in appearance only. Their son, Paulo, born in February 1921, kept the family together, as did their friendship with Igor and Vera. (In St Petersburg Vera had been close to Olga.) They attended Paulo's baptism, acting as godfather and godmother, and Picasso brought his son along to see Stravinsky off on his Channel and other flights. In 1922 the Picassos moved from Paris to Biarritz, as did Igor and Catherine, and not long after, when the painter went on to Juan-les-Pins, Igor and family moved to Nice while Vera stayed nearby in Le Lavandou. The foursome (Picasso, Olga, Igor, Vera) visited one another frequently until Picasso took up with Marie-Thérèse Walter.

The most important Stravinsky–Picasso year was 1920, during which they collaborated on the great and highly successful ballet *Pulcinella*, which compensated Diaghilev for the flop of *Parade*. The birthmarks of the ballet were inauspicious, however. At first Stravinsky did not take the project seriously, and when Picasso showed his initial sketches for the sets and costumes to Diaghilev the impresario threw them to the floor and stomped on them, incredible as this may seem to us now. Stravinsky somehow managed to reconcile the two men, and when he started work on the original music he was ecstatic with the pleasure of scoring for an eighteenth-century orchestra and injecting such musical jokes as the duet for a loud-mouthed trombone, and a weak-voiced string bass playing a syncopated melody. *Pulcinella* remains one of the most exquisite orchestrations in music history. After the premiere in May 1920 Picasso drew his second portrait of Stravinsky, and in gratitude the composer gave part of his *Pulcinella* manuscripts to him. In addition, Picasso gave to the composer a painting of two Harlequin musicians, a violinist and a guitarist. Picasso's third portrait of Stravinsky, the profile, was drawn on New Year's Eve, 1920. 1920 was also the year of Stravinsky's brief infatuation with Chanel, abetted by the encouragement of her good friend Picasso.

Even in the later 1920s the popularity of both figures waned somewhat due to the competition from other movements: in painting, the overnight Dada, the longer-lasting surrealism, then Swiss, German and Viennese expressionism as the great new painters – Klee, Schiele,

Matisse, De Chirico and others – arrived on the scene; in music, *Wozzeck* and Schoenberg's Variations. Yet the statures of Picasso and Stravinsky continued to tower over all others.

A divergence occurred in the 1920s with Stravinsky's neoclassicism, then an actual split in the mid-1930s with Picasso's *Minotauromaquia*[58] and *Guernica*, those potent indictments which revived art as politics (harkening back to Goya's own *Tauromaquia*, *Los desastres de la guerra*, *La carga de los mamelucos* and *El tres de mayo*). This time no reverberation registered on the Stravinsky side, only a renewed and purified dedication to classicism. In fact, the parallel ended ignominiously with Stravinsky's continuing support of Mussolini, an allegiance instigated by his champion Marinetti, and the retreat to the laissez-faire capitalist culture of the United States. In the same period Picasso became involved in the leftist causes, but in truth the artists continued to resemble each other in that neither embraced political philosophy on a deep level; both were disinterested opportunists trying to survive the vicissitudes of WWII. The millionaire Picasso joined the Communist Party to offset his reputation as a collaborationist who lived an untroubled, not to say lavish, life in occupied Paris, mingling and dealing with high-level Nazi art-lovers.

During his old age Picasso sculpted and painted masterpieces but also works of lesser quality, and the press exploited the minor scandals of his personal life while the impecunious Stravinsky looked on from the tinsel-tabloid Hollywood that he mostly managed to avoid. Not surprisingly, communication between the two friends ceased. In 1957 Francis Poulenc predicted that, 'Stravinsky will have a troubled old age because at seventy-five, he asked himself, "Is it my path to compose serial music?" Picasso, on the other hand, will have a serene old age because he doesn't give a damn about anything.' Until the very end, Stravinsky continued to experiment, even introducing in the Requiem Canticles the vibraphone, an instrument he had never used before. The last word from the composer concerning the painter

---

58   Stravinsky had a lithograph of this picture, a gift from Pierre Matisse in 1950, which the composer hung in his Hollywood living room, partly to terrify unwanted guests.

is inscribed in a 1964 copy of Françoise Gilot's *Life With Picasso*: 'Picasso is a monster, who at times, nevertheless, is right.'

Over the years in Europe Picasso gave a dozen paintings to Stravinsky, who proudly showed them to his Hollywood friends. All that remains of their correspondence in the composer's Basel archive, however, is a note of thanks sent to Stravinsky's home in Brittany with a photograph of Picasso and Olga in both of their handwritings. Although the artist seems to have been a voluble conversationalist, he was a man of few written words. When the duo-pianists Arthur Gold and Robert Fizdale visited Picasso shortly after World War II and mentioned that they were friends of Stravinsky, the painter questioned them for a considerable time about the composer's life in America and state of health. But his first words were, 'Toujours Vera?'

I spent the day of Stravinsky's death in his apartment at 920 Fifth Avenue reading telegrams of condolence from around the world. The first one that I remember opening read: 'ADIEU, CHER PÈRE, ET MERCI. PICASSO.'

T. S. Eliot

Stravinsky was our two months' lion…
Stravinsky, Lucifer of the season, brightest
in the firmament, took the call many times,
small and correctly in pince-nez.

T. S. Eliot, 1921

On 28 June 1921, the London *Times* reported that 'M. Stravinsky got a laurel wreath and the whole house roared itself hoarse.' Eliot's friend at the time, Robert Sencourt, added that after this 'performance of *The Rite of Spring* Eliot stood up and cheered'. Three years later the poet recalled in the *Criterion* his 'efforts, several years ago, to restrain (with the point of an umbrella) the mirth of my neighbors in a "family loge" which seemed united to deride the music of one of the greatest musicians, Stravinsky'.

T. S. Eliot's Parisian Year by Nancy Duvall Hargrove[59] quotes from Eliot's early writings about Stravinsky in the *Observer* and other publications, revealing the poet's acknowledgement that the puppet in *Petrushka* was the inspiration for the straw man in *The Hollow Men*. In September 1921 Eliot fulgently remarked in his 'London Letter' (*The Criterion*) that

> In the *Sacre du Printemps* Stravinsky's music did seem to transform the rhythm of the steppes into the scream of the motor horn, the rattle of the machinery, the grind of wheels, the beating of iron and steel, the roar of the underground railway, and the other barbaric cries of modern life... the spirit of the music was modern. [60]

I had assumed that before meeting Stravinsky, Eliot had read Ezra Pound's translation of Boris de Schloezer's book about the composer, most of which appeared in *The Dial*. Though Eliot frequently referred to 'il miglior fabbro' during our seven-year relationship, nothing was ever said about Stravinsky's opinion of this translation, Old Possum probably sensing (correctly) that the composer did not like the book.

The composer and poet began to learn more about each other in 1957 when Stravinsky sent excerpts of his *Conversations with Stravinsky* to Eliot for consideration at Faber & Faber, asking his opinion as to whether a short book consisting of this extended

---

59 University Press of Florida, 2010. This carefully researched volume requires at least one emendation. The author infers that Eliot attended a concert by 'a new music association' in Paris on 27 November 1911, in which the programme included Stravinsky's *Fireworks*. Eliot's year in Paris actually lasted nineteen months, from February 1910 to September 1911, when he returned to the U.S. A review in *Le Figaro* of this November concert by Robert Brussel is nevertheless of interest in its survey of such features of Stravinsky's rhythmic style and his 'shades of colour, vivacity, and instrumental seduction' continuing from *The Firebird*. The book cites a number of concerts in this period that Eliot did attend, most significantly a series of Beethoven quartets and a performance of piano pieces by Satie played by Ravel. The poet also may have been present when Siegfried Wagner conducted a Beethoven concert that provoked execrations in *Le Figaro*. Incidentally, Brussel had heard *Firebird* played by Stravinsky on the piano in St Petersburg weeks before the Paris premiere.

60 Not 100%. The first part of its penultimate dance reminds us of the 'Phrygian flute and the Berecinthian tambourine' (D'Annunzio). Eliot places Proust in opposition to the modern: 'Reconstruction of a past period and investigations of the unconscious do not appear to me relevant.' Proust's work is 'a wonderful commentary on the world that exists and has existed, not the discovery of a new one'. (Letter to Sydney Schiff, 6 April 1924.)

kind of dialogue could be published. Eliot's positive reply came immediately, together with his offer to edit the volume. When Stravinsky wondered if his correspondence with Jacques Rivière might be omitted as being of little general interest, Eliot persuaded him to retain the letters as being of historical importance. Another question arose concerning the French writer Julien Benda who had intrigued Stravinsky when they met on one of his transatlantic crossings. After reading Benda's *Belphégor*, Stravinsky asked Eliot for a copy of his essay on the author, a request that was quickly fulfilled. A part of dinner talk between the two artists was always devoted to contemporary French writers, among them Maritain and his *Art et scholastique*, and Saint-John Perse, regarded by both Stravinsky and Eliot as a good friend and learned gentleman but not a great poet (to my surprise, since Eliot had translated *Anabasis*). Both men had read Francis Picabia's *Jésus-Christ rastaquouère*[61] and both were Simenon addicts, Eliot admitting that he could read about Maigret when he could read nothing else.

When we first met Eliot in 1956 he was reserved but unable to conceal his curiosity. Vera broke the ice: 'Mr Eliot, you have something in common with my husband,' at which Mr Eliot straightened up, looking slightly alarmed. She continued: '*Time* magazine reviewed the premiere in San Marco of my husband's *Canticum Sacrum* under the title *Murder in the Cathedral*,' whereupon Eliot launched into his famously slow 'ha, ha, ha' laugh. He immediately felt comfortable with her. On a later occasion, after Vera had mentioned her husband's *Berceuses du chat*, she pointed out the two artists' love of felines. She told Eliot that her stepmother, during a drive from Victoria Ocampo's home outside Buenos Aires back to their hotel, had recited *Old Possum's Book of Practical Cats* by memory. This led to an appreciation of the names of favourite cats: Samuel Johnson's 'Hodge', Christopher Smart's 'Jeffrey', Poe's 'Caterina', Edward Lear's 'Old Foss' and Eliot's own 'Macavity'. The next morning

---

61 Vera de Bosset, who had shared an apartment in Paris with Picabia's wife, Gabrielle, for two or three years in the 1920s, was responsible for inducing Stravinsky to read this book by a painter whom he liked personally.

Eliot sent a copy of *Old Possum* 'Affectionately inscribed to Vera Stravinsky'.

Eliot venerated the composer but also cared for him personally, urging him to stop conducting concert tours and give his time to creative work: 'Let Robert do the conducting. You are an older man than I am but lead a much more strenuous life.' This last observation did not keep Eliot from asking Stravinsky a few years later to set the two stanzas of *The Dove Descending* to music, which Stravinsky did on 2 January 1962. Deeply grieved on hearing of Eliot's death, Stravinsky composed an *Introitus*, music distinguished in several ways from anything he had written before in its deep registration, its sonorities – viola, string bass, gong, bells, piano, harp, muffled timpani – and, above all, in the architectural divisions of a three-chord motif in complex, beautiful and never-before-heard harmonies.[62]

In August 1959 we flew from New York to London, dining the next day with Eliot and his wife Valerie in their apartment.[63] The purpose of this meeting was to discuss a projected opera collaboration, but nothing was said about the subject, partly because the prospective sponsor,[64] a New Mexican uranium magnate inspired by the Santa Fe Opera's production of *The Rake*, had withdrawn his offer.

On the last meeting of the two great men in December 1963 at Henri Soulé's Pavillon, the talk amongst the Stravinskys and the

---

62 Stravinsky wrote to his publisher that 'the music is very simple and very short... [T]he timpani notes... will be performed by two players. I consulted here with a specialist [the composer William Kraft, then the timpanist of the Los Angeles Philharmonic and a good friend]. Each player must have the two lines of the timpani before him. They will arrange between themselves how to distribute the notes.' On 3 March 1965 Stravinsky advised his publisher that he had completed the *Introitus*, which he described as 'the *Zaupokoynyi*, the chorale in memory of the unforgettable Eliot. The piece will be performed by the Chicago Symphony. Make certain that Leopold Spinner [the editor, a pupil of Webern] prints the tenor part in the treble clef since they cannot read the tenor clef.'

63 Knowing that Eliot was interested in any news concerning Henry James, I interposed at one break in the conversation that James's presence at the Paris *Firebird* in 1910 had recently been discovered.

64 John Crosby, director of the Santa Fe Opera, had brokered a high-figure commission, but Stravinsky was not really interested in the project. When he wrote to Eliot about it, the reply was equally unenthusiastic. The letter cannot be printed here because of its disobliging remarks about Auden's *Rake* libretto. In part Eliot blamed the unworkable mixture of Hogarth, *Everyman* and the year-and-a-day formula. (I once owned a copy of two pages of a first draft of the *Rake* libretto with Eliot's pencilled corrections of, respectively, an anachronism and a split infinitive.)

Eliots centred on Joseph Conrad, whose name arose when Stravinsky mentioned that his father and Conrad's father (Korzeniowski) had lived in the village of Chernigov. Stravinsky went on to ask if his accent resembled Conrad's, to which the answer was that Conrad's was thicker and more difficult to understand. I was hoping that the poet would say more about Conrad, while wondering how Stravinsky could have known that Eliot must have met the novelist (perhaps in the days of Conrad's collaboration with Ford Madox Ford). The composer had read *Under Western Eyes* and *Nostromo* and was aware of Eliot's indebtedness to Conrad in *The Waste Land*. I was also tempted to ask Eliot to comment on Junius, having recently learned that Eliot had quoted a passage from one of the letters in his *Homage to Aristophanes*.

I knew that Stravinsky was hoping to talk to Eliot about Valéry and other French writer friends such as Claudel and Céline, but the names did not come up. Eliot's published letters include a deflation of Valéry's reputation: 'He knows nothing whatsoever about dancing, not much about the soul, and very little about Socrates. It is the usual sort of French bluff. *Monsieur Teste* is also rubbish... I venture the idea that Valéry's poetry has merit, but the man cannot think.'

Nothing was said about politics, but after Eliot's death Stravinsky endorsed some remarks that the poet gave to an interviewer a short time later in his 'poet of adequation' phase:

> In our present mass entertainment culture which so far as I can see is without any values at all and yet is getting hold of the world... there is a deterioration, it seems to me, in the quality of amusement as it becomes mere mass entertainment... [I]t is profitable to appeal to the largest audience and therefore to the lowest common denominator... I don't think nihilism can be kept up indefinitely. A class society tends to equalise the responsibility, to atomise it into responsibility of the whole population - and therefore everyone becomes equally irresponsible.

On this evening at the Pavillon Stravinsky presented his manuscript of *The Dove Descending* to Eliot, who promised to donate it to the British Museum 'to exhibit the exquisite calligraphy as well as the music'. When departing, the two men were touchingly protective of each other and locked arms on their teetering walk to the vestière. As they approached, the maître d' said to an assistant rather too audibly: 'There you see the century's greatest composer and greatest poet together.' To spare them embarrassment, Vera responded: 'Well, they do their best.'

Aldous Huxley

Nothing so far has been said about the influence of Aldous Huxley on Stravinsky, but it was considerable, especially in questions of philosophy. Since he saw Aldous more frequently than almost anyone else, Stravinsky naturally wanted to know more about the writer's beliefs. In my early years in Hollywood, more evenings were spent in my reading aloud to the Stravinskys than in going to the movies or other diversions, which provided me with opportunities to acquaint them with their friend's works. Stravinsky was interested in Cardinal Richelieu and Père Joseph du Tremblay, the ascetic who preached the subduing of the self. Hence *Grey Eminence* was one of the first books I read to the composer, primarily because it was easier to understand than the off-putting language of *The Perennial Philosophy*. I also read *The Devils of Loudon* in which Stravinsky discovered Aldous's weakness, best described by Evelyn Waugh: 'There is no limit to the amount of knowledge you must have. The question is how much to impart. Aldous Huxley fails in this matter of taste. Particularly in *Devils of Loudon*, he can't resist giving irrelevant information.'

As a committed Mahayana Buddhist, Huxley naturally concludes the biography with a condemnation of the humble but powerful upstart monk for prolonging the Thirty Years' War in which millions died, mostly of starvation, and a large portion of Central Europe was devastated. In the end Richelieu and Père Joseph totally turned from their Catholic mysticism and supported the Protestants. Huxley repudiated violence, war and even political action.

Reviewing *Grey Eminence*, E. M. Forster traces Huxley's conclusion to the *Bhagavad-Gita* and Krishna's advice to Arjuna that it is his duty to fight for the just cause: 'In Huxley's judgment, mystics – whether Oriental or Christian – take a wrong turn when they believe that they can act and abstain from the fruits of action... [I]f the mystic oughtn't to turn politician, how can he help his fellows?' Unanswerable questions aside, Stravinsky shared Forster's mystical view that prayer should be private and would also have agreed with him on the political issue. Not politically minded except for a consistent opposition to Bolshevism, Stravinsky gave time, money and even free concerts for the war effort from the day that America, his new country, entered World War II. Though *Grey Eminence* fascinated Stravinsky, he criticised Huxley's thesis that mystics should not engage in politics.

Of all the artists, writers and musicians I met through Stravinsky, the one with whom I felt closest was Aldous Huxley, that kindest, most empathic and erudite of men. I was in his company more often than in that of any of Stravinsky's other illustrious friends, and we developed an affectionate relationship for which I shall always feel highly honoured. Huxley's conversation, fuelled by his insatiable intellect, was bewitching, eloquent and cheerfully misanthropic. He was multi-talented and born with exceptional musical gifts; music was intrinsic to his nature. Having been the *Westminster Gazette*'s music critic in his early twenties, he was wiser about the concert and opera repertoires than most of Stravinsky's professional musician friends. But Aldous's most phenomenal gift was his memory; the Broca's area may have increased during his teens as a result of the *keratitis punctata* that left him totally blind in his right eye (Virginia Woolf said it looked like 'the roe of codfish phosphorescence') and with only ten percent of normal vision in the left. How could he have written fifty books and read half a million of them in nine languages, some in Braille? Other people read to him, most devotedly his wife, Maria, who would recline on the fender of his chair whispering meaningless-to-her scientific and philosophical texts into his ear.

The Stravinskys and I dined with the Huxleys at each other's homes and at the Farmers' Market two or three times a week during my first six years in California. In a letter to her son of 13 May 1951, Maria describes the Stravinskys arriving at the Huxley home for a typical evening of listening to recordings. The composer

> was wearing blue jeans and a blue-jean zipper jacket open on a deep red wine jersey and silk scarf with pin. He looked enchanting and was really pleased with himself. As always he wore white socks and sandals. He reminded me of a voltigeur in a circus. Bob Craft, almost an adopted son of theirs, was with them. He is very clever, knows everything, terribly nervous, and not a pansy.[65] Aldous joins them and the three of them disappear to listen to recordings, leaving me alone with Vera for whom I have a very warm feeling.

Aldous regularly borrowed bits of my slang ('Let's get the hell out of here'). Exposure to me enabled him to study an American species heretofore unknown to him. With the discovery of his wife's fatal cancer at the beginning of 1952, Aldous asked me to witness their will and thanked me with a gift of Apollinaire's book of risqué verse inscribed with the comment that this would help me to improve my French, which had been his father's motive in giving it to him. During Maria's long illness[66] Aldous invited me to accompany him to movie-star parties and post-concert receptions – twice or thrice at Alma Mahler's, the lion-huntress he most dreaded. Her voice was strident, and she pestered him to taste sweet liqueurs from her large

---

65 When I asked Elizabeth Hardwick if I should delete this sentence, she answered, 'Most definitely not!'
66 After her death in 1955, Aldous married the violinist Laura Archera and the Stravinsky relationship all but came to an end. Huxley's social life spread to different kinds of people. When the Stravinskys returned from Japan in 1959, Huxley invited them to his home along with the novelists Lesley Blanch (*The Wilder Shores of Love*) and her husband, Romain Gary (*The Roots of Heaven*). The Stravinskys enjoyed this couple's company, at first because both understood and spoke Russian, and we saw them frequently for several weeks afterward until Gary, who was serving temporarily as the French Consul in Los Angeles, was recalled to Paris. His name is best known today for his marriage to the actress Jean Seberg who committed suicide a few years later, after she gave birth to a black baby. Gary later also committed suicide.

cupboard. Another factor in our camaraderie was that Aldous and I shared the same prurient imaginations and sexual predilections. (He had films of Bouguereau's most voluptuous nudes.) He knew about mine from his wife's much younger, much prettier and, as I did not yet know, much married sister who gossiped to him of my unsuccessful importunings of her.

In the early 1950s I often walked with Aldous in the forest that used to cover the summit of Doheny Hill. Having been detained by the Beverly Hills police for strolling on otherwise deserted sidewalks – his reason for perambulating there – Aldous had decided to return to the woods to avoid a possible charge of vagrancy. Maria asked me to accompany him in order to prevent a stumble or even fend off a reptile. (In my early years with Stravinsky he had encountered a rattlesnake near his Wetherly Drive house, had his home invaded for several hours by a possum, and his roof trodden upon and awnings clawed to tatters by a wildcat.) I immensely enjoyed these walks and talks with Aldous and soon felt comfortable enough to bring up moderately arcane subjects. After all, Stravinsky was now telephoning him for information as if Aldous were his personal *Encyclopædia Britannica*. Certainly he was highly regarded by Stravinsky as a medical advisor, both allopathic and alternative. Aldous was responsible for convincing Stravinsky of the efficacy of acupuncture, with which the composer received treatment for the rest of his life from Dr Sigfrid Knauer. When Stravinsky suffered from insomnia that the best of Scottish grains could not overcome, Aldous successfully practised his great skill as a hypnotist on the composer. I remember a period in the summer of 1950 when, still torn by the problem of Baba the Turk, Stravinsky would send me to fetch Aldous at midnight and then – after slumber had been induced – to drive the beleaguered genius back home. Aldous was Stravinsky's sleep therapist for the next two years.

One of our cultural ambles included a discussion of The Wilton Diptych, a subject much in the air at the time as the result of E. W. Tristram's revelations about this most impressive of English paintings. Every face in the diptych features the long, straight, Anglo-Saxon nose, including that of the kneeling Richard II, John the Baptist, and the angels. That the artist was a monk or friar named Gilbert Prince and the date of the picture was c. 1395 had only recently been determined. Since the king wears a collar made of broomcod, not then known in England, this is generally assumed to have been a gift from a French sovereign. My own interest in the diptych is its anticipation of Fra Angelico, who may have been the most musical of all painters. In the convent of San Marco in Florence, his angels play musical instruments, some of them trumpets *à bec* with flared bells. But Angelico's illuminated music manuscripts are no less stunningly beautiful. The square neumes themselves, whether alone or in groups, dancing happily on the manuscript, make lovely pictures, to my eye a more delectable form of abstract art than New York-period Mondrians.

On another rambling I inquired of Aldous why his *Perennial Philosophy* refers three times to the *Diamond Sutra* but never mentions the wonderfully frescoed Dunhuang cave in which it was found, nor the underlying argument of the *Sutra*, which is that 'the only reality is transience'. We switched to musical subjects. What was the chromatic scale famously employed in Agathon's tragedies? Aldous answered with a digression on this author's great personal beauty and his homoerotic friendship with Socrates, pointing out on the way that only about forty lines of Agathon's oeuvre survive. I turned to a simple topic. Why was the word *accelerando* not generally employed until after Beethoven, who used it in the *Grosse Fuge*? I had been trying to understand Nicholas Oresme's mean-speed theorem, which concludes that a uniform acceleration, beginning from rest or from an initial velocity, is equated to the mean speed of an accelerated motion.[67] Aldous perpended a moment, then expounded on Oresme as the first philosopher to touch on the idea of mathematical probability. But Aldous was certain that the musical term did not derive from the philosophical as I had naïvely suggested. On the drive home he promised to investigate the question, 'If I find

---

67 Two centuries before Galileo proved virtually the same theorem empirically, applying it to freefalling bodies, Oresme discovered the same thing. Oresme was Huxley's intellectual hero of the Trecento, the polymath of the early Renaissance, who also established the International Date Line 500 years before the geographers.

time before time finds me.' After Huxley's death in 1963, Gerald
Heard wrote a beautiful memorial tribute, *The Poignant Prophet.*
Henceforth Stravinsky and Gerald saw each other frequently, though
Gerald was absent for weeks at a time, staying alternately with Frank
Lloyd Wright in Arizona and Henry and Claire Boothe Luce in Hawaii.
Stravinsky and Gerald became increasingly close until the end of
their lives, only four months apart in 1971.

Edwin Hubble

...and other suns perhaps
With their attendant moons.

Raphael to Adam in *Paradise Lost*

On 22 May 1951 I drove the Huxleys and the Stravinskys to an
exhibition of Turner's watercolours at the Huntington Library
in Pasadena. Thanks to Aldous we were permitted to handle a
Shakespeare folio, an illuminated Chaucer manuscript, and a copy of
Haydn's Symphony No. 104 in the hand of the young Richard Wagner.

Edwin and Grace Hubble had invited us for tea afterwards. During
the drive Aldous explained that the astronomer had been a Rhodes
scholar but settled down as a small-town Midwest lawyer before
beginning his study of the sidereal situation. Aldous cautioned that
Hubble, a man of no small talk and few words, could be dour. Then
at the last moment Aldous revealed that Bertrand Russell was the
person Hubble most admired, and 'knowing that Bertie dined at our
home two days ago, Edwin will want news of him'. This proved to be
the case, to my relief since I also doted on the author of *The History of
Western Philosophy*, whose lectures I had attended at the New School
for Social Research in New York. As predicted, Hubble asked about
Russell and, at the end of our visit, actually loaned two of his books
to me.

During the drive, Aldous had also mentioned that he was seeking
Hubble's help in understanding a German treatise on the philosophy
of biology since the astronomer had studied in Germany and was

especially adept at reading scientific books in the language. Aldous and Hubble talked about Flammarion galaxies and the duration of the Big Bang (if indeed there was any duration, or any bang). Then the two men retreated to another room while Grace Hubble served tea and scones to the Stravinskys, Maria Huxley and myself.

Of that most memorable afternoon, I recall a portrait of Sir Arthur Eddington (perhaps because he was one of the rare readable physics popularisers) by Augustus John on the wall. I also remember Hubble's dark, furry cat, Nicolaus Copernicus, strutting into the room. (Nicolaus would outlive his master, who suddenly, shockingly, died of a heart attack only two years later, soon after he had begun to work with the 200-inch telescope.)

I saw the Hubbles next on 16 July 1951, at a dinner party in the portico of the Huxleys' North Kings Road home. It was a catered affair with such perfect decorum that I did not stray from the Stravinskys during pre-dinner talk. The seating arrangements placed the Hubbles across from each other at the centre of the table, thereby dividing it into Francophones and Anglophones. Gerald Heard, Christopher Isherwood and I were the only monolingual guests. Fortunately the Huxley brothers were at my end of the table, together with Gerald and Christopher, the latter addressing the novelist as 'Aldeuce'. An electrifying discussion of ideas followed, more scintillating than anything I had ever heard or expect to hear again. The subjects were exclusively noetic and far beyond my comprehension, but Hubble, who listened attentively, also remained silent, seeming to assume the stance of a moderator and reacting to some of Gerald's most far-fetched speculations (this was in his *Is Another World Watching?*) with a frown. Another reason for the silence could have been that Hubble's own flow of words was too deliberated for this swift Brit repartee. Watching the Huxley brothers together, I formed an indelible impression of Julian deferring to Aldous, beaming with pride at each of this younger sibling's inputs. Grace Hubble,[68] to my right, mercifully talked to me about Italy – the Hubbles having just

---

68 Her diaries record Aldous's invitations to go to bed with him as well as her rejections. She was a very attractive woman, with resemblances to Maria.

returned from there – where the Stravinskys and I were preparing to journey for the premiere of the *Rake*. Also at the table were the distinguished cardiac surgeon William Kiskadden and his beautiful wife, Peggy,[69] who had been so enchanted with Gerald when he was living in their house that he had been forced to flee. The other guests were Aldous's Belgian brother-in-law, Joep Nicolas, C. A. Hadow (the British consul in Los Angeles and son of the musicologist), and of course Igor and Vera Stravinsky.

On 25 July 1952 the Stravinskys and I again dined at the Huxleys' with the Hubbles and Mary Louise Kent, a jewel-bedecked nonagenarian bluestocking who smoked marijuana throughout dinner. In high spirits, Aldous gleefully told us that he had just discovered that the most popular words rhyming with his name were 'tremendous', 'stupendous', 'horrendous' and 'hazardous'. During dinner he remarked, apropos of I forget what, that lapiths and centaurs were apparently endowed with human emotions (sexual ones, anyway, in the only art I have seen).

A year later, on 27 July 1953, we celebrated Aldous's birthday with Gerald, the Hubbles, Chicago University's Robert Hutchins, and Julian Huxley. This was the third time we had been with Gerald that day, having attended his morning lecture, a defence of the Kinsey Report ('We can explain nature only by the accumulation of facts'), and afterward having lunched with him at the Bel-Air Hotel, where he had discussed the functions of the hypothalamus (a favourite topic) and told us that 'Aquinas gives twenty definitions of nature but contradicts them all in trying to prove why a woman could not become Pope'. At dinner the indefatigable Gerald's epicene felicity dominated even these professional lecturers. Hutchins followed this by an amusing imitation of Alfred North Whitehead, who apparently spoke so softly in his lectures that he could be understood only when he raised his head to say in a louder voice 'for example', after which he returned to a mumble. This was followed by an acutely observed imitation of

---

69   Peggy Kiskadden's elder son became the Harvard president Dr Derek Bok. Her younger son wanted to be a composer and through his mother became Stravinsky's pupil, but after the first lesson, in 1947, the young man told her that Stravinsky knew absolutely nothing about Schoenberg's techniques.

another mumbler, at least in English, Niels Bohr.[70] When Julian and Aldous momentarily disagreed about parapsychology and J. B. Rhine, Hubble dismissed the whole subject as credulity. We saw the Hubbles again with the Huxleys for the last time on 7 September 1953.

As a dilettante in the world of learning, except in some musical matters, I gained most of the smatterings I possessed concerning Hubble's work from Aldous, who had been close to the astronomer since 1937 and kept us abreast of each new discovery at the Mount Palomar and Wilson Observatories. Aldous explained the significance of Hubble's 1925 discovery that cepheid variable stars, in spiral-shaped nebulae, altered our cosmology. Hubble had estimated the speed of luminosity and calculated the distances that placed the cepheid variables beyond the boundaries of the planet Earth's galaxy, which multiplied the size of the universe by a factor of ten. The shock for us laymen was in learning that as late as 1916 Albert Einstein had concluded that the universe is static, and that quantum mechanics had long since brushed relativity aside and supplanted the great scientist's later work. In 1929 Hubble and his associates at Mount Wilson revealed that redshifts in the spectra of nebulae – generally accepted as Doppler shifts – are related to distance, thereby proving the correlation between velocity and distance. This relation established by Hubble showed that the more distant nebulae are receding from us at ever-greater speeds. Ergo, the universe is expanding, and redshifts can be measured even when stars and galaxies are too faint to distinguish.

Aldous continued to keep his brother, then the head of UNESCO, in touch with Hubble's discoveries. A letter to Julian in April 1940 notes that Hubble 'is very happy as he has just discovered the

---

70 Stravinsky dined with Bohr at a royal celebration in Denmark in May 1959 and confirmed the mumbling manner. The composer did not yet know that Bohr was widely regarded as the greatest scientific mind of the twentieth century, the man who had replaced relativity theory with quantum mechanics and virtually silenced Einstein for forty-three years. When told this, Stravinsky was unhappy, because Einstein had been so congenial to him when this most eminent of all scientists was brought to him after a performance of *Oedipus Rex* in Berlin conducted by Klemperer in 1928. The composer would have been interested to learn that Bohr himself would be outshone by his most brilliant pupil, the discoverer of the 'uncertainty principle', the young Werner Heisenberg. Perhaps Bohr's reputation was over-politicised when the U.S. Government brought him to Los Alamos in 1943.

answer to a problem that has defeated astronomers to date: which way the nebulae are revolving'. A letter of 26 February 1949 reports that Hubble had shown him the first pictures taken by the 200-inch telescope, which indicated that the latest nebulae detected go on with uniform density to a billion light years, and that five hundred million heretofore unknown galaxies are 'within range of the 200-inch. Crikey!' But this would be upset by another order of magnitude in the 1960s: the discovery of quasars.

In November 2009 physicists at CERN at last succeeded in sending beams of protons clockwise around the seventeen-mile underground racetrack near Geneva known as the Large Hadron Collider. The aim was to replicate the Big Bang by circulating and accelerating the beam to seven trillion electron volts, slamming the protons together in search of trans-dimensional particles. The machine is now expected to accelerate to 1.1 trillion volts, which is above the energy of the Tevatron (the failed rival project in Illinois). Sixteen years after launching, the Hubble Telescope has now been successfully installed with spectrographs, enabling astronomers to continue making measurements that have led to what the cosmologist Adam Riess of Johns Hopkins hailed as a 'triumph of metrology'. This refers to the discovery that for every additional million parsecs (about 3.26 million light years) that a galaxy is from us, it moves seventy-four kilometres per second faster. Hubble discovered cosmic expansion in 1929, and many physicists believe that some kind of dark energy is speeding up the expansion of the universe. The goal now is to proceed beyond the belief that width, height and depth are all that exist and that other dimensions will become perceptible. Hence the ultimate measurement of the 'Hubble constant' is still in the future. Since the universe is not constant the right number may never be found, but in January 2010 the CERN colliders collided. In the same month a year later, a galaxy older and farther than any others was discovered through the lens of the Hubble telescope. A patch of sky known as the Hubble Ultra Deep Field in the constellation Fornax reveals an immense number of heretofore unknown galaxies dating to 800 million years post-Big Bang. Since then the Higgs (temporarily so called) boson has been discovered; but I cannot comment on an invisible mass – in an unimaginable space. Meanwhile, earthlings (believers, that is) can meditate on what might be found of themselves and others and those yet undiscovered dimensions 'when we dead awaken'.

CD Tracklist

The Rite of Spring (1967 edition, with changes
incorporated from the original manuscript, 1913)   33:42

First Part – Adoration of the Earth

1	Introduction	3:32
2	The Augurs of Spring / Dances of the Young Girls	3:15
3	Ritual of Abduction	1:23
4	Spring Rounds	3:12
5	Ritual of the Rival Tribes	1:53
6	Procession of the Sage	0:41
7	The Sage	0:29
8	Dance of the Earth	1:16

Second Part – The Sacrifice

9	Introduction	3:53
10	Mystic Circles of the Young Girls	3:20
11	Glorification of the Chosen One	1:40
12	Evocation of the Ancestors	0:43
13	Ritual Action of the Ancestors	3:29
14	Sacrificial Dance (The Chosen One)	4:56

Total time 33:42

Philharmonia Orchestra
Robert Craft

Recorded at Abbey Road Studio 1, London, 3–5 January 2007
Producer: Philip Traugott
Editing: Floating Earth
Publishers: Boosey & Hawkes, reprinted with corrections, 1967
℗ 2007 & © 2013 Naxos Rights US Inc.

Index

IS refers to Igor Stravinsky

G

H

By the same author

Down a Path of Wonder: Memoirs of Stravinsky, Schoenberg
    and other cultural figures (Naxos Books, 2006)
An Improbable Life: Memoirs (Vanderbilt University Press, 2002)
Places: A Travel Companion for Music and Art Lovers
    (Thames & Hudson, 2000)
The Moment of Existence: Music, Literature, and the Arts 1990–1995
    (Vanderbilt University Press, 1996)
Stravinsky: Glimpses of a Life (St Martin's Press, 1992)
Small Craft Advisories: Critical Articles 1984–1988: Art, Ballet,
    Music, Literature, Film (Thames & Hudson, 1989)
Stravinsky: Selected Correspondence: Vol. 1 (Faber & Faber, 1981);
    Vol. 2 (Knopf, Faber & Faber, 1984); *Vol. 3* (Knopf, 1985)
Dearest Bubushkin: The Correspondence of Vera and Igor Stravinsky,
    1921–1954, with excerpts from *Vera Stravinsky's Diaries,*
    1922–1971, ed. Robert Craft (Thames & Hudson, 1985)
A Stravinsky Scrapbook: 1940–1971 (Thames & Hudson, 1984)
Present Perspectives: Critical Writings (Knopf, 1984)
Igor and Vera Stravinsky: A Photograph Album, 1921–1971
    (Thames & Hudson, 1982)
Stravinsky in Pictures and Documents (Simon & Schuster, 1978)
Current Convictions: Views and Reviews (Knopf, 1977)
Prejudices in Disguise: Articles, Essays, Reviews (Knopf, 1974)
Stravinsky: Chronicle of a Friendship (Knopf, 1972;
    revised and expanded, Vanderbilt University Press, 1994)
Themes and Conclusions (University of California Press, 1972)
Retrospectives and Conclusions (Knopf, 1970)
Dialogues and a Diary (Faber & Faber, 1968)
Bravo Stravinsky, with Arnold Newman and Francis Steegmuller
    (World Publishing, 1967)
Themes and Episodes (Knopf, 1966)
Expositions and Developments (Doubleday, Faber & Faber, 1962)
Memories and Commentaries (Faber & Faber, 1960)
Conversations with Stravinsky (Faber & Faber, 1959)